AMERICAN AMPHIBIOUS WARFARE

Titles in the Series

With Commodore Perry to Japan: The Journal of William Speiden Jr., 1852–1855

Whips to Walls: Naval Discipline from Flogging to Progressive-Era Reform at Portsmouth Prison

Crisis in the Mediterranean: Naval Competition and Great Power Politics, 1904–1914

Home Squadron: The U.S. Navy on the North Atlantic Station

The Sailor's Homer: The Life and Times of Richard McKenna, Author of The Sand Pebbles

Rough Waters: Sovereignty and the American Merchant Flag

New Perspectives on Maritime History and Nautical Archaeology

JAMES C. BRADFORD AND GENE A. SMITH, EDITORS

Rivers, seas, oceans, and lakes have provided food and transportation for man since the beginning of time. As avenues of communication they link the peoples of the world, continuing to the present to transport more commodities and trade goods than all other methods of conveyance combined. The New Perspectives on Maritime History and Nautical Archaeology series is devoted to exploring the significance of the earth's waterways while providing lively and important books that cover the spectrum of maritime history and nautical archaeology broadly defined. The series includes works that focus on the role of canals, rivers, lakes, and oceans in history; on the economic, military, and political use of those waters; on the exploration of waters and their secrets by seafarers, archeologists, oceanographers, and other scientists; and upon the people, communities, and industries that support maritime endeavors. Limited by neither geography nor time, volumes in the series contribute to the overall understanding of maritime history and can be read with profit by both general readers and specialists alike.

AMERICAN AMPHIBIOUS WARFARE

The Roots of Tradition to 1865

GARY J. OHLS

Naval Institute Press
Annapolis, Maryland

Naval Institute Press
291 Wood Road
Annapolis, MD 21402

Library of Congress Cataloging-in-Publication Data
Names: Ohls, Gary J., author.
Title: American amphibious warfare : the roots of tradition to 1865 / Gary J. Ohls.
Description: Annapolis, Maryland : Naval Institute Press, 2017. | Includes bibliographical references and index.
Identifiers: LCCN 2017043129 (print) | LCCN 2017043639 (ebook) | ISBN 9781682470909 (epub) | ISBN 9781682470909 (pdf) | ISBN 9781682470886 (hardcover : alk. paper)
Subjects: LCSH: Amphibious warfare—History—18th century. | Amphibious warfare —History—19th century. | United States—History, Military—18th century. | United States—History, Military—19th century. | Amphibious warfare—Case studies.
Classification: LCC U261 (ebook) | LCC U261 .O35 2017 (print) | DDC 335.4/6097309034—dc23
LC record available at https://lccn.loc.gov/2017043129

Maps created by Starlene Seargeant.

∞ Print editions meet the requirements of ANSI/NISO z39.48-1992 (Permanence of Paper).
Printed in the United States of America.

25 24 23 22 21 20 19 18 17   9 8 7 6 5 4 3 2 1
First printing

Contents

Maps

Acknowledgments

Among the many people who assisted in creating this book, I am particularly indebted to Dr. Gene Allen Smith of Texas Christian University and Dr. James Bradford of Texas A&M University. They provided professional and scholarly oversight and support throughout the long, intermittent writing and editing process. I am grateful to Dr. John Hattendorf of the U.S. Naval War College, who supported my efforts to complete an early draft and provided professional guidance and personal friendship over many years. Dr. Donald Stoker of the Naval War College's Monterey Program provided cheerful prodding to keep me motivated to see the project through to completion. Of course, there are other friends and colleagues too numerous to mention, who helped in various ways and to whom I owe a debt of thanks.

I would like to offer my gratitude to the staffs at the U.S. Army Heritage and Education Center, the U.S. Marine Corps Research Center, the Marine Corps History Division, the National Archives and Records Administration, the Naval War College Archives, the Dudley Knox Library at the Naval Postgraduate School, the Naval Historical Center, the Mary Couts Burnett Library at Texas Christian University, and the Monterey Public Library, Monterey, California. At these centers I always found cheerful professionals able and eager to assist in my research.

Author's Note on the History of Amphibious Warfare

ALTHOUGH NOT RAISED TO AN ESPECIALLY HIGH LEVEL OF proficiency by the United States until the twentieth century, the art of amphibious warfare has deep roots in early American military and naval tradition. The seven major battles studied in this book demonstrate how this amphibious tradition developed while analyzing its place in the strategic mosaic of each period. Through a case study approach, the operational and strategic significance of each amphibious action is analyzed and its impact on the development of our nation assessed. Of course, amphibious warfare does not begin in early America but goes back as far as recorded history. For example, amphibious operations constituted an important element of the Peloponnesian Wars, and Thucydides provides descriptions of important landings throughout his classical account of that conflict. In fact, one of the most significant triumphs of Athens over Sparta—a victory of sea power over land power—resulted from the amphibious landing on the island of Sphacteria in 425 BC.

The Spartan defeat at Sphacteria shocked the entire Hellenic world and forced Sparta to seek an end of the war and return of its prisoners, all to no avail.[1] Conversely, Athens' failed amphibious expeditions to Sicily and subsequent attack on Syracuse during 415–413 BC rank among her most disastrous defeats. Syracuse's effective resistance to the Athenian invasion introduces the question of defense against landing operations as an important element of amphibious warfare.[2] This aspect is particularly significant in studying early American wars where British forces possessed an offensive amphibious capability and the United States usually found itself on the defensive.

Two of the greatest commanders of ancient warfare—Alexander the Great and Julius Caesar—used amphibious warfare effectively when operational circumstances dictated. In Alexander's case, that great general found himself unable to conquer the Phoenician city of Tyre with only his army in 332 BC. Assembling a fleet of some 220 vessels at Sidon, he attacked and scattered the naval force defending the city's seaboard flank. He then conducted an amphibious assault that breached Tyre's walls and conquered the city, complete with great destruction and slaughter. This victory caused Alexander's prime adversary, Darius Codomannus, to offer a generous peace to the Macedonian commander, which he quickly rejected and continued his conquest of Egypt and the Persian Empire.[3]

Julius Caesar, like Alexander before him, is primarily known for his great land battles. But Caesar also conducted two of the most fascinating amphibious operations of antiquity in his efforts to conquer Britain. During his first invasion in 55 BC, the Roman general found a determined and hostile enemy awaiting him at the shoreline. With chariots drawn by specially trained horses, and augmented with cavalry and infantry, the Briton defenders attacked the Romans in the surf as they attempted to project their force ashore. With skillful maneuvering and furious assaults, Caesar's forces proved superior and eventually drove the defenders from the coast. Although Caesar established his landing force ashore, the lack of cavalry restricted his mobility, making it difficult to exploit the initial success. Damage to his amphibious ships by a devastating storm complicated Roman logistics so severely that Caesar found it necessary to negotiate an amphibious withdrawal. Dissatisfied with the outcome of his first incursion, Caesar conducted a second invasion in 54 BC, which met with a substantially different Briton concept of defense. Rather than oppose the invaders at the water's edge, as before, the defenders allowed their adversaries to come ashore and attempted a defense in depth, designed to cause attrition of the Roman army through a series of defensive battles. Unfortunately for the British defenders, this proved no more successful than their earlier effort as Caesar's forces consistently proved too strong. Yet despite a hard-won series of victories, Roman leaders found no great benefit from their successes and again departed British shores, not to return for nearly a century.[4]

For roughly a thousand years after the Roman era, the British Isles remained the focus of hostile amphibious assaults. Its inhabitants dealt with invasions from numerous sources, including Vikings, Anglo-Saxons, and ultimately the Norman Conquest by William the Conqueror in 1066.

Over many centuries, English society assimilated the people and methods of warfare of their invaders.[5] The nation that resulted from this diverse influx eventually grew into a seaborne empire in its own right, highly dependent on naval power and the ability to control the littorals of large parts of the world. Numerous imperial wars fought during the seventeenth and eighteenth centuries—usually between alliances headed by England and France—had worldwide implications, as their armies and navies engaged in far-flung operations. It is in this context that the inhabitants of North America first became involved in imperial warfare and the amphibious operations so key to its success.

The numerous imperial wars—worldwide wars—of the seventeenth and eighteenth centuries inevitably involved the European colonies in North America. Interestingly, these wars usually had two names: one used in Europe and a second used by Americans.[6] Although British leaders viewed these wars globally, most Americans—and many American historians—tend to see them in a narrower, hemispheric perspective. This is not to suggest they are unaware of the larger picture but rather that they attempted to understand these conflicts primarily from the point of view of their impact on political and military developments in North America.

From the perspective of amphibious warfare, the British attempted numerous landings in the Western Hemisphere throughout this era of imperial warfare. As Thomas More Molyneux laments throughout his masterful 1759 treatise on amphibious warfare, many of these actions failed.[7] Yet, toward the middle of the eighteenth century, Great Britain began to improve its effectiveness in littoral operations. Among the most interesting examples are the two operations against Louisbourg on Cape Breton Island, which constituted the Atlantic flank of French Canada. The first of these occurred in 1745, during King George's War, and the second in 1758, during the French and Indian War. These landings involved both British and colonial forces and constitute early pillars to the amphibious traditions that developed in the history of the United States.[8] Any naval invasion into the heartland of Canada had to first destroy or neutralize Louisbourg and take control of the St. Lawrence estuary. Although not the center of gravity for the conquest of Canada—that honor belonged to Quebec—strategists on both sides recognized Louisbourg's importance as a gateway into New France. They also realized that it could only be captured by an amphibious attack.

During King George's War (the American theater of the 1740–48 War of the Austrian Succession), leaders in both England and America recognized the need to capture Louisbourg and threaten French possessions along the St. Lawrence River. To colonial Americans, Louisbourg represented a French menace to New England. While British leaders also recognized this concern of their colonial subjects, they tended to focus more on the strategic advantage of possessing Louisbourg as a stepping-stone into Canada, and as an instrument for use in the peace negotiations that would eventually end the war. In short, New Englanders passionately viewed Louisbourg from a defensive perspective whereas British leaders thought of it primarily in terms of strategy and policy. New England support can be observed in the blessing the expedition received from George Whitefield, the most dynamic religious leader of the First Great Awakening, in which he called on God's assistance in achieving a victory over the Catholic French defenders of Louisbourg.[9]

The invasion force consisted almost exclusively of colonial militia and, initially, naval forces created from fishing and merchant ships. The British navy belatedly dispatched a squadron from the West Indies and eventually a few ships from England to support the operation, but it remained primarily a colonial affair. A wealthy Maine merchant and militia colonel, William Pepperrell, commanded the expedition. En route to Louisbourg, Pepperrell's force recaptured the English outpost of Canso on the northeast shore of Nova Scotia, which they used as an intermediate support base for the amphibious attack.[10]

The expedition to capture Louisbourg proved remarkably efficient and successful, especially considering the inexperience of the New England troops. On 30 April 1745, the Americans landed on an undefended beach a little more than a mile from the main French defenses. After rapidly establishing themselves ashore, the invaders quickly defeated a French force sent to interdict them and then captured a major artillery position turning its canon against the defenders. There followed a siege and blockade, which forced French capitulation in just under two months.[11]

The success at Louisbourg was the greatest British victory of King George's War. The primary reason for this great success lay in the detailed and precise planning that occurred in New England prior to departure of the expedition. Planning had been so thorough that the commanders even brought special ammunition that fit only the French artillery for use in case they captured enemy field pieces, which proved to be the case. The close cooperation between army and navy commanders also proved extraordinary for this period and provided another key to success of the mission. This is particularly significant since the army commander came from the colonial militia, and the naval commander, once the British squadron arrived on station, served as a regular officer of the Royal Navy. Yet Pepperrell—who received the temporary rank of lieutenant general for the mission—and Commo. Peter Warren worked together effectively and successfully. The third reason for the victory at Louisbourg involved the element of surprise. Pepperrell did not achieve surprise in the literal sense of the term, but he did achieve it in the military sense. Although the French became aware of his intentions when he attacked and recaptured the English city of Canso on the coast of Nova Scotia, they did not have time to reinforce or improve their defenses before the British-American force descended upon them.[12] Pepperrell then followed up his advantage by rapidly landing his force and moving against French defenses with such speed and flexibility that the defenders could only retreat into their prepared positions and submit to siege and blockade. Once this occurred, the only possibility of continued French resistance rested in the hope for reinforcements, which the British navy would not permit. The subsequent bombardment from artillery—including the captured French canons—and naval guns forced French capitulation.[13]

By any measure, the 1745 Louisbourg amphibious operation represented a significant achievement of British arms—all the more remarkable for the fact that colonial officers planned and led the expedition, and that militia troops executed the plan ashore. The New Englanders took great pride in the victory while believing passionately that they had removed the clear and present danger of French attack. These factors caused particular resentment among the colonists when, in 1748, British leaders unceremoniously returned Louisbourg to France in the Treaty of Aix-la-Chapelle, which ended the war.[14] In a decision based strictly on strategic and political considerations, the British government essentially traded Louisbourg for Madras, India, during the peace negotiations. Unlike most operations involving both regular and colonial forces during this period, the two elements worked together very well during the Louisbourg campaign and created a certain level of good will among the parties. The Treaty of Aix-la-Chapelle undercut that feeling and caused long-term resentments among colonial Americans, which would fester under the surface long into the future.[15] This diplomatic action negated the sense of pride that colonials felt in winning a great victory and restored the threat of French aggression or, equally fearsome, the likelihood of French-instigated Indian attacks.[16]

Less than a decade after the end of King George's War, the British and French again fought a major conflict known in America as the French and Indian War, and elsewhere as the Seven Years' War. Even more than the preceding imperial conflicts between the superpowers of that age, this truly qualified as a worldwide war. Although officially fought between 1756 and 1763, the maneuvering that brought it about started on the American frontier as early as 1753, with actual hostilities beginning in 1754. This early skirmishing grew into major combat, exemplified by Gen. Edward Braddock's expedition to Fort Duquesne in 1755 and then spread into full-scale warfare throughout the imperial system. Although the causes of this conflict ran very deep, the actual spark that ignited fighting occurred in the Ohio Valley—then coveted by both Virginia and France—in 1754 with an ambush triggered by a young militia officer named George Washington. This incident received attention at the highest levels of government in both Paris and London since Joseph Coulon de Villiers de Jumonville, a French officer of some importance, lost his life in the action. The French and Indian War would ultimately result in the expulsion of French colonial rule east of the Mississippi and initiate the dominance of the North American continent by English-speaking people.[17]

Initially, the French and Indian War did not go well for Great Britain and its American colonists. Even before the official declaration of hostilities, Edward Braddock's expedition against Fort Duquesne in the Ohio Valley suffered a crushing rout at the hands of the French garrison and its Indian allies. Following Braddock's defeat, French general Jean-Armand, Baron de Dieskau, suffered a reverse by British forces under William Johnson in the September 1755 battle—actually a series of battles—of Lake George. This constituted the last major fighting before the formal declaration of war in the spring of 1756. Once war became official, a brilliant and forceful commander, Louis Joseph, Marquis de Montcalm, scored key victories at Fort Oswego in August 1756 and at Fort William Henry in August 1757. Unfortunately for the marquis' reputation, the massacre of numerous British American survivors by Montcalm's Indian allies marred both triumphs.[18]

These victories marked the high point of French success in their effort to remain a colonial power on the North American continent. After the fall of Fort William Henry, the string of French victories began to end as the policies of William Pitt—"the Great Commoner," who acceded to the position of secretary of state and virtual prime minister in 1756—began to have an impact on British strategy. Pitt intended to destroy French power throughout North America as the strategic mainstay of his worldwide policy. His new approach to defeating Britain's archenemy started with a blockade of Toulon, France, to prevent reinforcements from sailing to America, followed by attacks against Ticonderoga in New York and Fort Duquesne in the Ohio Valley and a second assault against Louisbourg on Cape Breton Island.[19]

Maj. Gen. Jeffrey Amherst commanded the 1758 amphibious attack on Louisbourg with the able assistance of Brig. Gen. James Wolfe, who had already distinguished himself as an energetic and thoughtful young field commander. Wolfe served as the landing force commander in this operation and, like Amherst, represented part of the new look that Pitt had injected into the war effort.[20] In a sense, this engagement constituted the third attempt to conquer Louisbourg. In addition to the successful effort of 1745, the British commander in North America during the early years of the French and Indian War, Lord Loudoun, had organized an invasion force in the summer and autumn of 1757. That expedition actually got as far as Halifax, Nova Scotia, before bad weather, poor intelligence, and faintheartedness caused Loudoun to abort the operation and return his invasion force to New York. By the time of Amherst's attack on Louisbourg, Maj. Gen. James Abercrombie had replaced Loudoun as British commander in chief for North America. Although Abercrombie appeared somewhat superannuated, the new breed of younger and more energetic officer—as typified by Amherst and Wolfe—had acceded to most of the responsible command positions as the result of Pitt's incisive and forceful leadership.[21]

In June 1758 the British expeditionary force sailed for Louisbourg with 157 ships and approximately 12,000 men including 500 colonial rangers. In executing the amphibious assault, Amherst's landing force faced serious difficulties including heavy seas and strong defensive fire.

The French commanders had made substantial improvements in the Louisbourg defenses since its return at Aix-la-Chapelle. This made it difficult to replicate the rapid deployments of Pepperrell's assault thirteen years earlier. But the fortitude and aggressiveness of the troops and officers under Wolfe's direct command ensured a successful landing despite some initial confusion in the mind of the landing force commander.[22] Once ashore with his entire force, Wolfe suffered no further confusion, nor did Amherst or the other officers under his command. After consolidating his forces ashore, Amherst then conducted a campaign somewhat reminiscent of Pepperrell's earlier effort, defeating all French efforts to dislodge him and driving the defenders into the protection of Louisbourg's ramparts.[23]

Once Amherst controlled the land and sea accesses to Louisbourg, he moved rapidly to establish a classical eighteenth-century siege against the Vauban-style fortress, forcing French capitulation in just six weeks' time.[24] As Amherst tightened the siege on Louisbourg's fortifications, Adm. Edward Boscawen blockaded the French ships within the harbor, rendering them ineffective during the battle. At one point, the French commander sank four frigates at the harbor's entrance with the hope of keeping Boscawen's fleet at bay. But on the night of 25 July, Boscawen sent six hundred sailors in small boats into the harbor to burn one of the remaining French warships and capture the other.[25]

With Amherst's shells and mortars raining destruction into the city and Boscawen's fleet dominating the coastal approaches and preparing to enter the harbor, the French commander, Augustin, Chevalier de Drucour, asked for surrender terms. To his astonishment, Amherst offered harsh conditions with no honors of war for the French defenders. At first, Drucour refused to surrender under such terms but relented when he realized that Amherst and Boscawen were adamant and willing to destroy his force.[26] Under the conditions forced upon Drucour, the French soldiers became prisoners of war and the civilian population deported to France. These terms, which seemed so ungentlemanly to Drucour, resulted from the massacre visited on British and American defenders of Fort William Henry after its honorable surrender in 1757. Micmacs and Abenakis Indians under the command—but apparently not under the control—of the Marquis de Montcalm slaughtered numerous British and Americans living on the frontier in an infamous breach of the European rules of civilized warfare. This grated on British and colonial officers, and despite certain politeness of language associated with the interaction between the two adversaries at Louisbourg, the anger engendered by Fort William Henry had an impact on the thinking of British and American leaders in general, and Amherst in particular.[27]

The amphibious victory at Louisbourg in 1758 opened the St. Lawrence River—the avenue into French Canada—to British control. Authorities in London recognized Amherst's leadership role in the Louisbourg success and promoted him to replace Abercrombie—who failed in his attack on Fort Ticonderoga—as the supreme British commander in North America. Amherst went on to distinguish himself by capturing Ticonderoga in 1759, and, in the final campaign for control of Canada, he conquered Montreal the following year. Amherst's most important lieutenant at Louisbourg, James Wolfe, received promotion to major general and went on to immortal fame in his defeat of Montcalm and capture of Quebec during the summer and autumn of 1759. At Quebec, Wolfe and Adm. Charles Saunders used maneuver and deception to overcome a superior force entrenched in a defensive fortress that most observers considered impregnable.[28]

The battle for Quebec proved to be the critical victory of the French and Indian War, although important fighting remained. In the spring of 1760, the governor of French Canada, Philippe de Rigand, Chevalier de Vandreuil, failed in an attempt to recapture Quebec and in September suffered defeat in the battle for Montreal. It was the ability of Great Britain to capture and hold Quebec, not the fall of Montreal, that guaranteed the demise of French power in North America. The conquest of Quebec, like that of Louisbourg, resulted from an amphibious attack characterized by exemplary cooperation between the naval and landing force commanders.[29] Pitt's concept for conquering Canada in 1759 envisioned a three-pronged approach including the conquest of Fort Niagara in the west, an offensive against Montreal in the center of the colony, and an amphibious attack on Quebec up the St. Lawrence River in the east. The main French bastion of Quebec presented the most difficult objective of the war but also offered the greatest benefits if conquered. In prosecuting this operation, Wolfe and Saunders would face many challenges. Navigating the St. Lawrence River, facing the formidable French fortress and defensive lines at Quebec, and fighting against the highly professional

Montcalm constituted some of the greatest obstacles any commander would deal with in this war.[30]

Quebec rests along the St. Lawrence River near the point where it begins to broaden into a large estuary approximately a thousand miles from the Gulf of St. Lawrence. Saunders' ships not only served to transport Wolfe's army to the vicinity of Quebec but also continued to assist him as he maneuvered to gain advantage after arriving in the objective area. Saunders also used the awesome fire from his ship's guns to support Wolfe and deceive Montcalm throughout the operation. Unfortunately for Wolfe and Saunders, Montcalm's defenses offered no real openings to the amphibious task force, as they discovered in a failed assault on the French left flank.[31]

For several months Wolfe and his commanders searched for openings along the river defenses while teasing Montcalm with deceptive moves toward his right flank. In September 1759 Wolfe and Saunders undertook a cunning maneuver in which they threatened both of Montcalm's flanks, thereby pulling troops and attention away from the center. They then disembarked about 4,500 men at a relatively small cove named L'Anse au Foulon about one mile from the main Quebec defenses. Through a combination of deceit and stealth, Wolfe landed his troops, negotiated the steep cliffs, and deployed his force into battle array on the Plains of Abraham just west of the French defenses, catching Montcalm by complete surprise. At this point, Montcalm deployed the units under his immediate command and assaulted Wolfe's soldiers who now threatened his line of defense. What followed, of course, constituted a famous British victory that resulted in the deaths of both commanders.[32]

In retrospect, it is easy to claim that Montcalm erred in leaving his defensive positions to attack Wolfe. Critics point out that Montcalm's forces on the extreme right flank, under the command of Louis Antoine, Comte de Bougainville, were in position to threaten the British rear on the Plains of Abraham. Had Montcalm waited, the thinking goes, Wolfe might have found himself between two French forces and in grave danger. There is probably some wisdom in this point of view, but it does not give due consideration to Montcalm's problems. The strength of the French defense came from the tight linear positions running along the high cliffs on the north side of the St. Lawrence River. The fortress protecting Quebec was situated in the middle of this line with both flanks anchored on streambeds, making it extremely difficult to attack. Once Wolfe had penetrated this system, the entire dynamics changed. Montcalm's line had been broken, and any reaction to the penetration, such as bringing Bougainville to his rescue, would weaken French defenses elsewhere. Further, having reached the Plains of Abraham, Wolfe now had maneuver room to threaten French defenses all along the line, or to range out and destroy crops and facilities north of the river, just as he had previously done on the southern side. Montcalm had only a two-day supply of food remaining within Quebec, and Saunders' ships effectively blocked his only supply line. The British force now located on the Plains of Abraham would only get stronger over time because Wolfe could now reinforce his position, entrench, and bring up cannon.[33] With artillery ashore and Saunders' naval gunfire ships available, the British commanders could easily demolish the already battered walls of the lower portion of the city of Quebec. No guarantee existed that Bougainville's force could defeat Wolfe, even if it came up in time to cooperate with Montcalm. In fact, when Bougainville did arrive on the field after the defeat of Montcalm, the British sharply repulsed his attack and forced him to withdraw. For the French defenders, it was harsh reality that once Wolfe's army stood in battle formation on the Plains of Abraham, Montcalm had no good choices, only bad ones. Being a good and brave soldier, Montcalm chose the one he considered the most honorable.

Once Montcalm attacked Wolfe's forces on the Plains of Abraham, the superior quality of the British soldier decimated his formations. Yet, despite this display of tactical competence, it was the strategic and operational agility inherent in British amphibious forces that provided the key to defeat of French power at Quebec and with it the rest of North America. This striking power, coupled with the ability of the Royal Navy to control sea-lanes and limit—even eliminate—French resupply of its North American forces set the stage for the operational victories that turned the tide of the French and Indian War.[34] The success of Amherst and Boscawen in opening the St. Lawrence River through victory at Louisbourg, and of Wolfe's and Saunders' energetic operations at Quebec, changed forever the political face of North America. As illustrated by these successes at Louisbourg and Quebec, amphibious operations proved essential to Great Britain's victory over France during the French and Indian War and in the broader Seven Years' War as well. After the fall of Quebec, the fortunes of war increasingly favored the British Empire. Although the war continued to rage in Europe, India, Africa, Asia, and the Caribbean until the Treaty of Paris ended the conflagration in 1763, the die for the ultimate British victory was cast at Quebec.[35]

Victory in the French and Indian War created a new strategic reality in North America and new requirements in London. Americans now believed themselves more secure, with removal of the French threat and reduced risk of French-inspired Indian attacks. Seeing a reduced need for British troops in the colonies, they expected a reduction in defense spending. British leaders perceived a need to protect a much larger area in North America with the acquisition of French Canada and other territory east of the Mississippi. They believed that defense spending must increase to pay for this protection and, most importantly, to pay off the war debt accumulated in achieving this great victory.[36] The conflict that arose from these two new realities led to the next, and most critical, step in the building of a new American nation—the American Revolution. Amphibious operations had played an important part in achieving success in the French and Indian War. They also contributed to the convoluted political situation that resulted, and would play an equally significant role in the upcoming contest.

AMERICAN AMPHIBIOUS WARFARE

INTRODUCTION

THIS BOOK WILL FILL A GAP IN THE HISTORIOGRAPHY OF naval and military warfare. As the title implies, this book describes and analyzes early landing operations (from the Revolution through the Civil War) of American history, showing how they contributed to its rich amphibious tradition. No such study currently exists. Essentially, an amphibious action is—as defined in the U.S. Department of Defense *Dictionary of Military and Associated Terms*—"a military operation launched from the sea by an amphibious force, embarked in ships or craft with the primary purpose of introducing a landing force ashore to accomplish an assigned mission." This timeless definition applies to events of the past as well as to those of the present era.

This study does not attempt to describe every amphibious operation in early America. Rather it focuses on seven major battles or campaigns in American history that provide the reader with a strong appreciation for the roots of American amphibious traditions. It addresses other amphibious operations and various land and naval battles as necessary to place the seven major actions in proper historical context. For example, to understand the New York campaign of 1776, one must also appreciate the earlier operations at Bunker Hill and Boston. Therefore, they are included in abbreviated form in the chapter addressing New York.

Research for this work includes material from national and military archives, published primary sources material, published secondary sources, and military publications and directives. Many current concepts and terms used in this study have applicability over the long stretch of history even though they may not have existed during the period under examination. For example, the term "joint" refers to an operation involving more than one service of a single nation. Amphibious operations are usually joint unless the landing party comes exclusively from the Navy, and no such cases are included in this work. The term "combined" describes an operation involving services from more than one nation. The 1781 Battle of Yorktown is an example of a campaign that was both joint and combined—joint because it included Army and Navy units, and combined because it involved American and French forces.

The distinction between strategic and tactical levels of warfare existed in well-defined terms during the period of early America. In the last decades of the twentieth century, defense thinkers added a new level to the lexicon that fits between the tactical and strategic. This is the operational level of war and addresses actions oriented on a regional or theater level. Although the classification did not previously exist, the concept did. Military commanders fully realized that an intermediate level of war existed although they had not yet codified it in terminology. Using the term "operational level of war" in no way unfairly evaluates past historical events by applying current standards. The concept of "operational level of war" existed in the eighteenth and nineteenth centuries, even if a formal categorization did not.

A set of principles called the characteristics of amphibious warfare exists in recent and current Defense Department doctrine. The fundamental concepts they address apply to amphibious warfare throughout history. These four basic characteristics—integration between the Navy and landing force, rapid buildup of combat power from the sea to shore, task-organized forces capable of a range of missions, and unity of effort and operational coherence—are useful in evaluating the effectiveness of amphibious operations, and they help to explain success or failure. These characteristics provide one of several tools for use in assessing each of the major amphibious battles included in this study.

The principles of war came into the doctrine of most established military services during the first part of the twentieth century. They resulted from an effort to distill the teachings of military thinkers such as Carl von Clausewitz and Antoine-Henri Jomini—coupled with the hard lessons of war—into a relatively simple tool for students and practitioners of the art. Despite their checklist-like appearance, the principles of war serve only as a flexible basis for learning and assessment, nothing more. Yet they can be helpful in conducting an historical analysis of military and naval actions and are used throughout this study. The basic principles of war include the principle of the objective, the principle of mass, the principle of maneuver, the principle of the offensive, the principle of economy of force, the principle of unity of command, the principle of simplicity, the principle of surprise, and the principle of security.

The importance of military planning predominates much of the discussion of operations in this study. Planning is a component within the larger field of command and control that involves the process of identifying goals, gathering and organizing resources, and executing operations. Planning may be formal or informal but will always include such considerations as the mission, enemy capabilities, the quality and quantity of troops available to the commander, terrain and weather conditions, and time available for both planning and operations. For plans to be of value, the commander must communicate his plans in a manner that is both understandable and sufficiently detailed to ensure efficiency in execution.

In the case of the 1814 Battle of Bladensburg (a preliminary to the defense of Washington) the American commander developed a sound plan but failed to communicate it well enough to ensure success on the battlefield. During the 1847 landing at Veracruz in the Mexican-American War, planning often occurred on very short timelines, yet competent professionalism coupled with effective communications ensured an efficient and successful landing operation. The final arbiter of good planning is usually success on the battlefield although there are exceptions. George Washington, for example, consistently developed and communicated good plans, but his inexperienced and unstable army simply could not carry them out during the early phases of the Revolutionary War. Later, at Yorktown, his more capable army coupled with professional officers and units of the French army and navy could effectively execute his plans, bringing victory in the final major action of the Revolutionary War.

The chapter addressing the 1805 attack on Derna, Tripoli, introduces the concept of expeditionary warfare, a form of military action that has become very prominent among political and military leaders of the twenty-first century. Clearly, the idea of expeditionary warfare—like amphibious warfare—has deep roots in American history; and these two elements of the military art have an intertwined relationship.

Amphibious warfare is inherently expeditionary in nature, and the Derna campaign demonstrates important aspects of both. Such considerations as forward deployed forces, temporary advanced bases, sea basing, and forced entry into the objective area are expeditionary principles best achieved through amphibious actions. Since both expeditionary missions and amphibious operations are typically temporary measures, they easily meld into a common enterprise. Should a foreign mission require a long-term commitment ashore—such as the entry onto the European continent during World War II—it usually requires the establishment of bases and facilities ashore and quickly ceases to be expeditionary in nature. The operation takes on a more permanent flavor, requiring large army formations under diplomatic or political oversight, thereby replacing the initial amphibious forces. Conversely, the Derna campaign provides a rich example of expeditionary and amphibious warfare of a purer form in which American leaders used naval and military power for limited objectives on a temporary basis. The spirit of modern amphibious warfare in an expeditionary environment is captured in the U.S. Marine Corps white paper entitled *Operational Maneuver form the Sea: A Concept for the Projection of Naval Power Ashore*, and the Navy and Marine Corps white paper *. . . From the Sea: Preparing the Naval Services for the 21st Century*. Of course, these modern concepts built upon the successes experienced in early American warfare.

Occasionally this study introduces other concepts, such as the interrelationship of policy, strategy, and operations; interactions, adaptations, and reassessment of strategy and operations; the match between policy and strategy; and the adequacy of strategy to help analyze the outcome of an amphibious event. For the most part, these concepts are self-explanatory within the context of their usage in the text. In cases where they are not, an explanation accompanies the discussion.

The terminology of amphibious operations can be confusing unless the reader fully understands a few basic concepts. For example, when considering amphibious operations, most people think of an assault landing—such as those that occurred throughout World War II. This presumes a strike against prepared defenses, requiring the landing force to fight its way ashore. Yet many amphibious operations do not require such frontal action. It is actually preferable, when possible, to land unopposed and then to maneuver against the enemy force in a manner that provides advantages to the attacker. If naval gunfire and logistical support are used in such an operation, it fully qualifies as an amphibious attack, even though the landing may be unopposed. In other words, an amphibious attack need not necessarily be an amphibious assault. Other types of amphibious operations include raids, demonstrations, withdrawals, and various support missions. The key to an amphibious operation is that it projects power from the sea onto the land using both naval and ground forces.

It is important to remember that amphibious operations include both offensive and defensive actions, and that both, when viewed from the water's edge, can be instructive. Of the seven major amphibious campaigns examined in this book, five are offensive and two are defensive from the American perspective. (The New York and Baltimore campaigns were defensive, and the Yorktown, Derna, California, Veracruz, and Fort Fisher actions were offensive.) At the time that the United States fought the British—during the Revolutionary War and the War of 1812—England had the greatest amphibious capability known to history. Yet, despite initial success in the use of this capability, their amphibious efforts were decisively defeated in the last two major battles of the War of 1812—Baltimore and New Orleans. Although the Battle of New Orleans is the much better known of the two, the American victory at Baltimore provides keener insights and more important lessons for defending against an amphibious attack. That is why it, rather than the Battle of New Orleans, is included as a major case study in this work.

Lastly, it must be pointed out that this book is not a history of the U.S. Marine Corps although the Marines figure prominently in much of the story. The Marine Corps did not become the nation's primary amphibious force until after World War II. Prior to that time, the Marine Corps was too small to undertake major operations on its own. Of course, it usually participated in these large-scale operations and often performed smaller operations on its own—in conjunction with the Navy, that is. Because of the scope and size of World War II, the Marine Corps expanded vastly and undertook many major amphibious operations in the Pacific theater throughout the war. That, coupled with the work the Marine Corps had accomplished in amphibious planning and development during the interwar years, ensured a major role for the Marine Corps in the subsequent defense structure of the United States. Today the Marine Corps clearly stands as America's amphibious force in readiness, but during the early American Republic, it played a more ambiguous role.

Chapter 1

THE NEW YORK CAMPAIGN

THE 1763 PEACE OF PARIS THAT ENDED THE FRENCH AND Indian War altered the face of America and gave rise to conditions that would ignite even greater changes shortly thereafter. In an effort to raise revenue to balance its budget and consolidate control over its empire, British authorities in London initiated a series of ill-conceived acts that caused a tumultuous reaction in the North American colonies. The first of these actions involved the Proclamation of 1763 in which Great Britain closed the area west of the Appalachian Mountains to white settlement. Like many acts that followed, leaders in London had good intentions. They desired to avoid conflict between settlers and Indians long enough to arrange treaties with native tribes that would ensure an orderly and peaceful process of settlement. But Americans viewed the action very differently. They had fought the French and Indian War, in part, with the implicit understanding that the territory would become available for their future development.

Parliament followed with a series of equally unpopular measures, including the Currency Act of 1764, the American Duties Act (Sugar Act) of 1764, the Quartering Act of 1765, the Stamp Act of 1765, the Townshend Acts of 1767, the Tea Act of 1773, and ultimately the Coercive Acts (Intolerable Acts) of 1775. These measures and other actions by British leaders engendered intense resentment among colonial Americans, ultimately leading to the Declaration of Independence in July 1776. By that time, Americans were in open rebellion, having confronted British troops at Lexington and Concord, fought at Bunker Hill, captured Fort Ticonderoga, and invaded Canada. The resulting war pitted the loosely associated nation of thirteen former colonies against the most powerful nation in the world. As with the previous imperial wars, naval power and amphibious actions would play a key role in resolving the question of American independence.

Although the British navy had deteriorated badly since its unquestioned superiority at the end of the French and Indian War, the rebellious colonies started the conflict with no navy at all. This granted complete control of the seas and littorals of North America to Britain during the first three years of the war, which proved particularly vexing to George Washington. The situation changed somewhat over time, with the advent of "Washington's Navy," the establishment of the Continental Navy, the creation of state navies, and the issuance of letters of marque by both federal and state governments. Yet, despite some spectacular victories at sea—such as those of John Paul Jones later in the war—the British usually dominated naval warfare and joint operations in American waters. Not until the French recognized American independence and declared war on Great Britain in 1778 could the United States entertain any hope of mounting large-scale amphibious operations, and even then such actions remained problematic.[1]

After Spain and Holland joined the war as allies of France, Britain found itself outnumbered in total warships but still could usually maintain local naval superiority during key operations in North America.[2] The one exception was off the Virginia Capes during the Yorktown campaign in 1781. At all other times, its Royal Navy gave Britain control of North American waters and allowed its political and army leaders the flexibility to conduct operations virtually anywhere they wished.[3]

The value of naval superiority first became apparent to American leaders with the British amphibious withdraw from Boston in March 1776 and the subsequent amphibious campaign to capture New York.[4] If the withdrawal from Boston demonstrated the efficacy of one of the lesser types of amphibious operations, the offensive in New York exemplified its most important. And if the capture of New York did not end the war, it clearly gave Britain the strategic advantage during its first phase.

The conflict between Britain and her American colonies—both the political and violent dimensions—had from the very beginning centered in Boston. As a result, Boston also became the focus of British reaction and served as the initial base for its military activity. After the engagements at Lexington and Concord, militia from all over New England converged on Boston, placing the British forces in a virtual state of siege.[5] In an effort to alter this situation and remove a potential threat to transportation and communication lanes, Lt. Gen. Thomas Gage, commander of British force in North America, ordered Maj. Gen. Sir William Howe to attack the American fortifications located on the dominant high ground on Charlestown peninsula across Boston Harbor. On 17 June 1775, Howe landed a force of 2,200 soldiers and marines—later reinforced by 400 additional troops under Maj. Gen. Sir Henry Clinton—at the base of Breed's Hill. After three furious assaults, Howe's attack drove the militia from Breed's Hill to Bunker Hill and, after the defenders ran out of ammunition, from that position and off the Charlestown peninsula. This secured the high ground north of Boston.

British success in the Battle of Bunker Hill proved a Pyrrhic victory in every sense of that concept, succeeding at a terrible cost to the attacking force.[6] When forced to fall back, the Americans retreated in relatively good order, believing they had won a moral victory over the British regulars.[7] Clinton commented the night following the battle that Bunker Hill was "a dear bought victory, another such would have ruined us."[8] Equally important, in the judgment of some analysts, the bloody experience on Bunker Hill seemed to change Howe from an aggressive, daring warrior to a cautious, irresolute commander.[9] British casualties in the Battle of Bunker Hill amounted to 1,054, while the Americans suffered 411 killed and wounded plus 30 captured.[10] The dubious victory at Bunker Hill contributed to Gage's relief as British commander in North America and the elevation of Howe.[11]

Rather than loosening the siege-like conditions around British forces in Boston, the Battle of Bunker Hill caused them to tighten as militia continued to assemble in the surrounding hills.[12] In June 1775, the Continental Congress appointed George Washington commander in chief of the forces at Boston. A month later, when he took command of this "Continental Army," the Virginian was impressed by what he learned about its success at Bunker Hill but expressed concern about the men's state of training, discipline, and organization.[13] The shortage of weapons and gunpowder coupled with the complete absence of a quartermaster department—needed to ensure systematic procurement and resupply—further distressed the general. Washington energetically set out to correct these and other deficiencies and build an army for the new nation.[14] From an operational point of view, Washington focused on Gage's force bottled up in Boston. His instinct was to attack, and he frequently addressed the issue with his war council and members of the Continental Congress.[15] Yet concern that any major failure at this point could doom the Revolution before it had a chance to succeed caused him to delay, but not to forgo, the possibility of offensive action.[16] In this he found a cooperative opponent as Howe, who succeeded Gage in command at Boston on 10 October 1775, seemed satisfied to remain immobile within the confines of the city of Boston, awaiting reinforcements and unsure of what else to do.[17]

By February 1776 Washington decided to attack Howe's force in Boston, once additional cannon and ammunition then en route from Fort Ticonderoga reached his army. In an incredible feat of logistics in the face of forbidding weather and terrain, Col. Henry Knox delivered sixty-six field pieces and mortars to Washington's army, more than doubling its heavy weaponry.[18] With the guns from Ticonderoga and about 16,000 soldiers in camp, Washington believed the situation now demanded that he take the offensive against Howe's force in Boston.[19] Although the Continental Army still did not have a surfeit of powder, Washington felt he had enough to undertake an attack. His plan involved the bombardment of British positions for three consecutive nights. On 4 March—the third night of shelling—the artillery increased its intensity while Washington's soldiers occupied and fortified Dorchester Heights, which overlooked Boston and its harbor from the south. Howe awoke on 5 March to find a powerful American presence all along the Dorchester ridges and on other key terrain.[20] Howe and his commanders stood in utter amazement at the achievement of military engineering and in terror of its military implications. Washington had replicated on an even larger scale the threat Howe had previously faced from the heights on Bunker Hill.

Although not particularly heroic in appearance, amphibious withdraw can be an important strategic maneuver. Commanders conduct amphibious withdrawals to extract their troops from a hostile shore by sea. There are many reasons to conduct such an operation, including military pressure from an enemy, economy of force operations, and force redeployment.[21] All of these influenced Howe's withdraw from Boston, but the primary factor in the timing of his decision involved the military pressure that made his tactical situation untenable. Both armies claimed the British retirement from Boston as a victory. Howe departed with his army intact to fight again under circumstances more to his advantage and better under his control. Washington had maneuvered Howe out of his position and from the thirteen former colonies, and reclaimed Boston for the United States. For him, it had been a clear tactical victory, and a bloodless one at that.

But removal of the British army from New England proved a temporary respite. With a dominant navy and the ability to reintroduce his army at virtually any point along the American littorals, Howe held the advantage of initiative. Washington faced the disadvantage of having to determine his adversary's intentions with limited information. Although he recognized the necessity to be on guard for a variety of options, Washington felt certain that the next major blow would come at New York.[22]

Upon assuming command in New England, Washington created a small naval force—often referred to as Washington's Navy—to support operations throughout the northeast.[23] Additionally, on 10 November Congress had directed him to create two battalions of "American Marines to be considered as part of the Continental Army before Boston," but he deferred action due to manpower and recruitment shortfalls.[24] Recognizing the pressures and limitations on Washington, Congress took the first step to establish the Continental Navy on 13 October 1775 by ordering the construction of two armed vessels. On 28 November 1775, it provided for creation of the Continental Marine Corps.[25] While Washington remained preoccupied with future British strategy, the new Navy and Marine Corps conducted a successful amphibious raid on the Bahamian island of New Providence. Commo. Esek Hopkins commanded the squadron and Marine captain Samuel Nicholas led 234 Marines and 50 sailors ashore to capture two forts, the town of Nassau, the British governor, and large quantities of ordnance and military stores—all vital to the American war effort. The captured ordnance included 88 guns, 15 mortars, 16,535 rounds of shot and shell, and 24 casks of powder. Unfortunately, the take in powder did not prove as great as expected because two ships with approximately 150 casks (some sources report up to 200 casks) of powder had slipped out of port before Hopkins blockaded the harbor.[26] But this operation constituted one of the most

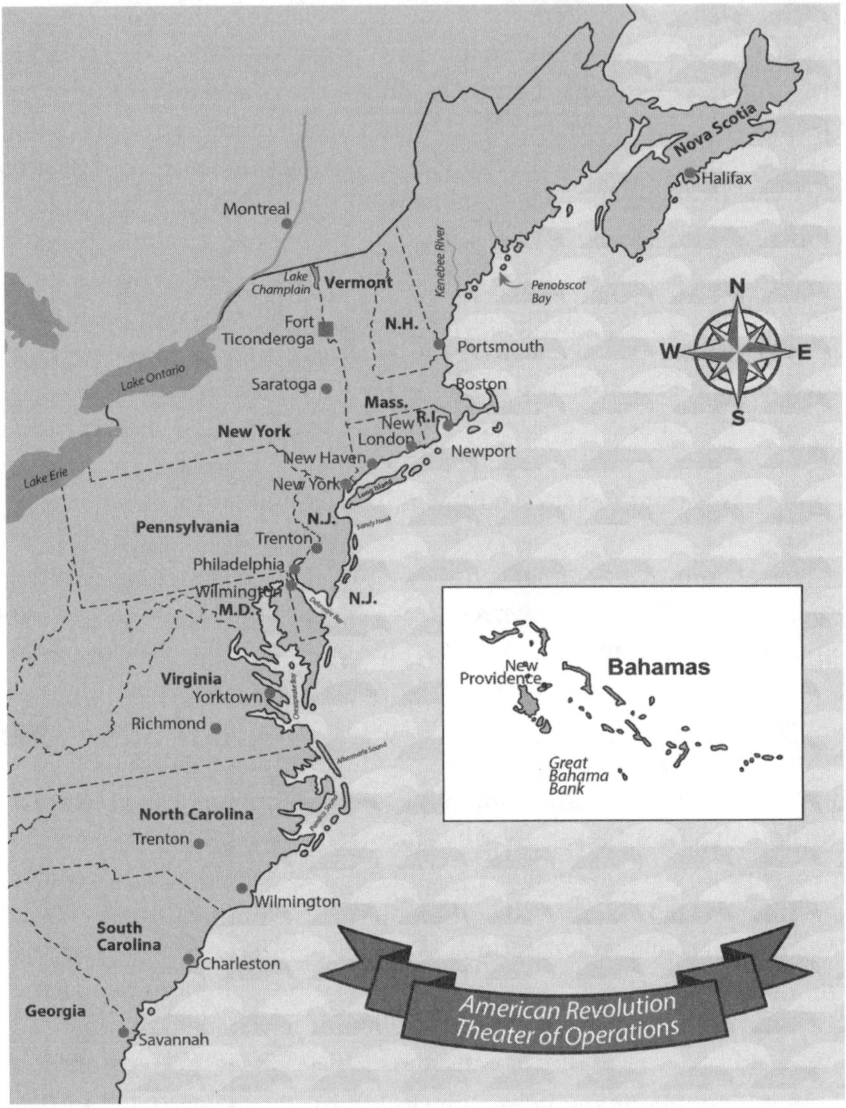

MAP 1. American Revolution Theater of Operations

successful American amphibious actions of the Revolution and one of its most important naval victories, boosting the morale of the new sea services. In addition to the stores of ordnance, Hopkins brought back three captured ships, along with Gov. Montfort Browne and two other British officials as prisoners of war.[27] This proved helpful later, during the battle for New York, when Washington exchanged Browne for the American generals Lord Stirling and John Sullivan, after their capture on Long Island.[28] And, of course, the raid provided much needed arms and military stores for Washington and his Continentals.[29]

Washington realized that the power of the British navy operating in conjunction with Howe's army along the Atlantic coast represented the greatest threat to the Revolution.[30] During his investment of Boston, Washington developed a sophisticated intelligence-gathering system that included agents operating within British lines.[31] Both his information and strategic instincts told him that an amphibious attack on New York would be Howe's next move. In fact, New York offered one of the best and most easily defended harbors in the northeast and could serve as an ideal base for future actions along the American littorals.[32] Moreover, it offered the British control of the lower Hudson River (also called the North River in the Manhattan area), which would be critical in severing New England—the hotbed of rebellion—from the rest of the nation. Additionally, much of the population of New York City and Long Island, unlike that of New England, favored the Tory cause, and Howe could expect better local support and a friendlier environment.[33]

Two months before the British withdrawal from Boston, in January 1776, Washington dispatched Charles Lee to develop a plan to defend New York and begin preparing positions. On 13 March, before the British had begun their withdrawal from Boston, Washington dispatched five regiments and one rifle battalion as an advance force for defense of New York.[34] After withdrawing from Boston, Howe initially moved his force to Halifax, Nova Scotia, where he awaited reinforcements, including a new naval commander for North America. Vice Adm. Richard Lord Howe, Sir William's brother, arrived to take charge of all naval forces in North American waters, including those soon to operate in the New York environs. During July and August of 1776, British forces began to assemble in the waters surrounding New York and established an advance base on Staten Island.[35]

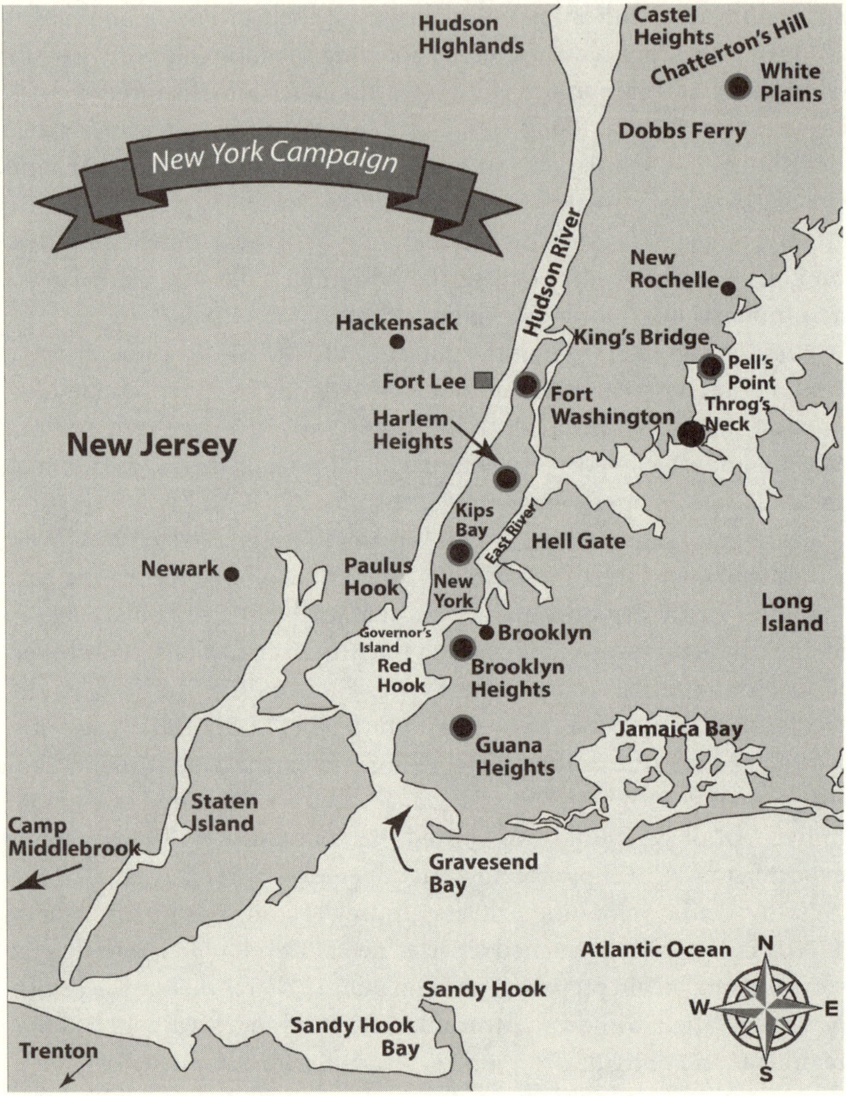

MAP 2. The New York Campaign

An additional force of 44 ships under Commo. Sir Peter Parker with about 2,500 troops under Lt. Gen. Charles Lord Cornwallis also arrived from the British Isles after a detour to the southern states of America. Prior to evacuating Boston, Howe had sent Clinton with a small troop of infantry to Virginia and North Carolina to join Cornwallis' force, which arrived at Cape Fear during May 1776. Howe intended for Clinton and Cornwallis to help British Loyalists there to reclaim North Carolina and Virginia.[36] This southern excursion proved unsuccessful because Congress had earlier taken Charles Lee from his duties in New York and dispatched him south to deal with Tory resistance. Lee organized American efforts at Baltimore, Williamsburg, and Norfolk while southern Patriots battered and disbursed Loyalist elements in battles at Great Bridge near Norfolk, Virginia, and Moore's Creek Bridge in North Carolina, all before Clinton and Cornwallis appeared on the scene.[37] With their primary mission in shambles before they even arrived, Parker, Clinton, and Cornwallis decided to capture Charleston, South Carolina, rather than give up completely on their southern venture. Upon hearing of Parker's fleet moving south, Lee immediately proceeded to Charleston, where he directed defensive efforts. After an inept landing attempt on Long Island (now called the Isle of Palms) and a subsequent mauling of Parker's ships—his flagship, HMS *Bristol*, was hulled seventy times—by the batteries of Fort Moultrie that protected Charleston Harbor, the British commanders acknowledged failure and limped back to New York, joining Howe's gathering forces.[38] This abortive effort undercut any prospect of a British southern strategy in 1776 and delayed further efforts in that quarter for two years. But the Howe brothers did not expect the war to last that long. They intended to end the rebellion in New York with the largest expeditionary effort ever assembled by Great Britain up to that time.

In addition to the already powerful British forces gathering around New York, Howe received 8,000 Hessian soldiers, bringing his total force to between 34,000 and 42,000 men, depending on which source one accepts. Although these Hessians are frequently referred to as mercenaries, they were actually well-trained and disciplined units of established armies from various German principalities—primarily Hesse-Cassel, Hesse-Hanau, Anspach-Beyreuth, Anhalt-Zerbst, Waldeck, and Brunswick. The British government contracted with German princes for the services of their troops, thereby justifying the term "mercenary." Yet the Hessians did not represent mercenaries in the twentieth-century concept of the term where freelance individuals sought work soldiering in various conflicts around the world. Ultimately, nearly 30,000 Hessians served the British Crown during the American Revolution to the financial benefit of their various sovereigns.[39]

To defend New York City, which was confined to Manhattan during the eighteenth century, Washington had roughly 23,000 Continentals and militia spread over key terrain on Long Island and Manhattan.[40] Washington could not defend New York simply by placing an army within the city because Manhattan was an island, and the British navy controlled the surrounding waters. If the British tired of laying siege to the American forces, they could land an army on Manhattan Island north of the city and launch a land attack. The Howe brothers rejected bombarding the city out of concern for Loyalists residents and concluded it would take too long to starve the Americans into surrender; instead they decided to launch a land attack.[41]

The tactically sound way to defend New York involved dominating the prominent ground on Harlem Heights to the north, controlling the high ground across the East River in Brooklyn and further out on Long Island, and occupying Governor's Island to the south. Howe's initial attack in New York focused on Washington's most forward positions across the East River on Gowanus Heights (also known as Guian Heights and Long Island Heights) and in Brooklyn. The American force there amounted to about nine thousand men under a fluid command structure.

Charles Lee had devised the defensive plan for New York and established the preliminary positions on Gowanus Heights and in Brooklyn prior to departing for the south. After Washington moved the bulk of his army into New York City, he assigned Nathanael Greene to command the defensive effort on Long Island. But Greene came down with a severe fever just before the British landing and therefore played no role in the subsequent fighting.[42] John Sullivan ascended to temporary command in Greene's absence. By the time of his arrival in New York, Sullivan already had a somewhat checkered career in the Continental Army. Replaced by Horatio Gates as senior commander in the Northern Department after the failed invasion of Canada, Sullivan had spent some time in the interim as a disgruntled officer.[43] But Washington retained confidence in him.[44] At the moment of the British attack, Washington placed Israel Putnam in overall command, with headquarters in Brooklyn, while Sullivan retained command of the most forward position located on Gowanus Heights. Putnam had held senior command at Bunker Hill, a battle that continued to influence thinking in both camps. Washington, Putnam, Sullivan, and other American commanders thought they could replicate that battle if they entrenched on favorable terrain and enticed the British to make frontal assaults.[45]

Howe and his commanders had similar memories about Bunker Hill and sought ways to attack the Americans without repeating that experience. Charles Lee, who had initiated work on the New York defenses, organized the battlefield so that American defenders could fight on favorable terrain rather than directly oppose the British landing at the beaches. Washington and Greene retained Lee's plan after arriving from Boston and continued defensive preparation along similar lines.[46] The forward American defenses on Long Island stretched from west to east—from the American right to left—along Gowanus Heights with forces under the command of William Alexander (known as Lord Stirling to his contemporaries) covering the right half and those under the direct command of Sullivan on the left. On his extreme left, Sullivan placed a Pennsylvania regiment under command of Col. Samuel Miles. The main American position on Long Island lay to the rear of Sullivan's defensive line in Brooklyn, where Putnam maintained his headquarters.[47] Washington and Greene envisioned a scenario where the soldiers in forward positions under Sullivan would inflict maximum casualties on the attacking British and Hessians and then conduct a fighting and orderly withdraw to the main position in Brooklyn, where the British advance would be defeated.[48]

During July and August, Lord Howe conducted a naval reconnaissance in the waters around New York and harassed Washington's communications north of the city in the area of the Tappan Zee. The relative ease with which they could operate on the multitude of waters surrounding New York pleased the Howe brothers as much as it dismayed Washington. American commanders had put considerable effort into creating obstacles and establishing shore batteries to control, or at least disrupt, British naval activity in the operational area, with little apparent success.[49] During this sparring period, the Howe brothers pursued a last-minute yet fruitless effort at peace negotiations. Although Washington agreed to some prisoner exchanges and left open the prospect of future talks, he rejected further talks, telling the British that they must deal with the Continental Congress.[50]

At sunrise on 22 August, the British fleet moved into the Narrows between Staten Island and Long Island while approximately 400 transports shuttled Howe's amphibious force to the landing beaches within Gravesend Bay. The initial landing inserted 4,000 soldiers, and by noon the British put 15,000 ashore achieving a very rapid buildup of combat power. This increased to about 20,000 within the next three days as Howe introduced his reserve forces into the beachhead. The advance element of the assault force under Cornwallis had immediately captured the township of Flatbush and began probing the American positions on Gowanus Heights. Faulty intelligence reports from the front tended to understate the number of troops ashore, causing Washington concern that the landings on Long Island could be a ruse.[51] The fact that Howe did not attack Gowanus Heights for five days after his initial landings, coupled with continuing naval activity in the Narrows, in the waters near Governor's Island, and around Red Hook peninsula tended to reinforce this idea.[52] Washington personally made frequent trips to Long Island, and, as he observed the forces arrayed against him, he came to realize that the landing at Gravesend Bay must surely be the British main effort.[53]

Despite the strength of the British landing on Long Island, the battle appeared to be developing as Washington had hoped. He rushed additional troops to reinforce the American defenses, expecting that British honor would demand that they attack his positions. But Howe's memory of Bunker Hill proved as good as that of his opponents, and he did not intend to repeat previous mistakes.[54] Recognizing the strength of the American positions, he chose to envelop to the east, sending a force through the unguarded Jamaica Pass on the extreme left of the defensive line. American commanders knew of this threat of envelopment, of course, and Sullivan had ordered Miles to patrol and observe the Jamaica road on that flank. Washington and Putnam apparently accepted Sullivan's arrangement, assuming they would have word of any British movement in that quarter in time to send reinforcements. Sullivan and Miles sent an observation team of five young militia officers to watch Jamaica Pass, and Washington ordered Miles to patrol toward Jamaica

Pass. For the most part, Miles complied with his orders, but he made the disastrous decision not to patrol during hours of darkness.[55]

In the early hours of 27 August, a British column of some ten thousand soldiers under command of Clinton and guided by local Tories and an impressed Patriot began moving to the east in an effort to get around the American left flank. By 0300 the British had captured the observation team protecting Jamaica Pass before its members could give the alarm, thereby denying Sullivan an opportunity to react before the British could menace his rear. At first light, British ships opened fire on American positions from the Narrows between Staten Island and Long Island to divert attention from the main effort. The Royal Navy also attempted to station several ships in the East River to attack the American rear in Brooklyn, but the wind and tide prevented this. As Clinton struck at Sullivan's rear with his enveloping force, Howe attacked all along the line. He sent Lt. Gen. Leopold Philip von Heister's (de Heister in some accounts) Hessians against the American left and center through Flatbush and Bedford Passes, and Gen. James Grant's Redcoats against Lord Stirling on the American right flank.[56]

With Clinton attacking their rear, Grant pressing on the right, and von Heister attacking the left and center, many of the inexperienced American troops broke and fled to the defensive position located on Brooklyn Heights where Putnam had his headquarters. Although the defeat on Gowanus Heights turned into a rout in some areas, in other cases units and individual soldiers stood their ground or retreated with good discipline. The fact that both Lord Stirling and Sullivan became prisoners of war amid stalwart units attempting to cover the retreat illustrates this fact. But isolated examples of courage and fortitude, no matter how noble, proved insufficient to stave off the British and Hessians. The psychological impact of rapidly shifting from a position of advantage to one of high risk proved too great for many of the inexperienced militiamen and Continentals. In addition, when competent and responsible officers such as Lord Stirling and Sullivan saw their units in danger of being surrounded and destroyed, they often ordered them to disperse into the woods and find a way back to Brooklyn, thus contributing to the impression of a rout.[57]

Feeling pressed from front and rear, the Americans fell back, and Putnam consolidated his forces on Brooklyn Heights. Washington, still hoping for a defensive battle against a British frontal attack, reinforced Putnam with several regiments from New York City, bringing his force on Brooklyn Heights to about 9,500 men. Although many British officers wanted to continue the attack and immediately assault Brooklyn Heights, Howe demurred. He and his engineer officers recognized the American defenses as even more formidable than those at Bunker Hill. He chose instead to conduct a siege, hoping he could use the guns of the fleet in conjunction with aggressive entrenchment to reduce the American positions through bombardment.[58] Following two days of waiting and hoping for a British frontal assault, Washington had second thoughts. After holding a council of war, he decided to move Putnam's force from Long Island back to Manhattan. Washington had long worried about the possibility of Howe conducting a landing on Manhattan while holding large numbers of American troops in place at Brooklyn. With this concern nagging his mind, he decided it was time to reunite his army on Manhattan. This involved a dangerous and tricky undertaking since the British navy controlled the waters and potentially could interpose.[59]

On the night of 29 August, Washington combined bold planning with stealthy movement to evacuate his forces on Long Island along with all their arms and ammunition across the East River into friendly lines on Manhattan. He accomplished this with the help of foul weather conditions and the superb work of Col. John Glover's regiment of Massachusetts fishermen-turned-fighters. Although never a part of the Marine Corps or involved in power projection operations, Glover's troops became known as Washington's "amphibious regiment" due to its work here and elsewhere. When British patrols probed American lines the next morning, they found only empty positions. Amazingly, the American forces on Long Island had escaped the trap that Howe believed he had closed.[60] The following day, Washington conducted a smaller yet equally remarkable evacuation of American forces and their equipment from Governor's Island in the face of British naval power.[61]

During a pause in combat, a second peace conference, known as the Staten Island Peace Conference, met on 11 September. Lord Howe initiated the meeting with John Adams, Benjamin Franklin, and Edward Rutledge, but it quickly ended because Howe was not authorized to recognize American independence and the three congressmen demanded such recognition before they would discuss any other topic. Unable to negotiate an end to the rebellion, British leaders resumed operations against the island of Manhattan to bring about its defeat. With the enemy in complete control of the surrounding waters, Washington and his officers considered the tactical problems of defending against British operations on Manhattan Island. Their alternatives included defending New York City, moving further north to Harlem Heights, or abandoning New York entirely and reverting to a Fabian strategy. Washington discussed the future of New York City with his generals and the Congress, evaluating both the feasibility of defending and the possibility of evacuation.[62]

On 7 September, Congress limited Washington's options by expressing its desire that the army defend New York City. Although strategically desirable, this proved a near tactical impossibility. Nathanael Greene—restored to health and duty—attempted to persuade Washington to abandon and destroy the city along with its suburbs. This, Greene pointed out, would deny its use to the British as a barracks for winter quarters and as a center for economic activity.[63] Washington agreed with Greene's assessment but felt constrained by the will of Congress. On 12 September, the situation changed when word arrived from Philadelphia authorizing abandonment, but not destruction, of the city. That same day Washington held a council of war at which he and his generals reaffirmed they could not hold New York City. Washington also learned that day that the British navy had moved into position at Hell's Gate, where it could interdict his possible escape route to the east.[64] This development required the Continental Army to maintain control of the avenue of access and egress at Kingsbridge across the Harlem River to the north.[65] Ever since moving into the New York area, Washington had gone to great lengths to keep open his northern avenue of escape over the Harlem River.[66] With the enemy at Hell's Gate to the east and in control of the Hudson River to the west, only Kingsbridge remained as a viable escape route from Manhattan Island.

Once Congress authorized the abandonment of New York, Washington began evacuating the American troops north to Harlem Heights. But a shortage of wagons and draft animals slowed the effort, and before he could complete the movement, Howe launched the British attack on Manhattan Island.[67] Again taking advantage of their unchallenged naval supremacy, the Howe brothers conducted an amphibious assault at Kips

Bay on 15 September with about four thousand Redcoats and Hessians under command of Clinton, with Cornwallis leading the primary assault element. This threatened the American army by interposing Clinton's force between Putnam's troops still in New York City and the forces already positioned on Harlem Heights. Although a very complex operation, the British landing proved extremely efficient due to Howe and Clinton's organization and planning. The British generals had orchestrated a movement involving the landing force, a deception operation, and the stationing of frigate fire-support ships in such a manner as to maximize their combat power while restricting American's ability to react.[68]

The British landing at Kips Bay came as a surprise since both Washington and Greene expected it to occur farther north, perhaps on the Harlem Plains or above Kingsbridge.[69] Howe actually intended to land at Horn's Hook, adjacent to Harlem Plain, but after receiving intelligence about its defenses, he considered the Americans too strong at that point. As a result, he chose Kips Bay, where the defenders consisted of the newest and least-experienced recruits in the American army, primarily Connecticut militia. New to the stress of combat, they panicked at the impressive—although ineffective—naval bombardment that preceded the British attack. This, coupled with the professional-looking Hessian and British regulars arrayed against them, unnerved many of the green troops. Regrettably, their panic spread along the line and set others into flight back to the defensive positions on Harlem Heights.[70]

Having rushed to the sound of battle, an enraged Washington personally attempted to stem the tide at considerable risk to his own safety, all to no avail.[71] Clinton and Cornwallis penetrated into the island less than one mile to Inclenberg Hill and then, acting in accordance with Howe's orders, began to consolidate their beachhead.[72] A more aggressive leader may have pushed across Manhattan Island and completely cut off Putnam's force, now marching from New York City to Harlem Heights.[73] Then again, a more aggressive leader may have stretched his landing force too thin and been defeated by the feisty Putnam, moving north out of New York City. This possibility is not an idle thought when one realizes that Col. William Smallwood's Maryland regiment repulsed repeated British attacks as it covered retreating American units subsequent to the British landing at Kips Bay. Smallwood's actions clearly demonstrate the vulnerability of a landing force when not concentrated. Had Clinton rushed across the island, he would have doubled the amount of terrain his forces would have to cover, making him weaker at all points.[74]

Upon hearing the firing at Kips Bay, Putnam set two brigades into motion to help defend against the landing. After the initial American rout by the landing force, "Old Putt" realized he must immediately try to slip past the developing British threat. Thanks to his aide's knowledge of the New York area and his own energetic leadership, Putnam found an open route leading out of New York west of the British beachhead at Kips Bay. This allowed Putnam's troops to elude Clinton's landing force and join Washington's main element on Harlem Heights. Putnam evacuated five thousand men from New York but could not remove all of the Continental Army's heavy cannon or stores due to pressure from the amphibious landing force.[75] That evening the still furious Washington consolidated his exhausted army on Harlem Heights and sent out reconnaissance patrols to assess the enemy situation. Although he demonstrated anger and frustration at the actions of his troops at Kips Bay, he remained hopeful that they might yet acquit themselves well.[76]

After establishing his landing force ashore, Howe quickly consolidated his beachhead at Kips Bay and moved on to occupy New York City. Meanwhile, Washington attempted to restore some confidence in his soldiers and create a sound tactical situation for continuing the battle. At this point, Washington had about 16,000 men available, of which he sent 6,000 to reinforce Maj. Gen. William Heath at Kingsbridge to protect his rear and secure the possible escape route.[77]

On the morning of 16 September, Washington's army regained some self-assurance when a reconnaissance patrol of about 150 rangers under Lt. Col. Thomas Knowlton observed an advanced British element vulnerable to isolation. Staging a feint in front of the enemy, Washington enveloped the British force with Knowlton's rangers and three rifle companies of Virginians—later reinforced with two regiments from Maryland and New England—driving them back into the main British lines. Washington believed the American victory could have been even greater had the enveloping force penetrated deeper to the British rear, as he had ordered. Yet his untrained soldiers had fought well and courageously, somewhat offsetting the embarrassment of Kips Bay the previous day and from the earlier action on Gowanus Heights. The engagement, resulting in some 230 British and 135 American casualties, had a noticeable impact on the morale of the army.[78]

Washington appreciated the improvement in his troop's performance but knew that the problems facing his army required more than local successes. He firmly believed that frequent dependence on militia units to augment his Continentals would ultimately prove disastrous. He also knew that short-term enlistments within the Continental Army would not provide a force able to contend with British power. He therefore began a relentless appeal to Congress for fundamental improvements, including long-term enlistments, less dependence on militia, and stronger articles of war with which to regulate his army.[79]

After the American victory at Harlem Heights, Howe again sought to destroy Washington through an indirect approach, fearing the American position too strong to storm directly without excessive losses. On 12 October, he sent Clinton and Cornwallis up the East River through Hell's Gate to Throg's Neck (also referred to as Frogg's Point during the Revolutionary War) where he conducted an abortive landing. American defenders under Heath's direction made excellent use of the difficult terrain coupled with rapid reinforcement to stymie every British effort to penetrate beyond their initial beachhead. Recognizing his tactical error, Howe reembarked the landing force at Throg's Neck and conducted a second landing at Pell's Point on the morning of 18 October.[80] This placed Howe in position to threaten Kingsbridge from either the east or north, with Washington's main army still south of the Harlem River.

With the exception of 2,000 soldiers under Col. Robert Magaw left behind at Fort Washington on northwest Manhattan, Washington moved his entire army across the Harlem River to a position where he could counter any action by Clinton and Cornwallis. Washington questioned the wisdom of maintaining a force at Fort Washington with the rest of his army north of the Harlem River.[81] But Greene argued that Fort Lee (previously known as Fort Constitution), across the Hudson River on the New Jersey bank, could support Fort Washington, and together these two forts could interdict British naval activity on the river. After a council of war supported Greene's position, Washington reluctantly agreed to garrison the forts, but only on a temporary basis. He viewed this as a tentative commitment and held the issue open for further review.[82] Washington sent one brigade to a forward position at White Plains and located his main body where it could react to British actions from the various watercourses surrounding the operational area. At this point, Washington had about 14,000 men under his immediate command, plus 3,500 across the Hudson River at Fort Lee in New Jersey.[83]

In addition to repositioning his army, Washington conducted a reorganization based on changes resulting from the recent fighting. Charles Lee had returned from his successful operations in the southern states. John Sullivan and Lord Stirling had returned from British captivity through a prisoner exchange worked out between Washington and Howe. Washington restructured his army into seven divisions under Nathanael Greene, William Heath, Charles Lee, Benjamin Lincoln, Israel Putnam, Joseph Spencer, and John Sullivan.[84] Greene's division occupied Forts Washington and Lee on opposite sides of the Hudson, and Washington positioned the rest of the army where it could maneuver against British forces north of the Harlem River. Washington deployed a brigade under Colonel Glover to engage Cornwallis' landing force after it came ashore at Pell's Point.

Possibly due to his own modesty, Glover is one of the unsung heroes of the American Revolution. Earlier his "amphibious regiment" had been key to moving the army across the East River to safety in Manhattan after Washington evacuated Brooklyn Heights. And his skillful and courageous delaying action against the British landing force at Pell's Point provides a classic model for defending against amphibious attack by a superior force. In a series of leapfrog-type retrograde movements, Glover drew the British and Hessians into one ambush after another, inflicting severe damage and delaying their movement. Despite his fighting withdrawal, Glover could not prevent the more powerful amphibious force from advancing to New Rochelle, where Howe concentrated his army for an attack on Washington near White Plains. But Glover's daylong fight at Pell's Point (sometimes called the Battle of Pelham Bay) impeded the British long enough for Washington to move his army into more favorable ground.[85]

On 22 October Washington's advance elements reached White Plains, and by 27 October he began to concentrate his forces. Throughout this period, constant skirmishing occurred between the opposing forces. On 28 October Washington engaged Howe's army of about 13,000–14,000 British effectives then located in Westchester County. After arriving at

White Plains, Howe observed the American positions on three hilltops north and west of the town. Determining the American right flank on Chatterton Hill to be the most vulnerable, he sent two regiments (one British and one Hessian) across the Bronx River to attack frontally while enveloping the American right with a regiment of Hessians under Col. Johann Gottlieb Rall, hoping to catch the defenders in a classic pincer movement. Initially, the militia and Continentals on Chatterton Hill withstood the assault, twice counterattacking and driving back the British and Hessians. But as British cannon fire began to take effect and British cavalry arrived on the scene, the Americans gave way. Howe's troops then occupied Chatterton Hill and established an artillery position from which they could bombard the entire American line. The British and Hessian forces had taken Chatterton Hill, but at a cost of 200 casualties to about 175 for the Americans. The determined resistance gave Howe pause, and he chose not to continue the attack against the entrenched Americans.[86]

Considering his positions untenable due to British cannon fire from Chatterton Hill, Washington moved his forces to prepared defenses about half a mile back and then to a set of entrenchments on North Castle Heights. After probing Washington's position for several days, Howe determined it was too strong to assault and on 4 November returned his army to Manhattan to consolidate his grip on New York City. Howe's move not only surprised American commanders, it also confused them. If Howe did not choose to fight at White Plains, what did he intend to do? Many American leaders thought this might presage a complete change in strategy. Opinion ranged from predicting a move to reinforce Canada in the north, to a possible redirection of effort toward the southern states, or an attempt to capture Philadelphia. Washington believed—correctly it turned out—that Howe would attempt to reduce Fort Washington on Manhattan and then turn his efforts to New Jersey. But he could not be certain of this and needed to guard against various possibilities. As a result, he sent Heath north to Peekskill with 4,000 men to reinforce the entrance to the Hudson Valley. He left Lee at North Castle Heights with 7,000 troops and personally took 2,000 across the Hudson River into New Jersey to join Greene's 3,500 troops at Fort Lee, where he also expected to receive substantial reinforcement from the New Jersey militia. At this point, neither Washington nor Greene considered giving up the fight against Howe's army located in the New York and New Jersey area.[87]

Greene continued to insist on the defense of Fort Washington across the Hudson on Manhattan and sent reinforcements increasing the garrison strength to nearly 2,800 men.[88] Even this effort would prove insufficient to defend the fort and all its outposts against the power Howe could bring against them. Congress continued to insist on obstructing passages up the Hudson River, and this required American possession of both Forts Washington and Lee. Therefore, against his better judgment and with great reluctance, Washington acceded to the continued occupation of Fort Washington. On 16 November, British and Hessian units launched a vicious assault on Fort Washington from the north, south, and east against stubborn American resistance. By 1500, the attackers had compressed Magaw's force into a much-reduced perimeter, and he agreed to surrender rather than experience the bloodbath that would surely have followed.[89]

The loss of Fort Washington constituted the greatest American defeat up to that point in the war. It was also Nathanael Greene's lowest point of the war although, for the most part, he escaped criticism for his role in the disaster.[90] Despite this debacle, Washington and Congress did not lose faith in the abilities and fidelity of Greene. Although he had insisted throughout that he could defend or at least evacuate Fort Washington by water if pressed by the enemy, American leaders did not lose sight of the fact that Greene's abilities would be crucial to ultimate success.[91] The losses at Fort Washington amounted to 78 killed and 374 wounded for the British and Hessians, and 59 killed and 96 wounded for the Americans. More critically, the disaster resulted in the capture of roughly 2,800 American soldiers—most of whom suffered terribly in British captivity—and the loss of all their weapons and equipment.[92]

After the fall of Fort Washington, the commander in chief knew he must also evacuate Fort Lee and the New Jersey shore. He immediately began removing ammunition and supplies in anticipation of a retreat across New Jersey. On 19 November a force of 6,000 under Cornwallis moved across the Hudson and attempted to capture Washington and Greene's force still at Fort Lee, but the Americans slipped away before Cornwallis could close his trap.[93] Thus began a march across New Jersey in which Cornwallis pressed Washington but could never quite catch him. Able to beat the British to Trenton, Washington evacuated his army across the Delaware River and destroyed or captured all boats and ferries to prevent further pursuit.[94]

Washington had lost the battle for New York but saved his army and the Revolution. He had also lost one of his most senior officers when a British patrol captured Charles Lee as he attempted to bring his forces south to join Washington. John Sullivan assumed Lee's command and ultimately brought that division into Washington's camp. By that time Washington had begun to have second thoughts about Lee's value to the war effort. Lee had been very slow in responding to orders, and when he did move, it lacked the energy and quickness that Washington expected.[95] In fact, among the major commanders on either side, only Washington acted with speed and agility during the entire episode following the fall of Fort Washington. This undoubtedly saved his army as Cornwallis, though slow, skillfully pursued with a large and determined force.[96] Washington demonstrated notable adeptness in getting his widely disbursed forces across the Delaware and establishing control over the river before Cornwallis and Howe could catch up and effect a crossing.[97] In fairness to Howe, his problems exceeded that of catching Washington before his escape into Pennsylvania. He needed to secure an all-weather port for harboring his brother's ships before the enclosed waters around New York began to freeze. Well before Washington began his retreat across New Jersey, Howe had begun preparing an army to move into Newport, Rhode Island, and gain control over the ice-free waters of Narragansett Bay.[98]

With Washington's escape across the Delaware, the amphibious aspects of the New York campaign essentially ended. The reversal of fortunes that resulted from Washington's attacks at Trenton on 26 December and Princeton on 2–3 January 1777 are, of course, among the most important American successes of the Revolution and two of the most brilliant tactical victories of the eighteenth century.[99] But a river crossing is hardly an amphibious operation, even with Glover's "amphibious regiment" manning the oars and controlling the boats.[100] And the dazzling maneuvers that brought victory at Princeton rests more in the category of land warfare than amphibious operations, despite the presence of Samuel Nicholas and three companies of Marines who joined Washington for the operation.[101] But the actions occurring throughout the New York campaign, including Long Island, Manhattan, and Westchester County, exemplify the nature and value of amphibious warfare and joint operations. At no time in the eighteenth century did any military force execute amphibious evolutions more completely or more skillfully than did the Howe brothers in the campaign for New York. Although often criticized as being too slow in execution, they conducted one of the most successful amphibious campaigns in history. If they were slow, they were also methodical, and they recognized that any major mistake could spell disaster.

Washington's army, although untrained, poorly equipped, inexperienced, and imperfectly disciplined, could be an effective—if erratic—instrument of war, as Howe learned at Harlem Heights, Pell's Point, and White Plains. Many observers suggest that Howe and his generals should have executed this campaign more aggressively. But bolder action would have also resulted in more opportunities for the Americans to exploit, as they did at Harlem Heights and Pell's Point. There is no guarantee that a more forceful approach by Howe, Clinton, and Cornwallis would have resulted in a more complete victory or in destruction of the American Revolution during the New York campaign. That assumption, although widely held by historians, remains speculative.

The decision to defend New York against British power made excellent strategic sense. Of all the deepwater ports along the American seacoast (Boston, Newport, New York, Norfolk, Charleston, Savannah), New York provided the best position to serve Britain's military and political objectives. It directly supported the British strategy of severing New England through control of the Hudson River Valley from New York to Canada. It also allowed the Howe brothers to leverage the relatively strong Loyalist sympathy that existed in that area. Defeating the British in New York would create great strategic benefits for the American war effort, and this certainly influenced the thinking of Washington and members of Congress. But despite its strategic importance, defending New York never made tactical sense in the presence of the Royal Navy. There simply existed too much water and shoreline available for amphibious operations. And at this point in history, no nation could conduct amphibious operations better that Great Britain.[102] The defense of New York may have been strategically desirable, but it proved tactically impossible given the power symmetry that existed between the adversaries.

Although the New York campaign ended with the crossing of the Delaware, the Howe brothers had undertaken an important adjunct amphibious operation designed to occupy Rhode Island and control Narragansett Bay.[103] In early December 1776 Lord Howe sent Parker to Newport with a force consisting of thirteen warships, fifty-one transports, and seven thousand troops under Clinton, where they conducted an unopposed landing and began a three-year occupation of the area.[104] The American garrison of about six hundred men felt unable to oppose Clinton's landing and retreated north across the Bristol Ferry. Although the troops evacuated most of their supplies and ammunition, the Americans left behind fifteen to twenty heavy cannon due to the speed of Clinton's amphibious operation.[105] In response to this amphibious thrust, Washington ordered Benedict Arnold and Joseph Spencer to Rhode Island, but they accomplished nothing more than to limit penetration of the countryside by the British and Hessians.[106] Control of Narragansett Bay not only provided the British with the best deepwater and ice-free harbor in America but also denied its use to numerous privateers operating from those waters. Due to the depth of Narragansett Bay and Newport Harbor, ship movement depended less on tidal considerations, thereby allowing for more free and aggressive naval operations. This provided an obvious advantage to whoever controlled Narragansett Bay. Additionally, establishing a base at Newport complemented naval operations conducted from New York and helped to tighten the blockade of the American coast.[107]

Beyond the strategic value of Newport, Howe hoped to gain a logistical advantage by acquiring food and fodder from the surrounding area. New York and New Jersey could not provide an adequate supply of these staples because of the destruction of fields and stores by retreating Americans. Additionally, Howe and his staff had misjudged the potential of that area as a supply base. Unfortunately for Howe and his army, New England Loyalists could provide very little beyond the needs of the local population and the troops occupying Newport. This, coupled with harsh winter weather conditions, caused the entire Narragansett Bay expedition to be a disappointment. Yet the capture of Newport accomplished British strategic goals and brought a knighthood to Sir Henry Clinton. Returning to New York in July 1777 after a triumphant visit to England, Clinton clashed with his immediate superior, Sir William Howe, regarding the next British move in subduing the American rebellion.[108]

This phase of the Revolutionary War—from Bunker Hill to the capture of Newport—represents a primarily amphibious campaign. Although the landing on the Charlestown peninsula and subsequent attack up Bunker Hill is amphibious only in a narrow sense of that concept, it is so fundamental to the Boston and the New York campaigns that it must be considered part of the whole. New York, of course, is the centerpiece of this first phase of the war and certainly the most important British victory of the Revolution. Washington became fixated with British occupation of New York, and it influenced his thinking—for better and for worse—throughout the war. The struggle for New York is a classic of amphibious excellence and could easily have ended the Revolution had it not been for Washington's operational agility. There are lessons for both offensive and defensive aspects of amphibious warfare in this campaign.

British forces proved successful at New York for numerous reasons. Obviously, they had superior naval and military power in every sense of that concept. But equally important, they applied their power prudently. At this point in the war, the British exercised a harmonious interrelationship of policy, strategy, and operations. The objective of Lord George Germain—the colonial secretary in London—and the Howe brothers in North America was well aligned and consistent. This would not be true in subsequent operations, and Britain later paid a high price for that at Saratoga. On the American side, this interrelationship proved less effectual. Congress placed numerous requirements on Washington—such as occupying New York City and maintaining free access along the North River—that constrained his operational and tactical decisions. Washington deferred to Congress while he argued for changes in their policies. He usually got his way, but this took time, and events on the battlefield moved faster than the decisions of Congress.

In addition to having good relations and effective coordination among the various operational and political elements, the Howe brothers performed well in the fundamental characteristics of amphibious operations. The integration between the navy and landing force proved excellent in all landings and immediate operations ashore. To some extent that may be attributable to the fact that the two component commanders were brothers. But in fact, the amalgamation of effort goes much deeper than that simple explanation. In every landing, the two elements developed mutually supporting plans at all levels, met timetables necessary for tactical implementation, and accomplished their missions with the synergy of a well-coordinated organization.

The ability to build up combat power rapidly is perhaps the most important element of an amphibious landing, and the Howe brothers accomplished this in a notable manner. Even at Throg's Neck, where Howe landed in an undesirable area, the entire landing force had quickly established itself ashore in a full combat posture. When withdrawn and reinserted at Pell's Point, the operation proved equally efficient. As Glover fought his delaying action against the British landing force, he faced its entire combat power.

One reason that British commanders could consistently build up combat power so rapidly involves the characteristic of task organization. Simply stated, this element allows commanders to properly configure the landing force based on the mission and capabilities of their fighting units. This structuring can include considerations regarding the mix of types of units, such as infantry, cavalry, artillery, and engineers. It can also include considerations among national forces such as English, Scottish, and Hessians. Each of these groups had a slightly different training and equipment makeup and could bring different skill sets to the battle. Task organizing to take advantage of all these attributes requires competent planning including mission analysis, evaluation of force structure, and the creation and dissemination of operation orders. British excellence in these areas is demonstrated by the fact that they always had the correct forces available when required. For example, Howe had artillery just when he needed it at White Plains, and engineers when wanted at Brooklyn Heights. When they operated outside the discipline of amphibious operations, they proved less reliable, such as arriving at the Delaware River without boats to cross. In that case, Washington simply needed to destroy or capture all boats along the river to halt Cornwallis' pursuit.

The final characteristic of amphibious operations involves unity of effort and operational coherence. Although the Howe brothers affected unity of effort very well, operational coherence proved more elusive for them. This is illustrated in the British failure to capture or destroy Washington's army despite outstanding amphibious landings and initial battle successes. On Long Island, Howe's force conducted an impressive landing and won a significant battle at Gowanus Heights only to have their offensive halted by the defenses on Brooklyn Heights. At Kips Bay,

Howe routed the defenders near his landing site and occupied New York City, but his force could not cut off Putnam's retreat from New York, and he suffered a setback when he engaged Washington at Harlem Heights. Again in Westchester County, Howe landed successfully at Pell's Point, drove Glover's defenders before him, won a victory against an isolated force on Chatterton Hill, and then ran out of steam against Washington's strong positions on North Castle Heights.

Historians give various reasons for the British lack of operational coherence in the New York campaign. Some contend that the high casualties at Bunker Hill traumatized Howe, causing him to become too cautious. Others suggest that the three key leaders—Germain and the Howe brothers—still hoped for reconciliation and therefore avoided delivering a crushing defeat that would humiliate the Americans beyond repair. Some believe that Washington's operational skills explain this phenomenon. They argue that, although he might have lost tactical engagements, Washington always planned for actions several moves ahead of the current event. He developed what we now call branch and sequel plans for every eventuality and placed his forces in such positions that they could always execute several options. If the British closed down one option, Washington could execute another.

Which of these theories best explains the British lack of operational coherence in the New York campaign? Undoubtedly all three—and more—played a role, but the third offers the best explanation. Throughout the war, Washington consistently avoided destruction of his army, even when faced with overwhelming superior force and flawless execution. Although Washington's performance at the tactical level may be mediocre compared to other great captains in history, his skill at the operational and strategic level was superior. It is the operational agility and strategic genius of Washington that best explains British lack of operational coherence during the New York campaign.

Chapter 2

NEW YORK TO YORKTOWN

AFTER LEAVING WINTER QUARTERS IN THE SPRING OF 1777, Sir William Howe spent several months maneuvering around New Jersey in an attempt to entice George Washington into open warfare. Rather than accept Howe's invitation to battle, Washington closely watched British movements from his fortified base at Middlebrook, New Jersey. In a Fabian-like operation, Washington struck small British detachments when he could and avoided battle where Howe would have the advantage. Washington reluctantly played this game throughout the spring and summer of 1777 because his lack of troops and supplies made offensive operations risky at best. Frustrated at his inability to bring Washington into a major battle and experiencing several minor yet sharp engagements resounding to the advantage of his adversary, Howe evacuated his army to Staten Island, leaving all of New Jersey except Paulus Hook to the Americans. Here he remained encamped, pondering his next move.[1] At this point, the British match among policy, strategy, and operations broke down due in part to the secretary of state for colonies Lord George Germain's ineffective leadership. The lack of effective coordination for the total war effort allowed the two main British armies in North America—Howe in New York and Gen. John Burgoyne in Canada—to act almost as independent forces rather than a synchronized team.[2]

Simultaneously with Howe's maneuverings in New Jersey during 1777, Burgoyne attempted to sever New England from the middle states by driving south along the Richelieu River, through Lake Champlain, and down the Hudson River. This river and lake avenue provided a water route for armies moving south from Canada, or north out of New York City. Germain and Burgoyne expected Howe to advance north along the

Hudson River in coordination with the southern thrust from Canada, but Sir William had other ideas. To resist Burgoyne's movement, Washington rushed reinforcements north to Philip Schuyler and Horatio Gates while keeping his remaining force in New Jersey, where he could defend Philadelphia from various possible British threats.[3] The presence of Washington's army in New Jersey coupled with the strong fortifications he had established along the Hudson Highlands undoubtedly contributed to Howe's decision not to move north and operate in conjunction with Burgoyne. He would have to fight his way past the American strong points at Stony Point, Peekskill, Forts Clinton and Montgomery, and West Point, with Washington in his rear—not an attractive prospect. But this decision left Burgoyne to face the full power of American military forces north of New York, which proved stronger than Howe had anticipated. In a series of defeats including Fort Stanwix, Oriskany, Bennington, and ultimately Saratoga, Burgoyne's effort failed utterly, bringing not only the surrender of an entire British field army but also French entry into the war as an American ally.

While Burgoyne attempted his penetration into American territory from the north, Howe moved against Philadelphia, the de facto American capital. Not wanting to attack across New Jersey with Washington on his flank, the general decided to make an amphibious thrust from south of the city. He left Clinton in New York with some 6,000 men to protect the city and provide what support he could to Burgoyne. That support proved to be little more than limited and ineffective probes against American positions along the Hudson Valley, particularly at Forts Clinton and Montgomery. On 23 July 1777, Howe sailed from New York with 260 warships loaded with 18,000 men, artillery, horses, and supplies for locations unknown to the Americans. This constituted the very thing Washington feared and envied most about British power: the ability to employ naval supremacy in conjunction with the army to conduct and support landing operations at any point along the American coastline.[4]

When Howe initially loaded his amphibious force in early July 1777, Washington believed he would move north up the Hudson to cooperate with Burgoyne's southward thrust.[5] When the British fleet sailed to sea rather than up the Hudson River, Washington felt certain that Howe would move south but could not yet be sure of his ultimate destination.[6] Would he enter the Delaware River or the Chesapeake Bay, or would he shift the focus of battle farther south to Charleston or Savannah? Although not entirely certain of Howe's main objective, Washington determined it prudent to concentrate his forces near Philadelphia.[7] Once he received reports that the fleet had arrived in the northern Chesapeake and had started off-loading at Head of Elk (present-day Elkton) in Maryland, Washington concluded that Howe would attack Philadelphia from the south.[8]

After landing on 25 August 1777, Howe advanced north toward Philadelphia while Washington moved south to protect the capital. Advanced detachments from Washington's army harried Howe's landing force as it moved from its beachhead including a particularly sharp engagement occurring at Cooch's Bridge.[9] Despite American interdiction efforts, Howe pressed on to the town of Kennett Square, Pennsylvania, where he deployed his force to engage Washington.[10] The main elements of the two armies met on 11 September at Brandywine Creek. In a partial replay of the Battle of Long Island, Washington selected good defensive ground on the east side of the creek, hoping to entice Howe into a frontal attack. In a series of intense clashes, the British advantage in numbers and position—including an effective flanking movement reminiscent of Gowanus Heights—overpowered the defenders, causing Washington to withdraw his force from the battlefield. Although recognized as a clear British victory, the Americans—with few exceptions—fought well at Brandywine and did not leave the field in despair.[11] Many felt pride in their efforts and confident regarding their ability to fight the regulars in the future, although Washington realized that his army was not yet a match for the British and German professionals.[12] Despite the defeat at Brandywine, Washington continued to oppose Howe's drive but could not prevent the British from occupying Philadelphia on 26 September.[13]

After the battle of Brandywine, the fighting between Howe and Washington ceased to be amphibious in nature. By the time subsequent operations occurred around Philadelphia—the Battle of the Clouds, Paoli, Germantown, Monmouth—Howe and Clinton (who replaced Howe as commander of British North American forces during June 1778) no longer maneuvered by sea to fight the Americans in the mid-Atlantic colonies. But to ensure an ongoing supply and communications system to support the occupation of Philadelphia, British commanders needed to open the Delaware River access to the city.

Lord Howe departed the Chesapeake on 14 September, three days after Brandywine, being satisfied that his brother had firmly established his position ashore and no longer required naval support. He then turned his attention to the American defenses along the Delaware River approaches to Philadelphia. During October and November, Lord Howe conducted a series of joint attacks that were more naval and riverine than amphibious. Despite determined resistance, Lord Howe reduced Forts Mifflin and Mercer, clearing the water access to Philadelphia just as Washington's forces tightened control of the overland access into the city.[14]

In February 1778, while Washington's army trained and endured conditions at Valley Forge, American diplomacy scored a major victory. Through a set of treaties of friendship and commerce, the United States essentially gained French recognition as an independent nation and set the groundwork for France to join the war as a belligerent against Great Britain. France had provided the United States covert aid in the form of munitions and money since 1775 with the implicit understanding that this could possibly lead to war. But not until the American victory at Saratoga and the determined but failed attack at Germantown during October 1777 did the efforts of Benjamin Franklin, Silas Dean, and Arthur Lee bring about French recognition. By May of 1778 Congress had approved the treaties, and by June France had become an American ally in the war against Great Britain.[15] Spain and the Dutch Republic would eventually join France, although each had its own set of war aims and ambiguous relations with the United States. For the British, this had the obvious effect of broadening the conflict well beyond the thirteen colonies and complicating their strategic planning. To a considerable extent, the focus of British attention shifted from subduing a rebellion on the continental mainland to an imperial war with worldwide implications. For America, French involvement offered the prospect of strong naval support and the fulfillment of Washington's long-held hope of being able to execute joint and combined operations. For both America and Britain, this presaged more of a naval focus in future operations.

Despite the importance of the strategic alliance, relations with France started poorly and caused frustration among American leaders before producing results. Yet the alliance influenced British thinking even before it became an effective instrument of war. Most importantly, the British army could not remain in Philadelphia once France officially entered the war. All communications between Philadelphia and New York, including supply support, had to move by sea because Washington's army controlled the country between the two cities. With the prospect of French ships plying American waters, the British occupation of Philadelphia became untenable, prompting Clinton to return his army to New York. In May 1778 Clinton replaced Howe as commander of the British army in Philadelphia and began his evacuation of the city. He loaded his noncombatants and all stores on transports, except for enough supplies for his main army as it moved overland to New York. The navy ferried Clinton's army across the Delaware River and then sailed for New York. During the march across New Jersey, Washington attacked Clinton at Monmouth on 28 June, winning a tactical draw but a moral victory as the Continentals fought well and the British withdrew from the field.

In July 1778 a French fleet under Adm. Charles Hector Théodat, Comte d'Estaing, arrived off the Virginia coast with instructions to cooperate with his American counterparts. D'Estaing came very close to catching Howe's fleet loaded with elements of Clinton's army and the bulk of his supplies at sea in a vulnerable situation. British leaders in London had dispatched a fleet under Vice Adm. John Byron to interdict d'Estaing and reinforce Howe. But Byron departed three weeks behind d'Estaing, giving the French commander a window of naval superiority in North America.[16]

Although Lord Howe reached New York Harbor before the French fleet could engage him, both d'Estaing and Washington intended to find a way to exploit their naval advantage. D'Estaing pursued Howe to New York, but his deeper-draft ships could cross the bar at Sandy Hook only during certain times, and then very slowly, making them vulnerable to British fire.[17] Lord Howe had emplaced shore batteries and stationed warships where he could dominate the avenues of approach at Sandy Hook, further complicating any effort to cross the bar into New York Harbor. Even if unable to enter the harbor, d'Estaing now controlled the waters outside Sandy Hook and around Long Island. Hoping for a joint and combined action against New York, Washington moved his army across New Jersey, linking up with a force from northern New York under Horatio Gates, and establishing strong positions north and west of Manhattan. Washington and d'Estaing now had Clinton's forces bottled up in New York, on Staten Island, and at Newport. But d'Estaing did not believe they could dislodge Clinton from New York and, seeing no advantage to an extended blockade, suggested an amphibious attack to reclaim Newport and Narragansett Bay.[18]

In August 1778 British general Sir Robert Pigot held Newport with some six thousand regulars. John Sullivan and a small contingent of Continentals watched Pigot from nearby Providence while Washington and d'Estaing planned a combined and joint operation. Their concept involved landing a few of d'Estaing's four thousand troops on Conanicut Island—across from Newport—to observe activities and serve as a staging area for the main attack. Sullivan would ferry his troops onto Rhode Island (Aquidneck Island) from the north and prepare to attack Pigot's force. As Sullivan moved into position, d'Estaing would land his main force on the western side of the island just north of Newport for a simultaneous assault on the British defenses. The ships of d'Estaing's fleet would support both the landing of French troops and the movement of Sullivan's force. But just before d'Estaing landed his troops on Aquidneck Island, Lord Howe, later reinforced by Lord Byron, arrived with British ships, threatening d'Estaing within Narragansett Bay. This forced d'Estaing to recall his troops from Conanicut Island and move immediately to engage Howe's fleet.[19]

For two days, the fleets maneuvered inconsequentially, each seeking the advantage of wind. Before any major combat occurred, a severe storm dispersed the ships, causing considerable injury to both fleets. With his fleet too severely damaged to conduct a major action, Howe returned to New York, and d'Estaing sailed briefly back to Narragansett Bay. When d'Estaing returned to Narragansett Bay, he decided his fleet had suffered too much impairment to resume amphibious operations or even remain in the area. On 22 August, despite extensive efforts by American leaders to dissuade him, d'Estaing sailed for Boston to make repairs.[20]

Sullivan now confronted British power alone in Rhode Island, with his officers and troops believing the French had abandoned them in the middle of a crucial campaign. Furthermore, the Royal Navy soon gained uncontested sea control in the waters of Narragansett Bay. Learning that Lord Howe's fleet approached Newport with Clinton and four thousand reinforcements, Sullivan decided to evacuate Aquidneck Island. While retreating from Newport, Sullivan repulsed repeated attempts by Pigot to destroy his force on Aquidneck Island, winning several major tactical victories over his adversary. John Glover's "amphibious regiment" ferried the Americans to safety at the Tiverton and Bristol crossings.[21] By the time Clinton landed his reinforcements and interdicted the channels, Sullivan's men had moved beyond his grasp.[22]

The initial effort at combined warfare involving American and French forces had been a major disappointment, leaving many Americans unsure of the commitment and reliability of their new ally.[23] Meanwhile, Howe and Clinton made use of their enhanced naval power by conducting a series of amphibious raids along the New England and New York coastlines designed to destroy stores and cause confusion regarding British intentions.[24] In November d'Estaing departed for the West Indies, ending any possibility for combined operations in the foreseeable future. Newport and its superb harbor remained in British hands for another fourteen months. But with the introduction of French naval power and improved coordination between French and American commanders, such outposts became more vulnerable to amphibious attack. This fact, coupled with increasing demands on British resources and a shift in operations toward the southern states, caused Clinton to order the evacuation of Newport in late 1779.[25] By then the focus of British strategy had shifted to the southern colonies and the West Indies.

While d'Estaing and British naval commanders directed their attention toward the West Indies, Clinton ordered Lt. Col. Archibald Campbell and a detachment of 3,500 troops including British regulars, American Loyalists, and Hessians to capture Savannah, Georgia. Campbell departed New York on 27 November 1778 on board a naval squadron commanded by Capt. Hyde Parker. Many leaders continued to think of southerners as more loyal to Great Britain than the inhabitants of northern states. By freeing them from the Patriots' grip, British leaders reasoned, the southern colonies would happily return to the Crown. Attempting to reclaim Georgia and South Carolina in the winter of 1778–79 made good sense to British planners, and Clinton initiated this effort by his attack on Savannah in late December. Clinton's southern strategy involved first capturing the city of Savannah and then moving up the Savannah River to take Augusta. After securing Georgia, he would attempt the more difficult task of capturing Charleston and reclaiming South Carolina. It seemed a well-conceived plan, and the operation got off to a good start. In a series of engagements on 27–29 December, Campbell defeated a disparate and inexperienced group of about 1,200 Continentals and militia under the confused command of the American major general Robert Howe, thereby capturing Savannah. After this defeat, Maj. Gen. Benjamin Lincoln—who had been within a few days' march of Savannah when the battle occurred—integrated remaining elements of the American force into his southern command.[26]

Before another major action occurred in the southern theater of war, American forces attempted an amphibious strike against Fort George on Penobscot Bay, in present-day Maine. During the summer of 1779, British commanders established a post on the Bagaduce Peninsula (present-day Castine, Maine[27]) under command of Gen. Francis McLean to assert British control of Maine, serve as a base for raiding the New England coastline, and counter the actions of privateers operating in nearby waters. Moreover, they also hoped to establish a colony there for the resettlement of displaced Loyalists.[28]

Officials in Massachusetts decided to move quickly against the intrusion before the British constructed permanent defenses and established a strong naval and army presence in the area. They designated Commo. Dudley Saltonstall as naval commander of the Penobscot expedition, which consisted of three ships of the Continental Navy (one frigate, one sloop, and one brig), three brigs of the Massachusetts Navy, one brig of the New Hampshire Navy, twelve privateers, and assorted transports and supply ships. The landing force would consist of nine hundred volunteers under Brig. Gen. Solomon Lovell and three hundred men from the Continental Marine Corps augmented by state marines. The marines were technically under Saltonstall, but Lovell used them freely, and they proved their worth as a professional force to spearhead the assault landings and conduct other essential missions. The total strength of the task force, including marines, sailors, and soldiers, amounted to some two thousand men. This included Lt. Col. Paul Revere's artillery unit, consisting of two eighteen-pounders, three nine-pounders, four four-pounders, and one howitzer. Saltonstall and Lovell served as co-commanders, thus denying the benefits of unity of command to the operating force. For this injudicious decision, the expedition would pay dearly.[29]

The expedition finally got under way on 19 July. Two days later it stopped at Townshend, Maine (present-day Boothbay Harbor), where it was joined by five additional ships and Maine militiamen (who made up the bulk of the ground force) before continuing to Penobscot Bay on 24 and 25 July. During the transit, Lovell finalized his invasion plan, designed to maximize the element of surprise. It called for an initial lodgment by an advance party, which would protect the flanks of three subsequent assault landings. The landing craft would sequentially return to their ships after each wave to embark and deliver the next assault element. Lacking adequate intelligence, a small detachment of marines went ashore during the night of 24 July on Fox Island at the mouth of Penobscot River to question local residents on the enemy situation. They learned that Fort George, the key British defense structure in the target area, was still under construction and that defenses were "feeble at best." This good news was somewhat offset by the unexpected presence of three British sloops of war in Majabigwaduce Harbor under the command of Capt. Henry Mowat. Mowat skillfully anchored his ships in the narrow part of the bay with his flanks covered by shore batteries located on Nautilus Island and Dyce's Point.[30]

During the afternoon of 25 July, Saltonstall ineffectually engaged Mowat's ships, after which Lovell's men commenced landing operations just north of Dyce's Head on the southwest side of the peninsula. But the lateness of the hour coupled with high winds and choppy seas caused concern in Lovell's mind that conditions would slow landing operations, leaving troops on shore without adequate support. Amid confusion and turmoil, he recalled his landing craft and abandoned the attack, leaving the British with the impression they had repulsed an American attack. The next day, despite intelligence that Fort George was vulnerable to attack from shipborne fires, Saltonstall refused to move against Mowat's ships to position his force for such an attack. The commodore felt constrained by the broadsides of Mowat's ships along with the vagaries of wind and current in the confined space of Majabigwaduce Bay. He did agree to an amphibious landing to capture Nautilus Island in the mouth of the bay located adjacent to Mowat's defensive line of ships. Late in the afternoon of 26 July a landing force of several hundred marines under Capt. John Welch assaulted and captured the island along with its battery of four cannons. This set the stage for fortifying the island and establishing additional gun positions from Revere's artillery in an exhaustive overnight effort by marines, sailors, and militiamen. This action placed Mowat's ships at risk, forcing him to move farther up the river, thereby clearing the way for Saltonstall' s ships to advance if he chose to do so.[31]

With Mowat's ships removed from the immediate scene of operations, Lovell ordered an assault for the early hours of 28 July consisting of Saltonstall's marines, Lovell's militiamen, and Revere's artillerymen. In a modification of Lovell's earlier landing plan, the landing force came ashore under supporting fire from navy ships, pressing every possible boat into service with the marines in the vanguard. Once ashore, the Americans faced a determined resistance from McLean's well-entrenched troops holding positions on the high ground behind the landing beaches. Lovell sent the marines, accompanied by a few militiamen, to the right toward Dyce's Heights and a force of militiamen to the left. A mixed force remained in the center to draw fire and provide support. After furious fighting against terrain and foe, the marines drove their opponents off Dyce's Heights and into the unfinished defenses of Fort George. The marines also captured a shore battery that had been dueling with Saltonstall's ships and then fanned out over the high ground in front of Fort George. At this point, McLean considered himself defeated and contemplated surrendering to preserve the lives of his remaining troops.[32]

Despite the hard-won success, Lovell—not realizing that his British counterpart was preparing to surrender—chose not to press on to total victory but ordered his command to prepare defensive positions against a potential counterattack.[33] While Lovell brought up artillery from the ships and Nautilus Island and Saltonstall skirmished ineffectually with Mowat's inferior ships, McLean improved his defenses and brought up additional guns from Mowat's transports. On 29 July a concerted artillery duel opened between the two forces. Lovell implored Saltonstall to attack and destroy Mowat's ships in Majabigwaduce Harbor, which he outgunned six to one, but to no avail. Saltonstall satisfied himself with cannonading and seeking shore-based sites, in addition to Nautilus Island and Dyce's Head, from which to destroy Mowat's sloops of war. The two commanders put all thoughts of offensive action against Fort George temporarily on hold. For the cautious American commanders, valuable time was lapsing, and their relaxed approach to warfare was about to cost them dearly.[34]

The impasse created by Lovell's lack of aggressiveness and Saltonstall's lack of commitment to the landing force resulted in a siege approach to the battle. The land commander believed the navy should lead with an attack on Mowat's ships and a bombardment against Fort George. The sea commander believed the ground forces should lead with an attack against Fort George, thereby preventing shore-based batteries from threatening his ships. After two weeks of inaction (other than cannonading and siege warfare), the two commanders were finally ready to cooperate in a simultaneous attack and were in the early phases of its execution when sails of the British relief force were spotted coming up the bay. The dilatory agreement between Saltonstall and Lovell had come too late; time had run out. On 13 August a British squadron under Commo. Sir George Collier arrived to intimidate and then defeated the entire expeditionary force.[35]

During the night of 13–14 August, Lovell began evacuating his men and equipment back to their transports. After a council of war on the morning of 14 August, Saltonstall—considering himself outmatched by Collier—ordered the squadron to flee up the Penobscot River, where he could establish a defensive position or land the crews and destroy his ships. Acting independently, the American ships, including the transports, sought safety up the Penobscot River. All American ships (seventeen warships and twenty transports) were eventually fired by their crews or destroyed by the British. Troops were set ashore without organization or leadership and forced to fend for themselves. Fortunately, despite the disastrous loss of ships and equipment, most men eventually made it home alive.[36] Penobscot stands with the Narragansett Bay operation of 1778 as an example of how irresolute leadership negated the advantages of military strength. At Narragansett Bay, failure resulted from d'Estaing's overconcern about the storm damage to his ships. At Penobscot Bay, it resulted from Saltonstall's focus on geography, wind, tides, and three British sloops of war.

As the Penobscot expedition and its aftermath played out in New England, operations in the southern states intensified. After Campbell had taken Savannah and Augusta, the new American commander of the southern department, Benjamin Lincoln, tried to challenge British forces in Georgia and the Carolinas. But Lincoln suffered a series of setbacks, beginning with a failed attempt—in conjunction with d'Estaing—to reclaim Savannah and the loss of Charleston. In September 1779 d'Estaing returned to American waters from French successes in the West Indies, intending to launch an amphibious attack against the British in Savannah.[37] Washington hoped d'Estaing would return to New York and join his army in an attack on British forces there, but d'Estaing chose to operate in Georgia. After being repulsed at Savannah, the French and Americans retreated, with d'Estaing departing for France and Lincoln returning to Charleston, where he found himself in the difficult position of preparing defenses with insufficient troops and uncooperative political support.[38]

As the war progressed Clinton came to believe that combining the perceived strength of southern Loyalists with a main force effort against Charleston provided the best opportunity to destroy American military power. Confirming that Savannah remained in British hands and that d'Estaing had departed American waters, Clinton departed New York for South Carolina on 26 December 1779 with a force of 8,500 men, including Charles Lord Cornwallis as his second in command.[39] According to British cavalry commander Lt. Col. Banastre Tarleton, Clinton selected Charleston because of the "mildness of the climate, the richness of the country, its vicinity to Georgia, and its distance from General Washington."[40] Clinton and Cornwallis had failed to take Charleston during their 1776 venture largely because of the battering of Adm. Sir Peter Parker's ships by the American defenders in Fort Moultrie at the mouth of Charleston Bay. But in 1780 Clinton and Cornwallis arrived on aboard Vice Adm. Marriot Arbuthnot's much more powerful fleet, consisting of 10 warships, 90 transports, and some 5,500 sailors and marines.[41] The British generals also commanded a much larger landing force, which they used more intelligently than on the previous occasion.

Believing he must leave at least 15,000 men in New York to counter any moves by Washington, Clinton completely evacuated Newport to augment his amphibious force for this mission. After landing his army south of the Charleston, Clinton moved methodically into positions north of the city and began constructing parallel siege lines.[42] Simultaneously, Arbuthnot's fleet ran by the guns of Forts Moultrie and Johnson. The American naval commander Commo. Abraham Whipple "scuttled several of his ships to serve as the basis of a log-and-chain boom between Charleston and a muddy island called Shute's Folly. The remaining Continental vessels, the sloop of war *Ranger* and the frigates *Providence* and *Boston*, stood guard at the northern end of the boom," but they were no match for the superior British fleet.[43] With Arbuthnot's ships in control of Charleston Harbor and British forces investing the city, the American commander had run out of options. Recognizing the hopelessness of his situation, Lincoln surrendered the city and his army on 12 May 1780.[44]

The surrender at Charleston proved to be the greatest American defeat of the Revolutionary War. It constituted such a huge loss that even Washington doubted the initial reports.[45] In addition to a terrible loss in manpower and matériel, the American cause lost its most important port in the south. The Continental Navy lost eight ships (five sunk and three captured), which, when added to the earlier losses at Penobscot Bay, reduced it to a minor influence during the remainder of the war. Recognizing the significance of his victory, Clinton quickly moved to consolidate his hold on the south by ordering Cornwallis into the countryside to reestablish British authority, discipline rebels, and destroy any lingering American fighting units. On 5 June, Clinton transferred command of the southern theater to Cornwallis and returned to New York.[46] In so doing, Clinton set in motion a series of events that would culminate in the Battle of Yorktown during October 1781, at which Washington and his French counterparts would conduct one of the most complex and successful concentration of forces occurring in the eighteenth century.

The year 1780 started very badly for the Patriot cause with the loss of Charleston and did not improve. Despite guerrilla action in the Carolinas, some of which proved successful, Cornwallis generally had his way with American forces sent south to fight him. In August Cornwallis inflicted a bloody defeat on American forces under one of its most renowned commanders, Horatio Gates, at the battle of Camden in South Carolina. As British forces overran Georgia and the Carolinas, Benedict Arnold attempted to betray the key American position in the Hudson Highlands at West Point. Although the capture of a British spy, Maj. John André, exposed Arnold's treason, the effort came very close to succeeding and presented Washington with one of his greatest shocks of the war.[47] In addition to nearly losing his key defensive position in the New York Highlands, Washington lost one of his most trusted lieutenants for whom he had genuine affection. Additionally, Washington's ongoing effort to persuade his French allies to cooperate in a joint and combined attack against New York met only with evasion and rebuff.[48] Lacking sufficient strength and funds to undertake offensive actions on his own, Washington reluctantly remained on the defensive. Yet, even under these constraints, Washington would strike boldly if he felt an opening presented itself, such as Lord Stirling's January raid on Staten Island.

If the year 1780 started badly for the American war effort, it began very well for the British, with major victories at Charleston and Camden coupled with numerous lesser successes in the south. Yet by the end of the year, any optimism Clinton may have possessed had evaporated. Despite major victories in the southern states, the population did not prove as loyal to the Crown, as expected. Vicious guerrilla activity continued, and American frontiersmen won an important victory at King's Mountain, North Carolina, on 7 October.[49] The failure of Arnold and André's effort to surrender West Point proved a major setback for the northern war effort. André served as Clinton's most trusted aide, and together they had worked long and hard to achieve this covert objective. Clinton believed the capture of West Point would unhinge Washington's defenses throughout New York and New Jersey, something he had been unable to do in three years of warfare.[50] Failing to capture West Point had the strategic and psychological effect of a major defeat to the British war effort.

Clinton was even more concerned in July 1780 when he learned of the arrival at Newport of Adm. Charles-Louis d'Arsac, Chevalier de Ternay, with seven French ships-of-the-line and Jean-Baptiste Doantien de Vimeur, Comte de Rochambeau, with 5,200 men. This expeditionary force resulted from a visit to King Louis XVI and his ministers by the Marquis de Lafayette, who persuaded the government of the need for direct French support to Washington. Upon landing, Rochambeau established a cordial and respectful relationship with Washington in which he deferred to Washington's position as commander in chief, and Washington displayed great respect for Rochambeau's professionalism.[51] Of course, Rochambeau often had his own ideas about operations and strategy and would occasionally work behind the scenes to get his way, particularly when important French assets such as the navy were involved.

Clinton believed he could destroy the French naval and military forces at Newport before they could join with Washington's troops around New York and undertake offensive operations. But the British army commander could not gain the support of Arbuthnot for such a venture. Thus, French forces remained in Newport undisturbed and available for the 1781 joint and combined operation at Yorktown, Virginia.[52]

While British naval and army commanders fell into bickering and disagreement, cooperation among American and French commanders continued to improve. Rochambeau proved an enthusiastic supporter of the American Revolution and worked closely with naval commanders to concentrate French power against the British enemy. Despite Rochambeau's stabilizing influence, the French navy in Newport experienced some disruption beginning with the death of de Ternay on 15 December 1780. In May Jacques-Melchion Saint-Laurent, Comte de Barras, arrived in Newport to take command from Charles René Dominique Souchet, Chevalier Destouches, and bring word that Adm. François-Joseph Paul, Comte de Grasse, would sail for America with twenty-six ships-of-the-line.[53] The principal task of de Grasse's fleet involved protection of French possessions in the West Indies, but he also had authority to operate off the North America coastline if it did not endanger his primary mission.[54] Taking advantage of this opportunity, Washington and Rochambeau requested that de Grasse bring his fleet to either New York or the mouth of the Chesapeake to support a major operation by their armies.[55] Washington preferred New York while Rochambeau favored the Chesapeake as a target, but the ultimate decision rested with de Grasse, who had to balance his obligations in the West Indies with their request for his assistance. While awaiting de Grasse's reply, Rochambeau's force joined Washington's army near White Plains, where they probed the British defenses of New York.[56] Finding British positions stronger than expected, and receiving de Grasse's reply that he could not operate as far north as New York, Washington cancelled his planned attack on the city.[57] But de Grasse did agree to bring his fleet into the Chesapeake, and on 19 August 1781 Washington and Rochambeau set out south to rendezvous with the French admiral. On 17 September the three principal commanders met on board de Grasse's flagship, where they laid plans to destroy Cornwallis' army, then concentrated in what Cornwallis considered a relatively secure enclave at Yorktown, Virginia.[58] At last Washington had achieved a joint and combined operation with the French fleet—a goal he had sought from the beginning of the alliance in February of 1778.

While Washington and Rochambeau planned strategy in New England during late 1780 and early 1781, Cornwallis, believing he could not pacify South Carolina as long as American forces there received support from North Carolina and Virginia, decided to invade North

Carolina. He believed this would also rally Loyalists in that region to support the British southern strategy. But that was not to be. In December 1780 Nathanael Greene replaced Gates as Continental Army commander in the south.[59] Demonstrating a capacity for strategic thinking, Greene shrewdly deployed his forces in such a way as to draw Cornwallis away from his supporting bases and gunships. These maneuvers set the stage for Daniel Morgan's defeat of Tarleton at the Battle of Cowpens on 17 January 1781. In the 15 March Battle of Guilford Court House, Cornwallis defeated Greene's army but at a cost he could not afford, suffering 532 casualties to 263 for Greene. Unlike at Camden seven months earlier, Greene retreated in good order with his army intact and very able to continue its southern campaign. Although winning a tactical victory at Guilford Court House, Cornwallis felt compelled to retreat some 175 miles to Wilmington, North Carolina, while Greene resumed his invasion of the Carolinas, attacking Loyalists along with British detachments and patrols.[60]

After the victory at Guilford Court House and retreat to Wilmington, Cornwallis turned his attention to Virginia while Greene moved into South Carolina, eager to link up with Thomas Sumter's guerrillas. By threatening South Carolina and Georgia, Greene hoped to force Cornwallis to abandon his ambitions in North Carolina and Virginia.[61] But Greene suffered a minor defeat at Hobkirk's Hill near Camden, South Carolina, on 19 April, which convinced Cornwallis he could safely move north into Virginia rather than return to South Carolina.[62] Although technically a British victory, the Battle of Hobkirk's Hill further strained British resources to the point that Lt. Col. Francis Lord Rawdon, the British commander, felt compelled to leave the field and return to Charleston. Rawdon's action had the effect of turning his tactical victory into a strategic defeat. These actions complicated the operational situation, but Cornwallis concluded he could best protect the Carolinas and Georgia by seeking and winning a decisive battle on the Chesapeake.[63] With Cornwallis' army in Virginia and Rawdon back in Charleston, Greene and his subordinate commander, Henry "Light Horse Harry" Lee, incrementally attacked and captured a series of isolated British posts during May and June 1781. In this effort Greene received support from the guerrilla bands of Thomas Sumter, Andrew Pickens, and Francis Marion.[64] In subsequent actions around Fort Ninety Six and Eutaw Springs, both sides gave a good account of themselves, with the British gaining the upper hand. But irreplaceable British losses coupled with growing American strength made it necessary for British forces to withdraw their forces into Charleston. Although American leaders did not consider these two battles tactical victories, they clearly perceived them as strategic successes.[65] By September 1781, the British controlled only Charleston and Savannah, leaving Greene to focus attention on subduing Loyalists in the rural parts of South Carolina and Georgia.

In April 1781 Clinton sent reinforcements under Maj. Gen. William Phillips to join Benedict Arnold (now a British brigadier general) in Virginia. In March a series of inconclusive naval actions involving Destouches and Arbuthnot had left the British in control of the entrance to the Chesapeake, allowing Clinton the freedom to send these additional troops into Virginia.[66] Arnold and Lt. Col. John Graves Simcoe had successfully raided American communities during the past four months while Lafayette attempted to meld militia units with his 1,200 Continentals to form a capable military force. Washington also sent Anthony Wayne with about 1,000 troops to reinforce Lafayette.[67] Phillips assumed command of all British forces assembled at Portsmouth upon his arrival and launched a series of raids, which Lafayette could only partially contain.[68] Cornwallis continued his movement north and, upon arrival at Petersburg, Virginia, added Phillips' troops to his own, bringing his force to about 7,000 men. Phillips died of typhoid fever in mid-May, and Clinton recalled Arnold to New York shortly thereafter, leaving Cornwallis in command of all British forces in Virginia. On 6 July Cornwallis inflicted a sharp check on Anthony Wayne, who had been dogging his army for more than a month, at Green Springs near the James River. But a desperate stand by Wayne's Continentals coupled with timely support from Lafayette permitted them to give a good account of themselves and remain an important force in eastern Virginia.[69]

While British and American forces sparred in the south, Clinton hoped to find a way to attack and destroy Washington's army around New York or, attack French forces at Newport. By the end of the summer of 1781, Clinton had given up on these strategic options and focused on Virginia, directing Cornwallis to establish a base on the Chesapeake, preferably at either Old Point Comfort or Yorktown. Clinton had serious reservations about continuing operations in Virginia, but he and Cornwallis felt confident that the Royal Navy could ultimately control the

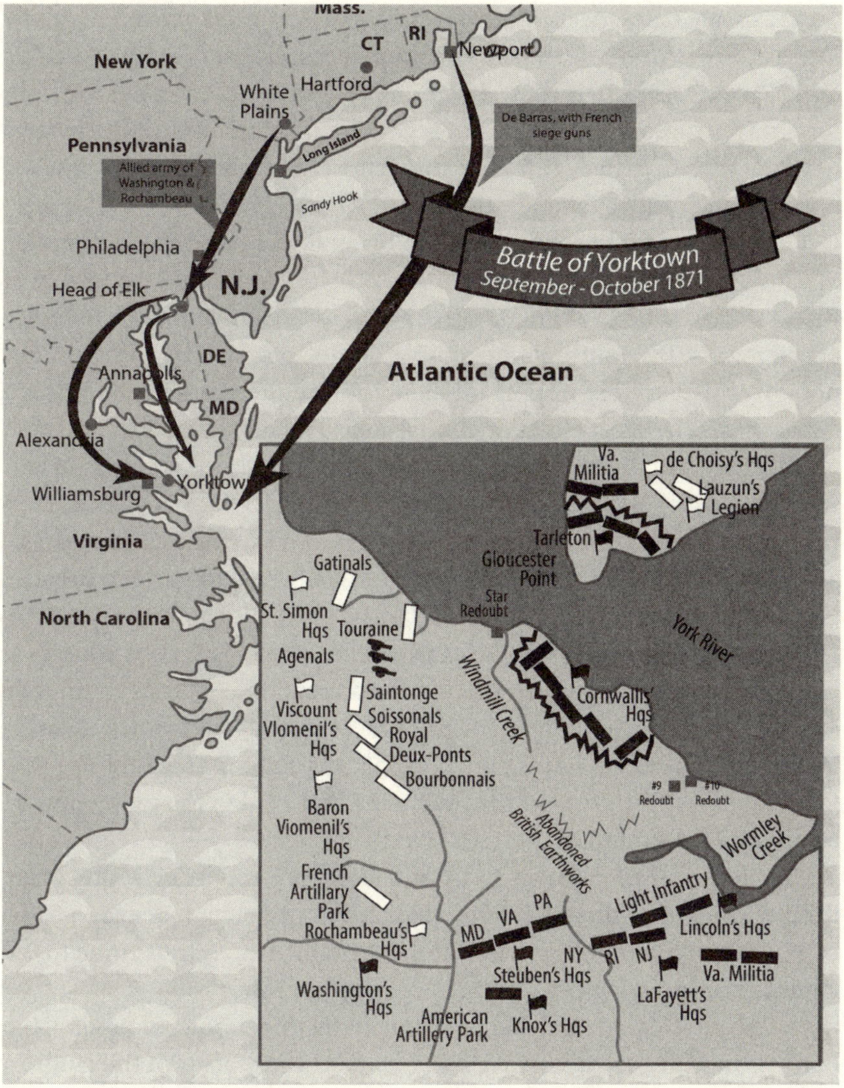

MAP 3. The Battle of Yorktown

waters of the Chesapeake. In early August, Cornwallis moved his army into Yorktown and a secondary position at Gloucester Point across the York River.[70] Although these positions provided an excellent location for a naval station, they had no prepared defenses, forcing Cornwallis to undertake an extensive fortification effort to create a support base for both ground and naval operations.[71]

Once de Grasse had committed to bring his fleet to the Chesapeake, Washington realized that conditions were ripe for a major victory over British forces if he could make all the disparate elements work together effectively.[72] This would be no simple matter because Washington did not control the most important element, the French fleet. Should de Grasse suffer a defeat at sea or choose not to challenge the British navy, it would reverse the tactical situation ashore and place Washington and Rochambeau in a compromising situation. On 15 August Washington instructed Lafayette to prevent Cornwallis from leaving the Chesapeake and marching south.[73] This proved more easily said than done because Cornwallis commanded a larger and more professional force than what Lafayette could muster. But the marquis harassed his British adversary while destroying local infrastructure and creating obstacles to impede any southern move by the British. Together with Rochambeau, Washington persuaded de Barras to transport the French siege train to the Chesapeake and then join his fleet with that of de Grasse in support of operations around Yorktown.[74] De Barras feared the more powerful British fleet operating in waters around New York could destroy his ships if he encountered them while moving south. As such, he needed to be convinced of the mission's value and then took a circuitous route to the Chesapeake, arriving off Yorktown on 10 September.[75]

Leaving William Heath behind with some three thousand men—the bare minimum—to protect West Point and the key posts of the Hudson Highlands, Washington initiated a series of deceptive ploys and began a forced march to join with de Grasse's fleet then en route to the Chesapeake from Saint-Domingue (Haiti).[76] By ordering his troops to carry pontoons and conducting a series of feints against British positions on Staten Island and near Sandy Hook, Washington kept Clinton confused about his real intentions.[77] Clinton's earlier interception of a message from Washington to Lafayette detailing his plan to attack New York in conjunction with the French navy added credence to Washington's deceptions. Not until he received reports of the movement of Washington's and Rochambeau's troops through Philadelphia could Clinton be certain they intended to attack Cornwallis on the Chesapeake. By 8 September, the Franco-American army had reached northern Maryland, in the upper reaches of the Chesapeake Bay. From that point and from docks at Baltimore and Annapolis, its major elements boarded transports sent by de Grasse and moved to the landing beaches near Williamsburg, where Washington organized his combined army for the siege of Yorktown.[78]

By the end of August, British commanders in New York recognized the seriousness of Cornwallis' position and dispatched a fleet under Adm. Thomas Graves—who had replaced Arbuthnot in July as the senior naval commander in North America—to evacuate Cornwallis from Yorktown. But on 30 August de Grasse's fleet of 28 ships-of-the-line arrived in the waters of the Chesapeake, and on 1 September he landed about 3,500 French troops under Claude-Anne de Rouvroy, the Marquis de Saint-Simon, to join Lafayette's Americans.[79] Although this combined force, coupled with the Franco-American army now in motion, outnumbered Cornwallis, British commanders did not consider the situation hopeless. They continued to believe the navy could support Cornwallis' position in Virginia despite the presence of de Grasse's fleet and the growing American ground strength. Additionally, now that Washington's intentions to concentrate against Yorktown had become clear, Cornwallis expected reinforcements from Clinton.[80]

One of the key battles of the Yorktown campaign occurred on 5 September when Graves' fleet, reinforced by the ships of Adm. Sir Samuel Hood, arrived at the mouth of the Chesapeake and engaged de Grasse in the Battle of the Capes. Adm. George Brydges Rodney had dispatched Hood from the West Indies to join Graves once he learned de Grasse had departed Caribbean waters. Hood sailed past the Chesapeake, noting the absence of French ships, and joined Graves at Sandy Hook on 28 August. When the British fleet departed New York for the Chesapeake on 31 August, they knew of de Barras' departure from Newport but not of the arrival of de Grasse, who had entered the Chesapeake after Hood's brief visit. When Hood returned to the waters off Virginia as part of Graves' fleet, the British admirals found not de Barras with eight ships-of-the-line, but de Grasse with twenty-eight. Graves and Hood engaged de Grasse at the entrance to the Chesapeake in a brief battle in which neither fleet lost a ship. Despite the inconclusive nature of the encounter in tactical terms, de Grasse gained a strategic victory because he retained control of the Chesapeake and maintained his superiority in warships.[81] In the days immediately following the battle, Graves and de Grasse eyed each other and sought the advantage of wind, but neither proved able to renew the fighting on favorable terms. On 10 September de Barras arrived on the scene, bringing French strength to thirty-six ships-of-the-line.[82] Needing extensive repairs to his ships and being overmatched by de Grasse and de Barras, Graves returned to New York, departing Virginian waters on 13 September.[83]

After the defeat of Graves in the Battle of the Capes, the vulnerability of British forces at Yorktown became obvious to both Clinton and Cornwallis. Clinton and the British naval commanders organized a second relief operation while Cornwallis contemplated a possible breakout by attacking Lafayette's army. But damage to the British fleet required more time to repair than initially expected, and despite the arrival of Rear Adm. Robert Digby with three ships-of-the-line and Sir Peter Parker with two ships-of-the-line, Graves could not respond in time to save the army at Yorktown. Although Cornwallis outnumbered Lafayette's force in the Yorktown area, the possibility of breaking out did not appeal to him because he still expected reinforcements from Clinton and relief from Graves.[84] Even if he could have broken free from Lafayette, Cornwallis did not have sufficient supplies to ensure his return to the Carolinas or to be in condition to fight Greene after arriving. As Washington's and Rochambeau's troops began to arrive and assume positions on 28 September, the possibility of a breakout faded. When de Barras landed the siege artillery on 6 October, the fate of Cornwallis and his British army had been sealed.

Washington had achieved his long-desired goal of isolating a major British force from its naval support and had set the stage for victory. Cornwallis held Yorktown and Gloucester Point with roughly 8,000 British and Hessian soldiers while Washington encircled him with an army of about 9,000 American and 7,800 French troops and de Grasse controlled the watercourses and sea lines of communication. Yet even this accomplishment did not ensure victory. De Grasse had made it clear that he could only stay in North American waters until the end of October (originally, de Grasse intended to remain only through mid-October).[85] Once he departed, Clinton and Graves could reinforce Cornwallis and provide the naval gunfire support that would pull victory from the grasp of disaster. In fact, Clinton intended to reinforce Cornwallis once Graves could take to sea, even if it meant again challenging de Grasse's superior fleet. After the arrival of Rochambeau's siege train, Washington had less than one month to destroy Cornwallis' force or compel it to surrender.[86] The siege operation consisted of a very sophisticated engineering and tactical evolution of which the basic plan included 55 specific and detailed instructions.[87] While siege operations commenced around Cornwallis' main army at Yorktown, Tarleton's force of about 700 cavalry was held in check at Gloucester Point by 1,200 Virginia militia under Maj. Gen. George Weedon, augmented by the legion of Armand-Louis de Gontant, Duc de Lauzun, and troops under Claude-Gabriel, Marquis de Choisy, who held overall command.[88]

Cornwallis may not have known of Washington's time constraints, but he had a sense that de Grasse's fleet could not remain in American waters for long. He therefore continued to believe, for some time, that relief would come through the gathering naval strength building up in New York Harbor. Thinking naval support a possibility and expecting promised reinforcements from Clinton, Cornwallis struck back at Washington with a series of raids and artillery attacks.[89] But his efforts proved ineffective in checking the increasing fury of the Franco-American siege.[90] On the night of 9–10 October, gunfire from French warships destroyed the frigate *Charon* along with several transport ships that guarded the passage between Yorktown and Gloucester Point.[91] As the bombardment of his positions intensified and Washington's siege lines constricted, Cornwallis faced the imminent destruction of his army.[92] On 14 October assault forces under command of lieutenants colonel Alexander Hamilton and Guillaume, Comte de Deux-Point, stormed and captured the final two redoubts that obstructed the advancement of siege lines, causing Cornwallis to recognize that his army was now beyond help.[93]

On 16 October Cornwallis attempted to escape across the York River to Gloucester Point where Tarleton's force of seven hundred remained contained by the Franco-American forces under de Choisy. Both Cornwallis and Tarleton realized that their last hope involved a breakout through Gloucester and a retreat to the north. But a severe storm prevented this scheme before it began. With the failure of the breakout attempt, in the words of Tarleton, "expired the last hope of the British Army."[94] The following day, Graves' refitted ships began loading about seven thousand of Clinton's troops at New York, and on 19 October he set sail with twenty-five ships-of-the-line. But Cornwallis had slipped beyond the ability of Graves and Clinton to save him. That same day, Cornwallis asked Washington for surrender terms, and the British and German troops from Yorktown and Gloucester Point marched out of the rubble and grounded their arms.[95] On 24 October Clinton arrived at the Chesapeake, but the continuing presence of de Grasse's superior fleet coupled with Cornwallis' surrender rendered his mission moot; after remaining on station for several days, he returned to New York.

The siege of Yorktown had been furious and devastating. Knowing he had superior firepower but limited time, Washington assaulted the British positions vigorously, determined to force either capitulation or complete destruction of his enemy. Once Cornwallis sought to terminate the contest and asked for terms, Washington offered the same "honors" granted to Lincoln at Charleston, causing consternation in the British camp. The British suffered some five hundred casualties during the siege and surrendered approximately eight thousand soldiers and seamen.[96] Clinton clearly recognized that the disaster at Yorktown resulted from French naval superiority, but he also felt Cornwallis could have held out longer with better fortifications.[97] He acted immediately to prevent another such disaster by dispatching Lt. Gen. Alexander Leslie to bolster the defenses at Charleston. Washington hoped to attack Charleston immediately but could not persuade de Grasse to cooperate in the venture.[98] He did obtain a provisional agreement from the admiral to support an action against Wilmington, North Carolina, but upon reconsideration, de Grasse chose not to carry out his tentative promise.[99] The French admiral had made assurances to his Spanish allies in the West Indies and believed any further actions in North America would delay his arrival beyond acceptable limits. The best Washington could wring out of de Grasse was a vague commitment to attempt another joint and combined operation sometime after May 1782. The frustrated Washington saw the prospect of eliminating all British power from Georgia and the Carolinas disappear over the horizon with the ships of de Grasse.

French naval superiority had existed just long enough to give Washington the victory he pursued so vigorously. Five months later, at the Battle of the Saintes near the channel between Guadeloupe and Dominica islands in the West Indies, Rodney and Hood defeated de Grasse's fleet and restored British command of the seas. But the victory came too late for the British war effort. On 12 April 1782—the same day as the Battle of the Saintes—British leaders opened negotiations with American representatives in Paris for an end to the conflict. Yet Washington remained anxious because he believed in "an old and true Maxim that to make a good peace, you ought to be well prepared to carry on the War."[100] Moreover, he now knew that there would be no French fleet to help replicate the Yorktown success elsewhere in North America.

Although Clinton evacuated Wilmington and most of North Carolina by mid-November 1781, Britain retained strong enclaves in New York, Charleston, and Savannah.[101] After the surrender of Yorktown, Washington sent reinforcements under Maj. Gen. Arthur St. Clair to Greene in South Carolina and returned with the rest of his army to New York in November 1781, strengthening the siege of British forces in that city.[102] Greene blockaded Charleston while sending detachments to secure the countryside in Georgia. Rochambeau remained in the Williamsburg, Virginia, area for the winter with orders to maintain close contact with Greene.[103] Clinton still had over 30,000 troops in North America, considerably more than could be mustered by his American and French enemies. Additionally, the virtual destruction of the small Continental Navy coupled with the inability of the French to maintain a fleet in American waters left the British in control of the sea. With this capability, offensive actions remained possible for British commanders, and this preyed on Washington's mind.[104] But Washington also believed that the return of a French naval force that could remain in American waters for an extended time and cooperate with his army would defeat British power in North America. He pressed Lafayette to make this case with the government of France during his return home in early 1782.[105]

Small-unit fighting consisting of forays out of Charleston and Savannah continued throughout 1782, often causing concern by Greene.[106] But with the fall of the Frederick Lord North government in London during March 1782, followed by the replacement of Clinton by Sir Guy Carleton that same month, British authorities thought more about evacuation than operations in North America. Washington and Greene believed they had to strive to remain strong despite the vexing problems they continued to face.[107] As information from John Adams and Benjamin Franklin trickled in from Europe, American leaders perceived a weakening of British resolve. Not only had Yorktown been a blow to British resolution but pressure from France in the West Indies and India, coupled with Spanish successes in West Florida and at Fort St. Joseph on Lake Michigan, also forced leaders in London to reevaluate their situation. Recognizing the change in strategic balance, Washington believed that further reinforcements from Britain to North America would be unlikely. Yet he closely watched British activities with the intention of responding to any action they might undertake with the forces on hand.[108] He also believed that any future offensive success by his army would likely come with a return of de Grasse's fleet. But Washington never had high expectation of that happening, even before learning of de Grasse's defeat at the Battle of the Saintes.[109]

The importance of naval power and amphibious operations to combat actions in the American Revolution can hardly be overstated. Throughout the war the ability of the British army and navy to operate along the North American littorals sustained their war effort and frustrated American hopes. The amphibious withdrawal from Boston in 1776 allowed Howe to redefine the symmetry of the conflict in North America. The damaging amphibious raids at Falmouth (Portsmouth), Maine, in 1775; along coastal Connecticut in 1777–81; in Chesapeake Bay in 1778; and along the James River in 1781 retarded American recruitment, destroyed stores, and impeded commerce. But the most important element for the British war effort was the ability to conduct large-scale amphibious operations, such as in the capture of New York and Newport in 1776, Philadelphia in 1777, Savannah in 1778, and Charleston in 1780. In each of these cases, the ability to project power ashore and support operations from the sea led to British victories and, on several occasions, nearly ended American resistance. Yet, despite this distinct superiority of naval and amphibious power coupled with the ability to win tactical victories and gain operational advantage, Britain could not force her rebellious adversary to capitulate. Britain's tactical and operational success could not overcome the superior strategic thinking of American commanders.

For the American revolutionaries, the amphibious experience came primarily from the defensive for most of the war. In defending against amphibious operations, the Americans had mixed results. The defeat at Savannah resulted in excessive loss of men and matériel, and the surrender of Charleston proved an unmitigated disaster. But in the New York, Newport, and Philadelphia campaigns, the American defenders lost battles and key positions but survived with sufficient strength and morale to sustain the Revolution. Through this process of survival evolved the American grand strategy of keeping its army in the field as a viable instrument of war, regardless of British successes or failures. The ability to turn tactical defeats into strategic successes served American commanders well throughout the war, especially during Greene's southern campaign. Conversely, British failures inevitability had a great and lasting impact on their war effort.

On the few occasions when American forces executed offensive amphibious operations, they also experienced mixed results. The successful operation at New Providence in the Bahamas could not offset the failure at Penobscot Bay. The failure to retake Newport in 1778 or Savannah in 1779 resulted from the weakness of the new Franco-American alliance (although many Americans preferred to blame the unreliability of d'Estaing). Throughout the war, Washington recognized that French naval power coupled with American ground forces provided the greatest hope for success in gaining American independence. As such, he maintained strong relations with his French counterparts, ever persuading, coaxing, requesting, and repairing frayed relationships in order to retain the prospect for a joint and combined operation that would have a major impact on the outcome of the war. This came to fruition in October 1781 with the most successful and most important American amphibious offensive operation of the war at Yorktown.

Of the many important battles of the Revolutionary War, only two proved decisive for either side—Saratoga and Yorktown. Of these two battles, only Yorktown involved naval and amphibious elements. Although the fighting at Freeman's Farm and Bemis Heights in New York—the actions that led to Burgoyne's surrender at Saratoga—involved some ancillary riverine operations, this American victory qualifies primarily as a ground battle fought between land armies. The Saratoga victory proved decisive not only because of the surrender of an entire British field army but also because it precipitated political recognition of the United States by France and the increased flow of military and matériel aid so crucial to sustaining the war effort. Saratoga does not stand alone in bringing about French recognition, of course, as French leaders looked beyond this single victory to assess American commitment and staying power. For example, Washington's failed attack at Germantown, Pennsylvania, had a positive influence on French decision makers because it demonstrated determination and tenacity.[110] Yet the success at Saratoga provided the actual impetus for formal French recognition and support, thereby validating its status as a decisive victory. After February 1778 the Revolutionary War changed as London confronted a worldwide threat, made even more critical when Spain and the Netherlands followed the lead of France by declaring war on Great Britain.

The Battle of Yorktown also proved decisive because it convinced British leaders that the cost of the struggle to retain their North American colonies had exceeded its worth. Britain faced a protracted and pervasive rebellion on the North American mainland that had proved a strategic, if not operational, match for its armies. At Yorktown, Washington gained both a strategic and operational victory—with the help of de Grasse's success in the Battle of the Capes—underscoring the American commitment to sustain its quest for independence. Washington orchestrated the use of naval power, amphibious evolutions, and traditional land operations to win a tactical and operational victory with great strategic implications. This occurred when Britain faced mounting pressure worldwide. It provided the catalyst to focus British attention on growing threats to its empire and status as a great power. Just as Saratoga served to coalesce French thinking toward recognition and support of the United States, the decisive and unequivocal Franco-American amphibious victory at Yorktown convinced British leaders that a change in policy and grand strategy must occur. Although it required eighteen more months of fighting before the Peace of Paris ended the struggle and granted American independence, within five months of the British defeat at Yorktown, the peace advocates in London had gained ascendancy. Yorktown had sealed the fate of Great Britain in North America and provided an opportunity for creation of an American republic—the United States of America.

The victory at Yorktown further demonstrates the importance of understanding the characteristics of amphibious operations. It also illustrates the flexibility of such concepts and the lack of rigidity in their application. The most important of these characteristics, integration between the navy and landing force, could hardly have been improved upon at Yorktown. The labors of Washington, Rochambeau, de Grasse, and de Barras in coordinating their effort proved exemplary in every sense. Although serious differences of opinion existed during the initial planning phase, they ultimately agreed upon a concept that all elements could support and execute. Subsequent to agreeing on the concept of operation, the unity of command throughout the operation—although dispersed and informal—proved effectual. All commanders deferred to Washington as the commander in chief, while Washington deferred to their professionalism and competence. This resulted in a unity of effort based on cooperation rather than pure authority, but it constituted a unity that worked very well.

The characteristic of task-organized forces applied at Yorktown, but in a somewhat limited manner. Washington and Rochambeau made every effort to ensure that de Barras would deliver siege weapons and engineers during the window of opportunity critical to the defeat of Cornwallis. Had de Barras failed to arrive (he could have been defeated en route) or arrived late, it would have unhinged the entire operation. But when de Barras did arrive with the siege weapons and their crews, he delivered the exact tactical units at exactly the right time to ensure victory. Yet the siege artillery would have been useless without engineers to construct the complex and sophisticated lines, trenches, and structures necessary to support the tactics required to reduce Cornwallis' defenses. Again, the availability of the key elements at the crucial time and place illustrates Washington's skill at task organization. Beyond these critical elements, task organization played a lesser role because Washington and Rochambeau simply used all forces available to engage Cornwallis.

Rapid buildup of combat power from the sea to shore is usually among the most important characteristics of amphibious operations. Ironically, Washington failed to achieve this in the Yorktown operation. The buildup of combat power occurred gradually because of time and space problems so typical of eighteenth-century warfare. This failed to undercut the operation for two basic reasons. First, the presence of Lafayette's army distracted Cornwallis to some extent thereby holding his army in place at Yorktown and Gloucester Point. Second, the landings occurred in areas where Cornwallis had no defensive positions, thus ensuring that the amphibious forces would not be at risk during the initial landings. Once de Grasse landed de Saint-Simon's force in early September and Washington's and Rochambeau's troops later that month, the window of vulnerability closed, and Cornwallis had missed his best opportunity to survive.

With ground forces ashore and in position for subsequent operations and with the navy in control of the waters surrounding the target area, Washington had achieved the initial objective of an amphibious operation. The operational coherence that followed proved outstanding as de Grasse protected the sea echelon and Washington and Rochambeau progressively devastated Cornwallis' force ashore. The pressure of time ensured that this must occur because anything less would not succeed. Only a vigorous and powerful bombardment capable of destroying British forces in a relatively short period could work in this situation. At a critical juncture, coordinated attacks by French troops on Redoubt #9 and American troops on Redoubt #10 carried both fortifications and opened another direction from which to train artillery upon the British. The operational coherence orchestrated by Washington created a culminating effect that left Cornwallis with a choice between surrender and destruction. Faced with that reality, Cornwallis chose the more humane option and, like Burgoyne before him, surrendered an entire British field army.

As well as demonstrating the characteristics of amphibious warfare in the Yorktown campaign, Washington also applied the principles of war advantageously. He clearly exhibited the principle of maneuver through the concentration of his forces and the isolation of Cornwallis on the Chesapeake. To accomplish this, Washington maneuvered his army by sea and land using every mode of transportation—including ships, boats, wagons, horses, and the feet of his soldiers—available in that era to create a favorable tactical situation at Yorktown. He also used tactical deception in New York and Lafayette's combat power in Virginia to shape the battlefield and support his efforts to maneuver Cornwallis into an unfavorable position while concentrating his own army to advantage. With his army ashore and the French navy controlling the sea echelon, Washington applied the principle of mass through the vigorous concentration of all his combat power at the British center of gravity in the southern theater—Cornwallis' army. In an effort that would have pleased Carl von Clausewitz—and may have influenced his thinking—Washington focused the entire effort of his firepower against "the hub of all power and movement, on which everything depends."[111] Washington's siege of Cornwallis at Yorktown provides a classic example of the application of the principle of mass against a Clausewitzian center of gravity.

Washington could maneuver so effectively and apply the principle of mass so well because he clearly defined the objective of his offensive campaign and achieved surprise (in the military sense of that term) by consistently acting faster than his enemy could react. He accomplished this in part through application of the principle of economy of forces in which he minimized troop levels elsewhere, especially in New York and South Carolina, thereby providing maximum combat power at the point of main effort. The principle of security also came into play as Washington ensured that his enemy never gained unexpected advantages and that he preserved his forces for the decisive action. The only principle of war not demonstrated in Yorktown is the principle of simplicity. In fact, Yorktown proved a very complex evolution with many potential failure points. Yet the unity of command and focus of effort achieved by French and American commanders proved sufficient to overcome any problems this necessarily complex operation may have created. We can clearly see in the Yorktown campaign a validation of the principles of war as applied in an amphibious operation.

Chapter 3

TO THE SHORES OF TRIPOLI

Once the Treaty of Paris ended the American Revolution and granted independence to the United States in September 1783, the new republic found itself in a state of near exhaustion. Needing to economize on expenses and having a weak central government under the Articles of Confederation, American leaders effectively disbanded the Continental Army, leaving only one regiment on active status. They also eliminated the remnants of the Continental Navy, auctioning off its last vessel in August 1785.[1] A variety of events such as Indian discord on the frontier and naval conflicts in the Mediterranean and West Indies forced the nation's founders to reconsider both the adequacy of their governmental structure and the commitment to national security. The debate on defense policy revolved around the issue of whether to protect the nation with regular, standing forces or with nonprofessional militias. More accurately stated, the question focused on where to place the emphasis. Should the United States rely on a small regular force that depended on substantial augmentation from militia units in time of need? Alternatively, should the nation build a regular establishment that would be less dependent on militia support? Few issues in the early days of the American Republic raised greater dispute, and the argument applied to both army and naval forces.[2]

The controversy surrounding the nature of military force structure not only dealt with national security but also with issues of republican ideology, which made the problem even more vexing. The Whiggish fear of standing armies becoming an instrument of oppression remained a strong influence in the thinking of American leaders of the Revolutionary era.[3] George Washington believed in a relatively small professional army with a federally trained and organized militia system to augment the active force in time of need.[4] In a memorandum to Congress, "Sentiments on a Peace Establishment," Washington acknowledged the concerns associated with a standing army while pleading for a core of professionals "well skilled in the Theory and Art of War, who will be ready on any occasion, to mix and diffuse their knowledge of Discipline to other Corps." He also believed that the government should provide funds to build and equip a navy "without which, in case of War We could neither protect our Commerce, nor yield that Assistance to each other, which, on such and extent of Sea-Coast, our mutual Safety would require."[5] By the end of the eighteenth century, Washington's thoughts for developing a systemic defense program had not come to fruition. But his concepts remained in the minds of many American leaders, and after the frustrations of the War of 1812, Secretary of War John C. Calhoun reintroduced a variation of Washington's ideas in his plan for an expandable army.[6] Moreover, Washington's concepts served as the basis for the debate over national defense policy for the next hundred years.[7]

Although the United States possessed no navy between 1785 and 1794, pressure had been mounting throughout that period to create a credible naval capability. The capture of American merchant ships and the enslavement of their crewmen by Algerian and Moroccan corsairs as early as 1784 drove pro-defense advocates to demand creation of a maritime service able to protect the American merchant fleet. Prior to the War of Independence, American vessels plying the Mediterranean and eastern Atlantic operated under protection of the Royal Navy and agreements made between London and various Barbary States.[8] With independence and the growing prospect of economic competition from American trade, British leaders had no incentive to protect merchantmen of the United States from North African raiders.[9] Indeed, it would better serve their interests to encourage attacks on American ships, and evidence suggests they did just that.[10] Additionally, the outbreak of the French Revolution in 1789 and the wars it spawned further moved the national security debate in favor of a strong U.S. Navy.[11] By the time American leaders began to address the problems of Barbary corsairs and the impact of the French Revolution on world affairs, the nation had a new form of government. The constitution of 1787 created a government within the United States more able to deal with its various problems, both internal and external.[12]

During March 1794 Congress passed an act that authorized the administration to either buy or construct six frigates, effectively laying the foundation for the U.S. Navy.[13] Ostensibly intended to protect American commerce from Barbary corsairs, the Navy Act of 1794 marked an important step forward in the creation of a professional navy.[14] Secretary of War Henry Knox (the office of secretary of the Navy did not yet exist) ensured that the design of these initial frigates would make them superior to any then on the sea. He also arranged for production of these vessels to take place at numerous locations along the eastern seaboard, spreading business opportunities as widely as possible and tying many American citizens to the naval project.[15] Treaties concluded with the dey of Algiers in March 1796 and with the pasha of Tripoli in 1797 seemed to hold promise for a general peace with the Barbary powers. A provision in the Navy Act of 1794 required construction of the frigates to stop once the president certified that peace existed with Algiers, but pro-defense advocates in Congress proved strong enough to retain three ships nearing completion.[16] The survival of these frigates—the *United States*, the *Constellation*, and the *Constitution*—provided the base for future naval expansion, which world events would soon dictate.[17]

Within the next twenty-five years, the United States found itself involved in no fewer than four wars. These include the Quasi-War with France fought mostly in the West Indies between 1798 and 1801; the Barbary War against Tripoli in the Mediterranean during 1801–5; the War of 1812; and a brief naval conflict with Algiers in 1815. Amphibious operations played only a minor role in the Quasi-War but proved a major element in the Barbary War and the War of 1812. During the War of 1812, as during the Revolutionary War, the United States usually found itself on the defensive as Great Britain conducted numerous amphibious landings along the American littorals, especially during 1813 and 1814. During the Barbary War—and to a lesser extent in the Quasi-War—the United States established roots in expeditionary warfare that would grow to become among the most important defense concepts of the twenty-first century. As we shall see, the amphibious operation at Derna, Tripoli, provides an ideal case study for this form of warfare, demonstrating virtually all of its important elements.

Although the 1796 treaty with the dey of Algiers theoretically ended the confrontation with that North African state, the release of American prisoners did not occur until the United States delivered all of the tribute agreed upon in February 1798. The United States also concluded treaties with the pasha of Tripoli in 1796 and the bey of Tunis in 1797, which included payment of tribute in both money and naval stores.[18] Yet despite these agreements, relations remained problematic between the United States and the Barbary powers as treaty compliance proved sketchy on all sides, and North African pirates continued to harass American interests whenever they chose.[19]

Despite ongoing problems in the Mediterranean, world conditions in the 1790s turned American attention to a new challenge closer to home and perceived as a greater threat. With the outbreak of war between Great Britain and Revolutionary France, the navies and privateers of both nations began to capture American merchantmen trading with enemy ports. Both the Washington and John Adams administrations declared neutrality in the wars of the French Revolution, hoping this would protect American vessels carrying noncontraband goods. But both Britain and France, interpreting international law concerning maritime rights of neutral nations in ways that suited their own interests, continued to seize American ships. Seeking a peaceful resolution to this and other outstanding issues, Washington dispatched John Jay to London, from which Jay returned with a controversial treaty that at least ameliorated the problem of commerce raiding.

French officials considered the treaty to be virtually an Anglo-American alliance and ordered the seizure of U.S. shipping. President John Adams responded by sending Charles Cotesworth Pinckney, John Marshall, and Elbridge Gerry to France in 1797, in hope of finding an accommodation. This effort resulted in the infamous XYZ Affair in which French foreign minister Charles-Maurice de Talleyrand-Périgord demanded a large amount of cash coupled with an even larger loan simply to open negotiations. When Americans learned of this, it caused an outcry that produced the catch phrase "millions for defense, but not one cent for tribute."[20] Ironically, Americans felt outrage at the thought of paying tribute to French leaders although they reluctantly did so to the "petty tyrants" of Barbary.[21]

French actions at sea and the XYZ Affair led to a shift in American opinion toward France.[22] The favorable attitude resulting from French support during the American Revolution and initial affinity for the French Revolution had already begun to erode when radicals took control of the French government and began executing aristocrats; now it turned positively hostile. In July 1797 Congress passed the Act to Provide a Naval Armament, which authorized the manning and employment of the three frigates initially built under the Naval Act of 1794.[23] Between May and July 1798 Congress authorized completion of the three additional frigates provided for in the 1794 act, created the Navy Department headed by a secretary of the Navy, reestablished the U.S. Marine Corps, and authorized American warships and privateers to take offensive action against French vessels.[24] Marines previously recruited under the various naval acts served on board ships from the beginning of this crisis. The 11 July 1798 act establishing a Marine Corps placed those Marines, as well as new recruits, under the commandant of the Marine Corps, who assigned Marine detachments to vessels and shore posts where they served under the operational orders of the ship or post commander to which assigned.[25]

Public fervor against France reached a high pitch by the spring of 1798, and Americans fully expected to go to war with their former ally.[26] Congress authorized a large increase in the army, and George Washington agreed to return as its commander in chief. To the chagrin of President Adams, Washington stipulated that Alexander Hamilton would serve as inspector general and second in command.[27] Although Congress never actually declared war on France, it did authorize attacks upon its ships worldwide. It also abrogated all accords between the two countries, including the 1778 treaties of friendship and commerce, declaring them invalid due to repeated French violations. Once American militancy became apparent, Talleyrand began to seek reconciliation.[28] But it would take nearly three years before the two republics came to an agreement.

During that time, each side prosecuted a limited naval war against the other in which operations were conducted primarily in the West Indies. Throughout the conflict, the U.S. Navy escorted American merchantmen, sought out and attacked French privateers, and attempted to retake American ships captured by French forces. Only rarely did the warships of the two navies directly engage each other. The most famous exception to this involved the battle between the American frigate *Constellation* and the French *Insurgente* near Nevis in the Leeward Islands of the Lesser

Antilles on 9 February 1799. Despite the superiority of the *Insurgente*, Capt. Thomas Truxtun and the *Constellation*'s crew outfought and captured the French frigate.[29] One year later, Truxtun and the *Constellation* repeated their victory off Guadeloupe, defeating the frigate *Vengeance*, although the French ship limped away under the cover of night and smoke. American officers on the scene during the battle thought that the *Vengeance* sank from battle damage.[30]

The U.S. Navy did not face the full force of French naval power in the Quasi-War because Britain's Royal Navy blockaded the French navy in port much of the time. Yet the newly established U.S. Navy performed well, as did its Marine Corps detachments serving on board fighting ships at sea. The Corps' primary contribution to combat operations involved providing musket fire from the quarterdeck and the fighting tops of the frigates and boarding or repelling boarders when ships came into close quarters, but it also contributed significantly to two small amphibious landings.

The most interesting amphibious incident of the Quasi-War occurred in May 1800 at the Spanish port of Puerto Plata, Santo Domingo, where French authorities held a captured British ship named *Sandwich*. When he learned of the situation, Capt. Silas Talbot of the frigate *Constitution* devised a cutting-out operation to capture the prize. The task presented a particular problem because the *Sandwich* had good protection from heavy cannons located at the principal fort protecting the harbor as well as having fourteen guns of her own. The deep-draft *Constitution* could not attack directly into the harbor, so Talbot decided upon a ruse coupled with an amphibious raid to accomplish his goal.[31] Talbot placed about ninety Marines and sailors under command of Navy lieutenant Isaac Hull and Marine captain David Carmick into an innocuous-looking sloop named *Sally*. He then ordered it to sail into Puerto Plata Harbor and come alongside the *Sandwich* without attracting undue attention, if possible.

The *Sally* had recently departed Puerto Plato, announcing that it would return shortly. With port authorities expecting the *Sally* and the landing force hiding below deck and out of sight, the ship came alongside the *Sandwich* and quickly captured the vessel. The sailors immediately began rigging the *Sandwich* for sea while the Marines went ashore to attack the fort protecting the harbor. Before French or Spanish authorities could respond to the assault, the Marines had captured the fort, spiked its cannons, and returned to the *Sandwich.* The task force initially planned to defend against a possible counterattack from within these two ships—*Sally* and *Sandwich*—until later in the evening when the prevailing wind would allow them to sail free of the port. But a favorable wind arose earlier than expected, allowing both ships to set to sea unassailed. The amphibious raid on Puerto Plata proved a model of speed, efficiency, and effectiveness, even if of dubious legality.[32]

The second amphibious raid occurred on 22–23 September 1800 on the Dutch island of Curacao. After the February 1800 battle between the *Constellation* and the *Vengeance*, the French frigate made its way to the port of Curacao seeking to refit and resupply.[33] During its battle with the *Constellation*, the *Vengeance* had suffered such a drubbing that she struck her colors three times and later reported that she had engaged a ship-of-the-line.[34] But American officers never noticed these acts of capitulation due to smoke, darkness, and the confusion of battle. When Dutch officials at Curacao refused to assist the severely damaged *Vengeance*, they evoked the ire of French officials who invaded the island driving its inhabitants into a single fort and began taking hostile actions against local Americans.[35] The U.S. Navy responded to a call for help from the U.S. Consul Benjamin H. Phillips by sending the sloops of war *Merrimack* and *Patapsco* to the area in September 1800. On 23 September Lt. James Middleton led a party of Marines ashore.[36] With naval gunfire support, the Marines compelled the French forces to withdraw during the night of 24 September and returned to Guadeloupe.[37] American amphibious operations, like the naval service in general, proved to be an effective tool of U.S. policy during the Quasi-War.

Much of the credit for American effectiveness in the Quasi-War is due to the efforts of the first secretary of the Navy, Benjamin Stoddert. A cost-conscious businessman and Revolutionary War veteran, Stoddert organized his new department into an efficient operation capable of holding its own with the powerful corporations in the shipbuilding industry.[38] Stoddert not only effectively managed the war effort but also built a capable fleet ultimately amounting to some fifty ships including fourteen frigates.[39] An additional frigate neared completion as Stoddert left office. His administrative and organizational skills, coupled with intense energy and incisiveness, had created and sustained the new

U.S. Navy throughout the Quasi-War. Stoddert's combatants effectively engaged French sea power, capturing more than ninety enemy vessels and usually besting their opponents in open combat.[40] Of equal importance, Stoddert and the Adams administration left behind a reduced yet capable naval force for President Thomas Jefferson as he faced the next challenge to American rights on the high seas—the Barbary State of Tripoli.[41] The outgoing Federalist Congress passed last-minute legislation, signed by Adams virtually as he left office, that preserved the frigate navy, although it eliminated most ships of lighter draft.[42] Contrary to the fears of Stoddert and his Federalist associates, Jefferson did not reduce the Navy beyond the recommendations of the outgoing administration. In fact, the new president retained fifteen frigates after the end of the Quasi-War, two more than Stoddert recommended before leaving office.[43]

The Barbary War of 1801–5 technically began on 14 May 1801, when the pasha of Tripoli, Yusuf Karamanli, ordered the American flagstaff cut down on the grounds of the U.S. consulate. This traditional declaration of war resulted in part from the Tripolitan leader's resentment that Algiers, Tunis, and Morocco received a larger tribute from the United States than his own country.[44] This was normal practice in the region where various Barbary rulers liked to be at war with at least one nation at any given time in order to justify seizure of "enemy" merchant vessels and holding their crewmen for ransom. They usually targeted lesser naval powers such as Sweden, Denmark, Venice, and other European principalities. Only naval powers of the status of Britain or France possessed sufficient strength to avoid this treatment, although they often considered it more cost-effective to purchase peace for their ships by paying tribute.[45] Some European nations also thought that the system gave them an edge in competing with their commercial rivals. Although an accepted custom by the eighteenth century, this practice of tribute, appeasement, and unpredictable warfare did not set well with the new American republic, and in June 1801 President Thomas Jefferson sought to end it.

Jefferson dispatched a naval squadron to the Mediterranean. Its commander, Richard Dale, had orders to reconnoiter conditions along the North African littorals.[46] At the time that Dale sailed for the Mediterranean, Jefferson and his advisers did not yet know that the pasha had declared war, although American consuls assigned to Mediterranean ports had alerted them of impending trouble.[47] More significantly, the dey of Algiers had commandeered an American frigate, the *George Washington*, in October 1800, forcing it to conduct a personal mission for himself between Algiers and Constantinople.[48] Not only did this act prove intolerable to the outgoing Federalists but Thomas Jefferson—incorrectly considered a pacifist by many people—also found it unacceptable.[49]

Although neither Jefferson nor his secretary of state, James Madison, wanted war with any of the Barbary States, both considered their leaders guilty of piracy and felt they must eventually be dealt with by force.[50] Jefferson had no doubt that the U.S. Navy could easily defeat the Barbary corsairs, but he did not relish the idea of keeping an American squadron permanently stationed in the Mediterranean. He also regretted America's having to deal with the Barbary threat without support and cooperation from major European powers.[51] In addition to the cost and exposure associated with fighting the Barbary States, Jefferson struggled with the constitutional separation of powers that granted Congress, not the president, authority to declare war.

When Dale's squadron, which consisted of the frigates *President*, *Philadelphia*, and *Essex* and the schooner *Enterprise*, arrived in the Mediterranean in July 1801, it had the dual mission of seeking reconciliation with Tripoli while intimidating the Barbary powers with American naval strength.[52] After visiting Algiers and Tunis and receiving assurance of their continuing friendship, Dale sailed to Tripoli, where he found a very different attitude. Unmoved by Dale's visit, the pasha insisted on his demands for increased tribute and persisted in his declared war against the United States.[53] This simply meant that he would continue to capture American merchant ships, keeping their cargos and holding the crews for ransom. Dale countered by blockading the coast of Tripoli.

On 1 August 1801 the *Enterprise*, commanded by Lt. Andrew Sterrett, decisively defeated the corsair *Tripoli*, inflicting at least sixty casualties at no cost to itself.[54] After taking the *Tripoli*, Sterrett cast its weapons and gunpowder overboard, stripped the ship of all rigging except one sail, and released it to make its own way home.[55] The victory received attention worldwide, praise in the United States, and contributed to congressional authorization for offensive (as opposed to strictly reactive) action against Tripoli.[56] The defensive and diplomatic nature of Dale's original mission allowed for naval action when arriving on the Barbary Coast, yet some uncertainty remained regarding his authority to act and the actions he could take.[57] All parties involved in this campaign, from Jefferson to Sterrett, felt constrained by constitutional issues. In February 1802 Congress eliminated this ambiguity by passing the Act for Protection of the Commerce and Seamen of the United States against the Tripolitan Cruisers.[58] Although not a formal declaration of war, this act provided the president and his Navy sufficient authority to take aggressive action against Tripoli and its ships.[59]

After Sterrett's victory there followed an extended period of relative inaction involving an ineffective blockade of Tripoli. In the spring and summer of 1802 a larger American naval force under command of Commo. Richard Morris gathered in the Mediterranean to relieve Dale's squadron.[60] Both Morris and Dale complained of the lack of gunboats, which hampered their efforts to conduct an effective blockade of Tripoli. Their deeper-draft combat ships had to remain too far at sea to maintain tight control over Tripoli's harbor and coastlines.[61] In February 1803 Congress responded to the need for gunboats and other requirements of war by authorizing the production of fifteen gunboats and four ships of war mounting twelve to sixteen guns (brigs).[62] Despite this and other efforts by the government to support operations along the Barbary Coast, enforcement of the blockade proved erratic and inconsistent throughout Dale's tour as American commander in the Mediterranean and did not improve under Morris. Other than some successful convoy escort duty, Morris' service on the Barbary Coast proved lackluster at best, and a failure at worst.[63] In fact, upon return to the United States, Morris faced a court of inquiry that found his performance censurable and cashiered him from the navy.[64]

The fact that Morris' tour as commander in the Mediterranean proved ineffective does not mean no action occurred. In addition to convoying American merchantmen and maintaining an erratic blockade, American ships chased and often captured Tripolitan vessels. The first amphibious action of the war occurred on Morris' watch during June 1803. On the last day of May the *John Adams* and *Enterprise* left their station on blockade duty in Tripoli Harbor to chase a ship spotted about thirty-five miles northwest of the city. When the American ships closed with the enemy vessel, they saw that it was off-loading wheat into ten small craft that were conveying it ashore. Standing offshore in deeper water, the American warships could do little to stop this action. That night a team led by Lt. David Porter reconnoitered the Tripolitan logistics site and exchanged gunfire with its defenders ashore. Returning to his ship, Porter recommended a landing to destroy the boats and cargo, which Morris approved.[65]

The next morning Porter led a party of fifty men equipped with a large amount of explosives to destroy the shuttle boats and their cargo of grain. The amphibious raiding force established itself ashore, engaged the enemy defenders, and attempted to set fire to the vessels and the wheat. After expending all their ammunition and combustibles, the landing party departed for its ships, hoping the fires they started would destroy the boats and their cargos. Although the timbers of the boats caught on fire, the grain resisted the flame, and many Tripolitan defenders rushed to extinguish the fires once the landing party departed. The *John Adams* kept firing at the Tripolitan troops ashore, making it difficult, but not impossible, for them to save their boats and grain. Five Americans, including Porter, received wounds during the raid, though all returned to their ships alive. The landing force and naval gunfire managed to kill some of the defenders and inflict damage to the grain boats. But other than these modest achievements, the amphibious landing had little effect in Tripoli or on the larger operation.[66] Three weeks after Porter's landing against the grain boats, Capt. John Rodgers and the *John Adams* engaged and destroyed a 22-gun cruiser, the largest and most powerful ship in the Tripolitan fleet.[67] Thinking that this spectacular victory would force the pasha to make peace, Morris called off the blockade of Tripoli. But the commodore had misjudged his enemy, and this decision proved to be another of his frequent mistakes.[68]

During September 1803 Commo. Edward Preble arrived at Cadiz, Spain, in command of a seven-ship squadron to relieve Morris' force.[69] Before proceeding to the Tripoli Coast, Preble sailed to Tangier, where he compelled the emperor of Morocco—whose officers had been guilty of instigating hostile actions—to enter into a treaty arrangement with the United States.[70] In addition to the powerful naval squadron he brought to the war effort, Preble planned to acquire gunboats and bomb ships (mortar ketches) from the Kingdom of Naples, which Jefferson and the Navy Department had authorized.[71] With gunboats working inside the harbors and near the coastlines, coupled with frigates and schooners controlling the sea-lanes, the commodore believed he could quickly achieve victory against Tripoli. Undoubtedly, Preble had the right idea, but before he could bring about the intended results, he experienced a major setback. While chasing a Tripolitan corsair in October 1803, Capt. William Bainbridge ran the frigate *Philadelphia* aground on uncharted rocks near the entrance to the harbor at Tripoli. Unable to move his ship off the rocks and pressured by hostile gunboats that closed in on his stationary vessel, Bainbridge surrendered the *Philadelphia* rather than suffer inevitable loss of life.[72] This fiasco proved to be a national disaster comparable to the *George Washington* incident of 1800. Ironically, Bainbridge served as the hard-luck captain of both vessels. Loss of the *Philadelphia* provided Tripoli with 307 American crewmen for ransom along with a modern frigate, although the pasha doubted his seamen could operate the vessel. Yusuf therefore authorized his consul at Malta to find a customer and negotiate the sale of the frigate. This incident distressed Preble very much, but he did not intend to allow the *Philadelphia* to be of service to Tripoli or any other Barbary State.[73]

The ineffectiveness of American naval power during 1801–3 under Dale and Morris did not persuade the pasha of Tripoli to alter his war-making course. The loss of the *Philadelphia* obviously did nothing to impress the pasha either. Yet despite the humiliation of this incident, it failed to dissuade Jefferson or Preble from their determination to achieve an American victory on the Barbary Coast.[74] To do this, they had to ensure that no Barbary ruler could make use of the *Philadelphia.* On 16 February 1804 Preble launched a dramatic attack to destroy the *Philadelphia*, which was moored under the guns of the main fort in Tripoli's harbor. Executing a plan devised by Preble and based on information provided by Bainbridge from his imprisonment in Tripoli through coded messages, Lt. Stephen Decatur led a crew of seventy volunteers, including eight Marines, in a daring raid that fired and destroyed the *Philadelphia*.[75] Decatur and his team sailed toward the frigate in a captured Tripolitan ketch originally named the *Mastico* and renamed the *Intrepid* by Preble. Using deception, the *Intrepid* pulled alongside the *Philadelphia* and the crew overpowered the Tripolitan guards and ignited combustibles at key locations within the ship before coming under fire from the shore batteries.[76] With the fire and explosions from the *Philadelphia* causing confusion, Decatur's party escaped from the scene without the loss of a single man, and America had a new naval hero. The boldness and efficiency of this action altered the situation on the North African Coast, changing the attitude of Barbary authorities, American leaders, and other international powers that operated in the Mediterranean.[77] American prestige rose in wake of the attack, and Preble intended to retain the initiative until he obtained victory over Tripoli. Among other actions designed to follow up this success, the American commander arranged with the king of Naples to borrow six shallow-draft gunboats and two mortar ketches. By combining these vessels with his frigates, brigs, and schooners, Preble believed he could control the harbor and blast Tripoli into submission.[78]

As spectacular as Decatur's raid on the *Philadelphia* had been, the next major operation—the joint and combined attack and capture of Derna, Tripoli, in April 1805—managed to exceed it in both drama and effectiveness. The capture of Derna and its impact on strategic and diplomatic efforts demonstrated the unique value of amphibious operations in expeditionary warfare. Additionally, the success of this action under incredibly difficult circumstances places the Derna operation among the most important events in developing the amphibious traditions of the U.S. Marine Corps. The attack on Derna sprang from an ongoing effort by Hamet Karamanli (sometimes spelled Ahmet Qaramanli) to regain control of Tripoli. Hamet believed himself to be the legitimate ruler of Tripoli, which his younger brother, Pasha Yusuf Karamanli, had usurped. Hoping to exploit the conflict between America and Tripoli to his advantage, Hamet offered a guarantee of lasting peace if the United States helped restore him to power.[79] Hamet had engaged the support of Richard Farquhar, a shady manipulator who operated out of Malta, to assist in his efforts to obtain American support.[80]

William Eaton, who had served as American consul to Tunis from 1799 to 1803, became an early advocate of returning Hamet to power as a means of ending Tripolitan piracy.[81] The first step in this process involved the capture of Derna, the largest and most important coastal city in the eastern part of the principality of Tripoli. This strategy fit nicely with Preble's plan for attacks against Tripoli by both land and sea. Attacking Derna not only opened another military front but also increased the political, economic, and diplomatic pressure on the pasha. Preble believed that supporting Hamet offered a good prospect for success and that restoring him to power would bring substantial benefits to the United States throughout the Barbary Coast.[82]

In September 1804 a powerful naval squadron under the command of Commo. Samuel Barron arrived in the Mediterranean with permission from Jefferson and the secretary of the Navy to support Hamet's efforts to achieve control of Tripoli.[83] During much of the previous year, Eaton had been in the United States, where he promoted his ideas for regime change in Tripoli. Although Eaton had convinced the administration in Washington of the efficacy of reestablishing Hamet in power, officials delegated the ultimate decision authority regarding this operation to Barron, not Eaton. Eaton returned to the Mediterranean on board Barron's flagship with the power to coordinate affairs with Hamet and oversee American support of the effort under Barron's overall leadership.[84] Through vigorous lobbying efforts and enthusiastic promotion of his plan, Eaton persuaded Barron to support his ideas for ultimate victory against Tripoli.[85]

While awaiting arrival of Barron's squadron and preparing for the attack against Derna, Preble did not remain inactive as his predecessors had done. During July 1804 he assembled all available naval power under his control and moved to inflict maximum destruction on the city and defenses of Tripoli. Before moving into Tripoli Harbor, Preble had acquired the gunboats and bomb vessels needed for his attack as a loan from the Kingdom of the Two Sicilies and procured other weapons and ammunition.[86] On 3 August Preble sent Decatur into Tripoli Harbor with six gunboats and two mortar ketches to attack enemy vessels and shore defenses. Decatur captured three Tripolitan gunboats, sank one, and damaged at least fifteen more. He also engaged in a celebrated incident of hand-to-hand combat with an enemy commander, which further cemented his standing as a naval hero.[87] Preble continued his attacks against Tripoli until early September, when Barron arrived with Eaton and the operation against Derna got under way.[88]

When Barron arrived to take command of American forces and operations in the Mediterranean, he possessed the largest naval force the United States had ever assembled up to that time. It included six frigates, two brigs, three schooners, one sloop, and as many gunboats as he or Preble could acquire in Italy. In addition to a powerful naval squadron, Barron carried instructions from President Jefferson directing, in the

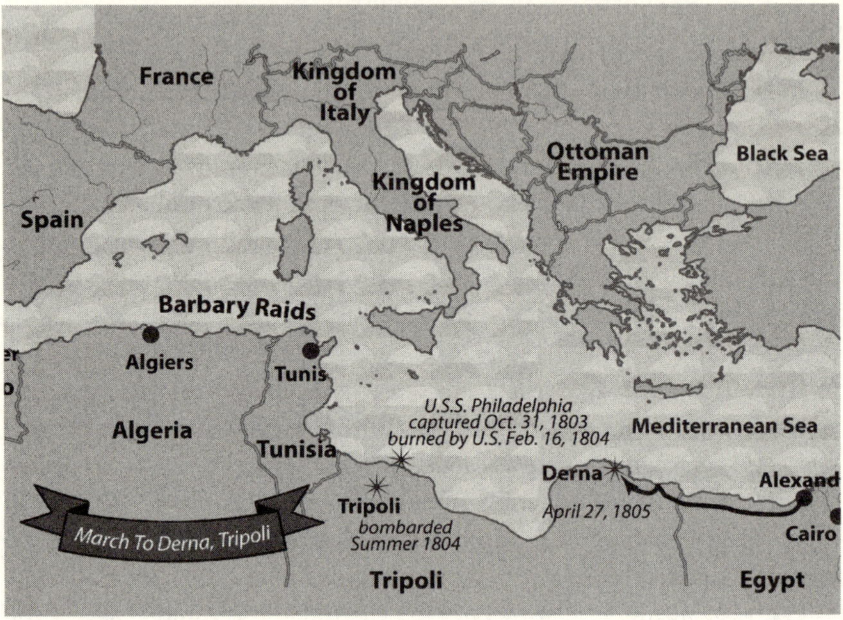

MAP 4. The North African Campaign (Tripoli)

strongest terms yet, aggressive and determined action against Tripoli and other Barbary powers if necessary.[89] Barron also brought with him Eaton, who held a commission from the secretary of the Navy as the U.S. naval agent to the Barbary Regencies, subject only to the orders of Barron.[90] To undertake the Derna operation, Eaton first needed to find Hamet, last known to be in Alexandria, Egypt.[91]

Barron ordered Master Comdt. Isaac Hull and the U.S. brig *Argus* to help Eaton locate Hamet and assist his operation against Derna.[92] Arriving in Alexandria on 29 November 1804, Eaton immediately proceeded on a dangerous trip to Cairo, where he believed Hamet had allied himself with a Mameluke faction. The Mamelukes once held great power throughout the Middle East, although their influence had diminished somewhat by 1804. During the time of the Tripolitan war, they remained one of several important factions contending for supremacy within Egypt. The Mamelukes' reputation as ferocious fighters made them a disruptive factor in Egypt, and they continued to fight Turkish rule until 1811 when Ottoman power finally destroyed their remaining forces.[93] In December 1804, while Eaton attempted to find Hamet in the interior of Egypt, fighting between the Turks and Mamelukes raged on, making his efforts more difficult and highly dangerous.[94] As Eaton perceived the situation, he faced perils in three areas including the "dangers of Robbery and assignation [*sic*] by the wild Arabs; danger of falling into the hands of the Arnaut Turks and being murdered as Enemys; and danger of being executed as Spies by the Mameluke Beys."[95] Despite the risky environment, Eaton and his small party ultimately found Hamet.

After meeting with Hamet, Eaton returned to Alexandria, where he made final his plans, coordinated with Hull for joint action, and recruited Greek soldiers and other Christian mercenaries to join his Marines and Hamet's Muslim supporters.[96] Hamet agreed that Eaton—a former captain in the U.S. Army—would hold the rank of general and command the force organized to capture Derna.[97] Once assembled in the Egyptian desert, Eaton's motley band constituted a diverse legion including American and Greek Christians along with Arab, Turk, and Tripolitan Muslims.[98] According to the plan developed by Eaton and Hull, the army would attack Derna from the land side while the maritime force under Hull would provide naval gunfire support from the sea.[99] The task force would then continue west along the coastline, repeat the operation at Benghazi, and finally capture the capital city of Tripoli.[100] As originally planned, this constituted more of a joint action than an amphibious operation. But as events played out at Derna, the battle took on more of an amphibious character. Eaton's entire force consisted of about five hundred to six hundred men, including the American detachment of seven Marines under command of Lt. Presley O'Bannon.[101]

Before departing Egypt for his march across the Libyan Desert, Eaton formalized the relationship between Hamet and the United States by creating a convention (written agreement) signed by both parties. Unfortunately for Hamet, Eaton, and U.S. credibility in the area, the American commander exceeded his authority and made commitments never intended by Barron or his government.[102] American leaders at the highest levels viewed the Hamet connection as a means of bringing pressure to bear on his brother, Pasha Yusuf. If successful, the United States would reward Hamet, but Barron and political authorities back in Washington considered the relationship to be a limited and conditional commitment.[103] Eaton disagreed, believing that once the United States sanctioned the restoration of Hamet, it should have the force of moral imperative. Whether because he genuinely believed the government would support this agreement or because he felt it would force the hand of American officials, Eaton created the convention with that objective in mind. He also conducted the operation against Derna with all the fervor of a committed zealot, often holding Hamet's army together by the strength of his personal leadership alone.[104] On 29 March 1805, while on the march about halfway between Alexandria and Derna, Eaton issued a dramatic and inspirational proclamation to the inhabitants of Tripoli declaring Hamet the rightful ruler and Yusuf a "treacherous scoundrel." Eaton called on the inhabitants of the kingdom to join hands with the forces of America and Hamet. This impassioned appeal clearly established Eaton's commitment to Hamet and his claim as the rightful ruler of Tripoli. It is obvious that Eaton did not consider his support of Hamet a mere tactic to gain advantage in negotiations with Yusuf.[105]

Although Pasha Yusuf knew of Eaton's efforts in Egypt and his intention to move against Derna, the effectiveness of the attack proved surprising because the defenders did not think American ships could get close enough to the shoreline to do any real damage to the city or its forts. Additionally, they did not expect an attack from the land side because that would require a six-hundred-mile march across the North African desert, which they considered unlikely if not impossible. The defenders of Derna proved to be wrong on both accounts. Eaton's naval support included three ships under Hull's command—the *Argus*, *Hornet*, and *Nautilus*—which had off-loaded all the arms and ammunition needed for Eaton's army in Alexandria and Bomba and then further lightened the ships so that they could get closer to shore and range the defensive structures and guns of Derna.[106]

While Hull prepared his ships for the assault, Eaton and O'Bannon undertook one of the most heroic and arduous marches in military history across a hostile desert with limited provisions and mutinous comrades.[107] At one point an intelligence report from Derna indicated that Pasha Yusuf had sent five hundred reinforcements to that city, causing panic among Hamet's Arab supporters in camp. In response to the near mutiny, Eaton suspended rations in order to reestablish discipline. This action, coupled with growing concerns about naval support for the mission, created the constant threat of desertion by the various Arab elements of Hamet's army during the march to Derna.[108] Despite the grueling and dangerous nature of the desert march, Eaton found time to examine ancient ruins and observe long abandoned artifacts telling of Greek and Carthaginian settlements from the distant past.[109] The intellectual stimulation of discovering historic attractions did not alleviate the taxing march that became so desperate at one point that the party found it necessary to kill and butcher a camel in order to feed the caravan.[110] During one of the worst moments of the march when mutiny and internecine warfare threatened, only O'Bannon, his Marine detachment, and a few Greek Christians within the army stood between Eaton and a revolt of Arab troops that included Hamet himself. But Eaton's strength of character and personal courage—and the help of a few Marines—kept the army together throughout the challenging and eventful march across the desert. Eaton credited O'Bannon as playing the key role in suppressing this potential disaster.

Before the situation within the army could deteriorate further, Hull and the *Argus* met Eaton's army at the coastal town of Bomba just forty miles short of Derna. Before the arrival of the American Navy, another mutiny appeared imminent, but the appearance of Hull's ships in the bay at Bomba helped avert disaster. With sails on the horizon, according to Eaton, "In an instant the face of everything changed from pensive gloom to inthusiastic gladness."[111] Not only did the American ship restore confidence and tranquility to Hamet's fighters, it also provided the supplies that permitted the army to arrive at Derna in a combat-ready state.[112] Most importantly, the supplies included rations to feed the troops and money for their pay.[113]

While refreshing his army at Bomba, Eaton and Hull laid final plans for the attack on Derna. His men rested and rearmed, Eaton left Bomba on or about 18 April 1805.[114] While en route, information reached the army that reinforcements had entered Derna. Consternation quickly spread among Hamet and his Arab supporters.[115] To calm their fears and get them to continue the march on Derna, Eaton promised to pay them an additional two thousand dollars. Hamet remained pessimistic, leading Eaton to comment that he "thought the bashaw [Pasha Hamet] wished himself back to Egypt."[116]

By 26 April Eaton and Hamet's force had arrived at the walls of Derna and coordinated with the ships of Hull's task force for the joint and combined attack against the city. Before launching the assault, Eaton invited the governor of Derna to accept Hamet as the legitimate sovereign and permit his army to enter the city. The governor rejected Eaton's request with the words "your head or mine."[117] The next day Eaton and Hull made final arrangements for naval gunfire support during the attack. Hull began a powerful naval bombardment of Derna and its forts that destroyed several batteries and eventually drove some of the Tripolitans from their guns and defenses. The marines then attacked the city along the beach with Hull's naval guns clearing the way. Concurrently, Hamet and his mounted Arabs circled south and west of the city, attacking from the opposite direction. Under the direct leadership of Eaton and O'Bannon, the Americans, along with a few Greek cannoneers, carried the hostile ramparts and entered the city. O'Bannon then turned the defenders' guns on the fleeing enemy just as Hamet's Arabs attacked from land side. This proved devastating for the defenders, and by the end of the day Eaton possessed both the fort and the city.[118] During the assault, Eaton received a painful but not incapacitating wound to his hand and wrist. Just before turning the fort's guns on the fleeing enemy, O'Bannon had removed the enemy flag from its staff and planted the American flag for the first time on a hostile foreign shore. The U.S. Marines had gone "to the shores of Tripoli."[119]

Determined and repeated efforts by forces loyal to Yusuf Karamanli attempted to retake Derna, but all failed due to the strong defense organized and directed by Eaton and O'Bannon, coupled with Hull's naval gunfire. Eaton and O'Bannon led several sorties against the hostile forces gathered around Derna, further discouraging their efforts to retake the city.[120] The loss of Derna, coupled with the bombardment of Tripoli by Preble and Barron and economic pressure created by the blockade, caused the pasha to seek peace negotiation through the offices of the Spanish consul in Tripoli.[121] On 4 June 1805 a treaty negotiated by Tobias Lear agreed on terms by which the United States would evacuate Derna and pay the pasha $60,000 in return for which Tripoli would release all Americans held prisoner and would release the United States from payment of any tribute in the future.[122] Never before had a Barbary State signed an agreement that did not include tribute or gifts in some form. Likewise, the treaty said nothing about Hamet's claim to rule Tripoli, and without American support he chose to depart North Africa for Syracuse where he lived for some time thereafter on an American pension.[123] The peace treaty with Tripoli did stipulate that Yusuf would release Hamet's wife and children—held for several years as prisoners by Yusuf—from their captivity in Tripoli. Unfortunately for Hamet's family, Lear agreed in a secret article to the treaty that allowed Yusuf to delay their release for four years.[124] Fortunately, the subsequent American consul to Tripoli proved able to effect their release two years early.[125] Many Americans—particularly Eaton—believed the United States had failed the rightful claimant to the title of pasha by not restoring Hamet to power in Tripoli.[126] Eaton considered the treaty with Yusuf premature and contended that his campaign would have achieved a much greater American victory if allowed to continue. He also believed that the United States had betrayed many supporters left behind in Derna when, under orders, he and Hamet slipped out of the city and harbor on board the *Constitution*.[127]

The American victory over Tripoli created a number of celebrities for the new republic, including Edward Preble, Stephen Decatur, William Eaton, and Presley O'Bannon, all of whom returned home to a hero's welcome.[128] Eaton used his new public status to vent resentment at what he considered a betrayal of Hamet Karamanli and his own strategy for the complete conquest of Tripoli.[129] In the process, he became a controversial figure—exploited by both Federalist politicians and Republican dissidents—and an ardent critic of both Tobias Lear and Thomas Jefferson.[130] O'Bannon's fame, although substantial, did not burn quite as bright as Eaton's at the end of the war with Tripoli. But he remains an icon within the Marine Corps to this day, revered for his contribution to the creation of a culture of dedication and courage. Although no documentary evidence exists to substantiate that Hamet awarded O'Bannon his personal sword, it remains a strong oral tradition, widely accepted by Marines. As a result, the Mameluke sword remains within the Marine Corps to this day, carried by commissioned officers as a standard item of dress uniform.[131]

Just as the war with Tripoli reached its favorable conclusion, the bey of Tunis threatened the United States with a new Barbary war. Upset by the capture of one of his xebecs and two of its prizes as they attempted to run the blockade of Tripoli, he demanded the United States return them or face a declaration of war.[132] But the time for bullying the United States on the Barbary Coast had passed. John Rodgers, who replaced

Barron as commodore of the Mediterranean squadron, concentrated a force of five frigates, three schooners, one brigantine, and one sloop at Tunis and gave the bey thirty-six hours to choose between war and peace.[133] The bey backed down, ending the Barbary War—at least for the time being.[134] Success against the Barbary corsairs proved inspirational to the new American republic. Ironically, it also marked the beginning of demise in American naval power.

When measuring the Derna action against the characteristics of amphibious operations and expeditionary warfare, several issues predominate. Most significantly, the integration between the Navy and landing force proved very effective, providing the most important factor for success. Although Barron endorsed the project halfheartedly, once he assigned Hull to support Eaton, the two commanders welded their efforts into a common enterprise. Hull assisted Eaton during his efforts to locate Hamet and recruit an army in Egypt and sustained him during the march across North African. Eaton could not have succeeded in either effort without Hull and his ships.

Upon arrival at Derna, Hull and Eaton task-organized their force by augmenting the assault element with artillery units as well as repositioning their troops for a beach attack against the sea-facing defenses. The fire support from Hull's guns coupled with Eaton's beach assault and Hamet's flanking attack exemplified the concept of unity of effort and operational coherence. Three of the characteristics of amphibious operations—integration between the Navy and landing force, task-organized forces, and unity of effort and operational coherence—are clearly demonstrated at Derna and explain the success of the operations. The fourth characteristic, rapid buildup of combat power from the sea to shore, occurred only in a vague manner. The actual tactics at Derna involved a joint and integrated attack with most of the forces already ashore when the assault occurred. Getting his army across the desert and in place at Derna's defenses constituted the concentration so important to an amphibious operation. Unlike the direct assaults against defended beaches of the twentieth century, eighteenth- and nineteenth-century amphibious landings primarily occurred at undefended sites from which the attacking force would move against the objective. In the case of Derna, the ground elements assembled at several points and converged—in conjunction with naval support—at the point of attack. These included several locations in Egypt and on the beaches at Bomba and Derna. Yet, even if this fourth characteristic of amphibious warfare fell short of perfection, the commanders addressed it well enough that, in conjunction with the other three, it served the purpose of the mission. Application of the characteristics of amphibious operations is not always perfect. It is desirable to achieve perfection in all four in every action, yet success remains possible so long as the amphibious force observes the preponderance of these principles. Such was the case at Derna.

In considering the expeditionary nature of the Derna operation, it clearly satisfies the defining characteristic of an expeditionary operation—the projection of forces into a foreign setting and their requisite support some significant distance from their home base. By gaining entry into the objective area by force—in this case through maneuver at sea and on land—the assault on Derna further exemplified the ideals of expeditionary warfare. Eaton effectively used Egypt and the Libyan Desert as forward bases while Hull's ships provided sea basing. For a successful assault on Derna, both forms of expeditionary basing were required. Additionally, the purposes for which the Derna operation had been conceived and launched—to secure policy objectives, to seize key physical objectives, to establish visible presence, and to (ultimately) rescue U.S. citizens—are all missions of expeditionary warfare. The most important of these missions is the securing of policy objectives, of course, which in this case involved ending the commerce raiding against U.S. shipping. Clearly, the success at Derna achieved this and other policy goals. Although Clausewitz is not normally associated with expeditionary warfare and amphibious operations, his overarching principle that war is policy by other means is clearly fundamental to these two modes of conflict.

Chapter 4

AMPHIBIOUS OPERATIONS IN THE WAR OF 1812

PRESIDENT THOMAS JEFFERSON AND SECRETARY OF THE Treasury Albert Gallatin constantly sought ways to reduce costs and eliminate unnecessary expenditures. The effectiveness of gunboats during the Barbary War with Tripoli coupled with the high cost of maintaining a frigate navy stimulated interest in developing a harbor defense system rather than maintaining a blue-water navy.[1] Although this concept seemed perfectly logical at the end of the Tripolitan War, the policy created problems for the United States when facing the Royal Navy during the War of 1812. The Jeffersonian gunboat fleet that augmented and replaced some of the frigate navy did not prove adequate to the needs of a renewed war against Great Britain, proving particularly vexing along the Atlantic and Gulf of Mexico littorals, where command of the sea allowed the British to conduct amphibious operations almost at will. Unfortunately, this did not represent the last time the United States sought a "peace dividend" after a long and arduous struggle that left the armed services inadequate for future security challenges.

In fairness to Republican leaders who promoted a shift from the deep-draft navy to a gunboat fleet, these vessels proved particularly valuable during the war with Tripoli. Initially, the friendly government in Naples loaned gunboats to the United States. As the war progressed, the United States began building its own gunboat fleet. During the final stages of the Barbary War, the secretary of the Navy had started sending American gunboats to the Mediterranean for combat duty.[2] The acquisition of Louisiana from France in 1803 and the consequent trepidation over security for New Orleans further stimulated interest in a defensive oriented gunboat policy. The prospect of creating an economically palatable gunboat fleet to secure new American territory proved particularly attractive to the U.S. Congress.

As the war with Tripoli wound down, Britain and France returned to war and both began seizing American ships trading with their enemy. In June 1805 Tripoli and the United States signed a treaty, after which many Republicans in Congress called for the reduction of the Navy. In September 1805 Secretary of the Navy Robert Smith publicly took issue with those who wished to remove virtually all frigates and sloops from active service, retaining only gunboats to provide coastal service. He believed the United States needed both blue-water and coastal warships and went so far as to recommend building six ships-of-the-line of seventy-four guns each.[3] Although Jefferson initially favored a balanced navy of both gunboats and seagoing vessels, the more frugal Congress did not support this approach, and economy trumped naval power in the budget battles that followed the Tripolitan War. Indeed, Jefferson's 1807 message to Congress requesting expansion of the gunboat fleet became the focus for future naval armament although the president had not intended it as a limiting factor.

As Britain expanded its fleet to counter the French, the Royal Navy once again turned to impressment to meet its need for sailors. On 22 June 1807 the U.S. frigate *Chesapeake* weighed anchor at Hampton Roads and set sail for the Mediterranean. HMS *Leopard* was waiting just outside U.S. territorial waters, and its captain, Salusbury P. Humphreys, demanded that the *Chesapeake* stop and return Royal Navy deserters believed to be on board the *Chesapeake*. When Capt. James Barron rejected the demand, Humphreys fired a broadside into the *Chesapeake*, killing three Americans and wounding eighteen others. Barron then allowed the British to take four sailors from the *Chesapeake* and returned to port.[4] Subsequently, Barron received a court-martial for failure to have his ship combat-ready, resulting in his suspension from the Navy for a period of five years.[5]

The episode caused outrage throughout the United States. President Jefferson resisted widespread demands for war and imposed an embargo on trade with both Britain and France, hoping that economic coercion would force both sides to respect American maritime rights.[6]

By 1811 Americans also believed that British agents were instigating Indian attacks in the region west of the Allegheny Mountains. These grievances—real or imagined—led many Americans to consider Britain a tormentor and generated demands for war with the former mother country.[7]

A faction of Republicans known as the "War Hawks" supported—even promoted—the movement toward war while most Federalists, particularly in New England, resisted. After a complex and rancorous debate, the Republican majority secured a declaration of war by a relatively close vote in Congress. War with Great Britain became official on 18 June 1812, when President James Madison signed the congressional declaration. The objectives of the war included ending British impressment of American seamen, eliminating or modifying the Orders in Council, and stopping Indian depredations on the American frontier by breaking British power in Canada.[8] Some leaders hoped to limit the fighting to naval actions—as happened in the Quasi-War—whereas others argued that Britain could be defeated quickly by invading Canada. Many Americans believed that conquering Canada would not only end British power in North America but also result in some or all of its provinces joining the Union.[9]

The initial campaign of the War of 1812 consisted of a three-pronged attack to conquer British Canada, including a drive against Detroit in the west, an offensive along the Niagara River in the center, and a main thrust against Montreal in the east. The strategy and assumptions underlying this approach seemed perfectly logical, but the militia-based army did not prove adequate for the task. The militia, and to some extent the small regular army, suffered from inadequate discipline, insufficient training, poor equipment, and deficient leadership. Many state officials and militiamen questioned the use of militia units outside their home state or in foreign lands such as British Canada. As a result, unity of command proved impossible, and the initial attacks against Canada in 1812 failed miserably.[10] Conversely, the U.S. Navy performed very well during the initial months of war. Despite the shift toward a gunboat fleet, the naval service had seven frigates and a dozen smaller warships in service at the start of the war.[11] In August 1812 the *Constitution* defeated HMS *Guerrière*, two months later the *United States* captured HMS *Macedonian*, and in December *Constitution* bested HMS *Java*. By the end of 1812 Americans had captured fifty British merchant ships.

Failure of the 1812 invasion of Canada convinced American leaders that they had to establish naval control on Lakes Erie and Ontario. These lakes provided the only effective avenues for transportation in the northwestern wilderness. Additionally, the most important population centers and military bases rested on the shores and tributaries of these lakes. To seize control of these waters, Isaac Chauncey, the senior American naval officer on the Great Lakes, converted available merchant schooners into combatants and began constructing new warships.[12]

While his shipbuilding effort progressed, Chauncey launched an amphibious attack that he believed would secure control of Lake Ontario. On 27 April 1813 a force of 1,700 Americans under Brig. Gen. Zebulon Pike attacked York (now Toronto), the provincial capital of Upper Canada. In a classic amphibious action, Chauncey landed the assault force west of the city, where it could maneuver against the defending army. His ships provided accurate naval gunfire to cover the landing, followed by maneuvers that drove the British and their Indian allies out of York and the surrounding area. Unfortunately, an explosion of the British powder magazine late in the battle killed more Americans than did the actual fighting, including Zebulon Pike, the renowned explorer who led the assault on York. This explosion infuriated the U.S. troops, who considered it an act of treachery, believing it occurred during the drafting of capitulation papers. For three days the troops looted and burned buildings, including the meeting place of the Upper Canada legislature, before American officers could fully restore discipline.[13]

The attack on York yielded outstanding results including the capture of one British ship and the destruction of another. The American force also captured large quantities of ordnance and stores and destroyed everything of military value they could not carry away. This created problems for the British navy on Lakes Ontario and Erie and the ground forces they supported.[14] One month later, on 27 May 1813, Col. Winfield Scott and Commo. Oliver Hazard Perry won an impressive amphibious victory at Fort George at the mouth of the Niagara River. Under the overall command of Maj. Gen. Henry Dearborn, who had also been Pike's superior at the Battle of York, Scott worked closely with his naval counterpart to plan and execute the assault landing. Not only did Scott conduct excellent detailed planning, he also personally led the first wave and established a reputation as an effective and courageous combat leader during the subsequent operation ashore.[15] On 28–29 May, British commodore Sir James Yeo attempted to restore the balance of power on Lake Ontario by attacking the American base at Sackets Harbor, New York. Both Yeo and his superior, Sir George Prevost, considered this a propitious opportunity as they knew Chauncey to be at the opposite end of the lake at the time. But the 750-man landing force suffered a sharp defeat by American defenders under the command of Brig. Gen. Jacob Brown, who forced them to return to their ships and retreat to Kingston.[16]

Alarmed by the attack on his base, Chauncey returned to Sackets Harbor and remained there until another sloop of war was completed, believing this made his flotilla stronger than that of the British. He then agreed to a second attack on York. On 31 July three hundred American troops met no opposition when they landed east of York, entered the undefended town, burned a British barracks, destroyed eleven bateau, and carried off five cannon, several barrels of flour, and other supplies before withdrawing without suffering casualties.[17]

The amphibious successes of Chauncey, Dearborn, and their subordinates temporarily turned the balance of power on Lake Ontario in favor of the United States. They also disrupted lines of supply and communications to Royal Navy forces on Lake Erie, thereby delaying preparations for the upcoming battle with Commodore Perry. The crowning victory of the 1813 Great Lakes campaign occurred on Lake Erie, where the U.S. Navy not only gained control of that lake but also established American strategic supremacy in the western theater. On 10 September Perry defeated the British naval force on Lake Erie under Capt. Robert Barclay in a savage battle lasting more than three hours.[18] Like the performance of Winfield Scott in the Battle of Fort George, Perry's conduct became legendary for its effectiveness and heroism. Perry's flagship, the brig *Lawrence*, bore the brunt of the fighting and suffered the greatest damage and highest casualties of the American fleet. The damage proved so great that Perry had to transfer his flag to the *Niagara* in order to continue the battle. After securing victory, Perry sent a laconic report to Maj. Gen. William Henry Harrison stating, "We have met the enemy, and they are ours: Two ships, two Brigs one Schooner & one Sloop."[19]

Perry's victory on Lake Erie (also known as the Battle of Put-in-Bay) paved the way for the reoccupation of Detroit and the destruction of

Indian power on the northwestern frontier. Harrison had maintained a defensive posture following an earlier American defeat at Frenchtown in January 1813, but Perry's victory changed the strategic and operational situation in the northwest. Within weeks of his victory on Lake Erie, Perry moved Harrison's army of about seven thousand effectives across the lake. When the Americans approached Detroit on 29 September 1813, Proctor left the city and retreated toward Moraviantown in an attempt to save his command. But Harrison caught and defeated the Anglo-Indian forces at the Battle of the Thames.[20]

British success in the eastern theater—arguably the most important area of conflict during 1813—more than offset the American successes on the western periphery of war. Maj. Gen. James Wilkinson's abortive scheme to attack down the St. Lawrence to threaten Montreal met with defeat at the Battle of Crysler's Farm in November 1813. Similarly, Wade Hampton's overland march toward Montreal met with defeat in the Battle of Chateauguay. The British remained strong in the Montreal–Lake Champlain area and on the Niagara frontier. The United States proved effective in controlling Lake Ontario and Lake Erie, and in destroying British and Indian power in the northwest. Only Mackinac Island on the northern extreme of Lake Huron remained an isolated British stronghold in this area. In the American south, a militant branch of the Creek tribe, known as Red Sticks, joined the conflict, bringing about the rise of Maj. Gen. Andrew Jackson. Although Jackson did not completely defeat the Red Stick Creeks until March 1814, he effectively destroyed Indian power in the south just as Harrison had done in the northwest.[21]

An important British objective of 1813 involved increasing pressure on the United States at sea and along the Atlantic littoral. With a fleet ultimately consisting of ten ships-of-the-line, thirty-eight frigates, and fifty-two craft of lesser draft, Adm. Sir John Borlase Warren tightened the blockade that Britain instituted at the beginning of the war and sought to confine American warships and commerce raiders within their harbors. Warren also intended to conduct amphibious raids along the Atlantic littorals and especially throughout the Chesapeake Bay. For this mission Warren assigned an amphibious task force under one of his most able officers, Rear Adm. Sir George Cockburn. During April–July 1813 the strength and mobility of the British task force allowed them to conduct amphibious raids at the times and locations of their own choosing.[22] But despite general success in the Chesapeake, British forces occasionally met with determined resistance such as the first attack against Norfolk, Virginia. In the early morning of 22 June, British troops sought to capture Craney Island as a base for attacking Norfolk, Portsmouth, and Gosport Navy Yard. In the sharp battle that followed, the American defenders used canister, grape, and round shot from the four guns of Fort Craney augmented by three guns removed from *Constellation* combined with American gunboats in the Elizabeth River to repel the British.[23]

By the end of 1813 both sides had experienced success and failure in their war efforts. During October 1813 Napoleon's defeat in the Battle of Leipzig presaged the end of war in Europe and redeployment of British forces against the United States, altering the balance of power for the remainder of the war. The fighting in 1814 involved increased amphibious action along the Atlantic coastline, particularly in Maine and within the Chesapeake. In northern Maine, where the border between the United States and Britain remained in dispute, Sir John Sherbrooke and Capt. Thomas Hardy launched a series of amphibious attacks in the summer of 1814 that captured Eastport, Maine, along the coastline, and Castine in Penobscot Bay. During September they drove up the Penobscot River, destroying property and taking control of large areas in that state. With British troops on the ground, Sherbrooke administered the area as if it were British territory, which caused great consternation among American leaders. Despite several plans to recapture that part of Maine, none came to fruition, and the occupied section remained in British hands until the end of the war.[24] British actions in 1814 also involved two of the most important amphibious landings of the war, including the Battle of Bladensburg followed by the destruction of Washington, and the battle for Baltimore, bringing mixed results to the combatants.

In April 1814, following a series of defeats, Napoleon abdicated, temporarily ending the European war and freeing 35,000 British troops for war in America.[25] British officials earmarked most of these men for a major push against the United States from Canada under command of Gov.-Gen. Sir George Prevost. But to distract American attention from their northern strategy, British authorities assigned a reinforced brigade under the command of Maj. Gen. Robert Ross to serve with Vice Adm. Sir Alexander Cochrane—who had replaced Warren as naval commander on the Atlantic and Gulf Coasts—and his joint expeditionary force then operating on the littorals of the United States. Cockburn, who served Warren so effectively, remained with the fleet as Cochrane's principal naval lieutenant although he retained a clear penchant for operations ashore. The Admiralty also assigned Cochrane an additional thousand marines organized into ten companies under the command of Lt. Col. James Malcolm to further enhance British amphibious capability.[26]

Ross' instructions clearly subordinated him to Cochrane, with the stipulation that he had the right to refuse any missions he considered imprudent. Ross commanded all ground forces while ashore and determined when they would return to their ships after completing combat actions. British authorities communicated their expectation regarding command relations to all principal commanders, and command relations did not seem to be a problem during the Chesapeake operations.[27] Yet, despite clarity regarding the lines of authority among the top commanders, true unity of command required cooperation, and individual personalities often played a role in decision making.

During the spring of 1814 Cochrane's enhanced amphibious task force intensified operations on America's Atlantic seaboard. Originally intended to distract attention from Prevost's attack southward along the Richelieu–Lake Champlain corridor against Plattsburgh, New York, the raids assumed a life of their own, especially those actions within the Chesapeake Bay.[28] Operations there had both military and economic implications. Strategically, they kept the American government guessing about British intentions. The possibility of a land campaign in the region also kept the Madison administration from transferring troops to northern New York to counter the invasion from Canada. Seizures of large quantities of tobacco and the destruction of plantations bordering Chesapeake Bay damaged the American economy, as did British attempts to free and recruit slaves during these raids.[29] During 1813 and early 1814 the British raids annoyed Americans and their government but had no significant impact on the war.

A campaign against the capital at Washington or the port of Baltimore could have a far greater impact on the war, and in early 1814 government leaders in London ordered an attack on Baltimore. Before initiating action aimed at Baltimore, the British had to neutralize the flotilla of gunboats and barges commanded by Commo. Joshua Barney.

A native of Baltimore, Barney had begun building the flotilla in the later part of 1813 in response to Cockburn's raids around Chesapeake Bay.[30] In early June 1814 Barney deployed his two gunboats and twelve barges at a point just north of the Patuxent River in a move designed to prevent the British from entering the upper section of Chesapeake Bay. When the lead elements of the more powerful British fleet appeared, Barney ordered his flotilla to seek refuge first in the Patuxent River and then in St. Leonard's Creek. Unable to reach Barney with his main fleet, Cochrane armed a series of barges and sent them upriver under escort of a schooner and two frigates with orders to destroy Barney's flotilla. Anticipating such an attack, Barney asked Secretary of the Navy William Jones to send land-based artillery batteries to provide fire support for his expected engagement with the British. Barney intended these batteries to augment the militia forces already supporting him from the banks of St. Leonard's Creek. Before the reinforcements arrived, Barney and his flotillamen repulsed a British effort to enter St. Leonard's Creek and destroy his flotilla. During the 20 June battle Barney lost a barge but inflicted serious damage on the eighteen-gun schooner HMS *St. Lawrence.*[31]

On 12 June, Jones dispatched Marine lieutenant (soon to be captain) Samuel Miller with about 110 Marines and 3 light 12-pounders to support Barney's flotilla and maintain security along the banks of St. Leonard's Creek. Jones had great faith in the training and professionalism of these Marines, whom he considered among the finest troops within the Washington area. He had also coordinated with the secretary of the Army, John Armstrong, for additional artillery and infantry to support Barney. Collectively, the joint force of Navy, Marine Corps, and Army units provided an adequate capability for Barney to launch an attack against British ships at the mouth of St. Leonard's Creek.[32]

During the early morning hours of 26 June 1814, British seamen woke to the sound of fire from the Army, Marine Corps, and flotilla guns directed at the frigates HMS *Loire* and HMS *Narcissus.* After a two-hour pounding, the British ships withdrew to new positions near the Chesapeake Bay. Barney then left St. Leonard's Creek and moved his flotilla up the Patuxent to a point where the river was too shallow for the British warships to follow.[33] As Cochrane continued to press Barney's gunboats, a large British amphibious force landed on 19 August

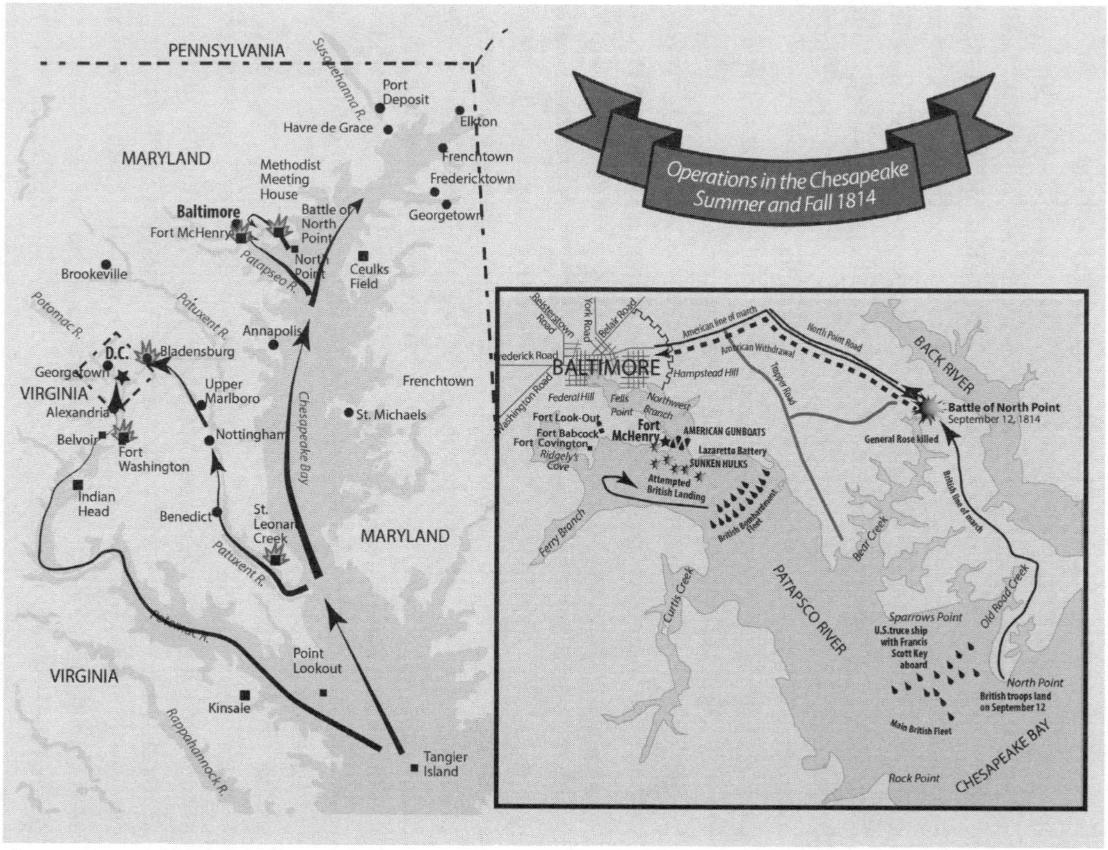

Map 5. Operations in the Chesapeake

at Benedict, Maryland, on the Patuxent River. The combined effects of these actions ultimately forced Barney to scuttle his flotilla and to use his sailors and Marines for other services in defense of Washington. The aggressive British action on the Patuxent coupled with the landing at Benedict convinced Barney that Washington represented the primary objective of the British campaign.[34]

Despite the landing of about four thousand British troops and their subsequent movement toward Washington, confusion about the strategic and tactical situations remained in the minds of American leaders. Some members of the Madison cabinet, led by Secretary of the Army John Armstrong, believed Washington offered no strategic advantage to the British and that the landing at Benedict could only be a feint. Others considered Washington the objective but remained confused about the tactical situation. This group included the commanding officer of the 10th Military District, Brig. Gen. William Winder, who had responsibility for the defense of Washington. The British used tactical deception very well in their march toward Washington, and the lack of good reconnaissance by American commanders enhanced their efforts. Uncertain of British intentions, Winder floundered under the fog of war and continually moved his troops around the countryside in the days approaching the battle. Uncertain where to position his force, Winder fell back to Washington on 23 August with most of his army, including the naval detachment under Barney and Miller.[35] On the morning of 24 August Winder finally realized that the British troops were marching on Washington along the Bladensburg Road and ordered the forces under his direct command to take up positions around Bladensburg to block the British advance.[36]

The town of Bladensburg sits near the upper forks of the eastern branch of the Potomac (now called the Anacostia River). The river did not represent a formable obstacle at that point, but crossing it would slow the British advance just as it passed a ridge to the west of Bladensburg. Occupying that ridge would place Winder's men in a strong defensive position, one from which they could fire down on the British as they crossed the bridge at Bladensburg or forded the river upstream from the town. Unfortunately, Winder's force did not arrive on the battlefield in time to organize their defenses properly or to prepare good positions.[37]

Both armies arrived at the battle site in a state of near exhaustion from the marching of that morning and the previous several days. In addition, both commanders introduced their forces into the battle in a piecemeal manner. But British commanders would do so more quickly and more effectively, and this had an impact during the early stages of the fighting. When British forces entered the town of Bladensburg, either side had the capability to win the battle. The British had the advantage of experienced regular troops, Congreve rockets, and the initiative of the offense. Yet their artillery lagged behind and did not arrive in time to provide fire support during the battle. The Americans had the advantage of occupying the high ground, artillery on the field, and a slight advantage in numbers, although very few regulars.[38]

First blood in the Battle of Bladensburg went to the Americans when their artillery and riflemen opened fire on British troops moving through Bladensburg. As the British moved across the Bladensburg Bridge, American cannon raked their forces but did not prevent passage. Failure to destroy the bridge across the East Branch and contain British troops within Bladensburg constituted the first major American mistake. The leading British elements charged across the bridge and conducted a frontal assault against the most forward positions while enveloping to the American left flank. The unexpected collapse of Col. Tobias Stansbury's Baltimore militia, which constituted the forward edge of the American defenses, facilitated the British envelopment. Concerned with the disjointed deployment of his forces, the exposure of his left flank, and the collapse of Stansbury's regiment, Winder ordered a retreat. At this point the tactical advantage shifted decisively to the British as confusion reigned within the American army. Winder's forward elements had reached the field just before the battle, and his follow-on forces were still arriving as the retreat began. Winder intended to regroup his force on the high ground farther to the rear of the battle area and again engage the attacking British, but the withdrawal quickly deteriorated from an orderly retirement, intended to reposition the army, into a disorganized rout.[39]

Just as Winder ordered his retreat, the flotillamen and Marines arrived and began establishing good defensive positions on terrain the British had not yet occupied. Winder hoped that a strong defense from these positions would weaken the enemy enough so that a reorganized defense from high ground at the rear of the battle area could repulse the British attack. Winder's idea was tactically sound and could possibly have worked considering the excellent performance of the naval detachment once it engaged the British advance. But Winder lost control of his forces as many of his retreating troops left the battlefield without restraint. Most of these soldiers simply did not know what their commander expected of them or where to go.[40]

The collapse of command and control over the American army resulted from inadequate planning and Winder's confused communications. He continually issued directions and then changed or withdrew what he had ordered. Adding further confusion was Secretary of State James Monroe, who was on the field as a volunteer scout and several times ordered troops to shift position without Winder's knowledge. This created uncertainty in the minds of his officers and men. Additionally, Winder had failed to explain his concept of defense in depth and had not designated rally points at which the retreating troops could reassemble. As a result, only the Marines and flotillamen stood their ground, and they provided a virtuoso display of combat effectiveness. Had the majority of Winder's force performed like his naval contingent, he could have prevailed at the Battle of Bladensburg.[41]

As the American forces fled the battlefield in disorder, the Marines and flotillamen took a position on the high ground about four hundred yards from the forward defenses. As the British approached, they recognized this new threat and momentarily halted their advance. Considering the condition of the American army at this point, the British did not expect a serious engagement. When the defenders held their fire, the British troops again moved forward against Barney's position. The flotillamen had established themselves astride the main road with the two 18-pounders that Miller acquired from the Navy Yard. Miller had positioned his Marines and a few flotillamen on excellent ground to Barney's right and retained three 12-pounders acquired from the Marine Park. Troops not required to serve the batteries provided musket fire to support and protect the big guns. Still farther to the right, a strong force of approximately seven hundred Maryland militiamen under the command of Col. William Beall occupied a commanding piece of terrain.[42]

When the British resumed their attack against Barney's position astride the main road, the flotillamen opened up with a withering fire that cleared the road and decimated the forward echelon of the British force. The British attempted two more assaults with disastrous results, and then moved by their left flank to envelop Barney's right. As they came within range, the Marines opened fire on them with devastating effect, forcing the British to halt. The battle then raged between the British and the Marines. At one point, British troops attempted to move farther to the right, but Miller ordered a counterattack, which drove them back and discouraged further effort in that quarter.[43] The nature of the immediate terrain coupled with the fields of fire available to the naval detachment forced the British to move by their left flank in an attempt to resume their attack.[44]

When that maneuver failed, the British were left with few options, the best of which was to attempt an even wider envelopment that would take them beyond the range of the Marines' fire into position to assault the right end of the American lines. There they would face Beall's regiment of Maryland militia. Since the Marylanders held strong positions, both Barney and Miller expected them to repulse any British effort in their front. But when the British appeared before Beall's force, the Marylanders fired several token shots and—to the astonishment of Barney and Miller—retreated before their enemy. This left the naval detachment as the only remaining American fighting unit on the field of battle.[45] It also exposed Miller's right flank to British attack at the same time the enemy began a wide envelopment to the left.

The Marines and flotillamen continued the fight until their ammunition ran out, and both Barney and Miller suffered serious wounds. With the enemy on all sides and moving toward their rear, Barney ordered the naval force off the battlefield, ending all resistance to the British advance. Although Barney and the flotillamen received considerable recognition for their stalwart effort, Miller and his Marines received the most widespread recognition for the fight they had staged. For his performance, Miller received promotion to brevet major from President Madison, being one of only four officers so honored at the Battle of Bladensburg.[46]

The Battle of Bladensburg remains controversial because of the quick defeat and disorganized rout that became general over most of the battlefield. The outcome of the battle, coupled with its culminating event—the burning of much of the nation's capital—engendered bitter recriminations at the time and ensured perpetual attention afterward. Further adding to the humiliation, a British naval element under Capt. James Alexander Gordon attacked other sites near the capital, including Fort Washington and Alexandria, Virginia. During these actions Gordon destroyed military facilities and captured merchantmen and cargos. The gallant though largely unsuccessful efforts of John Rodgers, David Porter, and Oliver Hazard Perry to harass Gordon's retreat down the Potomac offset—somewhat but not entirely—the disgraceful abandonment of Fort Washington and surrender of Alexandria. After the British burned much of Washington and inflicted other destruction along the Potomac, many leaders felt certain that Baltimore would be their next major objective.[47]

During the weeks immediately following the sacking of Washington, Cochrane, Cockburn, and Ross laid plans to attack Baltimore. Cochrane preferred to attack Rhode Island first and then return south to destroy Baltimore. In a private letter to the first lord of the Admiralty written immediately after the Battle of Baltimore, Cochrane expressed regret at not following his instincts, stating he only changed his mind at the insistence of Ross and to preserve unanimity between the two services. Throughout the Chesapeake operation, Cockburn proved the most aggressive and strong willed of the senior British officers. Most likely, Cockburn convinced Ross to attack Baltimore immediately, and collectively they persuaded Cochrane.[48]

Cochrane's regret at attacking Baltimore during September did not stem from any empathy for the city or its inhabitants. He considered Baltimore the richest and most democratic city in America and one that "ought to be laid in Ashes." Cochrane expected to receive further reinforcements during November to enhance his ability to "act with vigor." By raiding Rhode Island first, he could return south able to act against Baltimore with greater strength. But Cockburn and Ross convinced Cochrane to destroy Baltimore while still in the Chesapeake despite the smaller troop strength and concern for health risks associated with "the sickly season." In his official report Cochrane characterized the attack as a probe, intended to be converted into an attack should the opportunity appear advantageous. This is an obvious face-saving device as he committed his entire combat capability to the ill-fated mission, including three infantry brigades reinforced with artillery and Marines, and sixteen major combat ships.[49]

Immediately following the destruction of Washington, citizens and leaders in Baltimore became highly excited, fearing that the British would now move against their city. Throughout the summer of 1814, American authorities in Baltimore and the War Department conducted extensive planning for defense of that city.[50] On 25 August, at the urging of regular naval and Army officers in the vicinity, the Baltimore Committee of Vigilance and Safety—acting as the de facto city government—appointed militia Maj. Gen. Samuel Smith (who was also a U.S. senator from Maryland) as the overall commander of Baltimore defenses. On 26 August Gov. Levin Winder validated the appointment and further implied that Smith held federal service rank—not mere militia rank—because of President Madison's call-up order of 4 July 1814. As commanding general of the third division of Maryland militia, Smith had already taken control of defensive preparations without waiting for official sanction. Both military and civilian leaders on the scene generally accepted Smith's authority, but the potential for friction remained, given Smith's status as a militia officer.[51]

Following the destruction of Washington, citizens and leaders in Baltimore believed the British planned a similar fate for their city. But rather than take council of their fears, leaders in Baltimore and Washington redoubled their defensive efforts. Secretary of the Navy William Jones had already taken action on 19 August—before the Battle of Bladensburg—by ordering John Rodgers, then in Philadelphia, to "with the least possible delay . . . proceed to Baltimore with about 300 men . . . of the force under your command." Jones believed the British moves in the Patuxent River might be a feint designed to draw American forces away from the real British target, Baltimore. Rodgers and his men arrived too late to influence events at Washington but played a prominent role in the subsequent defense of Baltimore.[52]

During the final days of August, many American leaders remained uncertain about British intentions. As a result, Jones ordered Rodgers and the bulk of his force to the Washington area, where they could counter any moves by the British along the Potomac or Patuxent watercourses. At Smith's insistence, Jones authorized Rodgers to move to a point about midway between Washington and Baltimore, one from which he could also respond to the British should they be aimed at Baltimore. When American observers at Point Lookout reported that the British fleet was sailing up the Chesapeake Bay, Smith and Rodgers concluded that their target had to be either Baltimore or Annapolis. Jones ordered Rodgers to return to Baltimore, and by 8 September Rodgers and his seamen and Marines encamped amid the "Forts, Redoubts, and Entrenchments thrown up all round the Town."[53]

Although not convinced the British meant to attack Baltimore, Rodgers did all he could to improve the city's defenses. As commander of naval forces in the bay, he ordered the sloops of war under his command to move to positions where they could support Forts McHenry, Babcock, and Covington and placed barges and batteries in positions to provide additional support to these forts and to prevent the British from entering the Patapsco River. Rodgers also reinforced Smith's main defensive line on Hampstead Hill by emplacing batteries manned by sailors and Marines, to cover key avenues of approach along Philadelphia Road and Sparrows Point Road. Additionally, he stationed Marines—those not required to serve artillery pieces—into entrenchments located between the batteries to strengthen the defensive line that Smith laid out along Hampstead Hill. Other units involved in the defensive plan included numerous infantry and artillery units of Maryland militia, one division of Pennsylvania militia, one division of Virginia militia, and various detachments of U.S. infantry, artillery, and dragoons.[54]

Not all commanders cooperated as smoothly as Smith and Rodgers. When Winder arrived at Baltimore on 27 August, he fully expected to exercise overall command of American forces—including the militia units commanded by Smith. For his part, Smith could claim that the 4 July 1814 call-up by President Madison placing him into federal service meant Smith now outranked Winder on the field since Smith possessed a major general's commission and Winder held that of a brigadier.[55] The acquiescence of acting secretary of War James Monroe—who replaced Armstrong on 4 September—and President Madison to Smith's assumption of command resolved the issue, much to the chagrin of William Winder. It is to Winder's credit that he cooperated entirely with Smith during the period of adjudication and in all subsequent activities, despite what he considered an injustice.[56]

With reports of the British force sailing up the bay, Smith concluded that the British planned to attack Baltimore. On 9 and 10 September units of the fleet entered the Patapsco River, and on 11 September, anchored off North Point, Smith immediately dispatched a reinforced brigade under Brig. Gen. John Stricker to block any advance on Baltimore from that direction. During the early morning hours of 12 September the British began an unopposed landing at North Point, where the Patapsco meets the Chesapeake. The landing site lies roughly fourteen miles southeast of Baltimore. The route of march from North Point to Baltimore dissects a peninsula that juts southeast from the city between the Patapsco and Back Rivers.[57]

British plans called for the army to march up the peninsula and to attack Baltimore from either the east or north, depending on the situation they found. The second and equally important aspect of this plan involved sending a squadron of frigates and bomb ketches up the Patapsco to provide naval gunfire support for the attacking force and to bombard the city of Baltimore. By 0700 on 12 September the British had established their landing force of about 4,700 men ashore and quickly began the movement toward Baltimore. By the time Ross had his army in motion, Stricker knew of the landing and began preparing forward positions from which to counter the advance. For his main defensive line, Stricker selected a position at the narrowest point on the peninsula, about midway between North Point and Baltimore. His position lay adjacent to the Methodist meetinghouse, with its left flank tied into an inlet from Back River named Bread and Cheese Creek and his right protected by Bear Creek. Upon their arrival at the chosen position, Sticker's troops immediately started digging entrenchments, establishing fields of fire, and building obstacles. Meanwhile, Sticker sent a contingent of riflemen and cavalry forward to report on the size of the British force and to harass and slow its progress.[58]

Stricker's reinforced brigade consisted of the Fifth, Sixth, Twenty-Seventh, Thirty-Ninth, and Fifty-First Regiments of the Maryland Militia, the Fifth Maryland Cavalry Regiment, the First Maryland Artillery Regiment, the First Maryland Rifle Battalion, and a detachment of Pennsylvania infantry. As he prepared to challenge Ross' passage, Stricker had about 3,185 effectives and the advantage of a good position on the ground. Moreover, Stricker had a limited mission intended only to delay and inflict punishment on the British enemy. Smith intended the main defense of Baltimore to occur at the extensive entrenchments along Hampstead Hill and Rodgers' Bastion, not on the approaches to the city. Ross' force moving toward Stricker consisted of three reinforced regiments including infantry, artillery, and Marines totaling about 4,000 effectives.[59] If Stricker had the advantage of ground, Ross had the advantage of numbers. He also had benefit of well-trained, well-equipped, well-disciplined, and well-led veteran fighters.

The British army deployed from its beachhead in a single column of regiments with good tactical security to the front and flanks. Artillery batteries moved in the center of their column, providing protection during the march and the capability for rapid deployment upon contact. After a short time, the British passed a partially completed entrenchment line, which the American defenders had prepared but chosen not to occupy. This provided the British an important position three days later for protecting their force during its retreat to reembark. Just past this unfinished trench lay Gorsuch's farm about three miles in front of Stricker's line. One mile beyond Gorsuch's farm, Stricker's advanced force of riflemen had taken positions in a blacksmith shop and the surrounding woods.[60]

Initially, Ross had no knowledge of Stricker's force, due to deceptive information received from a captured American cavalryman. British leaders expected to meet only vedettes and skirmishers during the march to Baltimore. When the advance element of Ross' force approached the blacksmith's shop, American riflemen opened fire, causing confusion among the British troops. Due to the flat ground and heavy woods, British officers could not assess the situation without moving to the point of action. As Ross rode toward the sound of musketry, he received a fatal wound from the rifle of an American sharpshooter. But as Ross lay dying, his advanced guard began to drive the Americans from the woods, much to the chagrin of Stricker. This action brought about the Battle of Long Log Lane (also known as the Battle of North Point) just as Stricker intended. But Stricker expected the riflemen and cavalry to inflict greater casualties on his enemy before they reached his entrenchments.[61]

Stricker expected his riflemen to lay down a "galling fire" against the invaders, while the cavalry harassed their flanks. In Stricker's mind, the more his advanced element could degrade the enemy, the longer he could hold his position. The longer he held his position, the weaker the enemy would be upon arriving at the Baltimore defenses. Although this constituted sound tactical thinking, it failed to consider the inexperience of his soldiers. It also failed to consider that British commanders could rapidly deploy regimental-sized units against his advanced element, which amounted to little more than a harassment party. Yet, despite these factors, the American riflemen did not immediately break when the British moved against them. They maintained a desultory action until a rumor spread that the British had made an amphibious landing to their rear from Back River. Hearing this, they abandoned their positions and retreated to Stricker's line, where he placed both the rifle battalion and cavalry units in a position on his right flank.[62]

After driving the riflemen from the woods near the blacksmith shop, the British force pressed on until about two in the afternoon, when it confronted Stricker's main line of defense. The British leaders immediately recognized the strength of Stricker's position, noting his use of terrain and skillful deployment of artillery and infantry units. Most British officers overestimated the strength of the defenders and believed that they faced six thousand or more Americans. The new British commander, Col. Arthur Brooke, immediately advanced his force and deployed them in a position to launch a general attack on the American positions. As he did so, Stricker's vedettes and other advanced elements were forced to withdraw and an artillery duel began. American and British units exchanged fire for about half an hour, at which time Stricker ordered his men to cease firing and to reload their guns with grape and canister in anticipation that the British infantry would soon attack. At this point, the American defensive line consisted of one rifle battalion, the Fifth and Twenty-Seventh Regiments, and the artillery units forward deployed near the main defensive position. About half a mile to his rear Stricker had the Thirty-Ninth and Fifty-First Regiments preparing entrenchments, and one-half mile behind them he had placed the Sixth Regiment.[63] By positioning of his forces in this manner, Stricker intended to engage the British in successive actions, inflicting attrition throughout their march toward Baltimore. It is a classical application of the tactical evolution known as defense in depth.[64]

As the enemy assaulted his position, Stricker quickly discerned that the main effort would come against his left flank. Realizing that he did not have the necessary strength to defend all along the line while resisting a major thrust on his flank, Stricker ordered the Thirty-Ninth Regiment to move into position at the left end of his line and the Fifty-First to refuse (bend) his left flank from a position at right angles with the Thirty-Ninth.[65] Although this strengthened Stricker's main defensive line, it eliminated his second defensive position. That action left the Sixth Regiment as his only reserve and the only prepared position to which he could withdraw. In short, his three-phased defense in depth suddenly became limited to only two echelons. As the British pressed their attack,

Stricker's left gave way, but his center and right held fast until their position became untenable.[66] At that point the American and British accounts of the action differ substantially.

According to the British, after the collapse of the American left flank, the defenders took to their heels and fled as precipitously as they had at the Battle of Bladensburg. Most British observers contend the American force suffered between 500 to 600 casualties and retreated all the way to the Baltimore defenses. In fact, American casualties amounted to 24 killed and 139 wounded against British casualties of 39 killed and 251 wounded. Colonel Brooke admitted that the brief engagement had been sharp but believed he completely routed his enemy. He also suggested that he did not pursue the retreating Americans because of the lateness of the day and the fatigue of his own troops. Brooke's troops may have been tired, but they still had plenty of daylight left as the battle ended at about 1600 that afternoon.[67] Regardless of his reasons, the British army encamped the evening of 12 September on the field of battle.

The American account of the battle contends that the defensive line held very well until the Fifty-First Regiment failed to hold its position on the left flank. After moving from its reserve position to the main defensive line, the regiment immediately came under fire from the advancing British and "delivered one random fire [then] retreated precipitately," according to Stricker. In a message to Smith, he blamed the failure to check the enemy for a longer period entirely on the Fifty-First, calling its actions "senseless desertion." He acknowledges that some further disorder followed the collapse of the Fifty-First but insists that the remaining troops rallied, continued resistance for a time, and retreated in an orderly manner only when ordered to do so. Regardless of the manner of his retreat, Strickter established a new defensive position at the site occupied by the Sixth Regiment about one mile from the original line of battle. After seeing that the enemy had not pursued, Stricker decided to move his force back to the Baltimore defenses, where Smith assigned his brigade an area in front of the left flank, adjacent to the forces commanded by Winder.[68]

The next day, Brooke gingerly pushed his force forward through obstacles and foul weather, arriving at a position two miles in front of Hampstead Hill at about 1000 on the morning of 13 September. Upon conducting a reconnaissance of the defensive positions, British leaders concluded that they had engaged only a small portion of the American combat force during the previous day of fighting. Brooke and other British officers estimated the American army at between 15,000 and 20,000 effectives supported by vast amounts of well-placed artillery. The officers also recognized the formidable nature of the defensive entrenchments and the advantage that surrounding terrain offered to the defenders. If the British army felt any exultation from the Battle of Long Log Lane, the American positions at Baltimore severely dampened that spirit.[69]

As Brooke pondered the situation, he considered three options. A frontal attack against the American positions on Hampstead Hill offered no military advantage to the assaulting force. The British would have to move forward over a large open space for an extended period while being subject to massive firepower from well-protected defenses. To do this would invite slaughter on a massive scale. Additionally, the position of Winder's and Stricker's forces would threaten his flank and rear as his forces assaulted the prepared defenses on Hampstead Hill. Brooke believed he could minimize these disadvantages by conducting a night attack, thereby negating the American advantage of superior artillery. But even a night attack would require support from the Royal Navy within Baltimore Harbor. During the day of 13 September, Brooke still believed naval gunfire support would be available to support his attack on the city.[70]

A second option for British action involved a movement to the north, enveloping the strong entrenchments on Hampstead Hill and attacking the city at a weaker point. Initially, Brooke believed this to be his best choice although it also required naval gunfire support to ensure success. Additionally, the surrounding terrain limited the amount of maneuver space available to Brooke, and the forces under Winder and Stricker held ground from which they could dispute his passage. While engaged in any battle with Winder and Stricker, Brooke would offer his flank and rear to the American forces manning the palisades on or about Hampstead Hill. Given the vast numerical advantage of American forces on the battlefield, it would even be possible for them to threaten Brooke's army from the rear without weakening the defenses in the revetments. Brooke apparently recognized this as a high-risk option, as he concentrated his force in front of Smith's main defensive line in preparation for a night attack. In response, Smith moved Winder and Stricker to positions from which they could attack the British flank whether Brooke assaulted the ramparts or merely remained in place.[71]

The third available course of action amounted to a British retreat. Either of the first two options might be feasible, but only with substantial naval gunfire support.[72] Without it, the only good option involved moving back to North Point, reembarking on the ships, and placing the best possible face on their failure. But throughout the day, British leaders continued to seek a way of bringing the navy to bear. To provide the required naval gunfire support, British ships needed to destroy the guns and defenses of Fort McHenry, force their way through a set of obstacles at the mouth of the Northwest Branch, and position themselves to attack the American defenses around Baltimore. Fort McHenry provided the key to this battle because without its destruction or neutralization, the accumulated firepower that Rodgers had organized would destroy British ships before they could reach battle stations in Baltimore Harbor. Yet every time Cochrane's ships moved within range, the guns of Fort McHenry forced them to retreat. Not wanting to lose ships, the British admiral ordered his captains to bombard the fort from beyond two miles.[73]

British commanders knew their two-pronged attack on Baltimore could succeed only if executed in an integrated manner. The joint operation (combined operation, in British parlance of the time) began as two separate events designed to converge during the final assault on the city. But prior to the climatic event, each element found itself confronted with obstacles greater than it could overcome alone. Although the British army could hope to attack the Baltimore defenses only with support from the guns of the fleet, the navy could not pass Fort McHenry.[74]

As Ross landed his army at North Point and began to move up the peninsula on 12 September, Cochrane deployed sixteen ships to a position two and a half miles below Fort McHenry, just outside the range of its guns. Maj. George Armistead, a professional Army officer, commanded the fort and about one thousand men, both regular and volunteer. The defenders included artillerists, infantrymen, and assorted naval personnel from Commo. Joshua Barney's defunct flotilla. Armistead had worked closely with Smith, Winder, and Rodgers to ensure he had all the assets necessary to defend his position. The main structure of Fort McHenry consisted of a star-shaped bastion made primarily of brick, wood, and masonry. It sat at the end of Whetstone Point, where the Patapsco River splits into the Northwest Branch and Baltimore Harbor to the north, and Ferry Branch to the south. In addition to the batteries within the main structure, the fort included two powerful artillery positions outside the walls, which the defenders referred to as the upper battery and the lower battery. Armistead located his infantry in a lower ditch where the soldiers could respond to any British landing directed against the fort.[75]

As Brooke's rain-soaked army struggled through American obstacles toward Baltimore during the morning hours of 13 September, Cochrane's vessels began an incessant bombardment of Fort McHenry, which continued throughout the day and night. Finding the British ships beyond the effectiveness of his guns, Armistead ceased firing except when enemy vessels occasionally ventured into range. The British attack came primarily from mortars and rockets, both firing projectiles designed to explode upon impact or in the air over their targets. Fortunately for the American defenders, the rounds did not always explode due to the state of technology at that time.[76]

The British bombardment of Fort McHenry had mixed results on 13 September. The ships inflicted some damage on the fort and destroyed one 24-pounder, killing or wounding several men. Yet they could not suppress its guns, and every effort to move forward met with failure. Even if the British ships had been able to run past the guns of the fort, they would have been easy targets when they reached the Northwest Branch due to obstacles emplaced across the mouth of the inlet. Smith and Rodgers had created a barrier that ran from Fort McHenry across the river to Lazaretto Point. It consisted of sunken merchant ships, covered by guns at Fort McHenry and Lazaretto Point; sloops of war; and barges mounting naval guns and artillery. Undoubtedly, Cochrane could force a passage through the sunken ships, but not with the guns from the American forts and vessels covering them with fire. In an effort to break what had become a tactical stalemate, Cochrane devised a plan to conduct an amphibious assault against these American positions during the night of 13 September.[77]

Cochrane reasoned that if a force got ashore without being detected, it could move up the Ferry Branch under cover of darkness and attack Fort McHenry from the rear, rendering it ineffective. But doing so would not be easy, as several other defensive positions existed in the general vicinity where the landing would have to take place. Battery Babcock (sometimes called Fort Babcock) lay about a quarter of a mile up the Ferry Branch from Fort McHenry, and Fort Covington lay another quarter of a mile beyond that. Cochrane assigned navy captain Charles Napier to lead a force of 1,250 men intended as both a diversion for Brooke and a means to reduce Forts Covington and McHenry. At 0100 on 14 September the bomb ketches and rocket ships intensified their attack on Fort McHenry, and ships assigned to the assault force opened fire on its objective area. At 0200 boats carrying the assault force began moving toward the intended landing site. Alerted to the possibility of a night landing by the increased bombardment, the defenders at Fort Covington spotted the boats carrying the landing force as they approached their target and opened fire on them. Fire from the six guns of Battery Babcock soon joined that of Fort Covington. In the ensuing firefight, the British suffered severe casualties in men and vessels. Unable to suppress the American fire, or to reach the shoreline to effect a landing, Napier attempted to retreat to the protection of the fleet. As the British moved back down Ferry Branch, the guns at Fort McHenry and Lazaretto Point opened fire. Although no accurate accounting of the damage exists, Americans reported numerous bodies floating in the river and along the shoreline the next day.[78] Cochrane's order for this operation survives, but British commanders omitted any mention of it in their after-action reports for the obvious reason that it proved to be a disaster.[79]

Even before the repulse of his night attack, Cochrane had serious doubts about the efficacy of the operation. Knowing of the formidable defenses at Baltimore, he sent a message to Cockburn and Brooke during the day of 13 September indicating that his ships could not support an attack on the city and advising caution. Should Napier's night attack succeed in reducing Fort McHenry, they could always attack at some point in the future. Just before the setback on the Ferry Branch, Brooke, on the other side of Baltimore, held a council of war that decided to order a retreat. Leaving behind an element to deceive American defenders and serve as a rear guard, Brooke's army began its return to North Point about 0300 that day.[80]

Cochrane continued the bombardment of Fort McHenry until about 0700 on 14 September, at which time he began moving his ships down the Patapsco River. By 15 September all of Brooke's force had loaded on transports, and the British fleet began sailing down the Chesapeake Bay. During the twenty-five-hour bombardment, the British had fired between 1,500 and 2,000 shells and as many as 800 rockets at Fort McHenry. The fort suffered casualties amounting to 4 killed and 24 wounded. The British commanders did not include casualties in their reports, and American estimates of between 600 and 700 from all actions in the Baltimore campaign are possibly somewhat high. The British commanders claimed success in the action based on having created difficulties for the people of Baltimore and on Brooke's success in the battle of Long Log Lane. American commanders claimed victory due to the retreat of the British on both land and sea, and particularly because of the defeat of Napier's night amphibious attack at Ferry Branch.[81]

The most important characteristic of an amphibious operation involves the integration of effort between the navy and landing force.[82] The inability of the British expedition to accomplish this task is the most significant lesson from the Battle of Baltimore. American commanders planned and constructed their defenses to prevent any such joint concentration against the city. By blocking the mouth of the Northwest Branch and covering those obstacles with fire from Fort McHenry, Lazaretto Point, and sloops and barges, Smith and Rodgers prevented joint British actions at the culminating point of attack. By establishing formidable defensive positions around Baltimore, Smith created an objective too strong for the British army to attack by itself. Cochrane's idea of reducing Fort McHenry through a nighttime amphibious raid in a heavily defended area could be characterized as high risk at best and desperate at worst. Given the tactical situation they faced, the British commanders made the best possible decision in ordering a retreat. To press the attack without support from the fleet would invite defeat or, if it did succeed, would come at a cost beyond justification.

The lessons from the Battle of Baltimore demonstrate the pitfalls of landing operations. Amphibious actions are complex and begin from such a disadvantageous position that the landing force must do everything correctly to ensure success. At North Point the British succeeded in their seizure of the landing area, their rapid buildup of forces ashore, and their movement from troops toward the American defensive positions, but they failed to adequately task organize and never achieved operational coherence. Conversely, the American defenders did well in every area except that they failed to interpose with the British landing, and the delaying action at North Point proved insufficient. Collectively, the lessons from the Battle of Baltimore provided an enormous body of information upon which to base future amphibious actions.

Unfortunately for British ambitions, more bad news accompanied their failure at Baltimore. On 11 September, the day before Ross landed his amphibious force at North Point, Britain suffered a significant defeat on Lake Champlain in the battle for Plattsburgh, New York.[83] Failure of that campaign led officials in London to agree to the Treaty of Ghent, a *status quo antebellum* treaty, without waiting for the outcome of the planned operations against New Orleans. Coming on the heels of the American victory at New Orleans and British failures at Baltimore and Plattsburgh, news of the peace treaty caused many Americans to believe they had again defeated Great Britain.[84] Viewed from the overall war effort, that constituted an extreme interpretation of the outcome. But in the fullness of time, it is clear that the United States had fought the conquerors of Napoleon to nothing less than a stalemate.[85] Amphibious operations had played a major role in the fighting but never enough to tip the outcome in a decisive way for either side. Yet, by launching successful amphibious operations against York and Fort George, the United States expanded on traditions begun at New Providence and Yorktown during the Revolution. Moreover, by effectively repulsing British landings at Sackets Harbor, Baltimore, and New Orleans, military and naval leaders learned many vital lessons about how to conduct amphibious operations for future wars. The British amphibious attacks in the War of 1812 would be the last that Americans would face for 127 years. Not until 1942, when Japanese forces landed in the Philippines and on Wake Island, would the United States again be on the defensive side of an amphibious operation. With those two exceptions, offensive amphibious operations would become synonymous with American power projection from the middle of the nineteenth century into the twenty-first century. This pattern of offensive amphibious warfare, with its roots in early American wars from the Revolution to the Treaty of Ghent, was raised to yet a higher level in 1846 with the advent of the Mexican-American War.

Chapter 5

THE CONQUEST OF CALIFORNIA

AS THE WAR OF 1812 DREW TO A CLOSE, THE UNITED STATES did not experience an end to political strife. Despite the era of good feeling brought about during the presidency of James Monroe, issues of discord remained within the nation and on the world scene. American victories in the later part of the War of 1812, particularly at New Orleans, created a sense of nationalism, which the Republican Party used to sustain its control of domestic politics. The general reluctance of many Federalists to support the war effort, as exemplified by the Hartford Convention, contributed significantly to their demise as a major political force.[1] On 23 February 1815, only eight days after the Senate ratified the Treaty of Ghent ending the War of 1812, President Madison asked Congress to declare war on Algiers. Taking advantage of America's struggle with Great Britain, the dey had resumed depredations against American shipping in 1812. On 3 March 1815 Congress again authorized war against a Barbary power. A fortnight later, on 20 March, Stephen Decatur departed New York for North Africa with a squadron of three frigates, one sloop, four brigs, and two schooners. Shortly after arriving in the Mediterranean, Decatur captured two Algerine ships and sailed into waters off Algiers demanding peace on American terms. The power of the American squadron and determination of its commodore convinced the dey to accept peace and release the American prisoners. Decatur then sailed to Tunis and Tripoli, where he imposed similar terms and freed American and European prisoners. He not only forced the Barbary leaders to disavow tribute and ransom but also demanded and received compensation for American ships held in Tunisian and Tripolitan ports.[2]

Decatur's success in the Barbary conflict of 1815 did not involve amphibious operations due to the overwhelming naval power that intimidated the North African rulers. But amphibious operation remained a viable method for combating piracy and often found an application in other parts of the world. In the early years of the nineteenth century, the United States encountered piracy in the Western Hemisphere, particularly in the West Indies. To address the problem, the United States assigned one of its most aggressive officers, Commo. David Porter, to command the Navy's West Indies Squadron. Frustrated with the ineffective manner in which American courts dealt with the Caribbean pirates that he delivered for justice, Porter frequently preferred to hand over captives to British authorities who had a less formal and more permanent way of dealing with the miscreants. He also conducted landings against pirate camps and facilities when he could identify them. Always the aggressive commodore, Porter often pushed the boundaries of his mandate in carrying out this mission, and on 14 November 1824 he overstepped his authority by conducting a major amphibious operation against the Spanish fort at Foxardo (now Fajardo), Puerto Rico. Believing that Spanish authorities harbored and abetted pirates and that they had unlawfully held an American officer, Porter landed two hundred Marines and sailors, spiked the guns of the fort, and demanded an apology from the Spanish governor. The incident embarrassed the U.S. government, and a court-martial censured Porter and suspended him from duty for six months. Porter reacted by moving to Mexico to become commander in chief of the Mexican navy. Three years later he returned to the United States and the new president, Andrew Jackson, appointed him minister first to the Barbary States and then to the Ottoman Empire.[3]

Piracy in the Mediterranean and West Indies created challenge enough for American maritime interests, but seamen also faced threats in the East Indies. Most amphibious landings on the Pacific Rim—like those in Africa, Latin America, and the West Indies—amounted to minor incursions often involving little or no fighting. But in 1832 a force of about 250 Marines and sailors landed at Quallah Battoo (now Kuala Batu), Sumatra, destroyed five forts, killed about 450 people, and sank several native watercrafts in retribution for a lethal attack on an American merchantman. Although Commo. John Downes found it necessary to conduct other landings in the East Indies and on certain Pacific Islands during this period to protect American commerce, none rose to the level of violence attained at Quallah Battoo.[4]

During the 1830s a new set of problems confronted the United States as relations with Mexico deteriorated over the issue of Texas. After rebelling against Mexican rule in 1836 and establishing an independent republic, Texas petitioned for annexation to the United States. On 1 March 1845, in the last days of his presidency, John Tyler signed a joint resolution of Congress formally authorizing the annexation of Texas into the United States.[5] Relations between the United States and Mexico immediately moved from strained to hostile. By the end of the month, Mexico broke diplomatic relations with the United States, and Secretary of the Navy George Bancroft ordered Commo. David Conner's Home Squadron (formerly known as the U.S. West Indies Squadron) into Mexican waters. At that time Conner's squadron consisted of one frigate, one sloop of war, and two brigs. Shortly thereafter Bancroft sent an additional squadron under Commo. Robert F. Stockton consisting of one steamer, two sloops, and one brig to reinforce Conner near Veracruz.[6]

On 4 July 1845 Texans voted to ratify the annexation as specified in the congressional resolution of 1 March. On 29 December James K. Polk—who became president on 4 March 1845—signed a second joint resolution of Congress, which officially admitted Texas into the Union. During May 1845, in anticipation of trouble, Secretary of War William Marcy instructed Brig. Gen. Zachary Taylor to move his small army from Louisiana to a forward base near Corpus Christi, Texas, on the Nueces River. Taylor's force of some three thousand effectives began arriving in September and by March 1846 had moved south to the Rio Grande River.[7] Polk and the U.S. government contended that the Rio Grande constituted the southern border of Texas and the correct frontier between the two nations. The Mexican government did not recognize the independence of Texas or its subsequent integration into the United States. It also insisted that the Nueces River, not the Rio Grande, constituted the southern border of Texas, regardless of which country possessed it. Moving the Army into the area of contention supported the American assertion, whereas keeping it north of the Nueces would be tacit acceptance of the Mexican position. Critics of U.S. policy contend that Polk moved the Army into the disputed area specifically to provoke war with Mexico.[8] But Polk hoped to solve the crisis by purchasing the stretch of territory in question (the disputed land between the Nueces and Rio Grande and land extending to the west in Texas) along with New Mexico and California. He believed the presence of U.S. troops on the Rio Grande would increase pressure on Mexican leaders for a resolution of the issue, but by May 1846 efforts at negotiations had failed. Conner, who temporarily moved his squadron out of Mexican waters to facilitate discussions, returned to Veracruz.[9] As the drift toward war between the United States and Mexico moved toward a flash point in southern Texas, American leaders surveyed the entire theater of probable war. California became a paramount consideration because of its desirability and the prospect of bringing the Navy to bear in support of diplomatic or military actions.

The study of California during the Mexican-American War is particularly interesting in amphibious history because it provides an early example of a concept that became prominent in the last decade of the twentieth century. As the United States sought a new strategy of national defense to address issues of post–Cold War security, the Navy and Marine Corps published two white papers (essentially concept statements intended to provide planning and training guidance) that presaged a new approach to naval warfare. Entitled . . . *From the Sea* and *Operational Maneuver from the Sea*, these documents address combat in low- and mid-level intensity environments, which combine maneuver warfare with naval operations to provide rapid, flexible, and focused application of power projection across a wide range of geographical objectives.[10] The conquest of California exemplified these concepts 150 years before they were formalized in U.S. naval policy.

Major European powers, Great Britain, France, and Russia, had long coveted California. By the 1840s California had also come into the peripheral vision of American Manifest Destiny. Throughout the decade preceding war with Mexico, American frontiersmen entered and settled in California just as others had done in Texas during the 1820s and 1830s, though not in as large numbers. Moreover, by the 1840s the California coast had become a center for the hide trade and a layover point for ships of the Pacific whaling fleet. American leaders also considered California strategically important for protecting U.S. claims in Oregon and securing natural harbors on the Pacific coastline.[11] As early as 1842 the United States demonstrated its interests in the west coast when Commo. Thomas ap Catesby Jones occupied Monterey, California, under the mistaken assumption that war had broken out with Mexico. Although the incursion had been bloodless and subsequent relations with locals proved peaceful, the incident strained the increasingly delicate relations between the United States and Mexico. Reacting to official Mexican outrage over the Monterey incident, officials in Washington replaced Jones as commander of the Pacific Squadron but refused to take disciplinary action against him. Many high-level leaders, including presidents Tyler and Polk and Secretary of the Navy Abel P. Upshur, believed Jones had acted in good faith and possibly forestalled a British takeover of California.[12]

By 1846 the situation in California, like the relations between the United States and Mexico, had undergone considerable change. Native Californians had effectively—though not officially—achieved a form of independence in 1845 by ousting the appointed governor, Brig. Gen. Manuel Micheltorena, and installing Pío de Jesus Pico as governor and José María Castro as comandante (military commander). Pico relocated the seat of government to Los Angeles while Castro kept his headquarters in Monterey, creating a de facto partition of the province. Spanish and Mexican control of California had never been strong, and the local people had always considered themselves somewhat separate from the central government. All these factors served to weaken the leadership structure of California at a critical time in its history. The U.S. consul at Monterey, Thomas O. Larkin, believed conditions might support a peaceful conquest of California if handled with proper finesse.[13] But the presence of Army captain John C. Frémont and rebellious American settlers under the leadership of Ezekiel Merritt and William B. Ide presented complications for Larkin and his plans. The U.S. Pacific Squadron operating out of Mazatlán under Commo. John D. Sloat provided Larkin an important tool in dealing with the political crosscurrents under way in California. On 1 April, at the request of Larkin, Sloat dispatched the sloop *Portsmouth* to Monterey out of concern that machinations by Frémont and American settlers could upset the situation in California, causing reprisals and bloodshed.[14] At this point the United States and Mexico remained at peace although the expectancy of war prevailed.

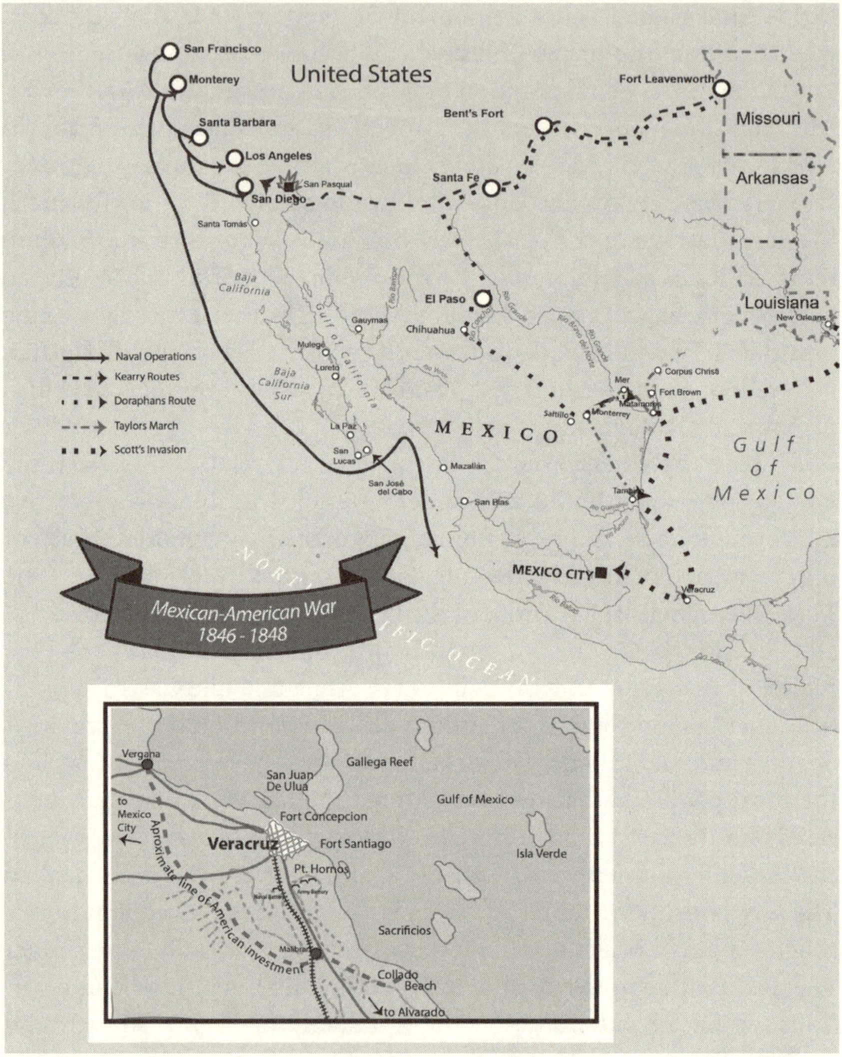

MAP 6. The Mexican-American War

On 23 April Mexican president Mariano Paredes declared war on the United States. Two days later two thousand Mexican troops moved into the disputed territory between the Rio Grande and Nueces Rivers, where they clashed with U.S. troops, killing eleven. On 8 May major fighting broke out in Texas, with Taylor defeating a larger Mexican force at the Battle of Palo Alto. Taylor won a second engagement the following day in the Battle of Resaca de la Palma. By the middle of the month the United States formally declared war.[15]

News of the fighting north of the Rio Grande soon reached Commodore Sloat in the Pacific. Less aggressive than Thomas ap Catesby Jones, Sloat chose a cautious approach to handling the immediate crisis. His orders from Washington were equivocal—they called for forceful action in case of war but cautioned against acts of aggression. Such directives protected the politicians back in Washington but failed to clarify expectations for commanders on the scene.[16] Sloat also received messages suggesting that the dispute over Oregon could lead to war with Great Britain. This possibly influenced his judgment because he knew the Royal Navy posed a greater threat to his squadron than the problems with Mexico.[17] Undoubtedly, the official reaction to Porter's incursion in Puerto Rico and Jones' at Monterey had a chilling effect on Sloat's thinking as well.[18] Once the United States declared war on Mexico, Secretary of the Navy Bancroft immediately sent orders to capture or blockade every port on the west coast of Mexico and California. These orders—as well as earlier instructions—specifically mentioned the taking of San Francisco, Monterey, and Mazatlán.[19]

On 1 July 1846 Sloat arrived in Monterey Bay to confer with Larkin. Bancroft's war directive had not yet arrived, and neither Sloat nor Larkin had received official notice that war existed between the two nations. But evidence had mounted to the point that Sloat and, to a lesser degree, Larkin considered it likely that war had broken out. Sloat knew of the fighting along the Rio Grande, and this knowledge coupled with Frémont's open support of the settler's rebellion then under way in the Sonoma Valley convinced him to act. On 7 July Sloat sent a message to Capt. Mariano Silva, the highest military authority in Monterey demanding surrender of the city. Silva refused, stating he had no authority to take such action. Anticipating an attack by the Americans, Silva and his soldiers withdrew from Monterey before the U.S. sailors and Marines landed and occupied the city. Later that morning, Sloat proclaimed California to be part of the United States (based on previous instructions from the secretary of the Navy for action in case of war) and established temporary military rule.[20] After completing formalities, the sailors returned to their ships, leaving a detachment of U.S. Marines under 2nd Lt. William A. T. Maddox to garrison the city.

Sloat next dispatched a communiqué to General Castro, demanding he surrender the forces under his command. Castro responded with a refusal to even meet with Sloat. While awaiting Castro's reply, Slat sent messages to Frémont and Ide (president of the recently proclaimed Bear Flag Republic in Sonoma) informing them of the situation in Monterey and requesting their support. Almost as an afterthought, Sloat sent a message to Pío Pico in Los Angeles, explaining his actions and inviting him to meet in Monterey.[21]

After deciding to capture Monterey, Sloat contacted Cdr. John B. Montgomery of the *Portsmouth*—now located in San Francisco Bay—explaining his plans and instructing him to seize San Francisco. On the morning of 9 July Montgomery landed a force of seventy Marines and sailors at Clark's Point to capture and occupy San Francisco. Unable to find anyone who could surrender the city, Montgomery marched his force to the customhouse, ran up the Stars and Stripes, and read Sloat's proclamation to those citizens sufficiently interested to listen. He assigned 2nd Lt. Henry Bulls Watson and a detachment of sixteen Marines to occupy the city. Montgomery also authorized Watson to organize a local militia force to serve under his command in time of need. Montgomery sent copies of Sloat's proclamation along with U.S. flags to Sonoma and Sutter's Fort announcing American primacy in California.[22]

Upon learning of the capture of Monterey, Frémont and his irregular force of "explorers" and frontiersmen departed to meet with Commodore Sloat. Marine lieutenant Archibald H. Gillespie—who had earlier delivered confidential dispatches from President Polk and Secretary of State James Buchanan to Sloat and Larkin—joined and remained with the Pathfinder as Frémont was commonly known. Gillespie had a confidential meeting with Polk prior to departing Washington to receive what the president described as secret instructions. These secret instructions have never been found and are the source of much speculation regarding

Frémont's activities in California. Locating Sloat and Larkin had not been a problem for Gillespie, but finding Frémont proved challenging. He finally located Frémont at Klamath Lake where he delivered messages both official and personal.[23] Gillespie remained with Frémont for some time thereafter and became a principal figure throughout the California campaign. Gillespie is one of the most colorful and interesting characters in the entire California saga. Although an officer in the U.S. Marine Corps, his role in the conquest of California involved him in a range of duties and responsibilities beyond those normally expected of a junior officer in the naval service.[24]

When Frémont arrived at Monterey for his meeting with Sloat, it became apparent that the two commanders held very different views about future activities in California. Sloat's innate caution clashed with Frémont's inherent aggressiveness, and the commodore resisted Frémont's plans for additional offensive operations. But Sloat would not constrain the Pathfinder for long, as a new naval officer arrived on the scene to take control of events. Commodore Stockton arrived in Monterey Bay on 15 July with orders to serve as Sloat's second in command. His orders also permitted Sloat to transfer command to Stockton and return to the United States, should his health so dictate. On 29 July Sloat did just that, handing over command of the Pacific Squadron to Stockton and departing for home. This change in command shifted American policy away from the methodical caution of Sloat and Larkin to the flamboyant aggressiveness of Stockton and Frémont.[25]

Stockton and Frémont believed that a campaign by both sea and land would be necessary to secure California. Stockton created the California Battalion of Mounted Rifles from Frémont's irregular team of explorers and frontiersmen located in the Sacramento Valley, making the Pathfinder its commander with the rank of major. He also promoted Gillespie to captain, assigning him as second in command. Frémont and his California Battalion served under Stockton's command throughout the campaign, functioning primarily as an amphibious adjunct to the Pacific Squadron. The administrative and legal aspects of this special organization required some correction after Brig. Gen. Stephen W. Kearny arrived in California. But in the interim, the California Battalion performed as a highly mobile naval power projection force operating in concert with Stockton's Marine and naval landing force.[26]

Stockton's first move to subdue California involved defeating Castro's military force then located near Los Angeles. To accomplish this, Stockton planned a series of amphibious landings designed to control key areas, isolate Castro's forces, and destroy all residual opposition. Stockton sent Frémont's California Battalion to San Diego where—preceded by a party of Marines—he conducted an unopposed landing on 29 July 1846. After obtaining horses from a relatively friendly populace, Frémont began moving north along the coast on 8 August while his support ship, the sloop *Cyane* under Cdr. Samuel F. DuPont, set sail for San Pedro. While Frémont and DuPont conducted the amphibious operation at San Diego, Stockton and Larkin sailed for San Pedro on board the frigate *Congress*. On 4 August, while en route to San Pedro, Stockton paused at Santa Barbara, where he sent a small party ashore to claim the town and establish a garrison. Two days later the *Congress* arrived at San Pedro, where 1st Lt. Jacob Zeilin led his Marines ashore and established a lodgment for the main body of the landing force. Stockton consolidated his amphibious force ashore and prepared to move toward Los Angeles, where he hoped to trap Castro between his force and Frémont's battalion moving north from San Diego.[27]

While Stockton moved to eliminate resistance in California through naval power, Larkin made a final attempt to find a peaceful settlement. He recommended to Governor Pico that California declare independence under American protection. Although Pico and Castro showed some interest in this approach and Stockton seemed amenable to it, nothing came from the effort.[28] On 11 August Stockton's landing force departed its encampment near San Pedro and headed to Los Angeles, arriving two days later. With American forces converging on Los Angeles and their own support dwindling, Castro and Pico fled south to Sonora and Baja California, while Juan B. Alvarado and a few of Castro's California soldiers fled north toward San Luis Obispo. Stockton entered Los Angeles to the accompaniment of a band from the frigate *Congress*, and Frémont arrived shortly thereafter.[29] The remaining elements of Castro's force surrendered to Stockton on 14 August, along with their weapons and equipment. Stockton paroled the prisoners captured at Los Angeles, then sent a small detachment under Maddox in pursuit of Alvarado, whom he captured near San Luis Obispo. On 17 August official notice arrived at San Pedro that a state of war existed with Mexico.[30]

After the victory at Los Angeles and the end of organized resistance, Stockton turned his attention to governing the province and blockading the Mexican ports on the Pacific. He planned ultimately to occupy Acapulco and from there to march on Mexico City from the west.[31] The first step in his grandiose plan called for sending the sloop *Warren* to blockade Mazatlán and the sloop *Cyane* to blockade San Blas (south of Mazatlán).[32] Upon arriving at San Blas, DuPont sent a landing party ashore that spiked twenty-four cannons. He then captured a Mexican sloop and brig and sailed on to Mazatlán to meet with the *Warren*'s captain, Cdr. Joseph B. Hull. At Mazatlán, Hull had captured two Mexican brigs and proclaimed a blockade of that port. The *Cyane* then sailed to La Paz on the Baja peninsula, where DuPont captured nine merchantmen as prizes of war and headed across the Gulf of California to blockade the port of Guaymas.[33]

While his sloops initiated the blockade of Mexican ports, Stockton returned to Monterey, where he finalized plans for capturing Acapulco. Frémont moved the bulk of his force into the Sacramento Valley, leaving a small detachment of forty-eight men under Gillespie to garrison Los Angeles.[34] At this point both Stockton and Frémont believed the United States had secured California. Before Stockton's plan for the conquest of Acapulco progressed beyond the initial actions of DuPont and Hull in the Gulf of California, problems arose that ended any hope for this strategic masterstroke. First, Frémont could not recruit the large number of soldiers needed for the venture. Although he persuaded some to join his ranks, he could not find enough to make his force sufficiently strong to carry out Stockton's broader mission. The second problem involved a counterrebellion that broke out in Los Angeles under the leadership of Mexican captain José María Flores. Some accounts blame Gillespie for causing the uprising by his tyrannical administration of the conquered city. Yet it remains difficult to be certain to what extent the problem was a reaction to rule by Gillespie and to what extent it resulted from his enforcement of Stockton's policies.[35] Flores—who violated his parole from Stockton to lead this rebellion—organized a force large enough to compel Gillespie to surrender his small garrison. Flores agreed that Gillespie and his men could keep their weapons and march unmolested to San Pedro. Upon arriving at San Pedro, Gillespie's force boarded an American merchantman, the *Vandalia*.[36] Flores moved to consolidate his control over southern California, and by October he controlled everything except a small enclave at San Diego. No longer able to think in terms of a bold stroke against Acapulco, Stockton now had to recapture an area he had believed already secure.

Initially Stockton had intended to retake Los Angeles with anther two-pronged attack. This time he planned to land Frémont's California Battalion at Santa Barbara while he moved to San Pedro in the *Congress*. While awaiting Frémont's arrival in San Francisco for embarkation, Stockton ordered Capt. William Mervine's frigate, *Savannah*, to San Pedro. Upon arriving, Mervine met with Gillespie—still in harbor on board the *Vandalia*—and they decided to attack Flores' forces immediately and reclaim Los Angeles on their own. On 7 October Mervine landed a force that included Gillespie's troops along with Marines and sailors from the *Savannah* and moved against Los Angeles. Having no horses or artillery, they faced a California force under José Antonio Carrillo at Dominguez Ranch that possessed both. After several attempts to break through Carrillo's well-conceived defense in depth, Mervine recognized the futility of the situation and returned with his men to their ships. He then sent a dispatch to Stockton and awaited his arrival at San Pedro. Carrillo and his Californians considered their check of Mervine and Gillespie a military victory, and some American leaders tended to agree.[37]

On 25 October Stockton arrived at San Pedro, and two days later he ordered his forces ashore for an advance on Los Angeles. After the initial landing party of Marines and sailors made a skillful lodgment against scattered resistance, the main body came ashore and established a beachhead. But as Stockton consolidated his landing force, Carrillo staged a series of deceptions that suggested he had a larger force than he really possessed. Concerned over the size of Carrillo's force and the lack of horses and cattle in the San Pedro area, Stockton reembarked his landing force before any serious fighting occurred and sailed for San Diego, where he believed conditions would better support his operations. Upon arrival, he had received reports that an attack on San Diego was imminent. Stockton decided to remain in San Diego, hoping his presence there would forestall any such attack by Mexican forces. Frémont also changed his point of debarkation from Santa Barbara to Monterey for similar reasons, as the garrison there feared an attack and requested reinforcements.[38]

The limited carrying capacity of Stockton's ships made it difficult to bring enough livestock to support his large landing forces. American commanders needed to procure horses for riding and draft as well as cattle and sheep for food from local suppliers. Both sides attempted to prevent their adversaries from acquiring these needed commodities, and the livestock shortage greatly affected tactics and strategy. But logistics did not constitute Stockton's sole problem. Throughout the months of October and November he struggled with the frustration of trying to execute a mission with inadequate resources. He simply did not have enough ships to conduct numerous amphibious operations on the California littorals while maintaining a blockade of the Mexican coast south of California. But that situation improved late in 1846 as Bancroft ordered reinforcements to the Pacific Squadron, which resulted in a substantial improvement in the military situation.[39] But acquiring sufficient livestock from local sources remained a problem throughout the California conflict.

On 3 December Stockton learned that another American force had arrived in California when he received a dispatch from Brigadier General Kearny, stating that he had just arrived at Warner's Ranch northwest of San Diego on the road between Los Angeles and Sonora. Stockton sent a forty-man detachment with one brass 4-pounder under Gillespie to meet Kearny's force and guide him into San Diego. In May 1846 the Polk administration had ordered Kearny to lead an overland expedition to capture and occupy New Mexico. After an easy conquest of Santa Fe, Kearny established a garrison and provisional government to control the territory. Exercising the next phase of his orders, Kearny pressed on to California, where he intended to establish a new government. He departed Santa Fe on 25 September with three hundred dragoons and ancillary engineers, guides, and hunters, thinking himself the senior American officer west of the Mississippi.[40] While Kearny marched overland to California, a regiment of New York Volunteers and a regular artillery company with weapons and provisions would be sent around Cape Horn to join him on the west coast.

While en route, Kearny met Kit Carson, who was heading east from California carrying dispatches from Stockton to officials in Washington. Carson told Kearny that California was already under American control, as appeared to be the case upon his departure. Thinking the conquest of California complete, Kearny believed his troops would be of greater use in back in New Mexico and kept only a detachment of one hundred dragoons to serve as his personal escort. On arriving in California, Kearny learned that, rather than arriving to govern a conquered province, he would be riding into a hostile environment with a much-reduced force. Kit Carson, whom he had persuaded (coerced) to guide him into California, accompanied Kearny into this cauldron.[41]

While crossing the Colorado Desert, Kearny and Carson met Archibald Gillespie and his thirty-man detachment. Gillespie reported that Capt. Andrés Pico, the brother of California governor Pío Pico, and a troop of Californians had moved to a position between his force and San Diego. On 6 December Kearny attacked Pico's forces in what became known as the Battle of San Pasqual. Kearny had superior numbers and one field artillery piece, but his attacking force engaged Pico in a disjointed manner, permitting the Californians to fight a series of separate actions. Gillespie attempted to rally the American troops by riding to the point of action, receiving three wounds and a brevet for his efforts. The Battle of San Pasqual ended with the Americans surrounded by the Californians, though not close enough to prevent Kit Carson from slipping through their lines and returning to San Diego, where he alerted Stockton of Kearny's precarious situation. Carson did not know that Pico lacked sufficient strength to follow up with offensive action. Thus, neither side renewed the battle.[42] Stockton quickly dispatched a relief column of about 180 Marines and sailors led by lieutenants Jacob Zeilin and Andrew V. F. Grey that accompanied Kearny on the final leg of his 1,043-mile, 78-day march from Santa Fe to San Diego.[43]

Upon arriving in San Diego in mid-December, Kearny conferred with Stockton, who proclaimed himself the senior American officer in California, to which Kearny temporarily acceded. Kearny carried orders from Washington authorizing him to take control of California and establish a government, yet he chose not to confront Stockton with the issue, intending to address the matter in due course.[44] While Stockton's troops foraged for livestock and Kearny's soldiers recuperated from their arduous trek, the two leaders developed a plan to regain Los Angeles. By 29 December Stockton's troops had completed their preparations and departed on the march north. His force consisted of Kearny's dragoons, elements of the California Battalion, an artillery detachment under Lt. R. Lloyd Tilghman, a detachment of Marines under Zeilin (who also served as adjutant for the force), sailors from various ships of the Pacific Squadron, and a native Californian element under the command of Santiago Anguilla. Stockton detailed Montgomery to remain in San Diego as commander of the station and American ships in the harbor. Just prior to departing, Stockton appointed Kearny as field commander for the expedition while he remained commander in chief. Expecting Frémont to advance on Los Angeles from the north, Stockton and Kearny pressed up from the south, engaging and defeating Flores and his Californians twice en route.[45]

The first action came on 8 January 1847—the thirty-second anniversary of the Battle of New Orleans—at the San Gabriel River, where the Americans forced a river crossing under fire and drove the defenders from the battlefield. When Stockton's column came within two miles of the San Gabriel River, it redeployed in a square formation. The front of the square was made up of dragoons and sailors under Capt. Henry S. Turner, the right flank contained Marines, sailors, and pikemen under Zeilin, the left consisted of Marines and sailors under Lt. Stephen C. Rowan, and the rear consisted of volunteers under Gillespie. Stockton placed all logistical support including stock and wagons inside the square, which moved forward as an integral body. Stockton and Kearny placed four cannons along the front line and two with the rear. The Californians occupied high ground north of the river from which their artillery could fire on Stockton's army as it approached and attempted to cross. Despite a bold effort to attack the American rear during the river crossing, the California troops could not halt the American advance. When Stockton's artillery established firing positions after crossing the river, it began to systematically destroy the Californian's field pieces. As the Americans reformed their square and resumed the attack, they received a determined charge on the left flank from Flores' cavalry. But musket fire broke the assault and the square resumed the attack, driving the Californians from the field. In the last action of the day, American firepower again halted a strong Californian effort against their right flank. That night Stockton's army camped on the heights previously occupied by Flores' rebels while Zeilin and a company of Marines conducted a nightlong reconnaissance.[46]

The next day fighting resumed as the American force continued to press forward toward Los Angeles. In the subsequent Battle of La Mesa,

Stockton essentially destroyed Flores' army and opened the way for reoccupation of Los Angeles. Early in the morning, Stockton and Kearny reconstituted the square formation, which the Californians called the infernal corral. At 0800 the formation began moving forward, and by 11:00 the enemy engaged the attackers with cannon fire from a strong position on the right flank. But the fire proved ineffective, and the Americans slightly adjusted their line of march, allowing them to bypass the Californian stronghold. This forced Flores to sally from his position and initiate a cavalry charge. Many American leaders considered Californians the best horsemen in the world, and Lt. Henry Bulls Watson described their attack formation as a beautiful sight. Notwithstanding their magnificence, the Californians could not break the American line despite determined assaults against both the left flank and rear. The volume and accuracy of American musket and cannon fire shredded the assault, emptying many saddles and forcing the Californians to retreat in confusion. As Flores retreated, Stockton pushed his force across the Los Angeles River, stopping within easy marching distance of the city of the angels.[47] On 10 January 1847 local officials surrendered the city, which the Americans immediately occupied along with the surrounding hills. As Stockton consolidated his tactical position, Gillespie once again raised the colors over Government House, which Flores had forced him to lower in capitulation the previous September.[48]

Although Frémont did not reach Los Angeles in time to participate in its capture, he accomplished several things on the way. After leaving San Juan Bautista, near Monterey Bay, in November, Frémont (now a lieutenant colonel) moved south, occupying San Luis Obispo on 14 December and capturing a California detachment of thirty-five men under Jesus Pico at nearby Wilson's Ranch. Jesus Pico—a relative of both Pío Pico and Andrés Pico—presented serious problems for Frémont because he, like Flores, had violated his parole by leading rebellious Californians. Stockton had earlier vowed to execute Flores for his role in the rebellion, and that fact surely rested on the Pathfinder's mind. Frémont ordered a court-martial for Pico, which found him guilty and sentenced him to death. But upon reflection, Frémont relented and pardoned Pico, thereby setting a precedent and generating good will among native Californians. Frémont then continued moving south, occasionally skirmishing with

California forces and reclaiming or capturing Santa Barbara, Mission San Buenaventura, and Mission San Fernando. At Rancho Los Verdugos Frémont came upon the remains of Flores' defeated force and invited them to discuss surrender terms. Flores turned over his command to Andrés Pico, recommended they negotiate with Frémont, and then departed for his native Mexico, where he might be beyond the reach of Stockton. In the subsequent Treaty of Cahuenga—signed on 13 January 1847—Frémont overstepped his authority by concluding an agreement that treated the defeated Californians with dignity and respect and provided them a degree of security. When Frémont and the California Battalion marched into Los Angeles on 14 January, the terms of his treaty were already in force, and Stockton had little choice but to accept the agreement.[49]

The Treaty of Cahuenga effectively ended the fighting between Americans and Californians in Alta (Upper) California. But it marked the beginning of a power struggle among U.S. officials regarding control of California. Both Stockton and Kearny believed themselves the ranking authority on the west coast. This resulted from the vagueness of their orders as well as their own sense of self-importance. Stockton appointed Frémont as the governor of California, who notified Kearny on 17 January that he would only accept orders from the commodore. Stockton also promoted Gillespie to the rank of major and assigned him to command the California Battalion as Frémont's replacement. But on 19 January a new naval officer—William Branford Shubrick—arrived in California to relieve Stockton and assume temporary command of the Pacific Squadron. Kearny met with Shubrick in San Diego, persuading the new commodore of his legitimate claim to govern California. By accepting Kearny's authority, Shubrick undercut Stockton's claim of seniority and Frémont's authority as governor.[50]

In February orders from both the Navy and War Departments arrived affirming Kearny's authority to establish a government in California and to command American forces ashore. The commodore of the Pacific Squadron would be responsible for all activities at sea as well as port and customs operations. On 2 March James Biddle arrived as the permanent commodore of the Pacific Squadron and issued a set of joint proclamations sustaining Shubrick's decisions and further clarifying the command situation in California. As Kearny took control of the California government, reinforcements began arriving and he soon had garrisons scattered throughout the territory. Despite the establishment of military authority in California, the various governors—Stockton, Frémont, Kearny, and (later) Robert B. Mason—consistently proclaimed their desire to return to civil government as soon as conditions permitted.[51]

The campaign for control of Alta California was complete by mid-January 1847. The area of Baja California and the Mexican coastline along the Gulf of California and Pacific Ocean had played only a minor role during that phase. After the Treaty of Cahuenga, the attention of leaders in both Monterey and Washington turned to the southern region. One of Stockton's last actions as commodore of the Pacific Squadron involved reestablishing the blockade of Mazatlán and capturing the Baja harbors at San José del Cabo (at the tip of the Baja peninsula), La Paz, and Loreto. The blockade of the Mexican Pacific Coast had questionable legal standing due to a lack of sufficient ships to ensure enforcement. This generated some criticism and created the possibility of conflict with British or French ships whose captains rightly believed they need not respect a "paper blockade" unenforced by ships.

On 17 February Montgomery and the *Portsmouth* arrived off Mazatlán and began to enforce the blockade. A month later they sailed to capture San José del Cabo. On 30 March a landing party of 140 men under Lt. Benjamin F. B. Hunter went ashore at San José del Cabo, and although local authorities refused to surrender the port, they offered no resistance. After running up the colors, the landing force reembarked on the *Portsmouth* and sailed to San Lucas to repeat the entire scenario. A similar action followed on 13 April at La Paz—the capital of Baja California—where Col. Francisco Palacios Miranda surrendered the city and signed articles of capitulation similar to those in the Treaty of Cahuenga. Three months later Lt. Col. Henry S. Burton and two companies of New York Volunteers occupied La Paz. Mexican forces under Capt. Manuel Pineda made three subsequent attempts to retake the capital without success. After the capture of La Paz, there followed a confused and erratic effort to blockade Mazatlán and the Baja ports that satisfied neither the interests of the United States nor the requirements of international law.[52]

As the United States began to assert itself in the Gulf of California through amphibious power projection, the American command structure in California began to stabilize. On 31 May Kearny transferred his authority and responsibilities to Col. Robert B. Mason, and on 16 June he and Frémont departed Sutter's Fort, returning overland to the United States. Upon arriving at Fort Leavenworth, Kansas, on 22 August, Kearny placed Frémont under arrest and charged him with insubordination for his defiant actions in California during Stockton's period of control. A subsequent court-martial held in Washington found Frémont guilty, although the court recommended clemency due to the confused command situation that had existed during the period in question. President Polk agreed with the recommendation for clemency, approved only one portion of the conviction, and restored Frémont to active duty. But Frémont believed the conviction entirely unjust and resigned from the Army rather than acknowledge any aspect of the charges. Many Americans sympathized with Frémont's view, and he remained a popular and influential leader who would play a prominent role in the affairs of his nation for another thirty years.[53]

Once Shubrick and Biddle accepted the authority of Kearny to govern California, joint command relations became stable and cooperative. But within the Navy important issues of command continued to create problems. Shubrick did not enjoy holding a secondary position after Biddle arrived on the scene.[54] On 1 June Shubrick requested that he be relieved of his duties with the Pacific Squadron. But before any action on the request could occur, Biddle departed after his short tenure as commodore. His orders contained an option to transfer command of the squadron to Shubrick once he believed the situation no longer required his services. On 19 July Biddle transferred command of the Pacific Squadron to Shubrick and shortly thereafter departed on board the *Columbus* for the United States. Shubrick remained commodore of the Pacific Squadron until the end of the war, when Thomas ap Catesby Jones relieved him of command on 6 May 1848.[55]

Consistent with the policy of shifting attention to the Gulf of California after securing Alta California, Shubrick issued a new blockade proclamation for Mazatlán, Guaymas, and San Blas on 6 August 1847. He also dispatched the *Dale* under Cdr. Thomas O. Selfridge to conduct amphibious incursions within the Gulf of California. On 1 October Lt. Tunis A. M. Craven led a landing party that attacked a Mexican force near Mulejé. With support from the guns of the *Dale*, Marines and sailors drove the Mexican defenders away from the city but accomplished little else. At the end of the day the landing party reembarked, and Selfridge then sailed to Loreto, where on 5 October Craven again landed a force of Marines and sailors. After capturing a few cannons and guns, the landing force reembarked and the *Dale* sailed to La Paz. These amphibious incursions accomplished very little other than to show American strength and arouse Mexican fighting spirits.[56]

On 17 October the *Congress* and *Portsmouth* arrived at Guaymas, and the following day Capt. Elie A. F. LaVallette of the *Congress* called on Col. Antonio Campuzano to surrender the 400-man garrison under his command. Campuzano refused, and LaVallette, after delaying his attack to allow for the evacuation of women and children, began bombarding the city in the early hours of 20 October 1847. After an hour and a half, LaVallette learned that the Mexican troops had withdrawn to Bocachicacampo, four miles north of Guaymas. Marines from the American ships intermittently occupied the town of Guaymas but did not maintain a constant presence. During early November, Campuzano made several attempts to infiltrate troops back into the city and on 17 November engaged the Americans in battle at Casal Blanca Hill. The Mexican force numbered some 250 men, but the American landing party supported by naval gunfire from the *Dale*—which had replaced the *Portsmouth* in Guaymas Harbor—drove them from the town. On 30 January 1848 Craven and his Marines and sailors from the *Dale* conducted a subsidiary landing at Cochori where they routed a Mexican detachment and captured fifteen soldiers including its commander and captain of the port. On 13 February a similar landing occurred under Lt. Fabius Stanly against Campuzano's remnant forces at Bocachicacampo, which defeated and disbursed the last Mexican position in the vicinity. Other than a minor skirmish on the Soldado River on 9 April, the destruction of Campuzano's force at Bocachicacampo ended the fighting in and around Guaymas.[57]

While Shubrick's naval forces struggled with subduing Guaymas and maintaining control of other Baja ports, a task force consisting of the *Independence*, *Congress*, and *Cyane* arrived in the water off Mazatlán on 10 November. The next day, when Shubrick called on officials to surrender the port and city, the Mexican commander, Col. Rafael Telles, refused. Within hours Shubrick landed a force of 730 men under LaVallette and raised the American flag over the port. Although not willing to surrender,

Telles chose to retreat rather than oppose the American incursion. The Americans then prepared defenses for the city and port and established a military government under LaVallette. Telles did not feel strong enough to attack the American defenses at Mazatlán, but he remained on its periphery maintaining the attention of American commanders.[58]

Within a few days LaVallette learned of a 90-man force at nearby Urias and on 20 November reacted with a two-pronged attack. Sending one element overland to attack the enemy flank and a second force by sea to conduct an amphibious landing, LaVallette caught the Mexican force between the two and compelled it to flee in confusion. The only other fighting that occurred at Mazatlán involved two skirmishes in which American patrols surprised and bested Mexican elements operating in the area.[59] By the beginning of 1848 the American position in Mazatlán had become too strong for Mexican forces to challenge.

While Shubrick and LaVallette established the American presence at Mazatlán, Mexican forces on the Baja peninsula were reinforced and reorganized under the leadership of Capt. Manuel Pineda, who had made several determined attacks against La Paz and San José del Cabo.[60] All failed, demonstrating that Pineda could not prevail in face of the U.S. Navy, whose ships always arrived in time to provide gunfire, reinforcements, and supplies. In early 1848 the balance of power began to favor the Americans. On 12 January a landing party commanded by Lt. Frederick Chatard destroyed the Mexican guns at San Blas. During February and March of 1848 Col. Henry Burton and his New York Volunteers began offensive operations out of La Paz with attacks against Pineda's camps at San Antonio, Todos Santos, and Santiago, resulting in the total defeat of Mexican resistance.[61]

Although fighting continued in Baja California during March and April 1848, the war had entered its terminal period. Negotiators had signed the Treaty of Guadalupe Hidalgo on 2 February, and commanders announced an armistice on 29 February. Although the ratification process in both the United States and Mexico remained, major operations had ended and only isolated skirmishes occurred. Shubrick's campaign in Baja had been in vain, as the treaty returned the entire peninsula to Mexico. But the amphibious campaign in Alta California had not been in vain as the joint efforts of naval and army forces ensured that California would remain in American hands.[62]

With only few exceptions such as the battles of San Pasqual, San Gabriel, and La Mesa, the entire conflict over California constituted an amphibious campaign. Even the battles of San Gabriel and La Mesa had amphibious aspects since Marines and sailors provided much of the manpower, and the operations received their logistical support from a forward expeditionary base and the ships of Stockton's Pacific Squadron. Although Kearny functioned as field commander after arriving in California, a naval officer—Stockton—served as commander in chief, and a Marine performed the duties of adjutant. In both a conceptual and literal sense, the conquest of California exemplified the theory of power projection and an early refinement of operational maneuver from the sea.

Among the most significant principles of operational maneuver from the sea as applied to the California campaign, use of the sea as maneuver space is most significant. From San Francisco to Monterey, San Pedro, San Diego, the littorals throughout the Gulf of California, and the Mexican Pacific coastline, American commodores inserted amphibious forces at points of enemy weakness, thereby avoiding direct attacks against strongly held defenses. Focusing on a series of key operational objectives that would eventually undermine the ability of Californians to continue the struggle, American forces integrated units (from all services), weapons, and logistical support to maximize combat power at the decisive points of battle. In the few cases where hostile forces presented a threat to the landing force, such as at San Pedro during the second effort to capture Los Angeles, Stockton simply back-loaded his amphibious force, moved to San Diego, and launched his operation from a new direction. Throughout the California theater of war, all-important objectives were situated on the coastline or within easy marching distance, providing a benefit that further enhanced the advantages of operational maneuver from the sea.

The use of maneuver at sea coupled with sea basing and integrated combat power allowed American commanders to retain the initiative, thereby generating an overwhelming tempo and momentum with which Californian and Mexican forces could not cope. Even during the brief counterrebellion in the Los Angeles area, it only required Stockton to forsake his Acapulco–Mexico City scheme and refocus his naval power in Alta California to subdue Flores and his followers. U.S. officers did not always apply these concepts perfectly, of course, as exemplified by the failed effort at Dominguez Ranch by Mervine and Gillespie. Yet, in general, senior commanders based the overall California campaign on the principles of operational maneuver from the sea, long before naval and Marine thinkers conceptualized them as a coherent doctrine for amphibious warfare.

Chapter 6

TO THE HALLS OF MONTEZUMA

As John Sloat and Robert Stockton undertook their amphibious conquest of California, Zachary Taylor followed up his victories in Texas with a drive into northern Mexico. During 20–24 September 1846 he assaulted a Mexican army under Gen. Pedro de Ampudia in the fortified city of Monterrey, winning a hard-fought victory at great cost to both sides. To President Polk's chagrin, Taylor agreed to an eight-week armistice following the battle, which allowed the Mexican army to retreat from Monterrey while providing respite for his own hard-pressed troops. American leaders hoped that a victorious U.S. Army on Mexican soil would force a negotiated settlement to the conflict. But Taylor's successes in Texas and at Monterrey, though impressive, did not convince Mexican authorities to end hostilities. As a result, leaders in Washington lost faith in the strategy of attacking overland and sought another way to force Mexico into negotiations.[1]

The ability of American leaders to focus on its problems with Mexico improved during June 1846 when the United States and Great Britain settled their boundary dispute in the northwest. Despite the popular call for a boundary of 54′ 40° ("54′ 40° or Fight"), President Polk and the Senate agreed on the forty-ninth parallel with several minor caveats. Not only did this remove a distraction for the United States but it also shattered any hopes that Mexican leaders may have entertained for an Anglo-Mexican alliance, or at least a diversion of American military power to the Pacific Northwest.[2]

The decision to assault Mexico at Veracruz resulted from both strategic and operational considerations. Although Taylor had won every engagement he fought against Mexican forces, the distance to Mexico

City and the difficult terrain along the route caused concern for Taylor as well as leaders in Washington. Pressing deeper into Mexico would stretch Taylor's lines of communication, making them more susceptible to guerrilla attack, already a growing problem.[3] By the winter of 1846 it had become clear that victory in northern Mexico would not be sufficient to bring Mexican officials to terms. Operational victories in Texas, Monterrey, and later at Buena Vista did not translate into the strategic advantage intended. Capturing and holding the more vital areas of central Mexico—even Mexico City, if necessary—made more strategic sense at this point in the war. Additionally, the Home Squadron had been blockading Mexican ports and operating freely throughout the Gulf of Mexico since the beginning of the conflict. With the war stalled in northern Mexico, the prospect of bringing naval power to bear along these littorals had strong appeal.[4]

Operationally, Veracruz presented the most viable location for invasion on the Gulf Coast. It offered good landing sites and accessible routes of egress from the beaches into the heart of Mexico. Like all military operations, landing at Veracruz also had disadvantages. The unprotected waters near the city required specialized landing craft. It would be necessary to design, build, and deliver these surfboats on very short notice. Even more challenging, the city's wall and protective forts made Veracruz the strongest fortified city in North America, in the minds of many observers.[5] Additionally, summer epidemics of malaria and yellow fever (*vomitó negro*) restricted the time when forces could concentrate along the coast. A common nineteenth-century view held that storms guarded the Mexican Gulf Coast during winter and disease during the summer.[6]

By November 1846 the idea of an amphibious attack at Veracruz had gained currency in political and military circles. Even powerful Missouri senator Thomas Hart Benton became a strong proponent of that option, and his influence among Democratic politicians proved essential to counterbalance Whig opposition to this apparent escalation in Polk's war strategy. Initially Polk had reservations about landing at Veracruz even though Commo. David Conner and other military and naval officers favored such an operation. But meetings with the former U.S. consul at Veracruz, Francis M. Dimond, helped convince him of the city's vulnerability and the prospect for a successful campaign.[7]

After discussing the concept with his cabinet during November 1846, the president decided to move forward with the operation.[8] Polk considered placing Benton in command of the expedition—with the rank of lieutenant general—but Congress would not agree to the proposition. Most Washington politicians—both Democrat and Whig—recognized Benton's lack of military qualifications despite his political brilliance. Ultimately Polk assigned Maj. Gen. Winfield Scott to command the expedition.[9] Scott's position as commanding general of the U.S. Army, coupled with a sterling record of achievement, made him the logical—even inevitable—choice. It did not make Polk happy to do so because he despised Scott both personally and professionally. Yet only Scott and Taylor had the credibility with Congress and the American public to command a mission of this magnitude, and Polk had come to despise Taylor even more than Scott. Under no circumstances would he consider giving Taylor such a prestigious assignment. Relations between Polk and his top generals proved deplorable throughout the conflict, with both sides believing the other played politics with military affairs.[10] Despite this rancor, Polk and his generals kept focused on their common objective and cooperated well enough to ensure ultimate victory.

Scott's amphibious force for the invasion of Veracruz consisted of new units arriving from the United States, Marines and sailors from the Home Squadron, and 9,000 troops transferred from Taylor's command in northern Mexico. This left Taylor with no more than 5,000 mostly green troops—not a large enough force to undertake offensive operations. This would not pose a problem for Taylor if he only had to deal with the remnants of Ampudia's force and a few guerrillas. But Gen. Antonio López de Santa Anna had recently returned to Mexico from Cuba—through intrigue and American help—and taken command of the Mexican armed forces. Seeing an opportunity to overwhelm Taylor's depleted force with his army of 20,000, Santa Anna set out from San Luis Potosí (located about halfway between Mexico City and Monterrey) to destroy the Americans

With the approach of the Mexican army, Taylor concentrated near the village of Buena Vista, where the two forces met on 22–23 February 1847. In another hard-fought engagement, Taylor withstood Santa Anna's repeated attacks, forcing him to withdraw back to Mexico City.[12] Upon his arrival at the Mexican capital, Santa Anna proclaimed his troops had won great victory at Buena Vista and accepted the presidency from the Mexican Congress.[13] The focus of war then shifted to the Gulf Coast, where Scott and Commodore Conner organized the largest and most innovative amphibious force the United States had ever assembled. Not only did the Americans develop uniquely designed landing craft, but they also used steam-powered ships for the first time in a major amphibious operation. The use of steamships and specifically designed surfboats also permitted American commanders to plan and execute the assault and support landings with greater precision than ever before.

Planning for the Veracruz invasion began as administration officials considered alternatives to advancing through northern Mexico and asked Scott for his input. An avid supporter of a waterborne approach, Scott developed a plan that impressed both the president and Secretary of War William L. Marcy.[14] Scott immediately ordered Q.M. Gen. Thomas S. Jesup to acquire transport ships and landing craft necessary for the operation. It quickly became clear to American leaders that the Veracruz operation required more troops and equipment than currently available in that theater of war. Due to the complexity of the operation, a strong professional—if not personal—relationship between Scott and Jesup needed to develop. Cooperation between Army and Navy components would prove equally critical. The fact that the Department of War, and not the Department of the Navy, acquired and controlled the transport ships and landing craft complicated this relationship and created potential for conflict.[15] Yet Scott established an excellent working relationship with Conner, whose Home Squadron supported the landing and subsequent operations. Together they worked as a professional team that negated the friction inherent in this operational environment.[16] Indeed, their cooperation exemplified that most important characteristic of amphibious operations, the integration between the Navy and landing force.

Scott designated a number of points of embarkation for his army including Mobile, New Orleans, Brazos Santiago (sometimes spelled San Jago or St. Iago) on the Rio Grande, and Tampico in Mexico. Those troops arriving from the United States would ultimately assemble at the mouth of the Brazos Santiago, and those arriving from Taylor's army would march south through Victoria to the port city of Tampico. Conner had captured Tampico on 14 November 1846 with an amphibious landing involving 300 Marines and sailors from the Home Squadron. After embarking his force, Scott moved to the island of Lobos (Isle de Lobos) south of Tampico, where he organized, equipped, and trained for the upcoming mission. Conner provided a sloop of war to guide Scott's transport and supply ships into secure anchorages, and officers for each ship to pilot them to the final staging area at Antón Lizardo, about twelve miles south of Veracruz.[17]

While Scott prepared his army for invasion, Jesup chartered 50 transport ships and acquired 65 new surfboats for the assault landings. He contracted to have these landing craft built to detailed specifications, which allowed them to fit compactly on the transports yet operate effectively in the unprotected waters (rough surf conditions) near Veracruz. These surfboats constituted the first American landing craft specifically designed for amphibious operations. The contract for the surfboats specified the type of wood, the metal fasteners required, and the method of caulking. It also specified three sizes for the boats including 35 feet, 37 feet 9 inches, and 40 feet in length, thereby allowing flexibility in planning the assault waves. Additionally, this allowed nesting the boats so as to take up less space in transporting them to Veracruz. Scott and Jesup originally ordered 141 landing boats, but only 65 arrived in time for the operation. With the army in control of the transport ships and landing craft, Scott could theoretically conduct the amphibious operation without naval help. Although some observers have suggested that he initially considered such action, there is no evidence to support that contention. In fact, the professional relationship that Scott and Conner developed during the planning and execution phases of this undertaking suggests just the opposite. Throughout the operation, cooperation between the two leaders and services proved to be exemplary.[18]

By early March 1847 Scott considered his army adequately prepared and equipped to commence operations. As the transport ships rendezvoused with the Home Squadron at the anchorage off Antón Lizardo, Scott and Conner accompanied by members of their staffs boarded the steamer *Petrita*, sailed along the coast to select a landing beach, and conferred on the operational plan.[19] Scott accepted Conner's recommended landing site at Collada, between two and a half and three miles southeast of Veracruz. Landing at Collada, the boats would be somewhat sheltered from dangerous surf conditions by Sacrificios Island, thereby making the landing safer. Additionally, Mexican artillery at Veracruz and Fortress San Juan de Ulúa (also spelled Ulloa) could not range the landing beach, although it remained within a short marching distance of the objective area.

Conner and his subordinate commanders had a good understanding of the Mexican coastline from their service on blockade duty and numerous amphibious incursions during the first year of the war, and Scott gladly took advantage of their expertise. Conner advised that a landing at Collada would first require transferring the landing force from their transports onto Conner's more tactically agile ships, which could maneuver into the proper position for debarkation near Sacrificios Island. Scott accepted this advice as well as Conner's suggestion that sailors should man the surfboats that would take the landing force ashore. These arrangements, coupled with the use of Connor's ships to provide fire support to the landing force, placed naval officers in complete control of the amphibious operation until Scott established his army ashore.[20]

Conner assigned the surfboats to his naval ships in five-boat units. For example, the sailing frigate *Raritan* received fifteen surfboats whereas the steamer *Princeton* received only ten. Each landing craft would be manned by at least seven sailors commanded by either a naval officer or petty officer. The surfboats used an anchor—or kedge—and line to prevent broaching and maintain stability during beach operations. The assault plan organized the surfboats in divisions of ten boats each. Each division would be commanded by a Navy lieutenant. Capt. French Forrest of the frigate *Raritan* commanded the overall ship-to-shore movement. The landing of the assault elements was to be executed in three waves, after which each individual boat made independent trips between the beach and ships.[21]

During the morning hours of 9 March 1847, Scott transferred his troops from their transports onto Conner's ships near Antón Lizardo while steamers towed the 65 surfboats that served as landing craft into position. That afternoon at Sacrificios Island, the landing force loaded into their surfboats for the ship-to-shore movement. The cross-decking of troops and their deployment into the surfboats proved a complex and detailed operation, all the more so because of last-minute changes in the operational plan. The efficiency of these evolutions is due entirely to the professionalism and leadership skills of Conner and his staff. Each landing boat carried between 25 and 70 soldiers with a naval officer in command and sailors manning the oars. Once the surfboats had all their troops on board, they moved in divisions to the predetermined line of departure marked by the *Princeton* about 450 yards off the beach. Seven of Conner's gunboats (2 steamers and 5 schooners), most carrying 32-pound shell guns, stood in line about 90 yards from the beach to provide fire support to the landing force.[22]

On signal—a cannon shot from the *Massachusetts* at 1730—the lines of surfboats began moving toward the beach. Within minutes a detachment of Marines under Capt. Alvin Edson and 5,500 army troops under the command of Brig. Gen. William J. Worth reached the beach almost simultaneously. To the surprise of many, the beach was undefended, and members of the first wave of Americans heard music drifting across the water from bands on board ships standing offshore, not cannon and gunfire from Mexican defenders. Reconnaissance boats had earlier detected Mexican lancers and artillery field pieces near the landing beach. Many Americans feared these forces might have staged behind the first set of sand dunes to attack the landing force before it could become established ashore, but none appeared during or after the landing. A detachment of cavalry observed on the beach just prior to the landing had been dispersed by fire from Conner's gunboats and did not reappear during the operation.[23]

Once the first assault wave loaded into their surfboats, some initial confusion developed due to a lack of rehearsals. This, coupled with an expectation that Mexican forces would oppose the landing, created anxiety among the officers and men of the amphibious force. But the aggressive Worth calmly ordered the regimental colors raised on the surfboats around which the assault line formed and began to pull ashore. Worth's personal leadership complemented the excellent work of Conner and his staff, ensuring an effective assault. In addition to his organizational and leadership skills, Worth set an example for courage and aggressiveness when he claimed the honor of being the first American on the beach. Immediately after disembarking the first wave of attackers, the surfboats returned to the ships, took on additional troops, and transported waves of reinforcements ashore. By 2200, Scott had his army of 12,000 ashore and ready for action.[24]

Scott and Conner had achieved another of the important characteristics of amphibious operations, the rapid buildup of combat power ashore. This is critically important, as the landing force is most vulnerable during the initial phase of the operation. Landing operations continued for several days until the Navy had delivered the bulk of artillery, horses, conveyances, and supplies to the beachhead. The efficiency and speed of the landing served as a tribute to effective planning and military-naval cooperation. Had Gen. Juan Morales, the Mexican commander at Veracruz, chosen to oppose the American landing, he could have inflicted casualties and complicated the operation. But the availability of fire from the gunboats close to shore and larger ships farther out, ensured that he would also suffer high casualties. Without the prospect of reinforcement anytime soon, Morales decided against fighting at the water's edge, believing his best hope lay within the defenses of Veracruz.[25]

The lack of resistance on the landing beaches created no illusions in the minds of Scott and Conner. Capturing Veracruz posed no small task, as its walls and protective forts—Fort Santiago to the south and Fort Conception to the north—presented a formidable challenge. The landward wall included nine strong bastions facing sand dunes and rising plains reaching an upland forest about three miles inland. The city's main defenses protected against an attack from the sea and included Fortress San Juan de Ulúa, which set on Gallego Reef about three-quarters of a mile from the coastline. These interlocking defenses possessed well-placed cannons, which provided defensive fires against hostile forces on land or sea. Yet, despite this impressive-looking defensive system, the structures had not been adequately maintained over time, and no system for sustaining the garrison at San Juan de Ulúa under siege conditions had been prepared. Regardless of these shortcomings, Scott recognized the defenses as daunting and knew he could not fight the battle for Veracruz on his enemy's terms.[26]

Despite objections from some of his subordinate commanders, Scott wisely decided to lay siege to the city rather than assault it directly. That decision had risks because Scott needed to capture the city and move his army away from the coast before the onset of yellow fever season. A direct attack might result in more initial casualties, but it would also bring about a quicker victory. A protracted siege that left his army lingering along the coast once the yellow fever struck could potentially be more costly in terms of casualties and morale. By deciding to invest the city rather than conducting an assault, Scott committed himself to an aggressive and powerful bombardment aimed at forcing surrender after a relatively short engagement.[27] This created a moral dilemma for Scott because of the collateral damage to civilians and property that such a barrage would surely inflict.

Upon his landing at Collada Beach, Scott quickly maneuvered the army to seal off Veracruz from the land side. Moving into siege positions proved challenging due to difficult terrain, chaparral, Mexican guerrillas, harassing fire from the forts, and a gale-force storm known as a "norther" that struck on 12–15 March. Placing his divisions in column, Scott ordered Worth to clear and occupy the southern portion of the force beachhead line. Following Worth, Maj. Gen. Robert Patterson's division then cleared and occupied the center portion, and Brig. Gen. David E. Twiggs' division cleared and occupied the northern part. Thus, Scott drove in all Mexican outposts and established a trench line—beyond effective range of artillery from the city—anchored at each end on the Gulf of Mexico at Collada Beach south of Veracruz and on Vergara to the north. He then advanced artillery-infantry teams into forward positions from which he could bombard the city.[28]

With the army investing Veracruz from land and the Navy blockading the city from sea, Scott had surrounded and isolated the objective area. As American forces moved into position and prepared to bombard the Mexican defenses, fear and fatalism gripped the people of Veracruz. They not only felt imprisoned by the American Army and Navy but also felt abandoned by their own government. Santa Anna could not send troops to attack the invaders. His army had been badly mauled and greatly reduced in size by its defeat at Buena Vista and its devastating march across the tough terrain of northern Mexico. With Taylor's army in northern Mexico, albeit considerably weakened, and revolution breaking out in the capital, the Mexican leader needed all his regular army and national guard troops in Mexico City. Santa Anna believed that if Veracruz fell, he could always stop Scott in the mountains west of the coast.[29] Mexican leaders on the coast recognized Santa Anna's position and realized they must face Scott with the resources on hand.[30]

Just before the siege began, Commo. Matthew Calbraith Perry relieved Conner as commander of the Home Squadron. Conner had proved to be a professional and cooperative naval officer, setting a high standard for close and continuous coordination. His positive attitude, coupled with the responsiveness of Scott, permeated the entire amphibious force and constituted one of the most important factors underlying its success. But after placing the amphibious force ashore, it remained necessary to fight and win the subsequent battle on the ground. The Navy played a crucial role throughout that action not only in providing gunfire support—both from naval batteries ashore and ships offshore—but also in serving as the logistical base for supplying Scott's army. For Secretary of the Navy John Y. Mason to relieve a key commander in the middle of a major combat operation from his distant post in Washington—especially a leader so highly respected by both Army and naval personnel—can only bring into question his competence as a service secretary. Certainly, the senior Army officers then engaging the enemy on a hostile shore resented the loss of Conner, whom they trusted implicitly. Perry had not been at Veracruz during landing operations—he had taken the *Mississippi* to Norfolk for maintenance and essential repairs—so the Army commanders did not know him.[31]

Fortunately for the war effort, and for the American troops ashore, Perry proved equal to Conner in both professionalism and cooperation. Although some historians have suggested otherwise, Conner's relief did not result from dissatisfaction with his performance. In fact, the Navy Department had already extended Conner's command of the squadron one year beyond the normal period. Polk and Mason had previously selected Perry to replace Conner and dispatched him to the Home Squadron to serve as vice commodore until Conner chose to turn over command. But once the Veracruz operation got under way, Conner had shown no inclination to surrender command, despite some ongoing health problems. Perry's critics suggest that he intrigued with Mason and Polk for an immediate change of command while back in the United States with the *Mississippi* during January–March 1847. They also contend that the decision to relieve Conner at that time had a political dimension. Active-duty military and naval officers of the nineteenth century tended to be more openly political than in our own time. Perry was a well-known Democrat, whereas most important commanders of the Mexican War (Scott, Taylor, and Stockton) had Whig affiliations and political ambitions. Having a Jacksonian Democrat in a key command position may well have made the Polk administration feel more comfortable with the political aspects of the war. Conner, for better or for worse, had no party connections and no known political ambitions.[32]

Conner had been criticized in the press due to three failed efforts to capture the port city of Alvarado during the summer and fall on 1846. Although the failures resulted more from issues of hydrography than from enemy resistance, it hurt his standing in the eyes of politicians and the public. To offset the failure at Alvarado, he had sent a task force to capture Tabasco during October. In a visible but militarily insignificant operation, Tabasco surrendered to the commander of the task force, Matthew Perry. The Tabasco operation restored confidence in the Home Squadron among Americans back in the states. But the credit redounded not to Conner, who ordered the operation, but rather to Perry, who carried it out. Whether because of press relations, political intrigue, or legitimate personnel rotation policy, changing commanders in the middle of a tactical operation is risky business. Credit for avoiding the potential disaster that such a change could create must go to Perry and Scott, not to Mason or the president. Ultimately the change of command did not have a disastrous impact, but it caused a period of confusion and uncertainty for the amphibious forces ashore and at sea. Regrettably, it also robbed Conner of the recognition he deserved as the most important single person involved in the landing at Veracruz. The more colorful and heroic Perry, with great exploits throughout his career, attracted greater attention in historical memory.[33]

In addition to poor judgment in relieving a commander during critical operations, logistical support for the Veracruz operation proved deplorable. While Scott and Conner worked well together and operations went smoothly at Veracruz, such was not the case in the United States, where individuals responsible for logistical support did not work well together and support did not go smoothly. Despite some good work in acquiring transports and custom-built surfboats, other aspects of support proved disappointing. Even the surfboats did not arrive in the quantities required to support the original landing plan. Less than half arrived in time for the amphibious assault.[34] This resulted in the surfboats returning to their ships to reload after landing each wave ashore. The time consumed in this operation could have proved costly if the Mexican army had made a determined defense at the waterline.

Had all 141 surfboats ordered been available, one wave could load while another landed on the beach. This would ensure a very rapid buildup of combat power ashore. With only 65 boats, the amount of time for the buildup more than doubled. The lack of enemy resistance, coupled with innovative planning and the hard work of sailors manning the boats, allowed the landing force to overcome the deficiency in numbers of landing craft. Whereas the buildup of combat power ashore proved rapid enough for the Veracruz operation, more surfboats would have made it even faster.

Imperfect logistical support plagued Scott throughout the war because reinforcements, equipment, weapons, and draft animals never arrived in the quantities promised and needed. Even by the most optimistic estimates, troop levels in Scott's army never exceeded 13,500 soldiers, despite Washington's promise of twice that number. The thousands of wagons, horses, mules, and supplies arrived in a fraction of the numbers needed, and those that did arrive were often too late to support the mission.[35] By sharing assets, Scott and Perry minimized the impact of this shameful lack of support, but only up to a point. Although the logistical problem initially resulted primarily from bureaucratic inefficiency, as the war progressed and Scott continued to win victories, many political leaders came to believe that the army could get by with less support than originally planned. Sympathy with Scott's constant requests for support waned, and he ultimately had to solve his own logistics problems as well as fight Santa Anna's resilient army.

On 22 March Scott asked General Morales to surrender Veracruz and its forts. Morales rejected the demand, as he had a similar request prior to the Collada landing. After Morales' rebuff, Scott opened fire on Veracruz and its forts while Perry's ships bombarded the target from the sea. The following day, Cdr. Josiah Tattnall took the steamer *Spitfire* within eight hundred yards of the main defensive castle and blasted away for several hours before returning to the main force. Tattnall's excursion—actually one of several—proved exciting, colorful, and risky. Despite a mild rebuke from Perry for recklessness, Tattnall's daring proved an inspiration to the entire amphibious force.[36] But, as in all wars, the horrors of battle counterbalance the glory of heroics. Both American and Mexican accounts of the bombardment of Veracruz describe a devastating experience for the occupants.[37] Scott had little choice other than to act aggressively, for to show mercy to his enemy within the city would ultimately be costly to his own army. He had to reduce Veracruz as quickly as possible and move inland in a race against the onset of disease and the movements of Santa Anna. If that meant the residents of the city must suffer, so go the fortunes of war.

The first several days of bombardment did not produce good results because the army's siege guns had not yet arrived. At Scott's request, Perry provided six heavy guns (three 68-pounder shell guns and three 32-pounder solid-shot guns) along with their crews for use on the line of battle. On 24 March these guns went into action.[38] The heavy naval guns provided the punch necessary to breach the defensive walls, making the city susceptible to infantry assault. Previous bombardment had failed to accomplish this, primarily inflicting damage to the structures and people within the walls. After the big guns came into play, the collective fire from cannon, mortars, rockets, and ships reached climatic levels, inflicting devastating punishment on the physical structures and mental condition of the Veracruz defenders. Despite a courageous effort at counter–battery fire from the forts and strongholds, the defenders could not suppress the American guns, and on 26 March Mexican leaders raised the white flag.[39]

Prior to the Mexican surrender, Scott had developed a plan to assault the city. The breaching of its walls by the heavy naval guns had made that an appropriate—even attractive—tactical choice. He organized the assault force into three columns consisting of regulars, volunteers, and Marines and sailors, respectively. Although this attack undoubtedly would have succeeded, the offer to negotiate presented a less costly alternative. After two days of discussions, Mexican general Jose Juan de Landero (Morales had slipped away in a small boat on the night of 25 March) surrendered Veracruz and Fort San Juan de Ulúa. The terms of capitulation made all Mexican officers prisoners but paroled the Mexican enlisted men and permitted them to march out of the city under full honors of war before surrendering their weapons. The agreement also protected the civil and religious rights of the Mexican citizens and permitted Mexican sick to remain in the city under their own medical care. While Veracruz passed into American hands, Scott looked west toward the National Highway and the route taken by Hernán Cortéz in 1519 through the Madre Mountains to central Mexico.[40]

As Scott built up supplies ashore, he extended his beachhead inland, created the Military Department of Veracruz, and ordered a major cleanup of the city to minimize the prospect of disease. Scott and Perry then launched a joint attack on Alvarado about thirty miles southeast of Veracruz under command of Brig. Gen. John A. Quitman. By attacking and capturing Alvarado, Scott believed he could strengthen his hold on the coastline as well as obtain horses, mules, and beef cattle to support his army. Quitman arrived at the city only to discover that Navy lieutenant Charles G. Hunter and his steamer, *Scourge*, had already accepted the surrender of Alvarado and nearby Tlacotalpán as well.[41] Although Quitman appeared to see the humor in one small naval steamer capturing the two cities before his division or Perry's force of thirteen vessels arrived, the commodore did not. Perry ordered Hunter court-martialed for contempt toward authority because he allowed the Mexican troops to take their livestock with them when they withdrew from the Alvarado area.[42] Despite that fact, Quitman returned to Veracruz with approximately five hundred horses. Hunter's penalty included dismissal from the squadron, but he became a folk hero back in the United States.[43] Most Americans believed that Hunter only followed orders, that Perry had sent him on the reconnaissance, and that he had simply exploited an opportunity presented on the field of battle, an act that deserved praise, not punishment, in the minds of most people. To many, Perry's actions seemed petty and vindictive, proving that even giants have flaws.

Concurrent with Scott's move to the west, Perry established headquarters in Veracruz, which became the center for regulating shipping and controlling activities throughout the harbor. He also took control of the customhouse and the collection of duties. Following the American occupation of Veracruz, traffic in its harbor recovered rapidly, increased in large part by ships carrying supplies for Scott's army then moving toward Mexico City.[44] To further tighten control over the Mexican littoral, Perry attacked and captured the fortified compound at Tuxpan, located between Veracruz and Tampico, with a landing force of about 1,500 Marines and sailors. Believing he could take the city only by joint land and sea action, Perry organized the landing party from the Home Squadron, which included his own son, Marine lieutenant William F. Perry. After capturing Tuxpan, Perry removed the guns and destroyed the fortifications designed to defend the town. Destroying the defenses of Tuxpan positioned him to control the key areas of Lobos, Soto de la Marina, and the Tabasco River basin.[45]

On 30 March Santa Anna received word of the fall of Veracruz. Several days later he set out from Mexico City to block the Americans' passage through the mountains and end their threat to the Mexican capital. Knowing the mountainous terrain between Veracruz and Mexico City favored the defense, Santa Anna felt very confident that he could stop Scott's army at any one of numerous places along the route. He first chose to defend at a narrow pass near the town of Cerro Gordo, where high ground protected both flanks and the Rio del Plan served as a natural obstacle to his front. Santa Anna deployed his army in a strong defensive position, which he believed would ensure a tactical victory against any American attack. Additionally, by holding the line at Cerro Gordo, he would keep his enemy on the yellow fever–plagued coastal plain.[46]

On 8 April 1847 Scott began his movement toward Mexico City along the National Highway. As he did so, operations in Mexico shifted from amphibious to expeditionary warfare. On 12 April Twiggs' division halted its advance when it made contact with the main enemy force near Cerro Gordo. Upon joining his lead element, Scott ordered Capt. Robert E. Lee to conduct a reconnaissance of the area to find an alternate avenue of advance against Santa Anna's formidable positions. Lee located a promising route, which offered an opportunity to surprise the Mexican left flank. Scott assigned Lee a detachment of pioneers to clear an avenue of approach by which Twiggs' division and several batteries of light artillery could advance on the enemy. Lee accomplished this with stealth and secrecy, thereby providing Scott's army the opportunity to flank, surprise, and defeat Santa Anna in the Battle of Cerro Gordo.[47] Scott's army defeated and routed the Mexicans at Cerro Gordo, capturing large numbers of prisoners and hotly pursuing the survivors westward toward Jalapa. He also captured so many field pieces that he could not move them from the battlefield due to a shortage of horses.[48]

After the Battle of Cerro Gordo and American forces had pushed on to Jalapa and Puebla, Scott initiated a strategic pause to entice Mexican authorities to enter into negotiations. Thinking the victories at Buena Vista, Veracruz, and Cerro Gordo might force concessions from Santa Anna, the U.S. government undertook a modest diplomatic initiative to end the war. The Polk administration had earlier sent Nicholas P. Trist

Gen. George Washington, commander in chief of the Continental Army. Washington had to fight the most powerful nation in the world with an army that had no structure, no regular pay, no long-term enlistments (it was constantly turning over), no regular supply and logistics system, and few experienced officers, with an unstable government and fragmented society. *Naval History and Heritage Command*

Maj. Gen. Sir William Howe, commander of British forces in North America after the Battle of Bunker Hill and during the Battle for New York. *Naval History and Heritage Command*

Vice Adm. Richard Lord Howe, Sir William's brother and commander of all British naval forces in North American waters during the New York campaign. *Naval History and Heritage Command*

Col. (later brigadier general) John Glover, whose Massachusetts fishermen evacuated Washington's Army from Long Island and later delayed the British landing at Pell's Point. *Naval History and Heritage Command*

Jean-Baptiste-Doantien de Vimeur Comte de Rochambeau commanded the French army of some 7,800 soldiers that fought under Washington at the Battle of Yorktown. *Naval History and Heritage Command*

Adm. François-Joseph-Paul, Comte de Grasse, whose victory over British naval forces in the Battle of the Capes allowed him to control the entrance to the Chesapeake Bay, thereby ensuring Washington's victory at Yorktown. *Naval History and Heritage Command*

Lt. Gen. Charles Lord Cornwallis surrendered a field army of some 8,000 British and Hessian soldiers to Washington at the Battle of Yorktown. *Naval History and Heritage Command*

William Eaton held a commission from the Secretary of the Navy as the U.S. Naval Agent to the Barbary Regencies. His six-hundred-mile march across the North African desert and subsequent attack on Derna, Tripoli, brought the pasha of Tripoli to submission. *Maryland State Archives*

Lt. Presley O'Bannon's Marine detachment not only enforced discipline on Eaton's polyglot army as it moved across North Africa, but also led the assault against the ramparts at Derna, Tripoli. *Naval History and Heritage Command*

Commo. Oliver Hazard Perry, whose victory on Lake Erie established American supremacy in the Northwest theater during the War of 1812. *Naval History and Heritage Command*

Rear Adm. Sir George Cockburn proved to be the most aggressive and strong-willed of the senior British officers throughout the Chesapeake campaign. *Naval History and Heritage Command*

Commo. Joshua Barney, who fought stubbornly on St. Leonard's Creek and whose Marines and sailors made a courageous but futile stand during the Battle of Bladensburg. *Naval History and Heritage Command*

Commo. John Rodgers played a key role in preparing the defenses of Baltimore on both land and sea. *Naval History and Heritage Command*

Maj. Gen. Samuel Smith (who was also a U.S. senator from Maryland) did not wait for orders to take command at Baltimore. His dynamic leadership ensured that Baltimore would not endure the same fate as Washington. *Portrait by Rembrandt Peale*

Capt. (later major general) John C. Frémont, whose activities during the conquest of California were both controversial and effective. *Naval History and Heritage Command*

Commo. John D. Sloat acted aggressively in proclaiming California for the United States but then became cautious and was replaced by the self-assured Commo. Robert Stockton. *Naval History and Heritage Command*

Commo. Robert F. Stockton's flamboyant aggressiveness was well suited for working with John C. Frémont. *Naval History and Heritage Command*

Commo. David Conner set a high standard for cooperation in joint operations by working closely with Winfield Scott during the planning and execution of the amphibious operation at Veracruz. *Naval History and Heritage Command*

Maj. Gen. Winfield Scott, in conjunction with David Conner, conducted one of the most successful amphibious operations of the nineteenth century. No lesser authority than the Duke of Wellington said of his Mexican campaign, "Scott is the greatest living soldier" and that his campaign "was unsurpassed in military annals." *Naval History and Heritage Command*

Commo. Mathew Calbraith Perry replaced David Conner shortly after the landing at Veracruz. The change of command was routine in nature, but of questionable wisdom in the middle of an important operation. Fortunately for the landing force (and to their relief), Perry continued Conner's policy of close cooperation with the Army. *Naval History and Heritage Command.*

Gen. Ulysses S. Grant ordered the attacks on Fort Fisher to close down the Confederate port at Wilmington, North Carolina, through which supplies reached Robert E. Lee's Army of Northern Virginia. *Naval History and Heritage Command*

Capt. David Dixon Porter was a bombastic yet effective naval commander. He did not work well with his Army counterpart, Benjamin Butler, during the first attack on Fort Fisher but had a productive relationship with both Grant and Butler's replacement, Gen. Alfred Terry. *Naval History and Heritage Command*

Maj. Gen. Benjamin F. Butler's lack of aggressiveness and commitment to the mission during the first attack on Fort Fisher infuriated Grant, who replaced him with the more effective Alfred Terry. *Library of Congress*

Maj. Gen. Alfred H. Terry, seated center, uncovered, with his staff. After the failure of the first attack on Fort Fisher, Grant turned to Terry, who worked well with Porter and led a successful amphibious attack against the formidable Confederate defenses. *Library of Congress*

An artist's rendering of the naval bombardment of Fort Fisher. *Naval History and Heritage Command*

to accompany Scott's army and act as commissioner plenipotentiary to negotiate peace terms with Mexican leaders. While the diplomats negotiated, Scott called in all his garrisons, including those guarding his line of communications with the Gulf of Mexico. When peace failed, Scott abandoned his links to Veracruz and resumed his march to Mexico City. It was a bold and risky move, one that would ultimately place Winfield Scott in the pantheon of history's great commanders. But at the time, many felt it was a disastrous mistake, including President Polk and the great British commander the Duke of Wellington.[49]

Scott soon defeated Mexican armies at Contreras and Churubusco, and—with their capital now at risk—Mexican officials agreed to resume negotiations. Again Scott temporarily suspended operations, but Mexican leaders could not yet pay the price for peace (the establishment of the Rio Grande as their northern boundary and cession of New Mexico and California), and the attack toward the capital resumed.[50] On 8 September 1847 Scott launched a series of assaults that resulted in the fall of Chapultepec Castle several days later, and on 13 September a detachment of Marines attached to Quitman's division overran the Halls of Montezuma. After the victory, Scott issued General Order No. 284, in which he appointed Quitman to be the civil and military governor of Mexico and exhorted his soldiers to remain disciplined and vigilant. It took the fall of Mexico City followed by its occupation by American troops to set in motion the negotiation that resulted in the Treaty of Guadalupe Hidalgo, signed on 2 February 1848.[51]

Success in the Mexican-American War came from numerous hard-fought battles and the will of many resolute leaders. But the successful amphibious operation at Veracruz created the strategic environment that made ultimate victory possible. One of the unique aspects of amphibious warfare is that it tends to function at all three levels of war (tactical, operational, and strategic) simultaneously. The fighting occurs on the tactical and operational levels, of course, but the impact of amphibious action is often strategic in nature. Whereas the payoff for success is often great, the complexity and vulnerability of amphibious operations also make them risky. The amphibious force must build up combat power ashore from nothing at all to a level capable of defeating an enemy force on its own ground. This requires support from strong naval forces coupled with extensive and detailed planning. In short, professionalism must permeate every aspect of the naval and ground forces involved. Cooperation between naval and ground elements must be strong and totally focused on mission accomplishment. Until the years between World War I and World War II, that cooperation tended to be ad hoc and personality driven. As amphibious doctrine became codified during the 1930s and tested throughout World War II, these critical issues of command relationships and integration of effort became developed and clarified. At Veracruz no such doctrine existed, and only the intelligent, professional, and results-oriented leadership of Conner and Scott provided the necessary direction. Undoubtedly, Scott benefited from his experience in the War of 1812, especially his successful amphibious attack against Fort George in May 1813.

At Veracruz, American leaders took every measure to mitigate the risk and provide conditions for a successful battle. Despite personality conflicts among Polk, Marcy, Scott, and Taylor, the amphibious commander received the support and freedom of action he needed to lead the invasion force. Despite the failure of Marcy and Jesup to provide the logistical support promised, they did provide enough to allow Scott to succeed, though by a narrow margin. Despite the lack of doctrine in joint operations (and a tradition of rancor between Navy and Army officers), Scott and Conner worked out the issue of unity of command so satisfactorily that it serves as a model for cooperative effort in joint operations.[52]

Not only did the command relations set a high example of effective leadership but also the entire Veracruz operation foreshadowed the American amphibious actions of World War II. Innovations in landing craft (surfboats in the 1840s, Higgins boats and tracked landing vehicles in the 1940s) provided an effective assault capability against the defensive capability of each enemy. Indeed, the Battle of Veracruz constituted the first case of special craft being built and used for amphibious operations. This allowed commanders to rapidly transfer combat power ashore and then sustain the landing force through the subsequent fighting. The innovation in sea-based fire support (steam-powered gunboats and frigates in the 1840s, close-in naval gunfire ships and carrier-based airpower in the 1940s) provided a force multiplier that degraded opposition on the beach and provided ongoing fire support to the landing force. Any student of World War II can clearly see the model for the amphibious campaigns in the Pacific and European theaters of war in the landing at Veracruz.

Veracruz not only served as a model for subsequent amphibious operations; it established the United States as the preeminent amphibious power in the world. America's previous experience with amphibious warfare had more often been on the defensive side of the action rather than on the offensive. This changed with Veracruz. After that successful landing, the United States remained an offensive power projection force. Since 1847 the United States has been the target of an amphibious attack only twice, at Wake Island and in the Philippines during 1942. During the years between 1847 and 1942, American amphibious power conducted hundreds of offensive landings, virtually all successful. Victory in the Mexican War established the United States as a continental power, spanning North America from the Atlantic to the Pacific Oceans. It established the conditions that would eventually ensure—despite a few detours—that the United States would become the preeminent naval and military power in the world.[53] It also created political and social conditions that led to a tragic civil war.

Chapter 7

THE FORT FISHER CAMPAIGN

THE FACT THAT THE AMERICAN CIVIL WAR WAS FOUGHT primarily on land has led historians and military professionals to focus on operations by the Union and Confederate armies. Yet the ultimate victory of Union forces resulted from a total war effort involving the use of political, diplomatic, economic, military, and naval power. The war began when Confederate batteries fired on Fort Sumter in Charleston Harbor on 12 April 1861. President Abraham Lincoln responded with a 15 April call for 75,000 volunteers to suppress Southern secessionists and, four days later, with an order to blockade Confederate ports. During the same period, the new president sought advice on strategy from Gen. Winfield Scott, the army commander at Veracruz and, in 1861, the senior officer in the U.S. Army. Scott sent Lincoln a three-part plan calling for (1) the creation of a large army both to defend Washington and counter Confederate forces gathering in Virginia; (2) the establishment of an effective blockade of the Confederacy; and (3) the division of the Confederacy by joint Army–Navy operations designed to divide the South along the Mississippi River. Although Scott's plan did not fit the tenor of the times in 1861, was derisively dubbed the "Anaconda Plan" by the Northern newspapers, and was never formally adopted, the operation and tactics outlined in Scott's plan became integral elements of Lincoln's wartime strategy as he sought to maintain pressure on the Confederacy at every point.[1]

Execution of the operations outlined in the plan led to joint Army–Navy operations on western rivers, naval support of Army operations along the rivers in Virginia, and amphibious assaults on the littorals of both the Atlantic Ocean and the Gulf of Mexico. The effects of this war strategy eroded Confederate strength in many areas, including the tactical power of their armies in the field. As Lt. Gen. Ulysses S. Grant and his lieutenants maneuvered against Southern armies, they faced smaller forces than they might have because of the Confederate strategy of defending all points, including the entire coastline, against a free-ranging Union Navy. In addition, as the Union Navy closed Southern ports to blockade runners, Confederate armies lost important sources of matériel and equipment needed to sustain their war effort.[2]

At the beginning of the American Civil War, leaders understood sophisticated concepts of naval strategy, but very little doctrine existed regarding amphibious operations. Yet a tradition of amphibious excellence had begun to germinate, crowned by the innovative and aggressive masterstroke at Veracruz in March 1847.[3] Despite this precedent set by David Conner and Winfield Scott, there was little institutional memory fifteen years later. American experience with amphibious operations during the Civil War produced mixed results until the final action at Fort Fisher in January 1865. Grant made good use of the Navy in maneuvering his army along the Tennessee, Cumberland, and Mississippi Rivers during the first two years of the war. These did not represent pure amphibious actions in the classic blue-water sense of the concept, yet they possessed many of the attributes of amphibious warfare, including the transport of troops, naval gunfire and logistical support, and close cooperation between Army and Navy commanders. In the era before the existence of joint doctrine, nothing required greater attention than cooperation between service leaders. No one in the Civil War did that better than Grant.[4] Unfortunately, other commanders did not always prove as skillful in applying this aspect of operational art.

The capture of New Orleans by amphibious forces early in the war established an important strategic advantage for the Union. Yet, despite operational success, cooperation between the Navy and Army elements had not been ideal. In April 1862 troops under Maj. Gen. Benjamin F. Butler arrived at New Orleans nearly one week after Flag Officer David G. Farragut initiated his naval attack on the city. This delay allowed Confederate officials to remove almost everything of military value, including an entire armament factory. Additionally, discord developed between Butler and Capt. David Dixon Porter, commanding a flotilla of mortar craft, regarding the role of each service in the conduct of tactical operations. This did not bode well for future relations between the two forceful commanders.[5] As a result, the New Orleans operation embodied both good and bad elements of amphibious warfare.

Union forces also conducted a series of amphibious operations along the Atlantic coastline early in the war. The 1862 operations of Flag Officer Louis M. Goldsborough and Brig. Gen. Ambrose Burnside on the Outer Banks of North Carolina proved highly successful and enhanced the reputation of Burnside, contributing to his subsequent promotion to command of the Army of the Potomac. But the lack of determined Confederate defense, coupled with superior Union firepower, created mistaken ideas about the ease of conducting amphibious operations, which led to costly errors during later landings.[6]

Throughout most of the war, the U.S. Navy and Army struggled with the problem of planning, organizing, and conducting effective amphibious operations against important enemy positions ashore. Such actions proved especially difficult when the entire support for an operation had to come from the sea.[7] Moving and sustaining large armies, such as George B. McClellan's on the York Peninsula in 1862 and Benjamin F. Butler's at Bermuda Hundred, Virginia, in 1864, contained important amphibious elements. From the perspective of power projection and sustainment, both of these operations proved highly successful, whatever failures occurred during subsequent operations ashore. But the real test of amphibious capability comes when fighting must occur against a determined defense during or shortly after the landing, as in the case of Fort Fisher.

The importance of Fort Fisher to the Confederacy lay in the role it played in protecting the port of Wilmington, North Carolina.[8] Throughout much of the war, the Army and Navy disagreed regarding what to do about Wilmington. Secretary of the Navy Gideon Welles consistently advocated a joint action against the city and its defenses, becoming more vigorous in his demands during 1864. Although eventually acceding to the operation, Secretary of War Edwin M. Stanton remained indifferent to it even until the first attack on the fort. When Grant was transferred to the east and given command of all Union armies in May 1864, he understood that capturing Fort Fisher would close Wilmington, the most important port through which foreign supplies reached Robert E. Lee's Army of Northern Virginia—with which the Union Army of the

Potomac was in nearly constant contact after May 1864. Additionally, the capture of Wilmington could possibly provide a base for supplying Sherman's army in his planned movement northward from Savannah to Virginia. After the failure of the first Union effort to capture the fort in December 1964, Grant became even more committed to the destruction of Fort Fisher and the capture of the port of Wilmington.[9]

By late 1864 only Wilmington and Charleston, South Carolina, remained open to blockade runners as Union forces had either captured or effectively blockaded all other Confederate ports. Of the two, Wilmington proved more important due to the difficulty it posed to blockading ships and its proximity to Lee's army. Located twenty miles up the Cape Fear River, Wilmington presented a particularly difficult challenge to the Union Navy. Its location made offshore bombardment of the city impossible, and the hydrography of the Cape Fear River estuary severely restricted avenues for the movement of ships attempting to attack upriver.[10] Access to the Cape Fear River consisted of two inlets separated by Smith Island and Frying Pan Shoals, which extended far out to sea. These conditions forced the blockading squadron to disperse its ships over a large sea space, thereby making it easier to penetrate.[11]

At the mouth of the river stood Fort Fisher, which was, in 1864, the most advanced fortification in the world. Indeed, many considered it the strongest earthwork ever built.[12] For more than two and a half years, Fort Fisher's energetic and brilliant commander, Col. William Lamb, labored to improve, strengthen, and expand its defenses. Working closely with his commanding officer, Maj. Gen. William Henry Chase Whiting, Lamb created a masterful defensive complex. As an observer during the Crimean War, Porter had visited formidable Fort Malakoff just after it surrendered to French and British forces. In his view, it did not compare to Fort Fisher in either size (the walls were nearly four thousand feet long overall) or strength.[13] As the naval commander during the attacks on Fort Fisher, Porter may have been inclined to overstate his case somewhat, but few would deny that the fort represented a strong defensive structure.

Fort Fisher lay on a peninsula jutting south from Wilmington in what looks like an elongated and inverted pyramid. Confederate Point—or Federal Point, depending on your persuasion—lies on the lower portion of the peninsula, which terminates at New Inlet, one of the two entrances to the Cape Fear River for deep-draft ships. The second entrance, Old

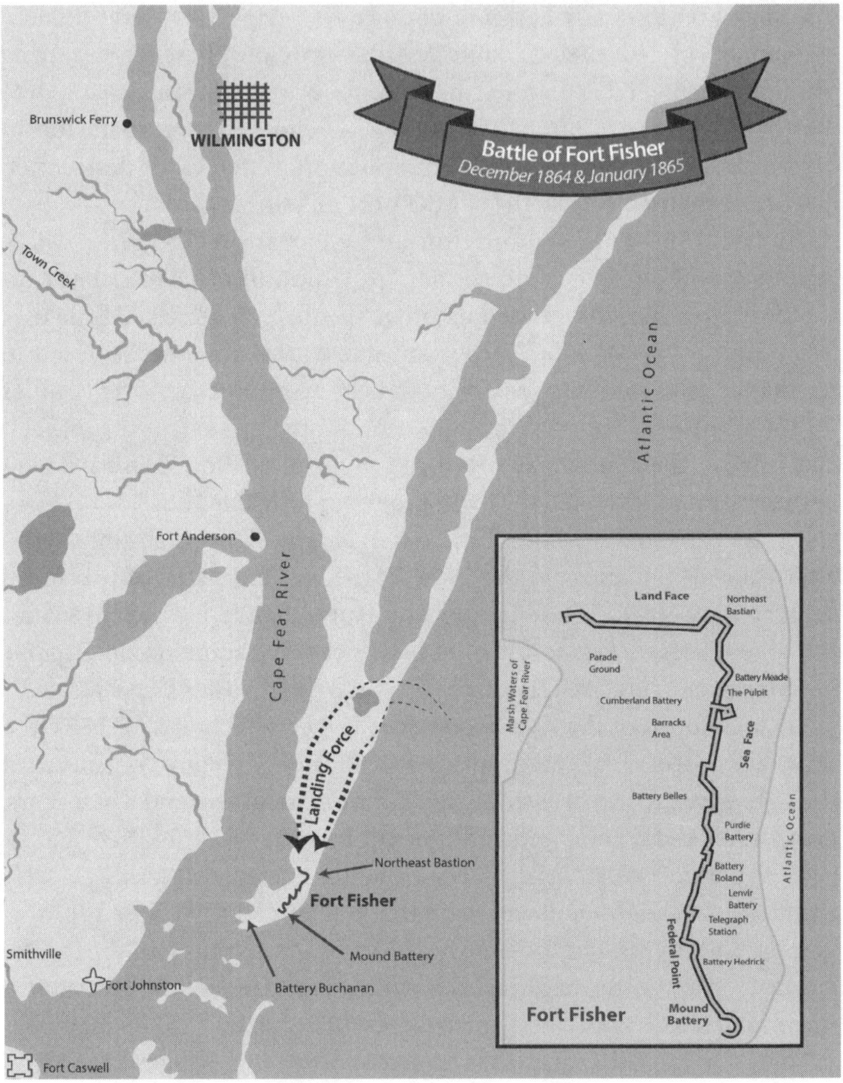

MAP 7. The Battle of Fort Fisher

Inlet, lay farther south, near Smith Island, and was defended by no fewer than four mutually supporting forts. Piloting through either inlet was slow and hazardous even under the best of conditions, and the guns of the various forts could either protect or destroy any ship attempting passage.[14] Fort Fisher dominated all traffic through New Inlet channel. But if Fort Fisher offered the advantage of strength and location to its Confederate defenders, these very qualities also offered Union strategists an operational center of gravity for taking Cape Fear and closing the port of Wilmington.[15] By neutralizing Fort Fisher, Union forces could control the entire region, just as David Farragut's capture of Forts Powell, Morgan, and Mobile blocked access by blockade runners into Mobile Bay.

The fort's design reflected the tactical and engineering skills of Whiting and Lamb. Fort Fisher was like a great numeral "7," with the horizontal top line stretching roughly from west to east about a thousand feet across the peninsula, and the longer vertical stem extending roughly north to south, parallel to the coastline for some three thousand feet. The horizontal, west–east portion faced north and protected the fort from land attack down the peninsula. Any force large enough to threaten the fortress had to deploy in the area to the north and assault that rampart, a formidable defensive challenge to Union commanders. Direct assault against the ocean-facing wall offered small prospect for success, given the weapons and equipment available to attacking forces of that era. An attack from the rear required passage through New Inlet, an unlikely avenue since the fort's guns could destroy the shipping before a landing force could get ashore.[16]

In early December 1864 Grant decided, in conjunction with naval leaders in Washington, to send a joint expedition to capture Fort Fisher. He assigned Maj. Gen. Godfrey Weitzel to lead the assault force but issued his orders through Major General Butler, who commanded the Department of Virginia and North Carolina as well as the Army of the James. Exercising command discretion, Butler chose to join the expedition off the coast of Fort Fisher and personally take charge of the operation. David Dixon Porter commanded the North Atlantic Blockading Squadron, with responsibility for actions at sea and against the Confederate littoral north of Cape Fear. It did not help subsequent operations that Porter and Butler still nursed grievances against each other from the time they served together in New Orleans.[17]

The overall plan of attack agreed upon by Grant and Porter involved moving 6,500 soldiers from Bermuda Hundred in Virginia to a rendezvous point off the North Carolina coast within striking distance of Fort Fisher. The force would wait in readiness until Porter exploded a powder boat near the fort and conducted extensive naval bombardment to destroy the fort's guns and defensive structures. When the defenders appeared sufficiently weakened, the landing force would go ashore and assault Fort Fisher from the north.[18]

The concept of operations seems sound, but the detailed planning proved utterly deficient. For example, detonation of the powder boat, naval "preparatory fires" (in modern parlance), and the infantry assault against the fortress required synchronized timing and fluid execution, creating shock for the defenders and momentum in the offensive. Instead, the efforts occurred disjointedly and spasmodically, allowing the defenders to concentrate their full attention on each in turn. The powder boat detonated at approximately 0200 on the morning of 24 December, with absolutely no effect on the troops, defenses, or subsequent battle. Throughout the day of 24 December, Porter's fleet conducted a slow bombardment of Fort Fisher, inflicting only minor damage on its structure and guns. The defenders spent much time in protective "bombproofs," emerging to serve their guns only when it appeared that the Union warships might up anchor and attempt to enter the river or when the naval gunfire ceased and Union troops began to press their attack.[19]

On Sunday, 25 December, while Porter resumed the naval bombardment, the landing force of some three thousand men went ashore about three miles north of the fort, out of range of its guns. Weitzel, the commander on the scene, pushed his force down the peninsula, capturing several small outposts along the way and scouting the approaches to Fort Fisher itself. In an act of courage and bravado, Lt. William H. Walling of the 142nd New York Infantry actually ascended the fort's parapet and returned with a Confederate flag knocked down by naval gunfire. Afterward Weitzel and Grant made much of this incident, along with the capture of a dispatch rider, neither of which was of real military significance.[20] Weitzel halted and deployed his main force about eight hundred yards from the base of Fort Fisher to evaluate the situation. An advance force of about five hundred skirmishers had already probed the fort's north-facing defenses only to be driven back by Confederate canister and musket fire.[21]

Weitzel was appalled by what he observed. Despite a later tendency to overstate the minor accomplishments of his attacking force against Confederate outposts and to understate the significance of the repulse of his skirmishers, Weitzel at the time considered Fort Fisher's north wall to pose a formidable challenge. Attacking it may have been the only viable option, but that did not make the task any more palatable. Any assault force had to first pass through an electrically detonated minefield, engage a line of infantrymen positioned behind the log-and-earthen palisade, and finally storm a twenty-three-foot rampart holding twenty-four guns and mortars capable of firing shot, shell, grape, and canister. The wall terminated at the west end adjacent to a slough covered by fire from field artillery, and on the east at the formidable Northeast Bastion, which mounted two 8-inch guns. Weitzel also noted that, despite the apparent accuracy of the naval gunfire, it had inflicted little damage to the guns or structure of the fort.[22]

The stout defenses reminded Weitzel of Fort Jackson (south of New Orleans in April 1862), Vicksburg (on the Mississippi, besieged May–June 1863), and Charleston (July 1863), where heavy bombardment had failed to destroy enemy defenses. His recollection of two bloody and failed assaults of 10 July 1863 on Battery Wagner in Charleston Harbor, "which were made under four times more favorable circumstances than those under which we were placed," weighed heavily on him. Weitzel took a boat to the Army transport *Chamberlain* to discuss the situation with Butler. He reported that it was his opinion—and that of his senior officers—that an assault under the present circumstances would be "butchery." Butler concurred, conjuring up, from Weitzel's vivid description of conditions, his own thoughts of Battery Wagner as well as Port Hudson, Louisiana, on the Mississippi (May–July 1863). After further conversation, Butler ordered the landing force to disengage and reembark on its ships.[23]

Porter disagreed with the decision to call off the assault on Fort Fisher and attempted to persuade Butler to reconsider. He explained that his ships had been bombarding at only a slow rate of fire; rapid firing, he felt confident, would suppress the fort's defenders until the assault force reached within twenty yards of the ramparts. He further informed Butler that he had dispatched his largest vessels to Beaufort, North Carolina, to fill up with ammunition in order to provide sustained support should Butler and Weitzel agree to resume the attack. Whether because of personal animosity or professional distrust, Butler rejected Porter's assessment. By 27 December all troops had left the beach, after which Butler's transports returned to Hampton Roads and Porter's fleet to Beaufort.[24]

On 28 December, after receiving Butler's preliminary after-action report, Grant telegraphed President Lincoln, stating that the expedition had "proven to be a gross and culpable failure." "Culpable" would prove to be the operative word. On 7 January 1865 Grant forwarded Butler's after-action report to Stanton, stating in his endorsement that he never intended for Butler to accompany the expedition and that his orders "contemplated no withdrawal, or no failure after a landing was made." It is clear from these two communications that Grant believed Butler had disregarded his orders and must assume responsibility for the failure at Fort Fisher. It is also clear that Grant's primary objection concerned the withdrawal of troops from the beach rather than the decision not to attack. Grant believed that simply establishing the landing force ashore constituted success because a subsequent siege would have been sufficient to guarantee ultimate victory.[25] Weitzel had recommended against launching an assault on the fort but did not become associated with the decision to evacuate the beachhead. Because of this and his prestige within the Army, he escaped the full force of Grant's wrath. Yet Weitzel had missed his opportunity and would have no role in future operations against Fort Fisher.

Even the men Butler and Weitzel had landed—3,000 of the 6,500 available—represented a strong and threatening presence ashore. Fort Fisher's garrison consisted of roughly 1,000 men including infantrymen, gunners, and engineers. The formidableness of the defenses would cause pause to any prudent commander but did not—as Grant pointed out—dictate evacuation of the beachhead. Nor did the developing weather conditions require evacuation, as Butler later contended, and Porter emphatically rejected. What better explains Butler's decision to withdraw his force was the arrival of Maj. Gen. Robert F. Hoke's division, dispatched from the Army of Northern Virginia by Lee.[26]

As Weitzel's troops came ashore north of Fort Fisher, the advance elements of Hoke's division began arriving through Wilmington and deployed to a position known as Sugar Loaf, six miles north of the fort. Commanded by Brig. Gen. William Kirkland, the Confederates initially engaged the lead brigade of the Union amphibious force under Brev. Brig. Gen. Newton Martin Curtis. Seeing himself outnumbered and not certain when the rest of his division would arrive, Kirkland pulled back. As Weitzel and Curtis began moving their troops south toward Fort Fisher, Kirkland established a cross-peninsula line north of the landing site and awaited reinforcements. Weitzel had no idea of Kirkland's strength, but interrogation of prisoners caused him to inflate it in his mind.[27] Thus, he probably feared being trapped between the two Confederate forces and decided to withdraw before they attacked.

In fact, the Confederates were weak both north and south of Weitzel. Braxton Bragg, the new commander of the Department of North Carolina, had pulled forces out of the Wilmington–Cape Fear area, including garrison troops belonging to Fort Fisher. Whiting and Lamb became alarmed, considering the fort dangerously undermanned. They also deplored Bragg's lack of urgency about the situation, which caused them to doubt his competence. Confederate weakness in the Wilmington area had prompted Lee to send Hoke's division to stiffen the defenses. Whiting and Lamb considered these reinforcements essential to the defense of their position. Despite Kirkland's timely arrival, the bulk of Hoke's division did not arrive until after Weitzel and Butler had evacuated their lodgment ashore.[28]

Union commanders did not appreciate their advantageous position on 25 December 1864 when they decided to end the operation. Similarly, neither Kirkland nor Bragg realized the vulnerability of Weitzel's force once it began to withdraw. Whiting severely criticized Bragg's failure to send Kirkland against the Union forces still ashore on 26 December. To Whiting and Lamb, the most important lesson from the first battle at Fort Fisher involved the need to coordinate a total military effort throughout the Wilmington–Cape Fear area. Unfortunately for the South, Bragg did not appear to understand the military situation and its impact on Fort Fisher. In fact, Whiting believed Bragg demonstrated incompetence throughout both battles for Fort Fisher and deserved the utmost censure. Nonetheless, Confederates had won a victory in December. In the words of Lamb, "December 27, the foiled and frightened enemy left our shores."[29]

The Union forces did not believe they had been defeated, but they could hardly deny they had failed. Joint planning existed only on a superfluous level, and independent action became commonplace during the operation, demonstrating the lack of coordination between the Army and Navy. Additionally, it is fair to state that both Butler and Weitzel exhibited tentativeness, if not outright timidity. Of course, they had no accurate information about true strength of the fort's garrison or of Hoke's division to their north.

At the same time, Porter's support of Butler and Weitzel had been erratic at best. Porter's coordination with the army in the explosion of the powder boat and the preinvasion bombardment had been abysmal.[30] Porter not only exploded the powder boat too early and without notifying army leaders, but he had also failed to establish any means of communicating with forces ashore to direct or evaluate the effectiveness of his gunnery. Additionally, his planning with respect to ammunition and fuel proved equally deficient. Butler may have known that Porter's warships had provided effective fire support during the probe against Fort Fisher's north wall on 25 December but lacked faith in Porter's commitment that he would provide continuous fire support should the army resume the attack.[31] Whatever the reason, Butler decided to abandon the operation and withdrew his forces. In general, both commanders failed in their obligation to ensure good integration of effort. They acted like separate commanders merely informing each other of their actions rather than as members of a cohesive and synergetic team.

Both Porter and Grant contended that the attack lacked vigor and commitment. Grant's disappointment at the failure of the operation is understandable, but his reaction appears somewhat disingenuous. Although he contended that he "contemplated no withdrawal or no failure after a landing was made," his initiating order to Butler had been ambiguous in that respect. It clearly states the objectives of the expedition but concluded, "Should the troops under General Weitzel fail to affect a landing at, or near Fort Fisher they will be returned to the army operating against Richmond without delay."[32] No doubt this sentence caused Butler to believe he had the discretion to abandon the lodgment ashore and return to Virginia. Since

Weitzel never landed more than half of his troops, he could rationalize that the landing had never been effected.

The only positive outcome of the first attack against Fort Fisher was that Union leaders learned from the failure. Despite their efforts to make Butler the scapegoat, both Grant and Porter realized that their own leadership needed improvement. Porter and Butler had held several meetings in early December but had conducted no real joint planning and did not communicate on an effective level. Grant had to recognize that his orders to Butler failed to clearly state his intentions and expectations.[33] Although it is possible to interpret Grant's directive as definitive, it did not appear so to Butler and Weitzel under the stress of combat. Generals like William T. Sherman or Philip H. Sheridan would probably have discerned Grant's intention better than did Butler or Weitzel. When Grant issued orders for the second attack on Fort Fisher, he made his expectations perfectly clear to everyone and required most emphatically close coordination between the Army and Navy.[34]

Grant had wanted to remove Butler from command for some time but had been prevented from doing so by political considerations—Butler enjoyed political support from Massachusetts—prior to the presidential election of 1864. After Lincoln's reelection, he removed Butler from command of the Department of North Carolina and Virginia and the Army of the James, and he replaced Godfrey Weitzel with Maj. Gen. Alfred H. Terry as commander of the Fort Fisher Expeditionary Corps.

The final lesson from the failure at Fort Fisher involved the problem of "operational security." The intention to capture Fort Fisher and close Wilmington Harbor in December 1864 had become general knowledge in both armies. Even worse, Confederate spies at Hampton Roads had reported specific intelligence about ship and troop movements to Lee, permitting him to send Hoke's division to interpose. Grant intended to keep the plans secret for the second attempt in January 1865. Only individuals with an absolute need to know would receive advance information about the mission. Even Terry, his new commander, was instructed to wait until he put to sea to open the orders explaining his mission and destination. Rightly perceiving that disinformation could also be helpful, Grant let the suggestion leak that Terry and his force had embarked to join Sherman's army in Savannah, thus providing a plausible explanation for all the naval activity.[35]

When the fleet assembled off Beaufort on 8 January 1865, Terry met with Porter to finalize plans for the amphibious operation. Porter respected Terry far more than he had Butler, and the two commanders developed a strong working relationship, which created the synergy so lacking in the first expedition.[36] After the planning sessions, they sailed through heavy weather toward Cape Fear, arriving off Confederate Point after dark on 12 January, too late to attempt a landing. At 0800 the next morning, Porter's ships began a bombardment of Fort Fisher, and landing operations commenced about 0830. By 1400 that afternoon, Porter and Terry had eight thousand men ashore—again north of the fort—with twelve day's provisions and all their equipment.[37]

Terry's advance element threw out pickets, who engaged Confederate scouts and captured a few prisoners. From these Terry learned that Hoke's division had not moved south to oppose Sherman's army (which had just seized Savannah, Georgia, and begun to move northward), as Union intelligence had previously indicated. Terry now had to concern himself with a strong force to the north as he moved south against Fort Fisher. He had planned a defensive line across the peninsula to protect his rear, but new information added urgency to that precaution and increased the size of the force needed.[38] Finding the best place to establish the line became more difficult than expected. Darkness set in before Terry could find ideal terrain, and a lake on the planning map—upon which he intended to anchor his defenses—proved to be a dried-up sand pit, providing no protection at all. In the end, Terry felt compelled to commit over half of his force to protect his rear.[39]

By 0800 14 January, Terry's men had constructed a strong breastwork across the peninsula, which his troops continued to improve upon by emplacing field artillery, creating interlocking fields of fire, and establishing naval gunfire "kill zones." He then conducted a reconnaissance of the fort in conjunction with his engineer officer, Col. Cyrus Comstock, and his assault force commander—the same brevet brigadier general who had led the attack in December—Martin Curtis. That evening he returned to Porter's flagship, reported his afternoon observations to the admiral, and recommended that they attack Fort Fisher immediately. Porter agreed, and the commanders began planning for operations to begin the next day, 15 January.[40] The attack would begin with a massive naval bombardment that would continue until the moment of assault. The assault would involve a two-pronged effort with army units on the right, attacking the western flank of the north-facing wall, and a detachment of sailors and Marines on the left, simultaneously attacking the Northeast Bastion. Terry assigned an army signal team to serve on board Porter's flagship so they could maintain communications throughout the battle.[41]

Terry had task organized his command into a provisional corps, which contained greater combat power than Weitzel's force of the previous month. In addition to Brig. Gen. Adelbert Ames' Second Division—which included Curtis' 1st Brigade—and Brig. Gen. Charles J. Paine's Third Division (consisting of "colored" troops), both of which had been with Weitzel in December, Terry had an additional brigade under Col. Joseph C. Abbott and a naval brigade of sailors and Marines under Lt. Cdr. K. Randolph Breese. The naval brigade, specially created by Porter for the attack, did not formally belong to Terry's command but was made available for his use. It consisted of 1,600 sailors and 400 Marines armed with cutlasses, revolvers, carbines, and Sharps rifles.[42] Porter's outstanding task organization of his squadrons on the sea space supporting the landing and subsequent operations ashore proved a model of effectiveness. The highly detailed fire support plan ensured that the right ships were at the right place at the right time with the right ordnance throughout the operation.[43]

At approximately 0900 15 January, most of Porter's North Atlantic Squadron began moving into position to bombard Fort Fisher. One naval division remained in position to support Terry's defensive line north of the fort. By 1100 the ships had opened fire, initiating a furious duel with the guns of Fort Fisher. The ground attack had been set at 1400, but not all of Terry's forces were in place by then. Thus, the warships continued firing on the fort until approximately 1500, when Terry signaled the fleet to shift to new targets and launched his two-pronged assault against the Confederate's northern line of defense.[44]

Furious fighting developed on both flanks over the next several hours as Terry ordered the advance of one unit after another in an attempt to break through the fort's outer defenses. Despite stiff resistance, Terry made progress on the Confederate left, due in part to the defenders' having mistaken the naval brigade at the other end of the line for the main Union effort and concentrated their combat power at that point.

Despite the courageous attack by Breese's bluejackets and Marines, confusion in the assault formation exposed it to devastating fire from the ramparts and ultimately forced the Union attackers to withdraw.[45] Breese believed that the failure of his attack resulted from organizational problems and lack of cohesiveness within his naval brigade. His force consisted of small squads from every ship in the fleet, thrown together to form a combat unit. They had no training as an integrated unit, and the first time they worked together involved storming the revetments of one of the strongest forts in the world. But Breese had no need to apologize or rationalize because his attack provided the diversion that allowed Terry to establish a lodgment at the other end of the Confederate line.[46]

As Breese and his brigade struggled with organizational problems and devastating fire on the Union left, Terry's brigades made gradual progress on the right. Having fed in all three brigades of Ames' division, Terry sent in an additional brigade and regiment drawn from his northern defensive line. Reinforced, Terry pressed the attack and entered the fort around 1800, although resistance continued well into the night.[47] Fearing an attack from Hoke, Terry moved Breese's spent naval brigade into the defensive line to replace the troops he had withdrawn. By 2200, the Union Army had taken Fort Fisher, having killed or captured all its defenders. Whiting and Lamb, both seriously wounded, became prisoners of war when the fighting finally ended at Battery Buchanan, roughly one mile from Fort Fisher proper.[48]

By any standard, the second attack against Fort Fisher stands as a superb example of naval competence, military efficiency, combat effectiveness, and the value of joint operations. But, like all great victories, the results at Fort Fisher reflect both competence in the victor and deficiencies in the defeated. Robert Hoke's division, sent to protect Fort Fisher and keep Wilmington open, numbered six thousand effectives.[49] Only Kirkland's lead brigade arrived during the first attack in December, and it did very little to oppose that landing, aside from the psychological pressure on Weitzel and Butler that its presence created. As it turned out, that presence, coupled with the strength of Fort Fisher's north wall, proved sufficient. In January 1865 Hoke's entire division was present and available for action, yet it proved of little value. The division remained in defensive positions well north of the fighting, posing a threat to Terry's force but taking no action against it. The most charitable view is that Hoke's proximity required Terry to maintain a strong defensive line in his rear, manned by over half of his troops. Yet even that had no impact on the outcome of the battle. Hoke and his division served as little more than spectators.

In Whiting's view, Fort Fisher fell to the Union for two principal reasons. First and most important, he believed Bragg's generalship during the battle to have been deficient. Bragg had first weakened the defenses of the area and then failed to use the replacements provided by Lee to good effect. Whiting's second reason involved the naval bombardment on 14–15 January, which he believed to have been the most powerful of the war. If Whiting thought the bombardment in December "diffused and scattered," the second attack he considered ferocious and tenacious. The shelling destroyed all the guns on the north wall, swept away the palisade, and plowed the minefield cutting most of the detonating wires. Nevertheless, Whiting believed the Confederate defenders could have held out if they had been supported by Bragg. Lamb believed that a fresh brigade could retake the fort immediately after it fell to the Union, but he had none in position. In Whiting's evaluation, ultimately the defeat at Fort Fisher resulted from Bragg's failure to order Hoke's division to attack Union forces while they were engaged at the fort.[50]

Whatever Hoke's division might have accomplished, the amphibious lessons are apparent. The most important prerequisite for an amphibious success is the effective integration between the Navy and landing force.[51] This element was not entirely missing in the first attack, as exhibited by the fire support provided during the probe of the north wall on 25 December. But compared to the overwhelming power of the bombardment on 15 January coupled with the integration of effort achieved by Porter and Terry throughout the second attack, it seems almost feeble. The army signal teams on board Porter's flagship in January illustrate the extent to which Terry went in order to coordinate their efforts. The close and continuous planning by Porter and Terry throughout the operation contrasts with the minimal communications in December. The potential existed for victory or defeat during both attacks on Fort Fisher. Integration of effort between the Army and Navy is an important reason why the first effort failed and the second one succeeded.[52]

The rapid buildup of combat power from sea to shore provides another key to success in landing operations. In the first attack, Butler and Weitzel took an almost leisurely approach to landing their force. They never got more than half their troops ashore, and even that element could not sustain itself beyond a few days. In contrast, Terry and Porter landed eight thousand troops in about five hours with all their equipment and supplies to last for twelve days. This illustrates the difference between a tentative effort and a determined commitment. Terry also task organized his force—including use of the naval brigade—in such a manner as to support his operations ashore with flexibility and fluidity.[53] He deployed his task-organized units in a manner that allowed reinforcement of his tactical evolutions without creating undue vulnerability elsewhere. Essentially, Terry deployed one element to establish a defensive line to protect the operations from attack from the north and two assault elements to simultaneous attack the Confederate left and right flanks. The defensive force served the additional function of tactical reserve and Terry used them as such during the fighting. There is no evidence that Butler or Weitzel gave any thought to task organization during the first attack.

Related to integration between naval and landing force is the concept of unity of effort and operational coherence.[54] Simply stated, this goes beyond integration of effort to include a unified approach at all levels coupled with a single-minded commitment to mission accomplishment. This unity and coherence emerged in the second attack in great part due to the failure of the first. Determined not to experience another setback, the secretaries of War and the Navy, Admiral Porter, and General Grant and General Terry realized they had to produce a common, unified effort and conduct a coherent operation. This resulted in a unity of effort at the highest levels that flowed down through all ranks and permeated the entire operation—perhaps more completely than any other episode of the Civil War. Certainly, it also stands in stark contrast to the disunity and disjointedness among the defenders. The concept of unity of effort and operational coherence appeared not to have entered into the thinking of the Confederate leadership during the struggle over the Wilmington–Cape Fear area.[55]

Despite the superb example of the Veracruz landing, naval and military commanders of the American Civil War had no doctrine or specially trained officers to plan or execute amphibious operations. Neither did they have a systematic way to capture, analyze, and document lessons from their own joint actions, such as those at Fort Fisher. As a result, the lessons of Veracruz were not recorded for use in the Civil War, and the lessons of Fort Fisher were not formally preserved for use during the next major conflict—the Spanish-American War of 1898. Nonetheless, it remains apparent that some institutional memory survived from one war to another. Of the four major landings undertaken by American forces in 1898, all proved successful even if not models of efficiency.[56] The commanders associated with these amphibious operations—George Dewey and William T. Sampson of the Navy; Nelson A. Miles, William R. Shafter, and Wesley Merritt of the Army; and Robert W. Huntington of the Marines—all had combat experience during the Civil War. In every case, the planners during 1898 ensured that the landings would be unopposed at the water's edge and that sufficient naval gunfire would support subsequent operations ashore.

Interestingly, the most outstanding example of interservice cooperation in both planning and support during the Spanish-American War occurred between Dewey and Merritt during complex amphibious actions in the Manila-Cavite area in the Philippines. Dewey served on the *Colorado* under Porter during the fight for Fort Fisher, bringing firsthand experience forward to America's next war. In comparison, the Daiquirí landings near Santiago, Cuba, lacked sound doctrine or officers with direct amphibious experience and appeared amateurish by comparison. Fortunately, the planning of Sampson and Shafter proved sufficient to permit establishment of the force ashore without enemy resistance.[57]

Fort Fisher, Veracruz, and, to a lesser extent, the Spanish-American War contributed to the U.S. amphibious tradition and historical record in ways useful to the future. They provided twentieth-century military and naval thinkers with solid examples on which to develop their theories, doctrine, and war plans. By then a melding of military history with the diligence of professional officers ensured that the amphibious experiences of the nineteenth century, and especially the example of Fort Fisher, would be available for future commanders. Today, even in a substantially changed operational environment, many of its lessons remain valid and instructive.

Postcript

Past and Future

For many Americans, the concept of amphibious warfare derives from the World War II model where landing forces assaulted foreign shores against determined resistance. These actions resulted in very high casualties yet proved uniformly successful for American operations. They involved isolating and preparing the amphibious objective area with naval and air power, then aggressively introducing landing forces to assault the defensive positions. Naval task forces not only inserted the amphibious troops but also sustained them with naval gunfire, tactical aircraft, and logistical support once ashore. This resulted in battles characterized by very high levels of violence and destruction. The circumstance of geography coupled with the weapons and equipment available at that time dictated this type of warfare. To make incremental progress in the war effort, military and naval forces of the United States needed to attack Pacific islands held by Japanese forces, and conduct forced entry on the European continent against beaches defended by the German army. Weapons such as attack aircraft and precision naval gunfire coupled with newly designed amphibious ships, landing craft, and tracked vehicles made these attacks possible. This type of amphibious warfare gave rise to the theory, principles, and doctrine that influenced officers, defense analysts, and historians throughout much of the twentieth century.

During the eighteenth and nineteenth centuries, no such equipment or weapons existed for assaulting defended beaches. Commanders attempted to land their forces in areas where the resistance would be light or nonexistent as illustrated in the cases of this study. Even at Veracruz and Fort Fisher—the two most sophisticated landings of the nineteenth century—the assault force did not have to fight its way ashore.

The initiative and maneuverability inherent in naval forces permitted the establishment of combat power ashore before having to engage the enemy. The naval echelon could deliver forces to the point of attack faster than land-based defenders could react. In cases where landing forces experienced opposition on the beach, it usually consisted of light resistance that only harassed and delayed the attack. The action at Pell's Point, New York, during the Revolutionary War clearly demonstrates this concept.

In cases where defenders could determine the landing site in time to prepare defenses at the water's edge, they often chose not to do so for fear of naval firepower. The defense of Baltimore provides an example where the entire concept of defense focused on avoiding naval gunfire. The decision to engage British major general Robert Ross' army at Long Log Lane rather than North Point coupled with the defenses created at Fort McHenry and Lazaretto Point all contributed to the goal of preventing Vice Adm. Sir Alexander Cochrane's naval guns from supporting British operations ashore. Typically in this era, both the attacking force and the defenders preferred to avoid direct engagement at the point of amphibious assault. The landing force did not want to face prepared defenses before it could concentrate combat power ashore, and the defenders did not want to face naval gunfire. Ironically, the weapons and equipment available in early America tended to prevent frontal amphibious battles, whereas modern weapons and equipment in the twentieth century led to such assaults. In the amphibious combat of World War II, both sides believed their superior weapons, equipment, and fighting spirit could destroy the enemy.

During the second half of the twentieth century—after the Korean War—a change in amphibious combat emerged. With the advent of larger and more agile amphibious ships, advanced landing craft, and helicopters, amphibious options expanded greatly. Harkening back to the amphibious warfare of early America, doctrine developed that called for unopposed insertions at landing sites where enemy forces were not concentrated. While retaining the ability to conduct forced entry against defended beaches, if required, American commanders no longer expected to conduct such operation. Modern technology and innovation has permitted amphibious warfare to progress forward into the past.

Although the modern concept of amphibious operations may compare with the earlier period, the actual conduct of combat is not the same. The modern Marine Corps—the world's preeminent amphibious force—typically conducts a landing with one element advancing in helicopters and two across the surface of the water in amphibious assault vehicles. When possible, commanders seek to launch amphibious attacks from over the horizon and support them with fixed-wing aircraft (AV8B Harriers now, and F-35B Lightening IIs in the future) based on the same amphibious ships that launch the attack. The advent of the air-cushioned landing craft (the LCAC) has also contributed to the flexibility of a modern landing operation by permitting heavy weapons—such as tanks and vehicle mounted weapon systems—and equipment to be delivered rapidly and with maneuverability. This newer approach to amphibious warfare focuses American strength against enemy weakness and depends greatly on the element of surprise.[1]

Whereas the equipment and weapons of the World War II era forced amphibious attacks into frontal assaults, subsequent advancements permit a return to the indirect approach, causing fewer casualties and inflicting less collateral damage. The latest generation of weapons and equipment are leveraged in this modern approach to amphibious warfare, permitting a more rapid buildup of combat power ashore while retaining the element of surprise. Such items as the V-22 Osprey tiltrotor aircraft (which can function as both an airplane and helicopter) along with advanced amphibious assault vehicles (currently under development as the Amphibious Combat Vehicle Program) provide greater speed of closure, choice of a wider range of landing sites, more flexibility for task-organizing, and greater sustainability once ashore. The ability to launch from over the horizon and rapidly close on the military objective is of particular importance in the current era, where potential adversaries are developing anti-access/area-denial capabilities along their littorals.[2] As stated in the commandant of the Marine Corps' planning guidance, "In partnership with the Navy, we will also continue to work to field high-speed, long-range, high-capacity systems of connectors and craft that are critical for amphibious operations and Joint Forcible Entry Operations. The capabilities we field will support our Ship to Objective Maneuver and Operational Maneuver from the Sea and will be fully incorporated into our service exercises and experimental program."[3]

A significant change that occurred in the post–World War II era is the prominence of the U.S. Marine Corps. During the amphibious warfare of early America, Marines played a relatively small role due to their size and the ambiguity of their mission. Even so, they created the roots of a tradition that allowed the Corps to grow into the world's premier amphibious force. Throughout the period of early America, Marines participated in exclusively naval amphibious operations as well as those involving Army forces. In the case of naval landing parties, Marines provided the core combat element, although often contributing fewer men than the Navy contingent. When participating with Army landings—usually large-scale operations—Marines often provided advance forces that secured initial lodgments for the main landing force, conducted amphibious reconnaissance, and undertook other special and adjunct operations ashore. The amphibious campaign for the conquest of California provides numerous examples of this, especially the landings at San Pedro and San Diego.

Over time the role of the Marine Corps changed and evolved into the force that exists today. One of the key reasons for that growth and maturation involves the important activities conducted by key officers in the 1920s and 1930s. During that era, senior officers of military forces throughout the world believed amphibious warfare had no important place in serious military planning due to the disastrous 1915 Gallipoli operation of World War I. But a small group of Marine officers thought otherwise and worked to develop the theory, concepts, doctrine, and equipment that proved so critical to the amphibious success of all services during World War II.[4] This intellectual undertaking, coupled with operational success in actual warfighting, established the Marine Corps as the lead service for amphibious warfare, a mission formally assigned in the National Security Act of 1947, which has grown even stronger since.[5] Despite a tendency since the 1980s to focus on the concept of expeditionary warfare, amphibious capability remains the mainstay of the Marine Corps and constitutes its unique contribution to the nation. The U.S. Marine Corps of the twenty-first century is the true inheritor of these roots of tradition established in early America.

The concepts presented in this study—the levels of war; the characteristics of amphibious warfare; the principles of war, expeditionary warfare, and operational maneuver from the sea—were structured into doctrine subsequent to the period of early America. But the ideas they embody are timeless and provide the historian and analyst a basis for evaluating military and naval events from any period. Although crafted to address the planning and educational requirements of the present era, there are few thoughts within these documents that military leaders from the Revolution up to our own time would not recognize. They continue to serve as excellent tools for both the professional officer and the analytical historian.

As the lines between traditional warfare and modern insurgencies, terrorism, and international criminal activity blur or combine into hybrid forms of conflict, we find much of the resulting chaos residing in the world's littorals.[6] The need for amphibious expeditionary forces in support of national objectives remains high and is increasing. In the words of Gen. James E. Amos, 35th commandant of the Marine Corps, "The future evolving and complex security environment will only increase the demands on the Marine Corps. The law requires and our heritage demands that we maintain a force that is naval in character and capable of conducting amphibious operations."[7]

Notes

AUTHOR'S NOTE ON THE HISTORY OF AMPHIBIOUS WARFARE

1. Robert B. Strassler, *The Landmark Thucydides: A Comprehensive Guide to the Peloponnesian War* (New York: Free Press, 1996), 242–46.
2. Ibid., 361–481.
3. John Keegan, *The Mask of Command* (New York: Viking Penguin, 1987), 75; N. G. L. Hammond, *A History of Greece to 322 B.C.* (Oxford: Clarendon Press, 1991), 611–13.
4. Julius Caesar, *The Conquest of Gaul* (London: Penguin, 1982), 97–115; Thomas More Molyneux, *Conjunct Expeditions: or Expeditions by the FLEET and ARMY, with a Commentary on a Littoral WAR* (London: R. and J. Dodsley in Pall-mall, 1759), 4–5.
5. Alfred Vagts, *Landing Operations: Strategy, Psychology, Tactics, Politics, from Antiquity to 1945* (Harrisburg, Pa.: Military Service Publishing, 1946), 122–49; and Winston S. Churchill, *The Birth of Britain,* vol. 1 of *A History of the English-Speaking People* (New York: Dodd, Mead, 1964), viii–xx.
6. For example, the 1689–96 War of the League of Augsburg became King William's War in America; the 1702–13 War of the Spanish Succession became Queen Anne's War; the 1740–48 War of Austrian Succession became King George's War; and Americans knew the Seven Years War fought between 1756 and 1763 as the French and Indian War. See Fred Anderson, *Crucible of War: The Seven Years' War and the Fate of Empire in British North America, 1754–1766* (New York: Knopf, 2000), xv, 11–12.
7. Molyneux, *Conjunct Expeditions.*
8. Historians and geographers cannot agree on how to spell Louisbourg, as it is often spelled Louisburg. It is possible to find either

spelling in both official and unofficial publications, and one can even find it occasionally spelled Louisburgh.

9. George A. Rawlyk, *Yankees at Louisbourg: The Story of the First Siege, 1745* (Englishtown, Nova Scotia: Breton Books, 1999), 44–45, 136; and Vagts, *Landing Operations,* 284–85.
10. Richard A. Brayall, *"To the Uttermost of My Power": The Life and Times of Sir William Pepperrell, 1696–1759* (Westminster, Md.: Heritage Books, 2008), 99–101; Rawlyk, *Yankees at Louisbourg,* 61–62; and Vagts, *Landing Operations,* 285–86.
11. Julian Gwyn, *An Admiral for America: Sir Peter Warren, Vice Admiral of the Red, 1703–1752* (Gainesville: University Press of Florida, 2004), 75–99; Brayall, *"To the Uttermost of My Power,"* 103–27; and Vagts, *Landing Operations,* 286–87.
12. Brayall, *"To the Uttermost of My Power,"* 103, 109, 131, 133–134; Vagts, *Landing Operations,* 286; and Gwyn, *An Admiral for America,* 91–102.
13. John Ferling, *Struggle for a Continent: The Wars of Early America* (Arlington Heights, Il.: Harlan Davidson, 1993), 139; and Vagts, *Landing Operations,* 487.
14. Stephen Brumwell, *Paths of Glory: The Life and Death of General James Wolfe* (Montreal: McGill-Queens University Press, 2006), 63–65.
15. Rawlyk, *Yankees at Louisbourg,* 158–59.
16. John Grenier, *The Far Reaches of Empire: War in Nova Scotia, 1710–1760* (Norman: University of Oklahoma Press, 2008), 138.
17. Winston S. Churchill, *The Age of Revolution,* vol. 3 of *A History of the English-Speaking People* (New York: Dodd, Mead, 1964), 148–56; and Ferling, *Struggle for a Continent,* 143–46.
18. Anderson, *Crucible of War,* 116–22, 150–57, 185–98; and Ferling, *Struggle for a Continent,* 56–60, 156–69.
19. Anderson, *Crucible of War,* 215–17; Churchill, *The Age of Revolution,* 152–54, 148–50; and Ferling, *Struggle for a Continent,* 170–72.
20. Ferling, *Struggle for a Continent,* 173–74.
21. Francis Parkman, *Montcalm and Wolfe* (New York: Atheneum, 1984), 326–33; Anderson, *Crucible of War,* 200–209, 232–33; Vagts, *Landing Operations,* 288–89; and Brumwell, *Paths of Glory,* 139–45.

22. Julian S. Corbett, *England and the Seven Years' War: A Study in Combined Strategy,* 2 vols. (London: Longmans, Green, 1918), 1:321–22; Ferling, *Struggle for a Continent,* 174–75; Vagts, *Landing Operations,* 288–89; and Parkman, *Montcalm and Wolfe,* 336.
23. Both Amherst and Wolfe visited Pepperrell and discussed his 1745 victory prior to setting sail for their own assault on Louisbourg. Brayall, *"To the Uttermost of My Power,"* 206; and Anderson, *Crucible of War,* 250–53.
24. The Marquis de Vauban was the most important military engineer of the seventeenth and eighteenth centuries. See Sebastian le Prestre de Vauban, *The New Method of Fortification, As Practiced by Monsieur de VAUBAN, Engineer-General of FRANCE.* (London: S. and E. Ballard in Little Britain; C. Hitch in Pater-nofter Row; and J. Wood under the Royal-Exchange, 1748); and Anderson, *Crucible of War,* 251–53.
25. Corbett, *England and the Seven Years' War,* 1:326, 329–28; and Parkman, *Montcalm and Wolfe,* 334–54.
26. Boscawen and Amherst to Drucour, letter of 26 July 1758, in Parkman, *Montcalm and Wolfe,* 345; Corbett, *England and the Seven Years' War,* 1:328; and Anderson, *Crucible of War,* 254–56.
27. Anderson, *Crucible of War,* 254–57.
28. Corbett, *England and the Seven Years' War,* 1:418–19; Julian S. Corbett, *Some Principles of Maritime Strategy* (London: Longmans, Green, 1911), 289, 301–2; Vagts, *Landing Operations,* 290; and Parkman, *Montcalm and Wolfe,* 523–24.
29. Corbett, *England in the Seven Years' War,* 1:472, 476; Alfred T. Mahan, *The Influence of Sea Power Upon History, 1660–1783* (Boston: Little, Brown, 1890), 294–95; Ferling, *Struggle for a Continent,* 195–97, 200–201; and Anderson, *Crucible of War,* 391–96, 400–409.
30. Corbett, *England in the Seven Years' War,* 1:474–75; Parkman, *Montcalm and Wolfe,* 442–56; and Mahan, *The Influence of Sea Power,* 296.
31. Brumwell, *Paths of Glory,* 217–48.
32. Anderson, *Crucible of War,* 344–62; Corbett, *England in the Seven Years' War,* 1:455–62, 470–72; Ferling, *Struggle for a Continent,* 192–93; and Brumwell, *Paths of Glory,* 261–65.
33. Anderson, *Crucible of War,* 359; and Ferling, *Struggle for a Continent,* 192–200.
34. Anderson, *Crucible of War,* 453–54.

35. Ferling, *Struggle for a Continent,* 197.
36. Ibid., 202–3.

CHAPTER 1. THE NEW YORK CAMPAIGN

1. Jeremy Black, *War for America: The Fight for Independence, 1775–1783* (New York: St. Martin's Press, 1991), 162.
2. Julian S. Corbett, *Some Principles of Maritime Strategy* (London: Longmans, Green, 1911), 210, 221–23.
3. Russell F. Weigley, *The American Way of War: A History of United States Military Strategy and Policy* (Bloomington: Indiana University Press, 1973), 9.
4. Douglas Southall Freeman, *George Washington: A Biography,* 7 vols. (Norwalk, Conn.: Easton Press, 1951), 4:70.
5. Ira D. Gruber, *The Howe Brothers & the American Revolution* (Chapel Hill: University of North Carolina Press, 1972), 20–22; and Andrew Jackson O'Shaughnessy, *The Men Who Lost America: British Leadership, the American Revolution, and the Fate of the Empire* (New Haven, Conn.: Yale University Press, 2013), 84–85.
6. George Washington to Samuel Washington, 20 July 1775, in *The Papers of George Washington, The Revolutionary War Series, June 1775–December 1783,* 20 vols. to date, ed. W. W. Abbot, Philander D. Chase, and Dorothy Twohig (Charlottesville: University Press of Virginia, 1985–), 1:134–36. Hereafter, *PGW RW.*
7. Nathanael Greene made the famous comment, "I wish we could sell them another hill at the same price we did Bunker Hill." Nathanael Greene to Jacob Greene, 28 June 1775, in *The Papers of General Nathanael Greene,* 13 vols., ed. Richard K. Showman (Chapel Hill: University of North Carolina Press, 1976–2005), 1:92–93. Hereafter, *PGNG.*
8. As quoted in Richard M. Ketchum, *Decisive Day: The Battle for Bunker Hill* (New York: Doubleday, 1991), 183.
9. John E. Ferling, *The First of Men: A Life of George Washington* (Knoxville: University of Tennessee Press, 1988), 121.
10. Douglas W. Marshall and Howard H. Peckham, *Campaigns of the American Revolution* (Ann Arbor: University of Michigan Press, 1976), 8.

11. Ferling, *The First of Men,* 136; and John Selby, *The Road to Yorktown* (New York: St. Martin's Press, 1976), 50.
12. Greene to Nicholas Cooke, 6 February 1776, *PGNG,* 1:192.
13. George Washington to John Hancock, 10–11 July 1775, *PGW RW,* 1:83–91; Hancock to Washington, 24 July 1775, *PGW RW,* 1:164–66; and Washington to Hancock, 21 September 1776, *PGW RW,* 2:24–30.
14. Richard Henry Lee to Washington, 26 September 1775, *PGW RW,* 2:51–53; and Ferling, *The First of Men,* 124–32, 126–28.
15. Council of War Report dated 18 October 1775, *PGW RW,* 2:183–84; and Proceedings of the Committee Conference, 18–24 October 1775, *PGW RW,* 2:185–203.
16. George Washington to John Hancock, 10 February 1776, *PGW RW,* 3:289; and Freeman, *George Washington,* 4:24.
17. Ferling, *The First of Men,* 132; and Freeman, *George Washington,* 3:505.
18. Henry Knox to Washington, 5 December 1775, New York, *PGW RW,* 2:495–96; and Knox to Washington, 17 December 1775, *PGW RW,* 2:562–66.
19. Washington to Joseph Reed, 26 February 1776, *PGW RW,* 3:369–75.
20. Plan for Attacking Boston, undated but believed issued 18–25 February 1776, *PGW RW,* 3:332; Washington to Jonathan Trumbull Sr., 9 March 1776, *PGW RW,* 3:444–46; Washington to Artemas Ward, 2 March 1776, *PGW RW,* 3:408–10; Rufus Putnam to Washington, 11 February 1776, *PGW RW,* 3:295; and Washington to Hancock, 7–9 March 1776, *PGW RW,* 3:420–26.
21. Department of Defense, Joint Publication 3–02, *Amphibious Operations,* Washington, D.C., 18 July 2014, IV-13.
22. Washington to Reed, 28 March 1776, *PGW RW,* 3:557; and Washington to John Augustine Washington, 31 March 1776, *PGW RW,* 3:566–70.
23. Washington to Hancock, 30 January 1776, *PGW RW,* 3:217; and John Glover to Gen. Washington, 15 October 1775, in William P. Upham, *A Memoir of John Glover of Marblehead* (Salem, Printed by Charles W. Swasey, 1863), 10.
24. Washington to Hancock, 24 January 1776, *PGW RW,* 3:180.
25. Journal of the Continental Congress, 9–10 and 28 November 1775, in *Naval Documents of the American Revolution,* ed. William Bell

Clark (Washington, D.C.: Department of the Navy, 1964), 2:957–58, 972; and James C. Bradford, "Samuel Nicholas: Senior Officer, Continental Marines," in *Commandants of the Marine Corps*, ed. Allan R. Millett and Jack Shulimson (Annapolis, Md.: Naval Institute Press, 2004), 17–18.

26. Gurdon Saltonstall to Washington, 8 April 1776; and Washington to Hancock, 15 April 1776, *PGW RW*, 69–70.
27. Charles R. Smith, *Marines of the Revolution: A History of the Continental Marines in the American Revolution 1775–1783* (Washington, D.C.: History and Museums Division, Headquarters, U.S. Marine Corps, 1975).
28. Washington to Jonathan Trumbull, 23 September 1776, *PGW RW*, 6:380–82; and Washington to Sir William Howe, 6 October 1776, *PGW RW*, 6:489–90.
29. Hopkins to Washington, 2 September 1776, *PGW RW*, 6:201.
30. Washington to Artemas Ward, 13 October 1776, *PGW RW*, 6:561–63; and Washington to Hancock, *PGW RW*, 6:587–88.
31. One of the more mysterious characters of the Revolution was the Boston merchant-turned-fisherman George Hewes. Information from Hewes and other agents in Boston, many of them members of the Sons of Liberty, not only helped Washington gather information but also validated the necessity for a counterintelligence program. See Thomas B. Allen, *George Washington, Spymaster: How the Americans Outspied the British and Won the Revolutionary War* (Washington, D.C.: National Geographic Society, 2004), 31–38.
32. Council of War Report, 13 March 1776, *PGW RW*, 3:459–60; Washington to Hancock, 13 March 1776, *PGW RW*, 3:461–64; Weigley, *The American Way of War*, 9–10; and Freeman, *George Washington*, 4:94–98, 110.
33. Charles Lee to Washington, 5 January 1776, *PGW RW*, 3:30–31; John Adams to Washington, 6 January 1776, *PGW RW*, 3:36–37; and Washington to Charles Lee, 8 January 1776, *PGW RW*, 3:53–54.
34. Washington to Hancock, 11 January 1776, *PGW RW*, 3:67–68; Council of War Report, 13 March 1776, *PGW RW*, 3:459; and Washington to Hancock, 13 March 1776, *PGW RW*, 3:461–64.
35. In order to avoid confusing the Howe brothers, Vice Adm. Richard Lord Howe will subsequently be referred to as Lord Howe, and his

brother, Sir William Howe of the army, will be called Howe. Gruber, *The Howe Brothers,* 27, 44–45.

36. Washington to Hancock, 30 January 1776, *PGW RW,* 3:217; Washington to Reed, 31 January 1776, *PGW RW,* 3:225; and Charles Lee to Washington, 5 February 1776, *PGW RW,* 3:250.
37. Charles Lee to Washington, 3 March 1776, *PGW RW,* 3;404–5; Lee to Washington, 5 April 1776, *PGW RW,* 4:42–45; Reed to Washington 23 March 1776, *PGW RW,* 3:518–19; and Ferling, *The First of Men,* 154.
38. Charles Lee to Washington, 1 July 1776, *PGW RW,* 5:168–71; General Orders, 21 July 1776, *PGW RW,* 5:411–12; Greene to Nicholas Cooke, 22 July 1776, *PGNG,* 1:259–60; and Selby, *The Road to Yorktown,* 58–60.
39. The actual number of soldiers available for combat operations for either side is difficult to determine because the sources vary and historians count troops differently. In the case of Washington's army, the numbers were always changing because of the constant rotation in and out of various militia units, the spasmodic expiration of short-term enlistments, and desertion due to either bad morale or ambiguous status. See Washington to Hancock, 7 August 1776, *PGW RW,* 5:605–6; Edward J. Lowell, *The Hessians and Other German Auxiliaries of Great Britain in the Revolutionary War* (New York: Harper and Brother, 1884; repr. Forgotten Books, 2012), 2–3, 20, 58, 299–300; and Rodney Atwood, *The Hessians: Mercenaries from Hessen-Kassel in the American Revolution* (Cambridge: Cambridge University Press, 1980), 51, 254, 256.
40. Ferling, *The First of Men,* 160; and Freeman, *George Washington,* 4:151.
41. Gruber, *The Howe Brothers,* 107.
42. Greene to Washington, 15 August 1776, *PGNG,* 1:287–89; and Greene to Jacob Greene, 30 August 1776, *PGNG,* 1:291–92.
43. Greene to Nicholas Cooke, 22 July 1776, *PGNG,* 1:259–60; and Charles P. Whittemore, "John Sullivan: Luckless Irishman," in *George Washington's Generals,* ed. George Athan Billias (New York: William Morrow, 1964), 140–42.
44. General Orders, 20 August 1776, *PGW RW,* 6:86–89.
45. General Orders, 23 August 1776, *PGW RW,* 6:109–11.

46. Charles Lee to Washington, 29 February 1776, *PGW RW,* 5:389–93; and Barnet Schecter, *The Battle for New York: The City at the Heart of the American Revolution* (New York: Walker and Company, 2002), 117–19.
47. William Alexander of New Jersey claimed title to a Scottish earldom and insisted on using the aristocratic name Lord Stirling. Ironically, his contemporaries in Revolutionary America, including Washington, addressed him as such with no apparent reluctance. He acquired his commission in the Continental Army through duty with the New Jersey militia and volunteers. Lord Stirling provided skilled, competent, and loyal service to American and the Patriot cause. Paul David Nelson, *The Life of William Alexander, Lord Stirling: George Washington's Noble General* (Tuscaloosa: University of Alabama Press, 2003), 1–2, 36, 174–75; and Freeman, *George Washington,* 4:156–60.
48. Ferling, *The First of Men,* 165; and John J. Gallagher, *The Battle of Brooklyn, 1776* (New York: Sarpedon, 1995), 85.
49. Council of War Report, 8 July 1775, *PGW RW,* 5:238; Washington to Hancock, 12 July 1775, *PGW RW,* 5:283–84; Washington to Hancock, 14 July 1776, *PGW RW,* 5:304–7; Gruber, *The Howe Brothers,* 104–5; Alfred Thayer Mahan, *The Major Operations of the Navies in the War for American Independence* (London: Sampson, Low, and Marston, 1912), 39; and Freeman, *George Washington,* 4:135–37.
50. Lord Howe to Washington, 13 July 1776, *PGW RW,* 5:296; Washington to William Howe, 30 July 1776, *PGW RW,* 5:521–22; William Howe to Washington, 1 August 1776, *PGW RW,* 5:532–28; Lord Howe to Washington, 19 August 1776, *PGW RW,* 676; Washington to Hancock, 12 July 1776, *PGW RW,* 5:284; Washington to Hancock, 14 July 1776, *PGW RW,* 5:305–6; Memorandum of an interview with Lieutenant Colonel James Paterson, *PGW RW,* 5:398–99; and Thomas J. McGuire, *Stop the Revolution: America in the Summer of Independence and the Conference for Peace* (Mechanicsburg, Pa.: Stackpole Books, 2011), 43–48.
51. Washington to Hancock, 22 August 1776, *PGW RW,* 6:102; Washington to Hancock, 23 August 1776, *PGW RW,* 6:111; and Schecter, *The Battle for New York,* 126, 128–29.

52. Freeman, *George Washington,* 4:156.
53. Washington to Hancock, 23 August 1776, *PGW RW,* 6:111–12; Washington to Trumbull, Sr., 24 August 1776, *PGW RW,* 6:123–24; Washington to Hancock, 26 August 1776, *PGW RW,* 6:129–30; and Schecter, *The Battle for New York,* 130.
54. Washington to Hancock, 8 September 1776, *PGW RW,* 6:248–52; and Freeman, *George Washington,* 4:157.
55. Schecter, *The Battle for New York,* 133–38; and Gallagher, *The Battle for Brooklyn,* 99–101.
56. Council of War, 29 August 1776, *PGW RW,* 6:153–54; Gallagher, *The Battle of Brooklyn,* 101–7; Schecter, *The Battle of New York,* 138; Gruber, *The Howe Brothers,* 111–12; Paul David Nelson, *General James Grant, Scottish Soldier and Royal Governor of East Florida* (Gainesville: University Press of Florida, 1993), 100–101; Nathaniel Philbrick, *Valiant Ambition: George Washington, Benedict Arnold, and the American Revolution* (New York: Viking, 2016), 14–15; and Freeman, *George Washington,* 4:164.
57. Lord Stirling to Washington, 19 August 1776, *PGW RW,* 6:159–60; Washington to the Massachusetts General Court, 19 September 1776, *PGW RW,* 6:344–47; Lt. Col. Robert Hanson Harrison to Hancock, 17 August 1776, *PGW RW,* 6:155–56; Washington to Hancock, 2 September 1776, *PGW RW,* 6:199–200; Washington to Hancock, 8 September 1776, *PGW RW,* 6:248–52; and Schecter, *The Battle for New York,* 152–53.
58. Freeman, *George Washington,* 4:169; Gallagher, *The Battle for Brooklyn,* 139–41; Schecter, *The Battle for New York,* 148–49, 156; and Selby, *The Road to Yorktown,* 66–67.
59. Council of War, 29 August 1776, *PGW RW,* 6:153–54, 177–78, 171–73; Washington to Hancock, 31 August 1776; and General Orders, 31 August 1776, *PGW RW,* 6:153–54, 177–78, 171–73.
60. Washington to Hancock, 31 August 1776, *PGW RW,* 6:177–79; and John Glover to his mother, letter dated 7 October 1776, in Upham, *A Memoir of John Glover,* 16–17.
61. Washington to Hancock, 31 August 1776, *PGW RW,* 6:177–78.
62. Washington to Hancock, 2 and 8 September 1776, *PGW RW,* 6:197–200, 248–52; and Gruber, *The Howe Brothers,* 118–20.
63. Greene to Washington, 5 September 1776, *PGW RW,* 6:222–25.

64. Hancock to Washington, 10 September 1776, *PGW RW,* 6:273; Lt. Col. Robert Hanson Harrison to Hancock, 12 September 1776, *PGW RW,* 6:294; Freeman, *Washington,* 4:188; and Ferling, *The First of Men,* 169.
65. Historians and historic figures often spell Kingsbridge as King's Bridge. As a general rule, when spelled "King's Bridge," an author is referring to the bridge as a structure, and when spelled "Kingsbridge," it includes the bridge and key terrain on both sides of the Harlem River at the bridge location. See Schecter, *The Battle of New York,* 79–80.
66. Numerous correspondence including Washington to Maj. Gen. William Heath, 8 September 1776, *PGW RW,* 6:157.
67. Washington to Hancock, 14 September 1776, *PGW RW,* 6:308–9; and Schecter, *The Battle for New York,* 177–78.
68. Gruber, *The Howe Brothers,* 122–23.
69. Washington to Hancock, 6 September 1776, *PGW RW,* 6:231–32; and Ferling, *The First of Men,* 170.
70. Schecter, *The Battle for New York,* 180–82; and George Anthan Billias, *General John Glover and His Marblehead Mariners: The Story of the Revolutionary War General Whose Fighting Fishermen Ferried Washington across the Delaware* (New York: Holt, 1960), 107–9.
71. Washington to the Massachusetts General Court, 19 September 1776, *PGW RW,* 6:344–47; Freeman, *George Washington,* 4:103–4; and Philbrick, *Violent Ambition,* 29–31.
72. Gruber, *The Howe Brothers,* 123–24; and Schecter, *The Battle for New York,* 184–86.
73. Ferling, *The First of Men,* 170–75; and Selby, *The Road to Yorktown,* 69–72.
74. Schecter, *The Battle for New York,* 192–93.
75. Aaron Burr was the aide who advised Putnam of the seldom-used road that made possible the escape of Putnam and his brigade, including Alexander Hamilton.
76. Washington to Hancock, 16 September 1776, *PGW RW,* 6:313–16; Freeman, *George Washington,* 4:192–94; and Schecter, *The Battle for New York,* 188–96.
77. Gruber, *The Howe Brothers,* 124.
78. Washington to Hancock, 18 September 1776, *PGW RW,* 6:331–33; Washington to the Massachusetts General Court, 19 September

1776, *PGW RW,* 6:344–47; Greene to Nicholas Cooke, 17 September 1776, *PGNG,* 1:300–302; General Orders, 17 September 1776; Washington to Nicholas Cooke, 17 September 1776; Washington to Abraham Gates, 17 September 1776, *PGW RW,* 6:320–25.

79. Washington to Hancock, 2 September 1776, *PGW RW,* 6:199–200; Washington to Hancock, 20 September 1776, *PGW RW,* 6:351–53; Washington to Hancock, 22 September 1776, *PGW RW,* 6:368–69; and Richard H. Kohn, *Eagle and Sword: The Beginnings of the Military Establishment in America* (New York: Free Press, 1975), 9–10.
80. O'Shaughnessy, *The Men Who Lost America,* 95, 97, 101; Green to Washington, 12 October 1776, *PGW RW,* 6:547–48; Schecter, *The Battle for New York,* 223–27; Gruber, *The Howe Brothers,* 131–32.
81. Washington to Greene, 8 November 1776, *PGNG,* 1:342–43.
82. Freeman, *George Washington,* 4:218–29; and Schecter, *The Battle for New York,* 225.
83. Lt. Col. Robert Hanson Harrison to Hancock, 20 October 1776, *PGW RW,* 6:592–93; Washington to Joseph Trumbull, 20 October 1776, *PGW RW,* 6:595–96; and Selby, *The Road to Yorktown,* 76.
84. Schecter, *The Battle for New York,* 244.
85. Greene to Hancock, 28 October 1776, *PGNG:* 1, 323–24; Extract of John Glover letter dated 22 October 1776 in Upham, *Memoir of John Glover,* 17–19; Harrison to Hancock, 25 October 1776, *PGW RW,* 7:27–29; Washington to John Augustine Washington, 6–19 November 1776, *PGW RW,* 7:102–5; Billias, *Glover and His Mariners,* xi–xii, 110–25, 200–201; and Schecter, *The Battle for New York,* 226–30.
86. Ferling, *The First of Men,* 173–74; Gruber, *The Howe Brothers,* 132; and Schecter, *The Battle for New York,* 239–42.
87. Washington to Greene, 7 November 1776, *PGNG,* 1:339–40; Washington to John Augustine Washington, 6–19 November 1776, *PGW RW,* 102–5; Washington to William Livingston, 7 November 1776, *PGW RW,* 7:110–11; Washington to Greene, 8 November 176, *PGW RW,* 7:115–16; Washington to Col. Richard Humpton, 5 December 1776, *PGW RW,* 7:265; and Schecter, *The Battle for New York,* 244–45.
88. Schecter, *The Battle for New York,* 245–47.

89. Greene to Washington, 15 November 1776, *PGW RW,* 7:162; Washington to Hancock, 16 November 1776, *PGW RW,* 7:162–65; and Washington to Hancock, 16 November 1776, *PGW RW,* 7:115–66, 7:162–65.
90. Greene to Henry Knox, 17 November 1776, *PGNG,* 1:351–52.
91. Theodore Thayer, "Nathanael Greene: Revolutionary War Strategist," in *George Washington's Generals,* ed. George Athan Billias (New York: William Morrow, 1964), 112–14.
92. Washington to Howe, 13 January 1777, *PGW RW,* 8:58–59; Washington to Howe, 13 January 1777, *PGW RW,* 8:59–60; and Washington to Howe, 10 June 1777, *PGW RW,* 9:661–66.
93. Greene to Nicholas Cooke, 4 December 1776, *PGNG,* 1:360–61; and Washington to Hancock, 19 November 1776, *PGW RW,* 7:181–83.
94. Washington to Hancock, 8 December 1776, *PGW RW,* 7:273; Washington to Hancock, 9 December 1776, *PGW RW,* 7:283–84; and Washington to Lund Washington, 10–17 October 1776, *PGW RW,* 7:289–91.
95. Maj. Gen. John Sullivan to Washington, 13 December 1776, *PGW RW,* 7:328; Washington to Lund Washington, 10–17 December 1776, *PGW RW,* 7:289–91; Washington to Sullivan, 15 December 1776, *PGW RW,* 7:350; Washington to Lee, 21 November 1776, *PGW RW,* 7:193–94; Washington to Lee, 1 December 1776, *PGW RW,* 7:249; Washington to Hancock, 2 December 1776, *PGW RW,* 7:251; Washington to Lee, 3 December 1776, *PGW RW,* 7:257; Washington to Colonel Richard Humpton, 5 December 1776, *PGW RW,* 7:265; and Freeman, *George Washington,* 4:260–90.
96. Black, *War for America,* 110.
97. Washington to the New York Convention, 16 November 1776, *PGW RW,* 7:355–57.
98. Gruber, *The Howe Brothers,* 136; and Schecter, *The Battle for New York,* 260–61.
99. General Orders, 25 December 1776, *PGW RW*, 7:434; General Orders, 27 December 1776, *PGW RW,* 7:448–49; and Gruber, *The Howe Brothers,* 153–57.
100. Gen. Henry Knox, speech to the Massachusetts legislature, in Upham, *Memoir of John Glover,* 21; Billias, *Glover and His Mariners,* 5–10, 129; and Schecter, *The Battle for New York,* 266.

101. General Orders, 30 December 1776, *PGW RW,* 7:484; Washington to Hancock, 5 January 1777, *PGW RW,* 7:519–23; Washington to Putnam, 5 January 1776, *PGW RW,* 7:484, 519–35; Alfred H. Bill, *The Campaign of Princeton, 1776–1777* (Princeton, N.J.: Princeton University Press, 1948), 121–22; and William S. Striker, *The Battles of Trenton and Princeton* (Boston: Houghton, Mifflin, 1898), 242, 305–7, 433, 435.
102. Washington to John Augustine Washington, 6–19 November 1776, *PGW RW,* 7:102–5.
103. Heath to Washington, 6 December 1776, *PGW RW,* 7:267; Jonathan Trumbull Sr. to Washington, 6 December 1776, *PGW RW,* 7:267–68.
104. Mahan, *Major Operations of the Navies,* 47–48; and Marshall and Peckham, *Campaigns of the American Revolution,* 30.
105. Nicholas Cooke to Washington, 8 December 1776, *PGW RW,* 7:272; Washington to Cooke, 21 December 1776, *PGW RW,* 7:391–93; and Black, *War for America,* 108.
106. Maj. Gen. Joseph Spencer to Washington, 12 January 1777, *PGW RW,* 8:51–52; Arnold to Washington, 13 January 1777, *PGW RW,* 8:55–56; Arnold to Washington, 31 January 1777, *PGW RW,* 8:197–98; Arnold to Washington, 7 February 1777, *PGW RW,* 8:267–68; Spencer to Washington, 26 March 1777, *PGW RW,* 8:640–41; and Greene to Nicholas Cooke, 21 December 1776, *PGNG,* 1:374–76.
107. Mahan, *Major Operations of the Navies,* 47–48; Billias, *Glover and His Mariners,* 164; and Gallagher, *The Battle for Brooklyn,* 15.
108. Marshall and Peckham, *Campaigns of the American Revolution,* 30; and Schecter, *The Battle for New York,* 286–87.

CHAPTER 2. NEW YORK TO YORKTOWN

1. Tench Tilghman to Hancock, 22 June 1777, *PGW RW,* 10:104–5; Washington to Reed, 23 June 1777, *PGW RW,* 10:113–15; Washington to Hancock, 25 June 1777, *PGW RW,* 10:123–25; Washington to Hancock, 28 June 1777, *PGW RW,* 10:137; Washington to John Augustine Washington, 29 June 1777, *PGW RW,* 10:149–50; and Lord Stirling to Washington, 3 July 1777, *PGW RW,* 10:176–77.

2. Andrew Jackson O'Shaughnessy, *The Men Who Lost America: British Leadership, The American Revolution, and the Fate of Empire* (New Haven, Conn.: Yale University Press, 2013), 106–14.
3. Washington to Putnam, 1 July 1777, *PGW RW,* 10:165–66; Washington to Hancock, 2 July 1777, *PGW RW,* 10:168–70; Washington to Schuyler, 2 July 1777, *PGW RW,* 10:170–72; and Washington to Lincoln, 24 July 1777, *PGW RW,* 10:385.
4. Washington to Hancock, 25 July 1777, *PGW RW,* 10:420–22.
5. Washington to Hancock, 22 July 1777, *PGW RW,* 10:356–57.
6. Brig. Gen. David Forman to Washington, 23 July 1777, *PGW RW,* 10:374–75.
7. Washington to Hancock, 25 July 1777, *PGW RW,* 10:410–11; Washington to Col. Theodorick Bland, 24 July 1777, *PGW RW,* 10:382; Washington to Col. Daniel Morgan, 24 July 1777, *PGW RW,* 10:390; Washington to Col. Stephen Moylen, 24 July 1777, *PGW RW,* 10:391; Washington to Putnam, 24 July 1777, *PGW RW,* 10:393; Washington to Stephen, 24 July 1777, *PGW RW,* 10:399; Washington to Lord Stirling, 24 July 1777, *PGW RW,* 10:399–400; Washington to Wayne, 24 July 1777, *PGW RW,* 10:401–2; and Washington to William Livingston, 25 July 1777, *PGW RW,* 10:412–13.
8. Hancock to Washington, 22 August 1777, *PGW RW,* 11:41; General Orders, 23 August 1777, *PGW RW,* 11:49–50; and General Orders, 5 September 1777, *PGW RW,* 11:147–48.
9. Washington to Hancock, 5 September 1777, *PGW RW,* 11:150; Washington to Brig. Gen. John Cadwalader, 28 August 1777, *PGW RW,* 11:82–83; Washington to Hancock, 30 August 1777, *PGW RW,* 11:93; and Washington to Hancock, 3 September 1777, *PGW RW,* 11:135–36.
10. Lt. Col. Robert Hanson Harrison to John Hancock, 10 September 1777, *PGW RW,* 11:182.
11. General Greene's Orders, 13 September 1777, *PGNG,* 2:156.
12. Washington to Hancock, 11 September 1777, *PGW RW,* 11:200–201.
13. Thomas J. McGuire, *The Philadelphia Campaign,* vol. 1: *Brandywine and the Fall of Philadelphia* (Mechanicsburg, Pa.: Stackpole Books, 2006), 263–327.
14. John W. Jackson, *The Pennsylvania Navy, 1775–1781: The Defense of Delaware* (New Brunswick, N.J.: Rutgers University Press, 1974), 225–81.

15. Washington, General Orders, 5 May 1778, *PGW RW,* 15:38–40; and Jonathan R. Dull, *A Diplomatic History of the American Revolution* (New Haven, Conn.: Yale University Press, 1985), 57–65, 89–94.
16. D'Estaing to Washington, 13 July 1778, *PGW RW,* 16:63; and Washington to President of Congress, Henry Laurens, 14 July 1778, *PGW RW,* 16:74–75.
17. Lt. Col. Alexander Hamilton to Washington, 20 July 1778, *PGW RW,* 16:109; Washington to Henry Laurens, President of Congress, 22 July 1778, *PGW RW,* 16:127–30; and Jonathan R. Dull, *The French Navy and American Independence: A Study of Arms and Diplomacy, 1774–1787* (Princeton, N.J.: Princeton University Press, 1975), 122–23.
18. Vice Admiral d'Estaing to Washington, 17 July 1778, *PGW RW,* 16:89–90; Washington to Sullivan, 17 July 1778, *PGW RW,* 16:92–93; Washington to d'Estaing, 22 July 1778, *PGW RW,* 16:125; Greene to Sullivan, 23 July 1778, *PGNG,* 2:466; and Green to Washington, 12–14 July 1778, *PGW RW,* 16:89–90.
19. Washington to d'Estaing, 12 August 1778, *PGW RW,* 16:297; Washington to Greene, 8 August 1778, *PGNG,* 2:478; Sullivan to Washington, 13 August 1778, *PGW RW,* 16:307–8; Greene to Henry Marchant, 25 July 1778, *PGNG,* 2:470–72; Greene to d'Estaing, 21 August 1778, *PGNG,* 2:480–82; John B. Hattendorf, *Newport, the French Navy, and American Independence* (Newport, R.I.: Redwood Press, 2005), 10–17; and Paul F. Dearden, *The Rhode Island Campaign of 1778: Inauspicious Dawn of Alliance* (Providence: Rhode Island Publishing Society, 1980), 66–80.
20. Sullivan to Washington, 21 August 1778, *PGW RW,* 16:350–55; Greene to d'Estaing, 21 August 1778, *PGNG,* 2:480–83; A protest of the General Officers on Rhode Island to Count d'Estaing, 22 August 1778, *PGNG,* 2:487–89; Lafayette to Washington, 25–26 August 1778, *PGW RW,* 16:369–74; and Hattendorf, *Newport, the French Navy and American Independence,* 24–29.
21. Sullivan to Washington, 31 August 1778, *PGW RW,* 16:450–51; Greene to Charles Pettit, 22 August 1778, *PGNG,* 2:491–92; Sullivan to Greene, 23 August 1778, *PGNG,* 2:492–93; Washington to Sullivan, 28 August 1778, *PGW RW,* 16:406–7; Washington to Sullivan, 29 August 1778, *PGW RW,* 16:417; Sullivan to Washington,

29 August 1778, *PGW RW,* 16:418–19; Colonel John Laurens to Washington, 2 September 1778, *PGW RW,* 16:479–80; and Greene to Washington, 31 August 1778, *PGNG,* 2:501–2.

22. David Syrett, *The Royal Navy in American Waters 1775–1783* (Aldershot, U.K.: Scolar Press, 1989), 109–10.
23. Dull, *The French Navy and American Independence,* 122–24.
24. Washington to Henry Laurens, 12 September 1778, *PGW RW,* 16:582–83; Sullivan to Washington, 14 September 1778, *PGW RW,* 16:614–15; and Greene to Washington, 7 September 1778, *PGNG,* 2:513–14.
25. Syrett, *The Royal Navy in American Waters,* 130.
26. John A. Tilley, *The British Navy and the American Revolution* (Columbia: University of South Carolina, 1987), 161, 167; and Syrett, *The Royal Navy in American Waters,* 133.
27. Bagaduce is the site of present-day Castine, Maine. Since the seventeenth century, it has been known variously as Bagaduce, Pentagoet, Penobscot, and Majabigwaduce. Michael M. Greenburg, *The Court-Martial of Paul Revere: A Son of Liberty and America's Forgotten Military Disaster* (Lebanon, N.H.: ForeEdge, 2014), 73; and George E. Buker, *The Penobscot Expedition: Commodore Saltonstall and the Massachusetts Conspiracy of 1779* (Camden, Maine: Down East Books, 2002), 1.
28. Greenburg, *The Court-Martial of Paul Revere,* 70–75; Buker, *The Penobscot Expedition,* 7–11; and Henry I. Shaw Jr., "Penobscot Assault—1779," *Military Affairs* 17, no. 2 (Summer 1953): 83–94.
29. Greenberg, *The Court-Martial of Paul Revere,* 80–91; Syrett, *The Royal Navy in American Waters,* 126; and Dale W. Burbank, "Want of Proper Spirit and Energy: The Penobscot Expedition of 1779" (Master's thesis, U.S. Army Command and General Staff College, 2011), 62–64.
30. Greenburg, *The Court-Martial of Paul Revere,* 90–95; and Burbank, "Want of Proper Spirit and Energy," 58–59, 66–69.
31. Greenburg, *The Court-Martial of Paul Revere,* 96–98; and Buker, *The Penobscot Expedition,* 37–41.
32. Greenburg, *The Court-Martial of Paul Revere,* 99–104; Buker, *The Penobscot Expedition,* 44–45; and Burbank, "Want of Proper Spirit and Energy," 74–78.

33. Buker, *The Penobscot Expedition,* 53–54; Greenburg, *The Court-Martial of Paul Revere,* 94–95; and Shaw, "Penobscot Assault," 91.
34. Greenburg, *The Court-Martial of Paul Revere,* 113; Buker, *The Penobscot Expedition,* 53–54; and Burbank, "Want of Proper Spirit and Energy," 79–82.
35. Washington to Horatio Gates, 17 August 1779, in John C. Fitzpatrick, ed., *The Writings of George Washington from the Original Manuscript Sources, 1745–1799,* 39 vols. (Washington, D.C.: U.S. Government Printing Office, 1931–1944), 16:117–18. Hereafter, *WGW.*
36. Buker, *The Penobscot Expedition,* 80–97; and Burbank, "Want of Proper Spirit and Energy," 90–93.
37. Washington to Lafayette, 12 September 1779, *WGW,* 16:267–69; and Washington to Lafayette, 30 September 1779, *WGW,* 16:368–76.
38. Washington to d'Estaing, 13 September 1779, *WGW,* 16:272–75; Washington to Maj. Henry Lee, 13 September 1779, *WGW,* 16:278–80; Washington to Lord Stirling, 14 September 1779, *WGW,* 16:287–88; Washington to d'Estaing, 4 October 1779, *WGW,* 16:409–14; and Greene to Colonel Ephraim Bowen, 7 November 1779, *PGNG,* 5:24.
39. Washington to Lafayette, 18 March 1780, *WGW,* 18:122–25.
40. Banastre Tarleton, *A History of the Campaigns of 1780 and 1781, in the Southern Provinces of North America* (Dublin: Colles, Exshaw, White, H. Whitestone, Burton, Moore, and Dornin, 1787), 4.
41. Marshall and Peckham, *Campaigns of the American Revolution,* 102.
42. John Collins to Greene, 2 May 1780, *PGNG,* 5:540.
43. Tilley, *The British Navy and the American Revolution,* 180, 187.
44. James Kirby Martin, with Christopher Smith, "The American Revolutionary War: 1775–83," in *Atlas of American Military History,* ed. James C. Bradford (Oxford: Oxford University Press, 2003), 29.
45. Washington to James Duane, 5 June 1780, *WGW,* 18: 478–79.
46. John D. Grainger, *The Battle of Yorktown, 1781: A Reassessment* (Woodbridge, Suffolk, U.K.: Boydell Press, 2005), 13.
47. Richard M. Ketchum, *Victory at Yorktown: The Campaign That Won the Revolution* (New York: Henry Holt, 2004), 38, 50–73.
48. Washington to Rochambeau, 30 April 1781 from New Windsor, *WGW,* 22:12–13.

49. Ketchum, *Victory at Yorktown* 98–105.
50. Ibid., 97.
51. Hattendorf, *Newport, the French Navy, and American Independence,* 58–62; and George C. Woodbridge, "Rochambeau: Two Hundred Years Later," in *Newport History: The French in Newport,* ed. James L. Yarnall (Newport, R.I.: Newport Historical Society, 2004), 85–86.
52. Ketchum, *Victory at Yorktown,* 27, 33–34, 36–37.
53. Hattendorf, *Newport, the French Navy, and American Independence,* 94–95.
54. Washington to Destouches, 14 May 1781, *WGW,* 22, 87–88; and James L. Yarnall, ed., *Newport History: The French in Newport* (Newport, R.I.: Newport Historical Society, 2004), 161, 165, 174.
55. Washington to Chevalier de la Luzerne, 23 May 1781, *WGW,* 22, 103–4; Notes from Conference with Rochambeau, 23 May 1781, *WGW,* 22:105–7; Circular to the New England States, 24 May 1781, *WGW,* 22:109–11; Rochambeau to Washington, 12 June 1781, *WGW,* 22:206; Washington to de la Luzerne, 13 June 1781, *WGW,* 22:205–6; Washington to Rochambeau, 13 June 1781, *WGW,* 22:207–9; Conference at Dobbs Ferry, 19 July 1781, *WGW,* 22:395–97; and Washington to de Grasse, 21 July 1781, *WGW,* 33:400–402.
56. Washington to the Army, Instructions for Reconnoitering the Enemy's posts at the North End of York Island, 13 July 1781, *WGW,* 22:370–72.
57. Washington, Thoughts on the Surprise of the North End of York Island, June 1781, *WGW,* 22:296–99.
58. Washington to de Grasse, 20 September 1781, *WGW,* 23:136.
59. Ketchum, *Victory at Yorktown,* 107–9.
60. Ketchum, *Victory at Yorktown,* 110–19, 129–31; Stephen R. Conway, "War of American Independence, 1775–83," in *A Companion to American Military History,* vol. 1, ed. James C. Bradford (Chichester, U.K.: Wiley-Blackwell Publishing, 2010), 32–33; Grainger, *The Battle of Yorktown,* 31; and Marshall and Peckham, *Campaigns of the American Revolution,* 108.
61. Greene to Colonel William Davies, 17 July 1781, *PGNG,* 9:23–24.
62. Washington to the President of Congress, 30 May 1781, *WGW,* 22:134–35; and Washington to Rochambeau, 3 June 1781, *WGW,* 22:154–55.

63. Washington to Rochambeau, 3 June 1781, *WGW,* 22:155–56.
64. General Orders, 15 June 1781, *WGW,* 22:215–16; Washington to Maj. Gen. William Heath, 15 June 1781, *WGW,* 22:217–18; Greene to Gen. Thomas Sumter, 14 July 1781, *PGNG,* 9:8–9; and Greene to Gen. Andrew Pickens, 15 July 1781, *PGNG,* 9:10–11.
65. Greene to Thomas McKean, President of the Continental Congress, 17 July 1781, *PGNG,* 9:27–31; and Gen. George Weedon to Greene, 11 November 1781, *PGNG,* 9:563–66.
66. Hattendorf, *Newport, the French Navy, and American Independence,* 86–94.
67. Washington to Baron von Steuben, 16 May 1781, *WGW,* 22:91.
68. Washington to Gov. Thomas Jefferson, 16 May 1781, *WGW,* 22:93–94; Washington to Lafayette, 31 May 1781, *WGW,* 22:139–40; and Washington to Rochambeau, 7 June 1781, *WGW,* 22:170–71.
69. Washington to Lafayette, 13 July 1781, *WGW,* 22:367–68; Washington to Lafayette, 30 July 1781, *WGW,* 22:431–34; Washington to Brig. Gen. Anthony Wayne, 30 July 1781, *WGW,* 22:435–36; Wayne to Greene, 7 August 1781, *PGNG,* 9:148–49; and Lafayette to Greene, 8 July 1781, *PGNG,* 8:507–8.
70. Lafayette to Greene, 12 August 1781, *PGNG,* 9:172–75; and Maj. James McHenry to Greene, 13 August 1781, *PGNG,* 9:178.
71. Greene to Col. Henry Lee Jr., 22 August 1781, *PGNG,* 9:222–23.
72. Washington to Comte de Grasse, 17 August 1781, *WGW,* 23:7–11; Washington Circular to States (New Hampshire, Massachusetts, Connecticut, New Jersey), 21 August 1781, *WGW,* 23:26–28; and Washington to Governor William Greene, 22–24 August 1781, *WGW,* 23:46–48.
73. Washington to Lafayette, 15 August 1781, *WGW,* 22:501–2; and Lafayette to Greene, 25 August 1781, *PGNG,* 9:246–47.
74. Washington to de Grasse, 24 August 1781, *WGW,* 23:39–40.
75. Washington to Comte de Barras, 15 August 1781, *WGW,* 22:499–500; Jeremy Black, *War for America: The Fight for Independence, 1775–1783* (New York: St. Martin's Press, 1991), 225; Grainger, *The Battle of Yorktown,* 59–60, 67; and Hattendorf, *Newport, the French Navy, and American Independence,* 101.
76. Washington to Heath, 19 August 1781, *WGW,* 23:20–22.
77. Washington to Rochambeau, 27 August 1781, *WGW,* 23:9–50.

78. Washington to Greene, 4 September 1781, *PGNG,* 9:295–97; Washington to the Superintendent of Finance, 17 August 1781, *WGW,* 23:11–12; Washington to Lafayette, 21 August 1781, *WGW,* 23:33–34; Washington to the Superintendent of Finance, 27 August 1781, *WGW,* 23:50–52; Washington to Lafayette, 27 August 1781, *WGW,* 23:52–53; and Washington to Brig. Gen. George Weedon or Alexander Spotswood, 10 September 1781, *WGW,* 23:110–11.
79. Washington to Chevalier de la Luzerne, 5 September 1781, *WGW,* 23:87; Washington to de Grasse, 6 September 1781, *WGW,* 23:92–93; and Lafayette to Greene, 2 September 1781, *PGNG,* 9:279–80.
80. Ketchum, *Victory at Yorktown,* 204–5.
81. Washington to de Grasse, 15 September 1781, *WGW,* 23:116–17.
82. Washington to the President of Congress, 15 September 1781, *WGW,* 23:117–18.
83. Ketchum, *Victory at Yorktown,* 206–7.
84. Ibid., 204–5, 208.
85. Washington to de Grasse, 17 September 1781, *WGW,* 23, 122–25; and de Grasse to Washington 17 September 1781, *WGW,* 23:125.
86. Washington to de Grasse, 25 September 1781, *WGW,* 23:136–39.
87. General Orders, 6 October 1781, *WGW,* 23:177–85.
88. Grainger, *The Battle of Yorktown,* 103, 119–22.
89. Washington to Greene, 28 September 1781, *PGNG,* 9:408–10.
90. Washington to the President of Congress, 16 October 1781, *WGW,* 23: 227–29.
91. Washington to Greene, 16 October 1781, *WGW,* 23:230–32.
92. Cornwallis to Clinton, 11 October 1781, in Black, *War for America,* 228–29.
93. Cornwallis to Clinton, 15 October 1781, in Black, *War for America,* 230; and Washington to the President of Congress, 16 October 1781, *WGW,* 23:227–29.
94. Tarleton, *A History of the Campaigns of 1780 and 1781,* 388.
95. Washington to Cornwallis, 18 October 1781, *WGW,* 23:237–38; and Washington to Greene, 24 October 1781, *PGNG,* 9:479–80.
96. Ketchum, *Victory at Yorktown,* 237–38, 242–45; Grainger, *The Battle of Yorktown,* 103, 155–59; and John Selby, *The Road to Yorktown* (New York: St. Martin's Press, 1976), 197.

97. Clinton to Germain, 24 October 1781 and summer 1782, in Black, *War for America,* 232–33.
98. Washington to de Grasse, 20 October 1781, *WGW,* 23: 248–50.
99. Washington to Greene, 31 October 1781, *PGNG,* 9:504–6; and Lafayette to Greene, 22 November 1781, *PGNG,* 9:609–11.
100. Washington to James McHenry, 11 December 1781, *WGW,* 23:381.
101. Acting governor Alexander Martin of North Carolina to Greene, 28 November 1781, *PGNG,* 9:634–35; and Washington to Greene, 15 December 1781, *PGNG,* 9:61–63.
102. Washington to the President of Congress, 27–29 October 1781, *WGW,* 23:294–95; Washington to Greene, 31 October 1781, *WGW,* 23: 309–12; and Washington to Greene, 15 December 1781, *WGW,* 23:389–91.
103. Washington to Greene, 31 October 1781, *WGW,* 23:309–12; Washington to Col. Timothy Pickering, 4 November 1781, *WGW,* 23:331–32; Greene to Rochambeau, 9 December 1781, *PGNG,* 10:20; and Greene to Washington, 9 December 1781, *PGNG,* 10:23.
104. Washington to Lafayette, 15 November 1781, *WGW,* 23:340–42.
105. Washington to Lafayette, 4 January 1782, *WGW,* 23:429–31.
106. Greene to Washington, 9 March 1782, *PGNG,* 9:471–72.
107. Greene to Washington, 24 January 1782, *PGNG,* 10:256–57.
108. Washington to Greene, 18 March 1782, *PGNG,* 10:524–25.
109. Rochambeau to Greene, 6 April 1782, *PGNG,* 10:591–92.
110. Dull, *A Diplomatic History of the American Revolution,* 91–96.
111. Carl von Clausewitz, *On War* (Princeton, N.J.: Princeton University Press, 1976), 595–96.

CHAPTER 3. TO THE SHORES OF TRIPOLI

1. Russell F. Weigley, *The American Way of War: A History of United States Military Strategy and Policy* (Bloomington: Indiana University Press, 1973), 40–41.
2. Don Higginbotham, *George Washington and the American Military Tradition* (Athens: University of Georgia Press, 1985), 101–5; Craig L. Symonds, *Navalists and Antinavalists: The Naval Policy Debate in the United States, 1785–1827* (Newark: University of Delaware

Press, 1980), 17–26; and Richard H. Kohn, *Eagle and Sword: The Federalists and the Creation of the Military Establishment in America, 1783–1802* (New York: Free Press, 1975), 2–7.

3. Glenn A. Phelps, "The Republican General," in *George Washington Reconsidered,* ed. Don Higginbotham (Charlottesville: University Press of Virginia, 2001), 174–76; Symonds, *Navalists and Antinavalists,* 18; and Ian W. Toll, *Six Frigates: The Epic History of the Founding of the U.S. Navy* (New York: W. W. Norton, 2006), 33.
4. Kohn, *Eagle and Sword,* 48.
5. George Washington to Alexander Hamilton, Chairman of the Committee of Congress on the Peace Establishment, 2 May 1783 from Newburgh with attachment entitled "Sentiments on a Peace Establishment," in *The Writings of George Washington,* ed. John. C. Fitzpatrick (Washington, D.C.: U.S. Government Printing Office, 1938), 26:374–98; and Higginbotham, *George Washington and the American Military Tradition,* 124–25.
6. Symonds, *Navalists and Antinavalists,* 207–8.
7. Higginbotham, *George Washington and the American Military Tradition,* 126–27; and Weigley, *The American Way of War,* 54–55.
8. The Barbary States of the eighteenth and nineteenth centuries include Morocco, Algiers, Tunis, and Tripoli. See Symonds, *Navalists and Antinavalists,* 41.
9. Ibid., 30; and Richard Zacks, *The Pirate Coast: Thomas Jefferson, the First Marines, and the Secret Mission of 1805* (New York: Hyperion, 2005), 12.
10. Peter Walsh of Dominick Terry and Company, Cadiz, Spain, to Secretary of the Navy, 20 September 1794, in *Naval Documents Related to the United States Wars with the Barbary Powers* [hereafter, *Naval Documents, Barbary Powers*], 6 vols., ed. Dudley W. Knox (Washington, D.C.: U.S. Government Printing Office, 1939), 1:82; Richard O'Brian to David Humphreys, U.S. Minister to Portugal, October 1794, *Naval Documents, Barbary Powers,* 1:82–86; Frank Lambert, *The Barbary Wars: American Independence in the Atlantic World* (New York: Hill and Wang, 2005), 80–81; and Joshua E. London, *Victory in Tripoli: How America's War with the Barbary Pirates Established the U.S. Navy and Shaped a Nation* (Hoboken, N.J.: Wiley, 2005), 13–15, 27.

11. William S. Dudley and Michael J. Crawford, eds., *The Naval War of 1812: A Documentary History,* vol. 1: *1812* (Washington, D.C.: U.S. Government Printing Office, 1985), xlv–xlvi.
12. John Ferling, *A Leap in the Dark: The Struggle to Create the American Republic* (New York: Oxford University Press, 2003), 291–92, 312–13; Lambert, *The Barbary Wars,* 4–6, 15, 71–72; and London, *Victory in Tripoli,* 34–35.
13. U.S. Statutes at Large, Third Congress, Sess. 1, 27 March 1794, "An Act to Provide a Naval Armament," *Naval Documents, Barbary Powers,* 1:69–70; and Toll, *Six Frigates,* 43.
14. London, *Victory in Tripoli,* 47; and Toll, *Six Frigates,* 40–45.
15. Secretary of War to Secretary of Treasury, 21 April 1794, *Naval Documents, Barbary Powers,* 1:71–74; Howard P. Nash Jr., *The Forgotten Wars: The Role of the U.S. Navy in the Quasi-War with France and the Barbary Wars, 1798–1805* (New York: A. S. Barnes, 1969); and Toll, *Six Frigates,* 49–55.
16. U.S. Statutes at Large, Third Congress, Sess. 1, 27 March 1794, "An Act to Provide a Naval Armament," *Naval Documents, Barbary Powers,* 1:69–70; and Nash, *The Forgotten Wars,* 36–37.
17. Lambert, *The Barbary Wars,* 55–56; Symonds, *Navalists and Antinavalists,* 46–49; and Weigley, *The American Way of War,* 42–43.
18. Treaty with Tripoli ratified by the United States, 10 June 1797, *Naval Documents, Barbary Powers,* 1:177–81; and Lambert, *The Barbary Wars,* 92–93.
19. Richard O'Brien, U.S. Consul General, Algiers, to Captain William Brainbridge, U.S. Navy, 9 October 1800, *Naval Documents, Barbary Powers,* 1:375–78; Brainbridge to the Secretary of the Navy, 10 October 1800, *Naval Documents, Barbary Powers,* 1:378–79; James L. Cathcart, U.S. Consul, Tripoli to Charles Lee, Secretary of State Protempore, 18 October 1800, *Naval Documents, Barbary Powers,* 1:382–84; Account of William Brown commanding the ship *Brutus* regarding voyage to Constantinople and Algierine Spoliation, 11 December 1800, *Naval Documents, Barbary Powers,* 1:385–88; Protest of James L. Cathcart, U.S. Consul, Tripoli, to All Whom It Doth Or May Concern, 20 October 1800, *Naval Documents, Barbary Powers,* 1:391–94; and Lambert, *The Barbary Wars,* 94–95.

20. William Stinchcombe, *The XYZ Affair* (Westport, Conn.: Greenwood Press, 1980), 4–5.
21. Jeffersonians coined the phrase "petty tyrants" during the 1780s in referring to the leaders of Barbary States. Lambert, *The Barbary Wars,* 7; and Toll, *Six Frigates,* 165.
22. George Washington to Secretary of the Navy Benjamin Stoddert, 26 September 1798, in *Naval Documents Related to the Quasi-War between the United States and France* [hereafter, *Naval Documents, Quasi-War*], vol. 1: *Naval Operations from February 1797 to October 1798* (Washington, D.C.: U.S. Government Printing Office, 1935), 455–56; and Secretary of War James McHenry to Honorable Samuel Sewall, 9 April 1798, *Naval Documents, Quasi-War,* 1:51–52.
23. Act to Provide a Naval Armament, 1 July 1797, *Naval Documents, Quasi-War,* 1:7–8.
24. An Act to make further appropriation for the additional Naval Armament, 16 July 1798, *Naval Documents, Quasi-War,* 1:211; An Act to establish an Executive Department, to be denominated the Department of the Navy, 30 April 1798, *Naval Documents, Barbary Powers,* 1:59–60; Act Pertaining to the Navy: An Act More Effectively to Protect the Commerce and Coasts of the United States, Act of Congress, 28 May 1798, *Naval Documents, Quasi-War,* 1:87–88; John Adams, President of the United States, Instruction to Commanders of Armed Vessels, 28 May 1798, *Naval Documents, Quasi-War,* 1:88; An Act Further to Protect the Commerce of the United States, Act of Congress, *Naval Documents, Quasi-War,* 1:181–83; and President of the United States and Secretary Stoddert, Instruction to Armed Vessels, 10 July 1798, *Naval Documents, Quasi-War,* 1:187.
25. An Act for the Establishing and Organizing a Marine Corps, 11 July 1798, *Naval Documents, Quasi-War,* 1:188–89; Thomas Pinckney to Major Commandant Burrows, USMC, 30 August 1798, *Naval Documents, Quasi-War,* 1:355–56; and Lt. Col. Commandant Franklin Wharton, USMC to 2nd Lt. Alfred Grayson, USMC, 8 April 1812, in Dudley and Crawford, *Naval War,* 1:94–95.
26. Henry Knox to the President of the United States, 26 June 1798, *Naval Document, Quasi-War,* 1:139–41; and Alexander DeConde, *The Quasi-War: The Politics and Diplomacy of the Undeclared War*

with France, 1797–1801 (New York: Charles Scribner's Sons, 1966), 74–108.

27. James McHenry to Samuel Sewall, 9 April 1798, *Naval Documents, Quasi-War,* 1:51–53; John Ferling, *John Adams: A Life* (Newtown, Conn.: American Political Biography Press, 1992), 356–62; and Allen R. Millett and Peter Maslowski. *For the Common Defense: A Military History of the United States of America* (New York: Free Press, 1984), 96–98.
28. DeConde, *The Quasi-War,* 145–47, 176–77, 331.
29. Capt. Thomas Truxtun to the Secretary of the Navy, 10 February 1799, *Naval Documents, Quasi-War,* vol. 2: *Naval Operations from November 1798 to March 1799* (Washington, D.C.: U.S. Government Printing Office, 1935), 326–28; Extracts from *Constellation*'s journal (log book) 9 February 1799, *Naval Documents, Quasi-War,* 2:328–29; Gardner W. Allen, *Our Naval War with France* (Boston: Houghton Mifflin, 1909, repr. 1962): 99–101; Michael A. Palmer, *Stoddert's War: Naval Operations during the Quasi-War with France, 1798–1801* (Columbia: University of South Carolina Press, 1987), 98–103; and Toll, *Six Frigates,* 117–23.
30. Capt. Thomas Truxtun to the Secretary of the Navy, 3 February 1800, *Naval Documents, Quasi-War,* vol. 5: *Naval Operations from January to May 1800* (Washington, D.C.: U.S. Government Printing Office, 1937), 159–61; Allen, *Our Naval War with France,* 163–70; Palmer, *Stoddert's War,* 184–87; and Toll, *Six Frigates,* 132–35.
31. Capt. Silas Talbot to the Secretary of the Navy, 12 May 1800, *Naval Documents, Quasi-War,* 5:503–4; and Nash, *The Forgotten Wars,* 136–64.
32. Capt. Silas Talbot to the Secretary of the Navy, 12 May 1800, *Naval Documents, Quasi-War,* 5:503–4; and Extract from journal of the U.S. Frigate *Constitution,* 12 May 1800, *Naval Documents, Quasi-War,* 5:509.
33. Allen, *Our Naval War with France,* 168–70.
34. Account of Capt. F. M. Pitot, commanding the French frigate *La Vengeance* during her engagement with the U.S. Frigate *Constellation,* 2 February 1800, *Naval Documents, Quasi-War,* 5:166–69.
35. Palmer, *Stoddert's War,* 196.

36. William D. Robinson to the Secretary of the Navy, 10 September 1800, *Naval Documents, Quasi-War,* 5:337–41; Letter to a Merchant in New York concerning the surrender of Curacao to Great Britain, 18 October 1800, *Naval Documents, Quasi-War,* 5:341–42; and Letter from an officer on board the U.S. Sloop *Patasco* to his friend in Philadelphia concerning conditions in Curraco [*sic*], 22 September 1800, *Naval Documents, Quasi-War,* 5:372–73.
37. B. H. Phillips, U.S. Consul at Curacao to the Commander of the U.S. Squadron, Guadeloupe, 10 October 1800, *Naval Documents, Quasi-War,* 5:451–52.
38. Toll, *Six Frigates,* 105–6.
39. Data Gathered from Official Sources Relative to U.S. Ships-of-War During the Quasi-War with France, *Naval Documents, Quasi-War,* vol. 7: *Naval Operations from December 1800 to December 1801* (Washington, D.C.: U.S. Government Printing Office, 1937), 364–71.
40. A List of French Armed Vessels Captured by United States Men-of-War, *Naval Documents, Quasi-War,* 7:372.
41. Palmer, *Stoddert's War,* 236–39.
42. London, *Victory in Tripoli,* 84; Palmer, *Stoddert's War,* 230–32; and Gene A. Smith, *"For the Purposes of Defense": The Politics of the Jeffersonian Gunboat Program* (Newark: University of Delaware Press, 1995), 7–8.
43. Secretary of the Navy Memorandum, 13–23 March 1801, *Naval Documents, Barbary Powers,* 1:455–60; Nash, *The Forgotten Wars,* 173–74; and Allen, *Our Naval War with France,* 255–59.
44. Circular issued by James L. Cathcart, U.S. Consul, Tripoli, 15 March 1801, *Naval Documents, Barbary Powers,* 1:454–55; Cathcart to the Secretary of State, 16 May 1801, *Naval Documents, Barbary Powers,* 1:455–60; Nash, *The Forgotten Wars,* 181; London, *Victory in Tripoli,* 95–96; and Zacks, *The Pirate Coast,* 12.
45. Lambert, *The Barbary Wars,* 90–91.
46. During this period, the highest rank in the U.S. Navy was that of captain. When several ships came together to form a squadron, the senior captain would take overall command and assume the title of commodore. Although he held the position and title of commodore, his rank remained that of captain.

47. James L. Cathcart, U.S. Consul, Tripoli, to Nicholas C. Nissen, Danish Consul General, Tripoli, 15 May 1801, *Naval Documents, Barbary Powers,* 1:453–54.
48. Secretary of State to William Eaton, U.S. Consul, Tunis, and Richard O'Brien, U.S. Consul General, Algiers, 20 May 1801, *Naval Documents, Barbary Powers,* 1:460–62; Ray E. Irwin, *The Diplomatic Relations of the United States with the Barbary Powers, 1776–1816* (New York: Russell & Russell, 1931, repr. 1970), 94–95; London, *Victory in Tripoli,* 1–9, 84–90; and Smith, *"For the Purposes of Defense,"* 27.
49. Secretary of State to William Eaton, U.S. Consul, Tunis, and Richard O'Brien, U.S. Consul General, Algiers, 20 May 1801, *Naval Documents, Barbary Powers,* 1:460–62.
50. Thomas Jefferson, President of the United States of America, to the illustrious and honored Bey of Tripoli of Barbary, whom God Preserve, 21 May 1801 from Washington, *Naval Documents, Barbary Powers,* 1:470.
51. Lambert, *The Barbary Wars,* 124–28.
52. Samuel Smith for Acting Secretary of the Navy to Captain Richard Dale, U.S. Navy, 20 May 1801, *Naval Documents, Barbary Powers,* 1:465–69.
53. Circular letter to U.S. Agents and Consuls in Europe from William Eaton, U.S. Consul, Tunis, 23 July 1801, *Naval Documents, Barbary Powers,* 1:528; and Eaton to Captain Richard Dale, U.S. Navy, 24 July 1801, *Naval Documents, Barbary Powers,* 1:528–30.
54. Secretary of the Navy to Benjamin Tallmadge, U.S. Congress, letter with Sterrett's report enclosed, 13 January 1802, *Naval Documents, Barbary Powers,* 1:536–37.
55. Irwin, *Diplomatic Relations,* 110; London, *Victory in Tripoli,* 102–4; and Nash, *The Forgotten Wars,* 185–87.
56. Article entitled "Capture of Ship of War *Tripoli* by U.S. Schooner, *Enterprize,*" in National Intelligencer and Advertiser, 18 November 1801, *Naval Documents, Barbary Powers,* 1:538–39; Act Pertaining to the Navy, United States Statutes at Large, "Resolutions Expressing the sense of Congress on the Conduct of Lieutenant Sterret,— the officers and Crew of the United States Schooner, *Enterprize,* 2 February 1802, *Naval Documents, Barbary Powers,* 1:539–40; and Lambert, *The Barbary Wars,* 128–33.

57. London, *Victory in Tripoli,* 100–101.
58. An Act for the protection of the Commerce and Seamen of the United States, against the Tripolitan Cruisers, United States Statute at Large 6 February 1802, *Naval Documents, Barbary Powers,* 2:51–52.
59. Thomas Jefferson, President of the United States, Instruction to the U.S. Ships of War, 18 February 1802, *Naval Documents, Barbary Powers,* 2:60.
60. Resume of the Squadron of Commodore Robert Dale dated 1806–1807, *Naval Documents, Barbary Powers,* 2:118–19.
61. Nash, *The Forgotten Wars,* 197–98; Smith, *"For the Purposes of Defense,"* 28; and Spencer C. Tucker, *The Jeffersonian Gunboat Navy* (Columbia: University of South Carolina Press, 1993), 12–14.
62. Act Pertaining to the Navy, United States Statutes at Large, dated 28 February 1803, *Naval Documents, Barbary Powers,* 2:366–67; and Tucker, *The Jeffersonian Gunboat Navy,* 13, 17.
63. Irwin, *Diplomatic Relations,* 128–29; Lambert, *The Barbary Wars,* 136–39; London, *Victory in Tripoli,* 115; and Smith, *"For the Purposes of Defense,"* 27–28.
64. Robert Smith, Secretary of the Navy, concerning Commodore Morris' squadron in the Mediterranean, Court of Inquiry, 31 August 1803, *Naval Documents, Barbary Powers,* 2:526–31; Nash, *The Forgotten Wars,* 206–8; and *Naval Documents, Barbary Powers,* 2:457–58, 526–27, 528; 4:105.
65. Extracts from journal of Midn. Henry Wadsworth, U.S. Navy, on board USS *New York,* Capt. Richard V. Morris, U.S. Navy Commanding, 31 May and 2 June 1803, *Naval Documents, Barbary Powers,* 2:432, 435–36.
66. Extract from journal of Midn. Henry Wadsworth, U.S. Navy, on board USS *New York,* Capt. Richard V. Morris, U.S. Navy Commanding, 2 June 1803, *Naval Documents, Barbary Powers,* 2:435–36; and London, *Victory in Tripoli,* 125–37.
67. Capt. John Rodgers, U.S. Navy to the Secretary of the Navy, 4 December 1803, *Naval Documents, Barbary Powers,* 2:459–60; Extract and translation form a journal kept in French by an unknown person on board the U.S. frigate *John Adams,* Capt. John Rodgers, U.S. Navy, commanding, from Tuesday, 28 to Wednesday,

29 June 1803, *Naval Documents, Barbary Powers,* 2:404; Rodgers to Morris, report dated 30 June 1803 from on board the *New York, Naval Documents, Barbary Powers,* 2:465–66; and Extract from the journal of Midn. Henry Wadsworth, on board the USS *New York,* 6 July 1803, *Naval Documents, Barbary Powers,* 2:469.

68. James Leander Cathcart, appointed U.S. Consul, Tunis, to Capt. Richard V. Morris, U.S. Navy, Naples, 1 August 1803, *Naval Documents, Barbary Powers,* 2:503–4; and London, *Victory in Tripoli,* 128–31.

69. Chipp Reid, *Intrepid Sailors: The Legacy of Preble's Boys and the Tripoli Campaign* (Annapolis, Md.: Naval Institute Press, 2012), 53, 61–62.

70. Resume prepared by the Navy Department in 1806 or 1807 concerning the U.S. Squadron in the Mediterranean, *Naval Documents, Barbary Powers,* 3:11–13; Declaration of Peace between the United States and the Emperor of Morocco under Imperial Seal, 8 or 9 October 1803, *Naval Documents, Barbary Powers,* 3:118; Emperor of Morocco to President Thomas Jefferson and the Senate of the United States, letter under Imperial Seal, 11 October 1803, *Naval Documents, Barbary Powers,* 3:124–25; Preble to the Secretary of the Navy, 5 to 17 October 1803, *Naval Documents, Barbary Powers,* 3:139–43; and Tobias Lear, U.S. Consul General, Algiers, to the Secretary of State, 18 October 1803, *Naval Documents, Barbary Powers,* 3:146–53.

71. Secretary of the Navy to Capt. Edward Preble, U.S. Navy, 13 July 1803, *Naval Documents, Barbary Powers,* 2:474–77.

72. Capt. William Bainbridge, U.S. Navy to the Secretary of the Navy, 1 November 1803, *Naval Documents, Barbary Powers,* 3:171–73; and Bainbridge to Preble, 12 November 1803, *Naval Documents, Barbary Powers,* 3:173–74.

73. Joseph Pulis, U.S. Consul, Malta, to Preble, 26 November 1803, *Naval Documents, Barbary Powers,* 3:236–37; Lambert, *The Barbary Wars,* 140–41; London, *Victory in Tripoli,* 155–58; Nash, *The Forgotten Wars,* 232–33; and Zacks, *The Pirate Coast,* 29–30, 77.

74. Smith, *"For the Purposes of Defense,"* 29–30.

75. Bainbridge to Preble, 5 December 1803, *Naval Documents, Barbary Powers,* 3:253–54; Bainbridge to Preble, 18 January 1804, *Naval Documents, Barbary Powers,* 3:346–47; Preble to the Secretary of

the Navy, 19 February 1804, *Naval Documents, Barbary Powers,* 3:413; Decatur to Preble, 17 February 1804, *Naval Documents, Barbary Powers,* 3:414–15; Lt. Charles Stewart to Preble, 19 February 1804, *Naval Documents, Barbary Powers,* 3:415–16; and Nash, *The Forgotten Wars,* 231, 234.

76. Preble to Stewart, 31 January 1804, *Naval Documents, Barbary Powers,* 3:375–76; Preble to Decatur, 31 January 1804, *Naval Documents, Barbary Powers,* 3:376–77; Preble to the Secretary of the Navy, 3 February 1804, *Naval Documents, Barbary Powers,* 3:384–86; Irwin, *Diplomatic Relations,* 135–36; Nash, *The Forgotten Wars,* 236–42; and Zacks, *The Pirate Coast,* 81–83.

77. Robert Smith, Secretary of the Navy, Statement concerning the destruction of the frigate *Philadelphia,* 13 November 1804, *Naval Documents, Barbary Powers,* 3:422–24; George Davis, U.S. Charge d'Affairs, Tunis, to the Secretary of State, 26 March 1804, *Naval Documents, Barbary Powers,* 3:524–35; and Extract from the journal of Surgeon Jonathan Cowdery, U.S. Navy, *Naval Documents, Barbary Powers,* 3:529–32.

78. Preble to the Secretary of the Navy, 17 January 1804, *Naval Documents, Barbary Powers,* 3:337–40; and Preble to the Secretary of the Navy, 11 March 1804, *Naval Documents, Barbary Powers,* 3:485–86.

79. Hamet, Lawful Bashaw of Tripoli to President Thomas Jefferson, 20 January 1803, *Naval Documents, Barbary Powers,* 3:347; and Zacks, *The Pirate Coast,* 86.

80. Richard Farquhar to President Thomas Jefferson, 15 November 1803, *Naval Documents, Barbary Powers,* 3:222; and Farquhar to Preble, 11 April 1804, *Naval Documents, Barbary Powers,* 4:19.

81. James Leander Cathcart, ex-Consul, Tripoli, to William Eaton, U.S. Consul, Tunis, 29 June 1801, *Naval Documents, Barbary Powers,* 1:493–95; Eaton to any American Commander or Agent in the Mediterranean, 29 March 1802, *Naval Documents, Barbary Powers,* 2:97; Eaton to Mohamet Caramelli [*sic*] Bashaw of Tripoli, 6 August 1802, *Naval Documents, Barbary Powers,* 2:227; and Irwin, *Diplomatic Relations,* 110–11.

82. Preble to the Secretary of the Navy, 17 January 1804, *Naval Documents, Barbary Powers,* 3:337–40; and Preble to the Secretary of the Navy, 11 March 1804, *Naval Documents, Barbary Powers,* 3:485–88.

83. Nash, *The Forgotten Wars,* 268–69.
84. Lambert, *The Barbary Wars,* 145–50.
85. Irwin, *Diplomatic Relations,* 143–45.
86. Sir John Acton, Prime Minister of State, the Two Sicilies, 13 May 1804, *Naval Documents, Barbary Powers,* 4:197–98; Preble to the Secretary of the Navy, 15 May 1804, *Naval Documents, Barbary Powers,* 4:103; and Preble to Joseph Barnes, U.S. Consul, Naples, 1 June 1804, *Naval Documents, Barbary Powers,* 4:140–41.
87. Recognition of Gallant Conduct of Personnel in Action of 3 August 1804 by Commodore Preble, *Naval Documents, Barbary Powers,* 4:361; Lambert, *The Barbary Wars,* 147–48; London, *Victory in Tripoli,* 173–82; and Nash, *The Forgotten Wars,* 250–54.
88. Preble to the Secretary of the Navy, detailed report of the attacks against Tripoli, 18 September 1804, *Naval Documents, Barbary Powers,* 4:293–310; Lambert, *The Barbary Wars,* 148–49; and Zacks, *The Pirate Coast,* 103–6.
89. Preble to the Secretary of the Navy, 30 May 1804, *Naval Documents, Barbary Powers,* 4:130–31; Secretary of the Navy to Capt. Samuel Barron, 6 June 1804, *Naval Documents, Barbary Powers,* 4:152–54; The relative Force of the four Squadrons sent to the Mediterranean, official listing of ships, 22 May 1805, *Naval Documents, Barbary Powers,* 4:30–31; and President Thomas Jefferson to Capt. Samuel Barron, 31 May 1804, *Naval Documents, Barbary Powers,* 4:132.
90. Secretary of the Navy to William Eaton, Appointment and Commission, 26 and 30 May 1804, Navy Department, Washington, *Naval Documents, Barbary Powers,* 4:120.
91. Farquhar to Barron, 1 November 1804, *Naval Documents, Barbary Powers,* 5:109–10; Salvatore Bufuttil, Consul of Hamet Caramanli, rightful Bashaw of Tripoli to Barron, 1 November 1804, *Naval Documents, Barbary Powers,* 5:110.
92. Barron to Hull, 13 September 1804 with Enclosure dated 15 September 1804, *Naval Documents, Barbary Powers,* 5:19–20; Barron to Hull, 10 November 1804, *Naval Documents, Barbary Powers,* 5:134; and Eaton to the Secretary of the Navy, 13 November 1804, *Naval Documents, Barbary Powers,* 5:140–41.
93. Extract from the journal of William Eaton, 1 December 1804, *Naval Documents, Barbary Powers,* 5:171; Extract from the journal of

William Eaton, 26 November 1804, *Naval Documents, Barbary Powers,* 5:162; and Eaton to the Secretary of the Navy, 28 November 1804, *Naval Documents, Barbary Powers,* 5:166–67.

94. Extract from the journal of William Eaton, 1 December 1804, *Naval Documents, Barbary Powers,* 5:171; and Extract from the journal of William Eaton, 7 December 1804, *Naval Documents, Barbary Powers,* 5:186–89.
95. Eaton to Hull, 8 January 1805, *Naval Documents, Barbary Powers,* 5:267–68.
96. Eaton to Hull, 24 December 1804, *Naval Documents, Barbary Powers,* 5:214–15; Eaton to Hull, 8 January 1805, *Naval Documents, Barbary Powers,* 5:268; Eaton to Preble, 25 January 1805–16 February 1805, *Naval Documents, Barbary Powers,* 5:300–305; and Eaton to Hull, 5 February 1805, *Naval Documents, Barbary Powers,* 5:333–34.
97. Hamet Caramanli, rightful Bashaw of Tripoli to Barron, 15 February 1805, *Naval Documents, Barbary Powers,* 5:356.
98. Extract from a letter to an officer on board U.S. Brig *Argus,* from Midn. Pascal Paoli Peck, U.S. Navy, 4 July 1805, *Naval Documents, Barbary Powers,* 5:361–63.
99. Eaton to the Secretary of the Navy, 13 February 1805, *Naval Documents, Barbary Powers,* 5:348–50.
100. Eaton to the Secretary of the Navy, 13 February 1805, *Naval Documents, Barbary Powers,* 5:350–51; and Eaton to Barron, 14 February 1805, *Naval Documents, Barbary Powers,* 5:353–54.
101. Extract from the journal of William Eaton, 2 April 1805, *Naval Documents, Barbary Powers,* 5:478.
102. Eaton to the Secretary of State, letter with enclosed Convention between the United States of America and his Highness, Hamet, Caramanly, Bashaw of Tripoli, 14 March 1805, *Naval Documents, Barbary Powers,* 5:367–69; and Irwin, *Diplomatic Relations,* 146–47, 149.
103. Barron to the Secretary of the Navy, 6 April 1805, *Naval Documents, Barbary Powers,* 5:485–86.
104. Eaton to the Secretary of State, letter with enclosed Convention between the United States of America and his Highness Hamet Caramanly, Bashaw of Tripoli, 14 March 1805, *Naval Documents, Barbary Powers,* 5:367–69; Barron to the Secretary of the Navy, 6

April 1805, *Naval Documents, Barbary Powers,* 5:485–86; Extract from the journal of William Eaton, 1 April 1805, *Naval Documents, Barbary Powers,* 5:475–76; and Extract from the journal of William Eaton, 2 April 1805, *Naval Documents, Barbary Powers,* 5:478.

105. Proclamation of William Eaton to the Inhabitants of Tripoli, 29 March 1805, *Naval Documents, Barbary Powers,* 5:467–70; Eaton to Barron, 29 April 1805, *Naval Documents, Barbary Powers,* 5:550–53.

106. Barron to Eaton, 15 April 1805, *Naval Documents, Barbary Powers,* 5:511–12.

107. Extract from the journal of William Eaton, 20 March 1805, *Naval Documents, Barbary Powers,* 5:432–33.

108. Extract from the journal of William Eaton, 26 March 1805, *Naval Documents, Barbary Powers,* 5:459; Extract from the journal of William Eaton, 27 March 1805, *Naval Documents, Barbary Powers,* 5:459; and Extract from the journal of William Eaton, 30 March 1805, *Naval Documents, Barbary Powers,* 5:472.

109. Extract from the journal of William Eaton, 5 April 1805, *Naval Documents, Barbary Powers,* 5:482–83; Extract from the journal of William Eaton, 14 April 1805, *Naval Documents, Barbary Powers,* 5:509–10; and Extract from the journal of William Eaton, 9 April 1805, *Naval Documents, Barbary Powers,* 5:495.

110. Extract from the journal of William Eaton, 13 April 1805, *Naval Documents, Barbary Powers,* 5:509.

111. Extract from the journal of William Eaton, 10 April 1805, *Naval Documents, Barbary Powers,* 5:498–99.

112. Extract from the journal of William Eaton, 15–22 April 1805, *Naval Documents, Barbary Powers,* 5:512–13; Extract from a letter to an officer on board the U.S. Brig *Argus,* from Midn. Pascal Paoli Peck, 4 July 1805, *Naval Documents, Barbary Powers,* 5:361–63; Barron to Eaton, 22 March 1805, *Naval Documents, Barbary Powers,* 5:438–41; Lambert, *The Barbary Wars,* 152; London, *Victory in Tripoli,* 204–7; and Zacks, *The Pirate Coast,* 223–26.

113. Hull to Eaton, 9 April 1805, *Naval Documents, Barbary Powers,* 5:493–94.

114. Irwin, *Diplomatic Relations,* 146–48.

115. Extract from the journal of William Eaton, 24 April 1805, *Naval Documents, Barbary Powers,* 5:538.

116. Extract from the journal of William Eaton, 25 April 1805, *Naval Documents, Barbary Powers,* 5:540–41.
117. Eaton to the Governor of Derna, 26 April 1805 (with reply), *Naval Documents, Barbary Powers,* 5:542; and London, *Victory in Tripoli,* 210–11.
118. Hull to Barron, 28 April 1805, *Naval Documents, Barbary Powers,* 5:547–48; and Eaton to Barron, 29 April 1805, *Naval Documents, Barbary Powers,* 5:553–55.
119. The first two lines of the Marines' Hymn, *From the Halls of Montezuma, To the Shores of Tripoli,* are among the most famous of any service hymn in the world. The second line obviously refers to the 28 April 1805 attack on Derna, Tripoli. Hull to Barron, 28 April 1805, *Naval Documents, Barbary Powers,* 5:547–48; and U.S. Senate, Resolution concerning Reward for March to and Capture of Derna, 18 March 1806, *Naval Documents, Barbary Powers,* 5:545–46.
120. Extract for the journal of William Eaton, 8 May 1805, *Naval Documents, Barbary Powers,* 6:6; Eaton to Barron, 15–17 May 1805, *Naval Documents, Barbary Powers,* 6:14–15; Extract from the journal of William Eaton, 28 May 1805, *Naval Documents, Barbary Powers,* 6:55; Eaton to Barron, 29 May–11 June 1805, *Naval Documents, Barbary Powers,* 6:58–63; Resume concerning the U.S. Squadron in the Mediterranean prepared in 1806 or 1807, *Naval Documents, Barbary Powers,* 5:8–11; and Irwin, *Diplomatic Relations,* 147–48.
121. Tobias Lear, U.S. Consul General, Algiers, to Captain John Rodgers, 1 May 1805, *Naval Documents, Barbary Powers,* 6:1–2; Resume concerning the U.S. Squadron in the Mediterranean prepared in 1806 or 1807, *Naval Documents, Barbary Power,* 5:8–11; and Irwin, *Diplomatic Relations,* 150–54.
122. Treaty of Peace and Amity between the United States and Tripoli, 4 June 1805, *Naval Documents, Barbary Powers,* 6:81–82; Lambert, *The Barbary Wars,* 169; and Zacks, *The Pirate Coast,* 273–77.
123. Eaton to Barron, 29 May–11 June 1804, *Naval Documents, Barbary Powers,* 6:58–63; Hamet Bashaw to the People of the United States of America, 1 September 1805, *Naval Documents, Barbary Powers,* 6:263–64; and Statement of the Account of Capt. Hugh G. Campbell, U.S. Navy, 7 June 1807–15 February 1808, *Naval Documents, Barbary Powers,* 6:531.

124. Treaty of Peace and Amity between the United States and Tripoli, 4 June 1805, *Naval Documents, Barbary Powers,* 6:81–82; and Resume concerning the U.S. Squadron in the Mediterranean prepared in 1806 or 1807, *Naval Documents, Barbary Powers,* 5:8–11.
125. George Davis, U.S. Consul, Tripoli, 12 May 1807, *Naval Documents, Barbary Powers,* 6:522–23; Davis to Hamet Caramanli, 7 October 1807, *Naval Documents, Barbary Powers,* 6:570; and Thomas Jefferson to the United States Senate, 11 November 1807, *Naval Documents, Barbary Powers,* 6:577–78.
126. Eaton to the U.S. House of Representatives, 3 November 1807, *Naval Documents, Barbary Powers,* 6:575–76.
127. Officers of the Expedition to Derna to Eaton, 20 May 1805, *Naval Documents, Barbary Powers,* 6:28–29; Eaton to Rodgers, 13 June 1805, *Naval Documents, Barbary Powers,* 6:116–17; Eaton to the Secretary of the Navy, 9 August 1805, *Naval Documents, Barbary Powers,* 6:213–19; and Eaton to the Secretary of the Navy, 5 December 1805, *Naval Documents, Barbary Powers,* 6:315.
128. Resolution in the Senate of the United States, 18 March 1806, *Naval Documents, Barbary Powers,* 5:545–46; Reid, *Intrepid Sailors,* 235–38; and Irwin, *Diplomatic Relations,* 158–60.
129. Eaton to the Honorable Stephen Row Bradley, Chairman of the Committee on the Application of Hamet Caramanli, United States Senate, 16 February 1806, *Naval Documents, Barbary Powers,* 6:370–71; President Thomas Jefferson to the Congress of the United States, 13 January 1806, *Naval Documents, Barbary Powers,* 6:344–45; and Zacks, *The Pirate Coast,* 319–29.
130. Zacks, *The Pirate Coast,* 345, 370.
131. James E. McDougall, "History of the Mameluke Sword of the United States Marine Corps," *Marine Corps Gazette* (Web Site Exclusive), November 2003.
132. Lear to George Davis, U.S. Charge d'Affairs, Tunis, 15 May 1805, *Naval Documents, Barbary Powers,* 6:16–17; Lear to Davis, 23 May 1805, *Naval Documents, Barbary Powers,* 6:44; and Hamuda Bey of Tunis to Barron, 28 May 1805, *Naval Documents, Barbary Powers,* 6:53–54.
133. Conversation between the Bey of Tunis and George Davis, U.S. Charge d'Affairs, (about) 1 August 1805, *Naval Documents, Barbary*

Powers, 6:200; Rodgers to Davis, ultimatum to the Bey of Tunis, 2 August 1805, *Naval Documents, Barbary Powers,* 6:202; and Irwin, *Diplomatic Relations,* 161–64.

134. Hamuda Bassaw Bey, the Bey of Tunis, to Rodgers, 14 August 1805, *Naval Documents, Barbary Powers,* 6:227; and Rodgers to Lear, 14 August 1805, *Naval Documents, Barbary Powers,* 6:228.

CHAPTER 4. AMPHIBIOUS OPERATIONS IN THE WAR OF 1812

1. Gene A. Smith, *"For the Purposes of Defense": The Politics of the Jeffersonian Gunboat Program* (Newark: University of Delaware Press, 1995), 30–31, 54–57; Craig L. Symonds, *Navalists and Antinavalists: The Naval Policy Debate in the United States, 1785–1827* (Newark: University of Delaware Press, 1980), 105–8; and Spencer C. Tucker, *The Jefferson Gunboat Navy* (Columbia: University of South Carolina Press, 1993), 17–20.
2. Secretary of the Navy to Barron, 7 March 1805, in *Naval Documents Related to the United States Wars with the Barbary Powers* [hereafter, *Naval Documents, Barbary Powers*], 6 vols., ed. Dudley W. Knox (Washington D.C.: U.S. Government Printing Office, 1939–1944), 5:395; and Circular letter to Commander of Gunboats from the Secretary of the Navy, 25 March 1805, *Naval Documents, Barbary Powers,* 5:451–52.
3. Secretary of the Navy to President Thomas Jefferson, 16 September 1805, *Naval Documents, Barbary Powers,* 6:280–82.
4. Capt. James Barron to the Secretary of the Navy, 23 June 1807, *Naval Documents, Barbary Powers,* 6:537–38; and Extract from the Log of U.S. Frigate *Chesapeake,* 22 July 1807, in *The Naval War of 1812: A Documentary History* [hereafter, *Naval War*], 3 vols., ed. William S. Dudley and Michael J. Crawford (Washington D.C.: U.S. Government Printing Office, 1985–2002), 1:27–28.
5. Secretary of the Navy to Barron, 12 September 1807, *Naval Documents, Barbary Powers,* 6:557–58; and Secretary of the Navy to Captain John Rodgers, 4 November 1807, *Naval Documents, Barbary Powers,* 6:561–70.

6. Proclamation by Thomas Jefferson, President of the U.S. of America, 2 July 1807, *Naval War,* 1:29–31.
7. President James Madison to Congress, 1 June 1812, *Naval War,* 1:73–81; James Fulton Zimmerman, *Impressment of American Seamen* (New York: Columbia University Press, 1925), 182–84; and Reginald Horsman, *The Causes of The War of 1812* (Philadelphia: University of Pennsylvania Press 1962), 17, 59–177, 267.
8. Orders in Council were a tightening of the British naval blockade on Napoleon's Europe that required neutral ships to visit Britain, pay a duty, and receive a license before preceding to Europe. Alan Taylor, *The Civil War of 1812: American Citizens, British Soldiers, Irish Rebels, and Indian Allies* (New York: Knopf, 2010), 116.
9. Providence Resolution, 7 April 1812, *Naval War,* 1:69–72; Horsman, *The Causes of the War of 1812,* 124, 225–36, 179; and Taylor, *The Civil War of 1812,* 5–6, 125–45.
10. J. C. A. Stagg, *The War of 1812: Conflict for a Continent* (New York: Cambridge University Press, 2012), 49–52, 60–74, 78; and Ronald J. Drez, *The War of 1812: Conflict and Deception* (Baton Rouge: Louisiana State University, 2014), 94–104.
11. Secretary of the Navy Hamilton to Langdon Cheves, Chairman of the Naval Committee, 3 December 1811, *Naval War,* 1:53–60.
12. Commo. Isaac Chauncey to Hamilton, 1 and 8 January 1813, *Naval War,* 2:406–7.
13. Chauncey to Secretary of the Navy Jones, 28 April 1813, *Naval War,* 2:449–50; Maj. Gen. Sir Roger Hale Sheaffe, British Army to Gov.-Gen. Sir George Prevost, 5 May 1812, *Naval War,* 2:455–57; Maj. Gen. Henry Dearborn, U.S.A., to Secretary of War John Armstrong, 28 April 1813, *Naval War,* 2:450–52; and Robert Malcomson, *Capital in Flames: The American Attack on York, 1813* (Toronto: Robin Brass Studio, 2008), 201–38.
14. Chauncey to Jones, 7 May 1813, *Naval War,* 2:452–53; and Lt. Robert H. Barclay, R.N., to Noah Freer, British Military Secretary, 9 May 1813, *Naval War,* 2:458–59.
15. Timothy D. Johnson, *Winfield Scott: The Quest for Military Glory* (Lawrence: University Press of Kansas, 1998), 29–33.
16. John R. Grodzinski, *Defender of Canada: Sir George Prevost and the War of 1812* (Norman: University of Oklahoma Press, 2013), xii,

112–17; Robert Malcomson, *Lords of the Lake: The Naval War on Lake Ontario, 1812–1814* (Annapolis, Md.: Naval Institute Press, 1998), 129–39; John D. Morris, *Sword of the Border: Major General Jacob Jennings Brown, 1775–1828* (Kent, Ohio: Kent State University Press, 2000), 40–48; and Patrick A. Wilder, *The Battle of Sackett's Harbour* (Baltimore: Nautical & Aviation Co., 1994), 85–120.

17. Malcomson, *Capital in Flames,* 309–12.
18. David Skaggs and Gerard Altoff, *A Signal Victory: The Lake Erie Campaign, 1812–13* (Annapolis, Md.: Naval Institute Press, 1997).
19. Capt. Oliver H. Perry to Maj. Gen. William Henry Harrison, U.S.A., 10 September 1813, *Naval War,* 2:553.
20. Morris Zaslow, ed., *The Defended Border: Upper Canada and the War of 1812* (Toronto: Macmillan, 1964), 61–83; and Sandy Antal, *A Wampum Denied: Procter's War of 1812* (Ottawa: Carleton University Press, 1997), 331–49.
21. Donald E. Graves, *Field of Glory: The Battle of Crysler's Farm, 1813* (Toronto: Robin Brass Studio, 1999), 98–112, 211–56; Richard D. Blackmon, *The Creek War 1813–1814* (Washington, D.C.: Center for Military History, 2014), 7–41; Mike Bunn and Clay Williams, *Battle for the Southern Frontier: The Creek War and the War of 1812* (Charleston, S.C.: History Press, 2008), 73–88; Malcomson, *Lords of the Lake,* 218–24; Barry Gough, *Fighting Sail on Lake Huron and Georgian Bay: The War of 1812 and Its Aftermath* (Annapolis, Md.: Naval Institute Press, 2002), 12–13, 54–56, 79–80; and Robert V. Remini, *The Battle of New Orleans: Andrew Jackson and America's First Military Victory* (New York: Penguin Putnam, 1999), 9–14.
22. Col. Sir Thomas Sidney Beckwith, British Army, to Adm. Sir John Warren, R.N., 5 July 1813, *Naval War,* 2:304–5; British officer Charles Napier quoted in Donald R. Hickey, *The War of 1812: A Forgotten Conflict* (Urbana: University of Illinois Press, 1989), 154; *Niles' Register* quotation from 1813 and 1814 in Hickey, *The War of 1812,* 154, 383n.
23. Capt. John Cassin to Secretary of the Navy Jones, 23 June 1813, *Naval War,* 2:359–60; Adm. Sir John B. Warren, R.N., to First Secretary of the Admiralty John Croker, 24 June 1813, *Naval War,* 2:360–61; and Christopher T. George, *Terror on the Chesapeake:*

The War of 1812 on the Bay (Shippenburg, Pa.: White Mane Books, 2000), 40–48.

24. Robert Aitchison, *A British Eyewitness at the Battle of New Orleans: The Memoir of Royal Navy Admiral Robert Aitchison, 1808–1827,* ed. Gene A. Smith (New Orleans: Historic New Orleans Collection, 2004), 49–52; and George F. W. Young, *The British Capture and Occupation of Downeast Main, 1814–1815/1818* (Stonington, Maine: Penobscot Books, 2014), 1–6, 16–23, 69, 86–88.
25. Hand Bill issued by the Portland Gazette on 2 June 1814, National Archives and Records Administration [NARA] Record Group [RG] 107, Microcopy No. 222 [M 222], Roll 14, 1814 (S–Z); Croker to Cochrane, letter No. 40, 4 April 1814, *Naval War,* 3:70; Croker to Cochrane, letter No. 61, 19 May 1814, *Naval War,* 3:71–72; and Bathurst to Maj. Gen. Edward Barnes, British Army, 20 May 1814, *Naval War,* 3:72–74. Although initially addressed to Barnes, this letter actually went to Robert Ross for action. Barnes remained with the British army in Spain.
26. Bathurst to Barnes, 20 May 1814, *Naval War,* 3:72; and Croker to Cochrane, 4 April 1814, *Naval War,* 3:70.
27. Bathurst to Barnes, 20 May 1814, *Naval War,* 3:72–73.
28. First Secretary of the Admiralty John W. Croker to Vice Adm. Sir Alexander F. I. Cochrane, R.N., 4 April 1814, *Naval War,* 3:70; Croker to Cochrane, 19 May 1814, *Naval War,* 2:71; and Secretary of State for War and the Colonies Earl Bathurst to Maj. Gen. Edward Barnes, British Army, 20 May 1814, *Naval War,* 3:72.
29. Capt. Thomas Brown, R.N., to Rear Adm. George Cockburn, R.N., 23 June 1814, *Naval War,* 3:121–22; and Gene Allen Smith, *The Slaves' Gamble: Choosing Sides in the War of 1812* (New York: Palgrave Macmillan, 2013), 99–105.
30. Secretary of the Navy William Jones to Capt. Joshua Barney, 18 February 1814, *Naval War,* 3:33–35; and Barney to Jones, 1 March 1814, *Naval War,* 3:35.
31. Barney to Jones, 3 June 1814, *Naval War,* 1:80–81; Rear Adm. George Cockburn, R.N., to Capt. Robert Barrie, R.N., 5 June 1814, *Naval War,* 3:84; Louis Arthur Norton, *Joshua Barney: Hero of the Revolution and 1812* (Annapolis, Md.: Naval Institute Press, 2000), 171–72; Capt. Joshua Barney to Secretary of the Navy William

Jones, 9 June 1814, *Naval War,* 3:84–85; Capt. Joshua Barney to Secretary of the Navy William Jones, 9 June 1814, *Naval War,* 3:84–85; Barney to Jones, 11 June 1814, *Naval War,* 3:88–89; and Barrie to Cockburn, 11 June 1814, *Naval War,* 3:89–91.

32. Secretary of the Navy Jones to Samuel Miller, 18 June 1814, NARA, Washington, D.C., RG 80, General Records of the Department of the Navy, Officer[s?] of the Marine Corps, 205; Secretary of the Navy Jones to Lt. Col. F. Wharton, Commandant of the Marine Corps, 10 June 1814, NARA, RG 80, 205–6; Jones to Barney, 10 June 1814, *Naval War,* 3:85–88; and Jones to Barney, 12 June 1814, *Naval War,* 3:97–98.

33. Barney to Jones, 26 June 1814, *Naval War,* 3:123; Joshua Barney to Louis Barney, 27 June 1814, *Naval War,* 3:123–25; Brown to Cockburn, 27 June 1814, *Naval War,* 3:127; and Barney to Jones, 26 June 1814, *Naval War,* 3:123.

34. Jones to Barney, 20 August 1814, *Naval War,* 3:188; Jones to Barney, 19 August 1814, *Naval War,* 3:186–87; and Barney to Jones, 20 August 1814, *Naval War,* 3:186–88.

35. Marine Corps Research Center, Quantico, Virginia, Archives, Samuel Miller Papers, The Battle of Bladensburg: In a Letter to Henry Banning, Esq., by an Officer of General Smith's Staff, 10 September 1814, 12 [hereafter, Staff Letter, Miller Papers); and Barney to Jones, 29 August 1814, *Naval War,* 3:207–8.

36. Staff Letter, Miller Papers, 3; and Anthony S. Pitch, *The Burning of Washington: The British Invasion of 1814* (Annapolis, Md.: Naval Institute Press, 1998).

37. Determined by personal observation of the author and the comments of Gen. Ross as quoted in Alfred Thayer Mahan, *Sea Power in Its Relations to the War of 1812,* 2 vols. (Cambridge: Cambridge University Press, 1905), 2:346; and Pitch, *The Burning of Washington,* 67–74.

38. Cockburn to Cochrane, 27 August 1814, *Naval War,* 3:220–23; Staff Letter, Miller Papers, 5.

39. Cockburn to Cochrane, 27 August 1814, *Naval War,* 3:220–23; Staff Letter, Miller Papers, 7–8, 13; Marine Corps Historical Library, Navy Yard, Washington, D.C., Archives, Rare Book Collection, Winder to Armstrong, 27 August 1814, in *Documents Accompanying the*

Report of the Committee to Inquire into the Causes and Particulars of the Invasion of Washington by the British Forces in the Month of August, 1814 (Washington, D.C.: A. and G. Way Publishers, 1814), 120–21.

40. Staff Letter, Miller Papers, 6, 9, 12.
41. Staff Letter, Miller Papers, 6, 12–13; and Barney to Jones, Report of the Battle of Bladensburg, 29 August 1814, Marine Corps Historical Center, Navy Yard, Washington, D.C., Archives, 1–2; and Norton, *Joshua Barney,* 180–82.
42. Barney to Jones, 29 August 1814, *Naval War,* 3:207; and Staff Letter, Miller Papers, 6.
43. Barney to Jones, 29 August 1814, *Naval War,* 3:207.
44. This conclusion is based on the author's personal observation and evaluation of the battlefield.
45. Barney to Jones, 29 August 1814, *Naval War,* 3:207–8.
46. Ibid.; and Citation of President James Madison 26 November 1814, NARA, RG 80.
47. *Documents Accompanying the Report of the Committee,* 24; Pitch, *The Burning of Washington,* 170–79; and Charles G. Muller, *The Darkest Day: The Washington-Baltimore Campaign during the War of 1812* (New York: J. B. Lippincott, 1963), 62, 154–66.
48. Cochrane to Croker, 17 September 1814, *Naval War,* 3:186; Rear Adm. Edward Codington to Jane Codington, 10 September 1814, *Naval War,* 3:271; Cochrane to Melville, 3 September 1814, *Naval War,* 3:269–71; Cochrane to Melville, 17 September 1814, *Naval War,* 3:289; and Codrington to Codrington, 10 September 1814, *Naval War,* 3:271.
49. Cochrane to Melville, 3 September 1814, *Naval War,* 3:269–70; Codrington to Codrington, 10 September 1814, *Naval War,* 3:271; Cochrane to Melville, 17 September 1814, *Naval War,* 3:289; and Cochrane to Croker, 17 September 1814, *Naval War,* 3:286.
50. Maj. Gen. Samuel Smith to Secretary of War John Armstrong, 30 June 1814, NARA, RG 107, M 221, Roll 66; Smith to Armstrong, 11 July 1814 regarding enemy sightings and requesting callout authority, NARA, RG 107, M 221, Roll 66; Smith to Armstrong, 19 July 1814, requesting rifles and power, NARA, RG 107, M 221, Roll 66; Smith to Armstrong, 20 July 1814, relating to command relations,

artillery support, and reinforcements for Fort McHenry, NARA, RG 107, M 221, Roll 66; and Smith to Armstrong, 28 July 1814, requesting his troops not be requisitioned upon call up, NARA, RG 107, M 221, Roll 66.

51. Smith to Armstrong, 24 July 1814, NARA, RG 107, M 221, Roll 66; Commodore John Rodgers to Secretary of the Navy William Jones, 27 August 1814, *Naval War,* 3:259–60; and Scott S. Sheads, *The Rockets' Red Glare: The Maritime Defense of Baltimore in 1814* (Centerville, Md.: Tidewater Publishing, 1986), 12–13, 61.

52. Jones to Rodgers, 19 August 1814, *Naval War,* 3:199; Commo. John Rodgers to Secretary of the Navy William Jones, 27 August 1814, *Naval War,* 3:259–60; and Commo. John Rodgers: General Orders issued at Baltimore, 28 August 1814, *Naval War,* 3:260.

53. Smith to Rodgers, 1 September 1814, *Naval War,* 3: 261; Rodgers to Smith, 1 September 1814, *Naval War,* 3:261; Smith to Armstrong, 5 September 1814, NARA, RG 107, M 221, Roll 66; Thomas Swann to Armstrong, report from observers at Point Lookout, 29 August 1814, NARA, RG 107, M 221, Roll 66; Smith to Rodgers, 1 September 1814, *Naval War,* 3:261; Rodgers to Smith, 1 September 1814, *Naval War,* 3:261–62; and Rodgers to Commo. Alexander Murray, 9 September 1814, *Naval War,* 3:263.

54. Rodgers to Commo. Alexander Murray, 9 September 1814, *Naval War,* 3:263; Rodgers to Master Cmdt. Robert T. Spence, 8 September 1814, *Naval War,* 3:263; Lt. Solomon Rutter, Flotilla Service, to Rodgers, 11 September 1814, *Naval War,* 3:264; Rodgers to Jones, 23 September 1814, *Naval War,* 3:298–302; George Robert Gleig, *A Narrative of the Campaigns of the British Army at Washington and New Orleans, under Generals Ross, Pakenham, and Lambert, in the Years 1814 and 1815; with some accounts of the countries visited* (London: John Murray, Albemarle-Street, 1821), 187; and Smith to acting Secretary of War James Monroe, 19 September 1814, NARA, RG 107, M 221, Roll 66. (President Madison appointed Monroe as acting Secretary of War as a replacement for John Armstrong on 4 September 1814.)

55. Smith to Armstrong, 27 August 1814, NARA, RG 107, M 221, Roll 66; and Rodgers to Jones, 27 August 1814, *Naval War,* 3:259.

56. Smith to Armstrong, 27 August 1814, NARA, RG 107, M 221, Roll 66; and Rodgers to Jones, 27 August 1814, *Naval War,* 3:259–60.
57. Thomas Swann to Armstrong, 29 August 1814, NARA, RG 107, M 221, Roll 66; Smith to Monroe, 19 September 1814, NARA, RG 107, M 221, Roll 66; Swann to Armstrong, 5 September 1814, NARA, RG 107, M 221, Roll 66; Gleig, *Campaigns of the British Army,* 164–65; John H. Schroder, *Commodore John Rodgers: Paragon of the Early American Navy* (Gainesville: University Press of Florida, 2006), 138–39.
58. Brooke to Bathurst, 17 September 1814, *Naval War,* 3:282–85; Brooke to Bathurst, 17 September 1814, *Naval War,* 3:282; Brooke to Bathurst, 17 September 1814, *Naval War,* 3:282; Brig. Gen. John Stricker to Smith, 13 September 1814, NARA, RG 107, M 221, Roll 66; Brig. Gen. John Stricker to Smith, 13 September 1814, NARA, RG 107, M 221, Roll 66; Stricker to Smith, 13 September 1814, NARA, RG 107, M 221, Roll 66; and Gleig, *Campaigns of the British Army,* 166–76.
59. Stricker to Smith, 13 September 1814, NARA, RG 107, M221, Roll 66; Stricter to Smith, 13 September 1814, NARA, RG 107, M221, Roll 66; Gleig, *Campaigns of the British Army,* 170–71; and Joseph A. Whitehorne, *The Battle for Baltimore, 1814* (Baltimore: Nautical & Aviation Publishing, 1997), 232–33.
60. Gleig, *Campaigns of the British Army,* 170–72; Smith to Monroe, 19 September 1814, NARA, RG 107, M 221, Roll 66; and Stricker to Smith, 13 September 1814, NARA, RG 107, M 221, Roll 66.
61. Gleig, *Campaigns of the British Army,* 172–73, 175; and Stricker to Smith, 13 September 1814, NARA, RG 107, M 221, Roll 66.
62. Stricker to Smith, 13 September 1814, NARA, RG 107, M 221, Roll 66; and Gleig, *Campaigns of the British Army,* 175–76.
63. Brooke to Bathurst, 17 September 1814, *Naval War,* 3:282; Cockburn to Cochrane, 15 September 1814, *Naval War,* 3:279; Brooke to Bathurst, 17 September 1814, *Naval War,* 3:282; Gleig, *Campaigns of the British Army,* 175–81; and Stricker to Smith, 13 September 1814, NARA, RG 107, M 221, Roll 66.
64. Department of Defense, Joint Publication 1–02, *Department of Defense Dictionary of Military and Associated Terms,* 14 September 2007, 147.

65. Stricker to Smith, 13 September 1814, NARA, RG 107, M 221, Roll 66. The word "refuse" is a tactical term that means to bend the end of a defensive line to protect it from a flanking attack.
66. Stricker to Smith, 13 September 1814, NARA, RG 107, M 221, Roll 66; and Gleig, *Campaigns of the British Army,* 180.
67. Brooke to Bathurst, 17 September 1814, *Naval War,* 3:282–85; Cockburn to Cochrane, 15 September 1814, *Naval War,* 3:180; Gleig, *Campaigns of the British Army,* 181–83; Gilbert Auchinlek, *A History of the War between Great Britain and the United States of America during the Years 1812, 1813 & 1814.* (London: Arms and Armor Press, 1855), 375; Muller, *The Darkest Day,* 190–91; Smith to Monroe, 19 September 1814, NARA, RG 107, M 221, Roll 66; and Stricker to Smith, 13 September 1814, NARA, RG 107, M 221, Roll 66.
68. Stricker to Smith, 13 September 1814, NARA, RG 107, Roll 66; and Smith to Monroe, 19 September 1814, NARA, RG 107, Roll 66.
69. Brooke to Bathurst, 17 September 1814, *Naval War,* 3:282–85; Cockburn to Cochrane, 15 September 1814, *Naval War,* 3:279–82; and Gleig, *Campaigns of the British Army,* 185–88.
70. Gleig, *Campaigns of the British Army,* 188; and Sheads, *The Rockets' Red Glare,* 93–97.
71. Brooke to Cochrane, 13 September 1814, *Naval War,* 3:277; and Smith to Monroe, 19 September 1814, NARA RG 107, M 221, Roll 66.
72. Brooke to Cochrane, 13 September 1814, *Naval War,* 3:277; and Gleig, *Campaigns of the British Army,* 188–89.
73. Armistead to Monroe, 24 September 1814, NARA, RG 107, M 221, Roll 59.
74. Schroeder, *Commodore John Rodgers,* 139.
75. Armistead to Monroe, 24 September 1814, NARA, RG 107, M 221, Roll 59; and Norman G. Rukert, *Fort McHenry: Home of the Brave* (Baltimore: Bodine & Associates, 1983), 26–32.
76. Armistead to Monroe, 24 September 1814, NARA, RG 107, M 221, Roll 59; Gleig *Campaigns of the British Army,* 185–86; and Muller, *The Darkest Day,* 197.
77. Armistead to Monroe, 24 September 1814, NARA, RG 107, M 221, Roll 59; Cochrane to Cocker, 17 September 1814, *Naval War,* 3:286–88; Rodgers to Master Cmdt. Robert T. Spence, 8 September 1814, *Naval War,* 3:263; Lt. Solomon Rutter, Flotilla Service, to Rodgers,

11 September 1814, *Naval War,* 3:264; Cochrane to Crocker, 17 September 1814, *Naval War,* 3:286–88; Cochrane to Ross, 12 September 1814, *Naval War,* 3:273; Rukert, *Fort McHenry,* 22; and Sheads, *The Rockets' Red Glare,* 82, 85–89.

78. Lt. Henry S. Newcomb to Rodgers, 18 September 1814, *Naval War,* 3:292–94; Rodgers to Jones, 23 September 1814, *Naval War,* 3:298–302; Armistead to Monroe, 24 September 1814, NARA, RG 107, M 221, Roll 59; and Smith to Monroe, 19 September 1814, NARA, RG 107, M 221, Roll 59.

79. Cochrane to Capt. Charles Napier, 13 September 1814, *Naval War,* 3:178; Cochrane to Croker, 17 September 1814, *Naval War,* 3:286–88; and Rukert, *Fort McHenry,* 27–28.

80. Cochrane to Cockburn, 13 September 1814, *Naval War,* 3:277–79; Brooke to Cochrane, 13 September 1814, *Naval War,* 3:279; Brooke to Bathurst, 17 September 1814, *Naval War,* 3:282–85; and Gleig, *Campaigns of the British Army,* 193.

81. Armistead to Monroe, 24 September 1814, NARA, RG 107, M 221, Roll 59; Smith to Monroe, 19 September 1814, NARA, RG 107, M 221, Roll 59; Smith to Monroe, 19 September 1814, NARA, RG 107, M 221, Roll 59; Rodgers to Jones, 14 September 1814, *Naval War,* 3:293; Rodgers to Jones, 14 September 1814, *Naval War,* 3:293; Rodgers to Jones, 23 September 1814, *Naval War,* 3:298–302; Cochrane to Croker, 17 September 1814, *Naval War,* 3:286–88; Brooke to Bathurst, 17 September 1814, *Naval War,* 3:282–85; Stagg, *The War of 1812,* 133; and Smith, *The Slaves' Gamble,* 128.

82. Department of Defense, Joint Publication 3–02, *Joint Doctrine for Amphibious Operations,* 19 September 2001, I-4.

83. Stagg, *The War of 1812,* 132; Drez, *The War of 1812,* 187, 190–95; and Sheads, *The Rockets' Red Glare,* 108.

84. Andrew Jackson, General Orders, 14 March 1815, in Arèsne Lacarrière Latour, *The War in West Florida and Louisiana in 1814–15, with Atlas,* ed. Gene A. Smith (Gainesville: Historic New Orleans Collection and University Press of Florida, 1999), 277–79; and Stagg, *The War of 1812,* 154–55.

85. Allan R. Millett and Peter Maslowski, *For the Common Defense: A Military History of the United States of America* (New York: Free Press, 1984), 113–14.

CHAPTER 5. THE CONQUEST OF CALIFORNIA

1. Convened in Hartford, Connecticut, on 15 December 1814, the Hartford Convention met to express dissatisfaction with "Mr. Madison's War" and with Southern domination of national politics. Although radical elements called for secession and a separate peace with Great Britain, more moderate representatives prevailed and the convention resolutions were somewhat less strident. James M. Banner Jr., *To the Hartford Convention: The Federalists and the Origins of Party Politics in Massachusetts, 1789–1815* (New York: Knopf, 1970), 348–50.
2. Max Boot, *The Savage Wars of Peace: Small Wars and the Rise of American Power* (New York: Basic Books, 2002), 27–28; and Spencer C. Tucker, *Stephen Decatur: A Life Most Bold and Daring* (Annapolis, Md.: Naval Institute Press, 2005), 153–66.
3. Michael Birkner, "The 'Foxardo Affair' Revisited: Porter, Pirates and the Problem of Civilian Authority in the Early Republic," *American Neptune* 42, no. 3 (July 1982): 165–78; and David F. Long, *Nothing Too Daring: A Biography of Commodore David Porter, 1780–1843* (Annapolis, Md.: Naval Institute Press, 1970), 229–57, 256–57, 288–89.
4. Boot, *The Savage Wars of Peace,* 47; and David F. Long, "'Martial Thunder': The First Official American Intervention in Asia," *Pacific Historical Review* 42 (1973): 143–62.
5. Richard Peters, ed., *The Public Statutes at Large of the United States of America* (Boston: Charles C. Little and James Brown, 1850), 5:797–98.
6. K. Jack Bauer, *Surfboats and Horse Marines: U.S. Naval Operations in the Mexican War, 1846–48* (Annapolis, Md.: U.S. Naval Institute, 1969), 4–7.
7. Amy S. Greenberg, *A Wicked War: Polk, Clay, Lincoln, and the 1846 Invasion of Mexico* (New York: Knopf, 2012), 84–85, 101.
8. John Schroeder, *Mr. Polk's War: American Dissent and Opposition, 1846–1848* (Madison: University of Wisconsin Press, 1973), 8.
9. Allan Nevins, ed., *Polk: The Diary of a President 1845–1849 Covering the Mexican War, the Acquisition of Oregon, and the Conquest of California and the Southwest* (New York: Longmans, Green, 1952), 63–69; and Bauer, *Surfboats and Horse Marines,* 9–15.

10. . . . *From the Sea: Preparing the Naval Service for the 21st Century* (Washington, D.C.: Department of the Navy, September 1992); and *Operational Maneuver from the Sea: A Concept for the Projection of Naval Power Ashore* (Washington, D.C.: Headquarters, U.S. Marine Corps, 1996).
11. Norman A. Graebner, *Empire on the Pacific: A Study in American Continental Expansion* (Claremont, Calif.: Regina Books, 1983), 65–72, 108–16, 220.
12. Gene A. Smith, "The War That Wasn't: Thomas ap Catesby Jones's Seizure of Monterey." *California History,* June 1987, 104–13, 155–57; and Claude Hampton Hall, *Abel Parker Upshur: Conservative Virginian, 1790–1844* (Madison: State Historical Society of Wisconsin, 1963), 180–88, 254n.
13. Thomas O. Larkin, Description of California report dated 20 April 1846, in George P. Hammond, ed., *The Larkin Papers: Personal, Business, and Official Correspondence of Thomas O. Larkin, Merchant and United States Consul in California* (Berkeley: University of California Press, 1953), 4:30–32; Harlan Hague and David J. Langum, *Thomas O. Larkin: A Life of Patriotism and Profit in Old California* (Norman: University of Oklahoma Press, 1990), 112–35; and John Adam Hussey, "The Origin of the Gillespie Mission," *California Historical Society Quarterly,* March 1940, 47.
14. Manuel de Jesus Castro to Thomas O. Larkin, letter dated 8 March 1846, in Hammond, *The Larkin Papers,* 5:238–39; Larkin to James Buchanan, letter dated January 14, 1947, in Hammond, *The Larkin Papers,* 6:8–11; Neal Harlow, *California Conquered: War and Peace in the Pacific, 1846–1850* (Berkley: University of California Press, 1982), 70–73, 79–80, 97–98, 110; Richard R. Stenberg, "Polk and Frémont, 1845–1846," *Pacific Historical Review* 7, no. 3 (September 1938): 222–23; and Henry Bulls Watson, journal entries for 10, 11, 14, and 20 June 1846, in Charles R. Smith, ed. *The Journals of Marine Second Lieutenant Henry Bulls Watson,* (Washington, D.C.: History and Museums Division, Headquarters, U.S. Marine Corps, 1990), 139, 144–45, 147; hereafter, *Journals of Watson.*
15. Nevins, *Polk,* 126; and Larkin to Stockton, letter dated 24 July 1846, in Hammond, *The Larkin Papers,* 4:159–60.

16. Secretary of the Navy Bancroft to Sloat, 24 June 1846, as quoted in Bauer, *Surfboats and Horse Marines,* 138–39.
17. Sloat to Bancroft, 29 July 1845 as quoted in Robert Erwin Johnson, *Thence Round Cape Horn: The Story of United States Naval Forces on Pacific Station, 1818–1923* (New York: Arno, 1980), 71; and Bauer, *Surfboats and Horse Marines,* 138–42.
18. Edwin Allen Sherman, *The Life of Rear-Admiral John Drake Sloat, of the United States Navy, Who Took Possession of California and Raised the American Flag at Monterey on July 7th, 1846* (Oakland, Calif.: Carruth & Carruth, 1902), 40–41.
19. Bancroft to Sloat, directive dated 15 May 1846, in George Winston Smith and Charles Judah, eds. *Chronicles of the Gringos: The U.S. Army in the Mexican War, 1846–1848, Accounts by Eyewitnesses and Combatants* (Albuquerque: University of New Mexico Press, 1968), 149; hereafter, *Chronicles;* George Tays, "Frémont Had No Secret Instructions," *Pacific Historical Review* 7, no. 3 (September 1938): 169; and James M. Cutts, *The Conquest of California and New Mexico by the Forces of the United States in the years 1846 & 1847* (Philadelphia: Carney & Hart, 1847), 103.
20. Commodore Sloat, General Order, 7 July 1846, in Bauer, *Surfboats and Horse Marines,* 150–51, 153–54; Larkin to Abel Sterns, letter dated 8 July 1846, in Hammond, *The Larkin Papers,* 5:115–16; Watson, 8 July 1846, *Journals of Watson,* 158–60; Sloat to Bancroft, 31 July 1846, *Chronicles,* 150–51; Secretary of the Navy to Commo. John D. Sloat, directive dated 12 July 1846, in Cutts, *The Conquest of California,* 165–66; and John Drake Sloat, proclamation dated 7 July 1845, in Hammond, *The Larkin Papers,* 5:105–6, 142.
21. William Brown Ide, proclamation dated 18 June 1846, in Hammond, *The Larkin Papers,* 5:53–54; Greenberg, *A Wicked War,* 122; Bauer, *Surfboats and Horse Marines,* 152–54, 170; Harlow, *California Conquered,* 125; Justin Harvey Smith, *The War with Mexico* (New York: Macmillan, 1919), 2:335; Sloat to Bancroft, 31 July 1846, *Chronicles,* 150–54; Harlow, *California Conquered,* 125; and Cutts, *The Conquest of California,* 114–15.
22. Sloat to Montgomery, 7 July 1846, in Sherman, *The Life of Rear-Admiral John Drake Sloat,* Official Reports and Correspondence, ii. Prior to 30 January 1847, the village of San Francisco was known as

Yerba Buena. For purposes of clarity and simplicity, this study uses the name San Francisco throughout. Bauer, *Surfboats and Horse Marines,* 143, 154–57; Cutts, *The Conquest of California,* 115–17; Watson, 9 July 1846, *Journals of Watson,* 160; Montgomery to Watson, 9 July 1846, *Journals of Watson,* 160–63; and Montgomery to Sloat, 9 July 1846, in Sherman, *The Life of Rear-Admiral John Drake Sloat,* Official Reports and Correspondence, ii–iii.

23. Fremont to Senator Thomas Hart Benton, 15 July 1846, in *Chronicles,* 144–48; Harlow, *California Conquered,* 124–25; Sherman, *The Life of Rear-Admiral John Drake Sloat,* 53; Stenberg, "Polk and Frémont," 216–19, 222–23; Tays, "Frémont Had No Secret Instructions," 160; Nevins, *Polk,* 22; Gillespie to Larkin, letter dated 25 May 1846, in Hammond, *The Larkin Papers,* 4:393–94; and Harlow, *California Conquered,* 77–78, 81–82.
24. Larkin to Buchanan, letter dated 1 June 1846, in Hammond, *The Larkin Papers,* 5:2–4.
25. Johnson, *Thence Round Cape Horn,* 78–79; David F. Long, *Sailor-Diplomat: A Biography of Commodore James Biddle, 1783–1848* (Boston: Northeastern University Press, 1983), 228–30; Harlow, *California Conquered,* 131–32; Sloat to Bancroft, 31 July 1846, in *Chronicles,* 150–54; and Bauer, *Surfboats and Horse Marines,* 158–59, 162.
26. Stockton to Bancroft, 28 August 1846, *Chronicles,* 154–55; and Greeley and McElrath, "The Polka Dance—Annexation of Mexican Territory—Exciting Debate," *New-York Tribune,* 9 December 1846.
27. Stockton to Fremont, 23 July 1846, in Sherman, *The Life of Rear-Admiral John Drake Sloat,* ii; Capt. Jacob Zeilin, USMC, to Brig. Gen. Archibald Henderson, Commandant of the Marine Corps, 7 April 1848, Mexican War General File (MWGF), Marine Corps Historical Division (MCHD), Quantico, Virginia; Zeilin to Henderson, 7 April 1848, MWGF, MCHD; and Larkin to Able Sterns, letter dated 6 August 1846, in Hammond, *The Larkin Papers,* 5:184–95.
28. Harlow, *California Conquered,* 147–48; and Smith, *The War with Mexico,* 2:337.
29. Stockton to Bancroft, 28 August 1846, *Chronicles,* 154–55; Harlow, *California Conquered,* 151; Smith, *The War with Mexico,* 2:337; and Philip St. George Cooke, *The Conquest of New Mexico and*

California: An Historical and Personal Narrative (Oakland, Calif.: Biobooks, 1952), 112–13.

30. Bauer, *Surfboats and Horse Marines,* 168–69; and Harlow, *California Conquered,* 154.
31. Stockton to Mervine, 19 September 1846, in Johnson, *Thence Round Cape Horn,* 82; Harlow, *California Conquered,* 155; Smith, *The War with Mexico,* 2:338; and David Roberts, *A Newer World: John C. Fremont and the Claiming of the American West* (New York: Simon & Schuster, 2000), 173.
32. Greeley and McElrath, "The Military Polka—Annexation of Mexican Territory," *New-York Tribune,* 9 December 1845.
33. Bauer, *Surfboats and Horse Marines,* 170–73.
34. Zeilin to Henderson, 7 April 1848, MWGF, MCHD; Bauer, *Surfboats and Horse Marines,* 173–74; Stockton to Gillespie, Orders dated 31 August 1846, in *A Sketch of the Life of Commodore Robert F. Stockton; with and appendix, comprising this correspondence with the Navy Department respecting his conquest of California; and extracts from the defense of Col. J. C. Fremont, in relation to the same subject; together with his speeches in the Senate of the United States, and his political letters* (New York: Derby & Jackson, 1865), app. A, 2–3; Harlow, *California Conquered,* 159; and Cooke, *Conquest,* 114.
35. Watson, 2 February 1847, *The Journals of Watson,* 287–91; Johnson, *Thence Round Cape Horn,* 83; and Smith, *The War with Mexico,* 2:339.
36. Cutts, *The Conquest of California,* 127–28; Bauer, *Surfboats and Horse Marines,* 174–75; Harlow, *California Conquered,* 163–67; and Johnson, *Thence Round Cape Horn,* 83.
37. Bauer, *Surfboats and Horse Marines,* 178–79; Stockton to Bancroft, report dated 11 January 1847 and Stockton to Bancroft, report dated 18 February 1847, in *Sketch of the Life of Stockton,* app. A, 8–9, 17–30; and Watson, 2 February 1847, *The Journals of Watson,* 287–91.
38. Zeilin to Henderson, 7 April 1848, MWGF, MCHD; and Bauer, *Surfboats and Horse Marines,* 180–82.
39. Bauer, *Surfboats and Horse Marines,* 184.
40. Ibid., 147, 184–85; and Nevins, *Polk,* 106–9.
41. Cory S. Hollon, "A Leap in the Dark: The Campaign to Conquer New Mexico and California, 1846–1847," *Army History* (Winter

2015): 18; and Kearny to Brig. Gen. Roger Jones, Adjutant General, Washington, D.C., 12 December 1846, *Chronicles,* 156.

42. Harlow, *California Conquered,* 183–88; Watson, 10 December 1846, *The Journals of Watson,* 255–58; Stephen W. Kearny, official report in Cooke, *Conquest,* 134–36; and Letter of John M. Stanley, 19 January 1847 cited in the Saint Louis *Reveille, Chronicles,* 157–59.
43. Zeilin to Henderson, 7 April 1848, MWGF, MCHD; Bauer, *Surfboats and Horse Marines,* 186–89; Harlow, *California Conquered,* 175, 180–92; Watson, 11 and 12 December 1846, *The Journals of Watson,* 258–59; and Durwood Ball, Stephen W. Kearny, in *Soldiers West: Biographies from the Military Frontier,* ed. Paul Andrew Hutton and Durwood Ball (Norman: University of Oklahoma Press, 2009), 57.
44. Hollon, "A Leap in the Dark," 21; Harlow, *California Conquered,* 198–201; and Tom Chaffin, *Pathfinder: John Charles Freemont and the Course of American Empire* (New York: Hill and Wang, 2002), 368–71.
45. Watson, 16–29 December 1846 and 1 January 1847, *Journals of Watson,* 259–63, 264; Stockton to Bancroft, report dated 11 January 1847, in Cutts, *The Conquest of California,* 129–31; and Kearney to Brig. Gen. R. Jones, report on the Battles of San Gabriel and La Mesa, in Cooke, *Conquest,* 140.
46. Brev. Maj. William H. Emory, Notes on a Military Reconnaissance from Fort Leavenworth in Missouri to San Diego in California, *Chronicles,* 159–65; Stockton to Bancroft, report dated 11 January 1847, in *Sketch of the Life of Stockton,* app. A, 8–9; Watson, 8 January 1847, *The Journals of Watson,* 268–76; and Zeilin to Henderson, 7 April 1848, MWGF, MCHD.
47. Brev. Maj. William H. Emory, Notes on a Military Reconnaissance from Fort Leavenworth in Missouri to San Diego in California, *Chronicles,* 159–65; Watson, 9 and 10 January 1847, *The Journals of Watson,* 276–281; and Smith, *The War with Mexico,* 2:344.
48. Stockton to Bancroft, report dated 11 January 1847, in *Sketch of the Life of Stockton,* app. A, 8–9; Stockton to Bancroft, report dated 5 February 1847, in *Sketch of the Life of Stockton,* app. A, 12–16; Brev. Maj. William H. Emory, Notes on a Military Reconnaissance from Fort Leavenworth in Missouri to San Diego in California, *Chronicles,* 159–65; Watson, 9 and 10 January 1847, *The Journals*

of Watson, 191–99; Bauer, *Surfboats and Horse Marines,* 191–99; and Harlow, *California Conquered,* 208–18.

49. Watson, 11 January 1847, *The Journals of Watson,* 267, 282; Stockton to Bancroft, report dated 15 January 1847, in Cutts, *The Conquest of California,* 133–34; Bauer, *Surfboats and Horse Marines,* 199–201; and Harlow, *California Conquered,* 225, 231–32, 236.
50. Nevins, *Polk,* 221; Watson, 14 January and 2 February 1847, *The Journals of Watson,* 287–91; and Commo. W. Branford Shubrick, General Order dated 1 March 1847, in Cutts, *The Conquest of California,* 139–40.
51. Nevins, *Polk,* 252; Long, *Sailor-Diplomat,* 231; Bauer, *Surfboats and Horse Marines,* 202–4; and Harlow, *California Conquered,* 250–53, 278, 313.
52. Watson, 17 February, 4 and 30 March, 3 and 13–14 April 1847, *The Journals of Watson,* 296, 303–4, 313–15, 318–20; and Henry W. Halleck, *The Mexican War in Baja California: The Memorandum of Captain Henry W. Halleck Concerning His Expeditions in Lower California, 1846–1848,* ed. Doyce B. Nunis Jr. (Los Angeles: Dawson, 1977), 23–90.
53. Nevins, *Polk,* 301–2; Harlow, *California Conquered,* 272–75; and Roberts, *A Newer World,* 179–83.
54. Johnson, *Thence Round Cape Horn,* 87.
55. Ibid., 89–90; Long, *Sailor-Diplomat,* 231–32; Bauer, *Surfboats and Horse Marines,* 209–10, 232; and Harlow, *California Conquered,* 275.
56. Craven to Cdr. Thomas O. Selfridge, report dated October 3, 1847, in Halleck, *The Mexican War in Baja California,* 153–55; Halleck, *The Mexican War in Baja California,* 94–97; Bauer, *Surfboats and Horse Marines,* 201, 212–13; and Gabrielle M. Neufeld Santelli, *Marines in the Mexican War* (Washington, D.C.: History and Museums Division, Headquarters, U.S. Marine Corps, 1991), 23–24.
57. Watson, 17, 18, 19, and 20 October 1847, *The Journals of Watson,* 355–59; Zeilin to Henderson, 7 April 1848, MWFG, MCHD; and Bauer, *Surfboats and Horse Marines,* 214–19.
58. Zeilin to Henderson, 7 April 1848, MWGF, MCHD; and Watson, 16 November–31 December 1847, *The Journal of Watson,* 368–69.
59. Bauer, *Surfboats and Horse Marines,* 221–26; and Smith, *The War with Mexico,* 2:207.

60. Lt. Charles Heywood to Commo. W. Branford Shubrick, report dated 25 November 1847, in Halleck, *The Mexican War in Baja California,* 168–72.
61. Bauer, *Surfboats and Horse Marines,* 226–30.
62. Richard W. Amero, "The Mexican-American War in Baja California," *Journal of San Diego History* 30, no. 1 (Winter 1984), https://www.sandiegohistory.org/journal/1984/january/war/.

CHAPTER 6. TO THE HALLS OF MONTEZUMA

1. Maj. Gen. Zackary Taylor to Roger Jones, Adjutant General of the Army, 25 September 1846, in *Joint Forces Staff College, Case Study: Mexican War* (Norfolk, Va.: National Defense University, January 2006), 40, hereafter, *Staff College Case Study;* and Allan Nevins, ed., *Polk: The Diary of a President 1845–1849 Covering the Mexican War, the Acquisition of Oregon, and the Conquest of California and the Southwest* (New York: Longmans, Green, 1952), 161, 156.
2. Nevins, *Polk,* 110, 114–16.
3. Zackary Taylor, letter published in the New York *Express,* 9 November 1846, in George Winston Smith and Charles Judah, *Chronicles of the Gringos: The U.S. Army in the Mexican War, 1846–1848, Accounts of Eyewitnesses & Combatants* (Albuquerque: University of New Mexico Press, 1968), 169; and Correspondence of the New Orleans *Picayune,* 14 November 1846, in Smith and Judah, *Chronicles of the Gringos,* 166–67.
4. Nevins, *Polk,* 161–65; and Raphael Semmes, *Service Afloat and Ashore during the Mexican War* (Cincinnati: W. H. Moore & Co., 1851), 75–76.
5. K. Jack Bauer, "The Veracruz Expedition of 1847," *Military Affairs* 20, no. 3 (Autumn 1956): 162.
6. Philip S. P. Conner, *The Home Squadron under Commodore Conner in the War with Mexico: Being a Synopsis of Its Services* (Philadelphia: Privately printed, 1896), 12.
7. Semmes, *Service Afloat and Ashore,* 77; and Nevins, *Polk,* 154.
8. Nevins, *Polk,* 154.

9. Ibid., 169–71, 176–77, 178, 190; John S. D. Eisenhower, *So Far from God: The U.S. War with Mexico, 1846–1848* (New York: Random Hours, 1989), 117–43; Winfield Scott, *Memoirs of Lieut-General Scott, LL.D., Written by Himself,* 2 vols. (Freeport, N.Y.: Books for Libraries Press, 1970 [1864]), 1:400–401; and Secretary of War, William L. Marcy to Gen. Winfield Scott, 23 November 1846, in Scott, *Memoirs,* 1:397–98.
10. Marcy to Scott, 23 November 1846, in Scott, *Memoirs,* 1:397–98; Scott, *Memoirs,* 1:401–15; and Nevins, *Polk,* 163, 166–67, 169–71, 173–74, 185–86, 197–99.
11. Eisenhower, *So Far from God,* 175, 176–77; Semmes, *Service Afloat and Ashore,* 117–20; and Ulysses S. Grant, *Personal Memoirs of U.S. Grant* (New York: Charles L. Webster & Company, 1885), 1:122–23.
12. Taylor to Marcy, 6 March 1847, in *Staff College Case Study,* 82–91; Nevins, *Polk,* 208–9; and Semmes, *Service Afloat and Ashore,* 122.
13. Semmes, *Service Afloat and Ashore,* 122–24.
14. Timothy D. Johnson, *Winfield Scott: The Quest for Military Glory* (Lawrence: University Press of Kansas, 1998), 156–59; and John Fleming Polk, "Vera Cruz, 1847: A Lesson in Command," *Marine Corps Gazette,* September 1974, 74.
15. William G. Temple, *Memoir of the Landing of the United States Troops at Veracruz in 1847,* included as attachment in Conner, *The Home Squadron,* 63–65.
16. Scott to Conner, 23 December 1846, in Smith and Judah, *Chronicles of the Gringos,* 171; Eisenhower, *So Far from God,* 255; John Fleming Polk, "Vera Cruz, 1847," in Merrill L. Bartlett, ed., *Assault from the Sea: Essays on the History of Amphibious Warfare* (Annapolis, Md.: Naval Institute Press, 2014), 76; and Temple, *Memoir,* in Conner, *The Home Squadron,* 64.
17. Scott, *Memoirs,* 1:413–14; Justin H. Smith, *The War with Mexico,* 2 vols. (New York: Macmillan, 1919), 17–18; Conner to Capt. John H. Aulick, 28 February 1847 in Temple, *Memoir,* in Conner, *The Home Squadron,* 3–64, 80; and Semmes, *Service Afloat and Ashore,* 78, 124–25.
18. Temple, *Memoir,* in Conner, *The Home Squadron,* 60–62; Samuel Eliot Morison, *"Old Bruin": Commodore Matthew C. Perry, 1794–1858* (Boston: Little, Brown, 1967), 207; Russell F. Weigley, *The*

American Way of War: A History of United States Military Strategy and Policy (Bloomington: Indiana University Press, 1973), 76; Cornelius C. Smith Jr., "Our First Amphibious Assault," *Military Review* 38 (February 1950): 23–24; Polk, "Vera Cruz, 1847," in Bartlett, *Assault from the Sea,* 75; and Scott, *Memoirs,* 1:429.

19. Conner, *The Home Squadron,* 18; and Brev. Maj. George Archibald McCall, account in Smith and Judah, *Chronicles of the Gringos,* 178–79.
20. Semmes, *Service Afloat and Ashore,* 125; Jay Slagle, *Ironclad Captain: Seth Ledyard Phelps & the U.S. Navy, 1841–1864* (Kent, Ohio: Kent State University Press, 1996), 61–64; Temple, *Memoir,* in Conner, *The Home Squadron,* 12, 19, 64; and Bauer, "The Veracruz Expedition of 1847," 165–66.
21. Conner to Capt. French Forrest, 7 March 1847, in Temple, *Memoir,* in Conner, *The Home Squadron,* 82; Maj. Gen. Winfield Scott, General Order No. 17, 7 March 1847, in Temple, *Memoir,* in Conner, *The Home Squadron,* 79; Temple, *Memoir,* in Conner, *The Home Squadron,* 64–66, 68; and Smith, "Our First Amphibious Assault," 24.
22. Temple, *Memoir,* in Conner, *The Home Squadron,* 57; Polk, "Vera Cruz, 1847," in Bartlett, *Assault from the Sea,* 76; Commo. David Conner, General Orders, 7 March 1847, in Temple, *Memoir,* in Conner, *The Home Squadron,* 81–82; Semmes, *Service Afloat and Ashore,* 126–27; Smith, *The War with Mexico,* 2:25–26; Scott, *Memoirs,* 1:419; and Bauer, "The Veracruz Expedition of 1847," 167.
23. Maj. Gen. Winfield Scott to Secretary of War William L. Marcy, 12 and 13 March 1847, in Conner, *The Home Squadron,* 19–20, 41–42; Nevins, *Polk,* 208; and Polk, "Vera Cruz, 1847," 76.
24. Accounts differ regarding the size of Scott's landing force at Veracruz, with some being as low as 8,600 and others as high as 12,000. Semmes, *Service Afloat and Ashore,* 128; Conner, *The Home Squadron,* 19–20; and Bauer, "The Veracruz Expedition of 1847," 167–68.
25. Scott to Marcy, 17 March 1847, in Conner, *The Home Squadron,* 20, 42; and Scott, *Memoirs,* 1:420–21.
26. Grant, *Personal Memoirs,* 1:127; Scott, *Memoirs,* 1:422, 428; Johnson, *Winfield Scott,* 175; Morison, *"Old Bruin,"* 206–7; Semmes, *Service Afloat and Ashore,* 102, 105–6; and Smith, *The War with Mexico,* 2:19–20.

27. Scott, *Memoirs,* 1:423–25; Semmes, *Service Afloat and Ashore,* 129–30; and Smith, *The War with Mexico,* 2:23.
28. Smith, *The War with Mexico,* 2:27; Scott, *Memoirs,* 1:425–26; Semmes, *Service Afloat and Ashore,* 129; and Brig. Gen. David E. Twiggs, Account of Siege, in Smith and Judah, *Chronicles of the Gringos,* 188–89.
29. Eisenhower, *So Far from God,* 261–63; Joseph Wheelan, *Invading Mexico: America's Continental Dream and the Mexican War, 1846–1848* (New York: Carroll & Graf, 2007), 310–15; and Walter K. Borneman, *Polk: The Man Who Transformed the Presidency and America* (New York: Random House, 2008), 259.
30. Wheelan, *Invading Mexico,* 314–15; and Borneman, *Polk,* 259.
31. Conner, *The Home Squadron,* 5–6, 29; Temple, *Memoir,* in ibid., 70; Secretary of the Navy John Y. Mason to Conner, 23 April 1847, in ibid., 37; Scott to Marcy, 17 March 1847, in ibid., 42; Scott to Marcy, 21 March 1847, in ibid., 42–43; Brig. Gen. William J. Worth to Conner, 28 March 1847, in ibid., 44; Slagle, *Ironclad Captain,* 63; and Polk, "Vera Cruz, 1847," 77.
32. Conner, *The Home Squadron,* 4–6; Semmes, *Service Afloat and Ashore,* 128; and Morison, *"Old Bruin,"* 212–13.
33. K. Jack Bauer, *The Mexican War, 1846–1848* (New York: Macmillan, 1974), 248; and Eisenhower, *So Far from God,* 262–63.
34. Temple, *Memoir,* in Conner, *The Home Squadron,* 62.
35. Scott, *Memoirs,* 1:429, 430–31; and Grant, *Personal Memoirs,* 1:122.
36. E. Kirby Smith to his wife, 22 March 1847, in E. Kirby Smith, *To Mexico with Scott: Letters of Captain E. Kirby Smith* (Cambridge, Mass.: Harvard University Press, 1917), 121–25; Conner, *The Home Squadron,* 47; and Semmes, *Service Afloat and Ashore,* 130–32.
37. "Mexican Narrative of Events at the Heroic City of Vera Cruz, while Besieged by the American Army," published at Jalapa, 1847, and "War with Mexico," New Orleans *Delta,* 17 April 1847, in Smith and Judah, *Chronicles of the Gringos,* 192–95.
38. Conner, *The Home Squadron,* 47; and Semmes, *Service Afloat and Ashore,* 133–34; Temple, *Memoir,* in Conner, *The Home Squadron,* 69; and Morison, *"Old Bruin,"* 215–18.
39. Gen. Scott's General Order No. 80, 30 March 1847, in Conner, *The Home Squadron,* 43–44; Wheelan, *Invading Mexico,* 315; Grant,

Personal Memoirs, 1:127; and Semmes, *Service Afloat and Ashore,* 135–42.

40. Scott to Marcy, 29 March 1847, in Semmes, *Service Afloat and Ashore,* 141, 143–44; Conner, *The Home Squadron,* 47; Nevins, *Polk,* 211; Semmes, *Service Afloat and Ashore,* 142, 145–47; George Ballentine, *Autobiography of an English Soldier in the United States Army,* in *To Mexico with Taylor and Scott 1845–1847,* ed. Grady McWhiney and Sue McWhiney (Waltham, Mass.: Blaisdell Publishing, 1969), 117–19; and Scott, *Memoirs,* 1:427–28.
41. R. Blake Dunnavent. *Brown Water Warfare: The U.S. Navy in Riverine Warfare and the Emergence of a Tactical Doctrine, 1775–1970* (Gainesville: University Press of Florida, 2003), 48–49; Semmes, *Service Afloat and Ashore,* 147–48; and K. Jack Bauer, *Surfboats and Horse Marines: U.S. Naval Operations in the Mexican War, 1846–48* (Annapolis, Md.: U.S. Naval Institute, 1969), 100–101.
42. Morison, *"Old Bruin,"* 223.
43. Johnson, *Winfield Scott,* 180.
44. Secretary of the Treasury R. J. Walker to President Polk, letter regarding collection of duties in Mexican ports, 30 March 1847, and Polk implementation, 31 March 1847, in *Staff College Case Study,* 96–100; Morison, *"Old Bruin,"* 224; and Semmes, *Service Afloat and Ashore,* 148–49.
45. Perry to Mason, 26 April 1847, in Semmes, *Service Afloat and Ashore,* 156–57; and Dunnavent, *Brown Water Warfare,* 48–49.
46. Eisenhower, *So Far from God,* 272; and Semmes, *Service Afloat and Ashore,* 175.
47. Ballentine in McWhiney, *To Mexico with Taylor and Scott,* 127–28; Smith, *The War with Mexico,* 2:48–49; Grant, *Personal Memoirs,* 1:130–32; Scott, *Memoirs,* 1:430–33; and Semmes, *Service Afloat and Ashore,* 176.
48. General Order No. 111, 17 April 1847; Scott to Marcy, 19 April 1847; Scott to Marcy, 23 April 1847, all in Scott, *Memoirs,* 1:433–51; Nevins, *Polk,* 221, 228, 232; and Semmes, *Service Afloat and Ashore,* 180–82.
49. At the time both Polk and Wellington criticized Scott's decision to cut off from his base and advance as an independent force. Polk proclaimed that Scott had "committed a great military error."

Nevins, *Polk,* 249–50. Wellington said, "Scott is lost—he cannot capture the city (Mexico City) and he cannot fall back upon his base." Amy S. Greenberg, *A Wicked War: Polk, Clay, Lincoln, and the 1846 Invasion of Mexico* (New York: Knopf, 2012), 208. After Scott's great victory, Polk could not bring himself to give Scott credit for his achievement, but Wellington stated that "Scott is the greatest living soldier." Bauer, *The Mexican War, 1846–1848,* 322. Wellington also stated that his campaign "was unsurpassed in military annals." Weigley, *The American Way of War,* 75.

50. Nevins, *Polk,* 212–13, 215, 218, 262–63.
51. President James K. Polk, Third Annual Message to Congress, 7 December 1847, in *Staff College Case Study,* 132–59; Grant, *Personal Memoirs,* 1:147–49, 161; Polk to the Senate of the United States, 22 February 1848, and Polk to the Senate of the United States, 29 February 1848, in *Staff College Case Study,* 165–66 and 167–68; General Order No 284, Headquarters of the Army, Mexico, 14 September 1847, the Aztec Club archives, 1847–1964, OCLC 47922580, Box 3, Folder labeled Aztec Club copies of Gen. Taylor's Order # 30, Gen. Scott's G.O. # 284, U.S. Army Historical Center, Carlisle Barracks, Pennsylvania.
52. Paul C. Clark and Edward H. Mosely, "D-Day Veracruz, 1847—A Grand Design," *Joint Forces Quarterly* 10 (Winter 1995–96): 102–15; and Polk, "Vera Cruz, 1847," in Bartlett, *Assault from the Sea,* 77–78.
53. Semmes, *Service Afloat and Ashore,* 474.

CHAPTER 7. THE FORT FISHER CAMPAIGN

1. Donald Stoker, *The Grand Design: Strategy and the U.S. Civil War* (New York: Oxford University Press, 2010), 38, 411.
2. James M. McPherson, *Battle Cry of Freedom: The Civil War Era* (New York: Oxford University Press, 1988), 370–72; Rear Adm. David D. Porter to Secretary of the Navy Gideon Welles, after-action report (AAR) dated 22 January 1865, in Naval War Records Office, *Official Records of the Union and Confederate Navies of the War of the Rebellion,* 30 vols. (Washington, D.C.: Government Printing Office, 1894–1922) (hereafter, *ORN*), ser. 1, vol. 11 (S# 11) (Carmel:

Guild Press of Indiana, 1999, republished by Oliver Computing); Ulysses S. Grant, *Personal Memoirs of U.S. Grant* (New York: Charles L. Webster & Company, 1885), 2:387; and Stephen R. Wise, *Lifeline of the Confederacy: Blockade Running During the Civil War* (Columbia: University of South Carolina Press, 1988), 3, 6–8.

3. K. Jack Bauer, *Surfboats and Horse Marines: U.S. Naval Operations in the Mexican War, 1846–48* (Annapolis, Md.: U.S. Naval Institute, 1969), 83–97; Matthew Forney Steele, *American Campaigns*, 2 vols. (Washington, D.C.: United States Infantry Association, 1943), 1:105–26; and Russell F. Weigley, *The American Way of War: A History of the United States Military Strategy and Policy* (Bloomington: Indiana University Press, 1973), 73–76.

4. James M. McPherson, *War on the Waters: The Union & Confederate Navies, 1861–1865* (Chapel Hill: University of North Carolina Press, 2012), 3, 74–82; John D. Milligan, *Gunboats down the Mississippi* (Annapolis, Md.: Naval Institute Press, 1965), 27–28, 38–49; 143–60; Dudley Taylor Cornish and Virginia Jeans Laas, *Lincoln's Lee: The Life of Samuel Phillips Lee, United States Navy, 1812–1897* (Lawrence: University Press of Kansas, 1986), 96, 105; Department of Defense, Joint Publication 3–02, *Joint Doctrine for Amphibious Operations* (Washington, D.C., 19 September 2001), xi, II-1, VII-1; and Department of Defense, *Joint Staff Officer's Guide*, AFSC Pub 1 (Norfolk, Va.: National Defense University, 1984), 142–43.

5. Chester G. Hearn, *The Capture of New Orleans, 1962* (Baton Rouge: Louisiana State University Press, 1995), 255–57, 266–67; and Rowena Reed, *Combined Operations in the Civil War* (Annapolis, Md.: Naval Institute Press, 1979), 195.

6. Reed, *Combined Operations*, 39–43, 141, 190; and McPherson, *War on the Waters*, 52–54.

7. Department of the Navy, U.S. Marine Corps, Marine Corps Doctrinal Publication 1–0, *Marine Corps Operations* (Washington, D.C., 27 September 2001), 2–8.

8. Robert M. Browning Jr., *From Cape Charles to Cape Fear: The North Atlantic Blockading Squadron during the Civil War* (Tuscaloosa: University of Alabama Press, 1993), 271, 301–2.

9. Secretary of the Navy Gideon Welles to President Abraham Lincoln, 28 October 1864, *ORN*, ser. 1, vol. 11 [S# 11]; Reed, *Combined*

Operations, 331–32; Grant, *Personal Memoirs,* 2:387; and Ron Gragg, *Confederate Goliath: The Battle of Fort Fisher* (New York: HarperCollins, 1991), 34–35, 107.

10. Wise, *Lifeline of the Confederacy,* 124, 205.
11. Chris E. Fonvielle Jr., *The Wilmington Campaign: Last Rays of Departing Hope* (Campbell, Calif.: Savas, 1997), 21; and Gragg, *Confederate Goliath,* 11–12.
12. Charles M. Robinson III, *Hurricane of Fire: The Union Assault on Fort Fisher* (Annapolis, Md.: Naval Institute Press, 1998), 188–89; Gragg, *Confederate Goliath,* 12, 18–20; Reed, *Combined Operations,* 336; and David D. Porter, *Naval History of the Civil War* (Secaucus, N.J.: Castle, 1984), 694.
13. Gragg, *Confederate Goliath,* 17–26; Robinson, *Hurricane of Fire,* 32–40; and Porter to Welles, 16 January 1865, *ORN,* ser. 1, vol. 1 [S# 11].
14. Reed, *Combined Operations,* 336; and Porter, *Naval History of the Civil War,* 694.
15. Porter to Welles, 27 December 1864, *ORN,* ser. 1, vol. 11 [S# 11].
16. Weitzel to Turner, 31 December 1864, in U.S. War Department, *The War of the Rebellion: A Compilation of the Official Records of the Union and Confederate Armies* (hereafter, *ORA*) (Carmel: Guild Press of Indiana, 1997, Republished by Oliver Computing LLC), ser. 1, vol. 42/1 [S# 87]; and Porter, *Naval History of the Civil War,* 694.
17. Grant, *Personal Memoirs,* 2:388–90; Richard S. West Jr., *Lincoln's Scapegoat General: A Life of Benjamin F. Butler, 1818–1893* (Boston: Houghton Mifflin, 1965), 280; David D. Porter, General Order No. 70, 10 December 1864, in *ORN,* ser. 1, vol. 11 [S# 11]; and Wayne Wei-siang Hsieh, "The Civil War on Rivers and Coastal Waters," in *America, Sea Power, and the World,* ed. James C. Bradford (Chichester, U.K.: Wiley Blackwell, 2016), 114–15.
18. Benjamin F. Butler to Ulysses S. Grant, 3 January 1864, *ORA,* ser. 1, vol. 42/1 [S# 87]; Porter to Welles, 26 December 1864, *ORN,* ser. 1, vol. 11 [S# 11]; and Grant, *Personal Memoirs,* 2:390.
19. *Joint Doctrine for Amphibious Operations,* I-1–II-1, XV-1–XV-4; Grant, *Personal Memoirs,* 2:391–393; Butler to Grant, 3 January 1865, in *ORA,* ser. 1, vol. 42/1 [S# 87]; Porter to Welles, 26 December

1864, *ORN,* ser. 1, vol. 11 [S# 11]; Col. William Lamb to Maj. James H. Hill, Chief of Staff, 27 December 1864, *ORA,* ser. 1, vol. 42/1 [S# 87]; and Craig L. Symonds, *The Civil War at Sea* (New York: Oxford University Press, 2009), 158–60.

20. Maj. Gen. Godfrey Weitzel to Brig. Gen. J. W. Turner, Chief of Staff, 31 December 1864, *ORA,* ser. 1, vol. 42/1 [S# 87]; Weitzel to Turner, 31 December 1864, *ORA,* ser. 1, vol. 42/1 [S# 87]; Porter to Welles, 26 December 1864, *ORN,* ser. 1, vol. 11 [S# 11]; Fonvielle, *Wilmington Campaign,* 155–57; and Grant, *Personal Memoirs,* 2:393.
21. Weitzel to Turner, 31 December 1864, *ORA,* ser. 1, vol. 42/1 [S# 87]; Maj. Gen. W. H. C. Whiting to Lt. Col. A. Anderson, adjutant, cover letter to Lamb's AAR, 31 December 1864, *ORN,* ser. 1, vol. 11 [S# 11]; Lamb to Hill, 27 December 1864, in *ORA*, ser. 1, vol. 42/1 [S# 87]; Butler to Grant, 27 December 1864, *ORA,* ser. 1, vol. 42/1 [S# 87]; and Lamb to Hill, 27 December 1864, *ORA,* ser. 1, vol. 42/1 [S# 87].
22. Weitzel to Turner, 31 December 1864, *ORA,* ser. 1, vol. 42/1 [S# 87]; and Grant, *Personal Memoirs,* 2:391–92.
23. Grant, *Personal Memoirs,* 2:391–92; and Butler to Grant, 3 January 1864, in *ORA,* ser. 1, vol. 42/1 [S# 87].
24. McPherson, *War on the Waters,* 215–16; Porter to Butler, 26 December 1864, *ORN,* ser. 1, vol. 11 [S# 11]; Porter to Welles, 26 December 1864, *ORN,* ser. 1, vol. 11 [S# 11]; Porter to Welles, 27 December 1864, *ORN,* ser. 1, vol. 11 [S# 11]; Lamb to Hill, 27 December 1864, *ORA,* ser. 1, vol. 42/1 [S# 87]; and Grant, *Personal Memoirs,* 2:391–95.
25. Grant, *Personal Memoirs,* 2:394–95; Grant to Secretary of War Edwin Stanton, endorsement on Butler's AAR, 7 January 1864, *ORA,* ser. 1, vol. 42/1 [S# 87]; and Horace Porter, *Campaigning with Grant* (New York: Bonanza Books, 1897), 362–63.
26. Porter to Welles, 26 December 1864, *ORN,* series 1, vol. 11 [S# 11]; Lamb to Hill, 27 December 1864, *ORA,* ser. 1, vol. 12/1 [S# 87]; Porter to Welles, 22 January 1865, *ORN,* ser. 1, vol. 11 [S# 11]; Grant, *Personal Memoirs,* 2:392, 394–95; and West, *Lincoln's Scapegoat General,* 289–90.
27. Weitzel to Turner, 31 December 1864, *ORA,* ser. 1, vol. 42/1 [S# 87].
28. Whiting to Anderson, cover letter to Lamb's AAR, 31 December 1864, *ORN,* ser. 1, vol. 11 [S# 11]; and Gragg, *Confederate Goliath,* 59–61.

29. Porter to Welles, 22 January 1864, *ORN,* ser. 1, vol. 11 [S# 11]; Butler to Grant, 27 December 1864, *ORA,* ser. 1, vol. 42/1 [S# 87]; Whiting to Lee, 18 January 1865, *ORA,* ser. 1, vol. 46/1 [S# 95]; Whiting to Butler, 22 February 1865, *ORA,* ser. 1, vol. 42/1 [S# 87]; and Lamb to Hill, 27 December 1864 *ORA,* ser. 1, vol. 42/1 [S# 87].
30. Lamb to Hill, 27 December 1864, *ORA,* ser. 1, vol. 42/1 [S# 87]; and Porter to Welles, 22 January 1865, *ORN,* ser. 1, vol. 11 [S# 11].
31. Grant, *Personal Memoirs,* 2:392; Lamb to Hill, 27 December 1864, *ORA,* ser. 1, vol. 42/1[S#87]; and Porter to Butler, 26 December 1864, *ORN,* ser. 1, vol. 11 [S#11].
32. Grant to Stanton, cover letter to Butler's AAR, 7 January 1865, *ORA,* ser. 1, vol. 42/1 [S# 87]; and Grant to Butler, 6 December 1864, *ORA,* ser. 1, vol. 42/1 [S# 87].
33. Grant to Butler, 6 December 1864, *ORA,* ser. 1, vol. 42/1 [S# 87]; and Reed, *Combined Operations,* 354.
34. Grant, *Personal Memoirs,* 2:396.
35. Porter, *Campaigning with Grant,* 367; Grant, *Personal Memoirs,* 2:396; Maj. Gen. Alfred H. Terry to Brig. Gen. John A. Rawlins, Chief of Staff, 25 January 1865, *ORA,* ser. 1, vol. 46/1 [S# 95]; Grant, *Personal Memoirs,* 2:396; Maj. Gen. Alfred H. Terry to Brig. Gen. John A. Rawlins, Chief of Staff, 25 January 1865, *ORA,* ser. 1, vol. 46/1 [S# 95]; Gragg, *Confederate Goliath,* 60; Robinson, *Hurricane of Fire,* 147; and Craig L. Symonds, *Lincoln and His Admirals: Abraham Lincoln, the U.S. Navy, and the Civil War* (New York: Oxford University Press, 2008), 348–49.
36. Terry to Rawlins, 25 January 1865, *ORA,* ser. 1, vol. 46/1 [S# 95]; Porter to Welles, 17 January 1865, *ORN,* ser. 1, vol. 11 [S# 11]; Grant, *Personal Memoirs,* 2:395–96; Porter to Grant, 14 January 1865, *ORN,* ser. 1, vol. 11 [S# 11]; Porter to Welles, 14 January 1865, *ORN,* ser. 1, vol. 11 [S# 11]; and Porter to Welles, 15 January 1865, *ORN,* ser. 1, vol. 11 [S# 11].
37. Terry to Rawlins, 25 January 1865, *ORA,* ser. 1, vol. 46/1 [S# 95]; and Porter to Welles, 17 January 1865, *ORN,* ser. 1, vol. 11 [S# 11].
38. Terry to Rawlins, 25 January 1865, *ORA,* ser. 1, vol. 46/1 [S# 95]; and Gragg, *Confederate Goliath,* 118.
39. Terry to Rawlins, 25 January 1865, *ORA,* ser. 1, vol. 46/1 [S# 95].
40. Ibid.; and Porter to Welles, 17 January 1865, *ORN,* ser. 1, vol. 11 [S# 11].

41. Terry to Rawlins, 25 January 1865, *ORA,* ser. 1, vol. 46/1 [S# 95]; and Porter to Welles, 17 January 1865, *ORN,* ser. 1, vol. 11 [S# 11].
42. Porter, Landing Order, 15 January 1865, *ORN,* ser. 1, vol. 11 [S# 11]; Organization of U.S. Forces, commanded by Maj. Gen. Alfred H. Terry, at Fort Fisher, N.C., 13–14 January 1865, *ORA,* ser. 1, vol. 46/1 [S# 95]; Lt. Cdr. K. Randolph Breese to Porter, 16 January 1865, *ORN,* ser. 1, vol. 11 [S# 11]; and Porter to Welles, 17 January 1865, *ORN,* ser. 1, vol. 11 [S# 11].
43. Reed, *Combined Operations,* 378.
44. Porter to Welles, 17 January 1865, *ORN,* ser. 1, vol. 11 [S# 11]; and Terry to Rawlins, 25 January 1865, *ORA,* ser. 1, vol. 46/1 [S# 95].
45. Terry to Rawlins, 25 January 1865, *ORA,* ser. 1, vol. 46/1 [S# 95]; Breese to Porter, 16 January 1865, *ORN,* ser. 1, vol. 11 [S# 11]; Whiting to Lee, 18 January 1865, *ORA;* Porter to Welles, 17 January 1866, *ORN,* ser. 1, vol. 11 [S# 11]; and Whiting to Lee, 18 January 1965, *ORA,* ser. 1, vol. 46/1 [S# 95].
46. Breese to Porter, 16 January 1864, *ORN,* ser. 1, vol. 11 [S# 11]; Whiting to Lee, 18 January 1965, *ORA,* ser. 1, vol. 46/1 [S# 95]; Terry to Rawlins, 25 January 1865, *ORA,* ser. 1, vol. 46/1 [S# 95]; and Symonds, *The Civil War at Sea,* 163–64.
47. Terry to Rawlins, 25 January 1865, *ORA,* ser. 1, vol. 46/1 [S# 95]; and Whiting to Lee, 18 January 1865, *ORA,* ser. 1, vol. 46/1 [S# 95].
48. Breese to Porter, 16 January 1865, *ORN,* ser. 1, vol. 11 [S# 11]; Terry to Rawlins, 25 January 1865, *ORA,* ser. 1, vol. 46/1 [S# 95]; and Whiting to Lee, 18 January 1865, *ORA,* ser. 1, vol. 46/1 [S# 95].
49. Robinson, *Hurricane of Fire,* 116, 150.
50. Whiting to Lee, 18 January 1865, and 19 January 1865, *ORA,* ser. 1, vol. 46/1 [S# 95]; Brig. Gen. A. H. Colquitt to Lt. Col. Archer Anderson, Assistant Adjutant General of the Army of Northern Virginia, 17 January 1865, *ORA,* ser. 1, vol. 46/1 [S# 95]; and Whiting to Lee, 18 January 1865, and 19 January 1865, *ORA,* ser. 1, vol. 46/1 [S# 95].
51. *Joint Doctrine for Amphibious Operations,* I-4.
52. Doris Kerns Goodwin, *Team of Rivals: The Political Genus of Abraham Lincoln* (New York: Simon & Schuster, 2005), 65.
53. *Joint Doctrine for Amphibious Operations,* I-4.
54. *Joint Doctrine for Amphibious Operations,* I-5–I-6.

55. Colquitt to Anderson, 17 January 1865, *ORA,* ser. 1, vol. 46/1 [S# 95]; and McPherson, *War on the Waters,* 219.
56. Graham A. Cosmas, "Joint Operations in the Spanish-American War," in *Crucible of Empire: The Spanish-American War & Its Aftermath,* ed. James C. Bradford (Annapolis, Md.: Naval Institute Press, 1993), 104; and Alfred Vagts, *Landing Operations: Strategy, Psychology, Tactics, Politics, From Antiquity to 1945* (Harrisburg, Pa.: Military Service Publishing, 1946), 452–58.
57. Cosmas "Joint Operations in the Spanish-American War," 110, 116, 145.

POSTSCRIPT

1. Department of Defense, Joint Publication 3–02, *Joint Doctrine for Amphibious Operations,* I-1–I-8, XIV-1–XV-6; and Department of the Navy, U.S. Marine Corps, Marine Corps Doctrinal Publication 1–0, *Operations,* 2–2–2–11.
2. Milan Vego, "On Littoral Warfare," *Naval War College Review,* Spring 2015, 32.
3. Department of the Navy, U.S. Marine Corps, *U.S. Marine Corps, 36th Commandant's Planning Guidance, 2015* (issued February 2015), 12.
4. For a detailed account of the development of amphibious thinking during the interwar years of the 1920s and 1930s, see Gary J. Ohls, *Changing Modes of Warfare: Amphibious Doctrine and the Interwar Years* (Master's thesis, Texas Christian University, 2004).
5. The National Security Act of 1947, Pub. L. No. 80–253, 61 Stat. 496. Various subsequent amendments over time continue to validate the missions assigned to the Marine Corps in this basic document.
6. Vego, "On Littoral Warfare," 31.
7. Department of the Navy, Headquarters U.S. Marine Corps, *Expeditionary Force 21,* 4 March 2014, 3.

Bibliography

ARCHIVAL SOURCES

Archive ARCH Col 01 Restricted Circulation Aztec Club Archives OCLC 47922580.

Collection 258, Levi Twiggs Papers.

Collection 1668, Jacob Zeilin Jr. Papers.

Collection 3275, Thomas Yardley Field Papers.

Collection 3975, Mexican War Collection.

Documents accompanying the Report of the Committee to Inquire into the Causes and Particulars of the Invasion of Washington by the British Force in the Month of August 1814.

Document Clippings 1843-2002, Biography Section.

General Board File 408, Microfilm Collection.

Historic Summary AQ35-1265-HPH-hph dated 25 May 1953 titled *Louisiana and Marine Corps Highlights.*

Lt. Col. Samuel Miller File.

Manuscript Collection 105, Richard S. West Jr. Papers.

Manuscript Item 108, David Porter Letter of 9 August 1822.

Manuscript Item 121, Matthew C. Perry Letter of 26 May 1823.

Marine Corps History Division, Quantico, Virginia

Marine Corps Research Center, Marine Corps University, Quantico, Virginia

Mexican War General File.

Monterey Public Library, California History Room and Archives

National Archives and Records Administration

Naval War College Archives, Newport, Rhode Island

Record Group 8, Intelligence and Technology Archive.

Record Group 15, Lectures.

Record Group 80. General Records of the Department of the Navy, Officers of the Marine Corps.

Record Group 107. Letters Received by the Secretary of War, Registered Series, 1801–1860. Microcopy No. 221.

Record Group 107. Letters Received by the Secretary of War, Unregistered Series, 1789–1860. Microcopy No. 222.

Record Group 127. *Records of the U.S. Marine Corps.*

Samuel Miller Papers.

U.S. Army Heritage and Education Center (USAHEC), Carlisle, Pennsylvania

Published Sources

Abbot, Henry L. *Beginning of Modern Submarine Warfare under Captain Lieutenant David Bushnell.* Hamden, Conn.: Archon Books, 1966.

Abbot, W. W., et al., eds. *The Papers of George Washington: The Revolutionary War Series, June 1775–December 1983.* 24 vols. Charlottesville: University of Virginia Press, 1985–2015.

Ainsworth, W. L. "Amphibious Operation that Failed: The Battle of New Orleans." U.S. Naval Institute *Proceedings*, February 1945, 192–201.

Aitchison, Robert. *A British Eyewitness at the Battle of New Orleans: The Memoir of Royal Navy Admiral Robert Aitchison, 1808–1827.* Edited by Gene A. Smith. New Orleans: Historic New Orleans Collection, 2004.

Aldridge, Fredrick S. "Marine and Sailors Defend Washington: An Account of the Battle of Bladensburg." *Marine Corps Gazette* 34, no. 3 (March 1950). http:www.mca-marines.org/gazette/marine-corps-gazette-archives.

Alexander, Joseph H., Don Horan, and Norman C. Stahl. *A Fellowship of Valor: The Battle History of the United States Marines.* New York: HarperCollins, 1997.

Allen, Gardner W. *Our Naval War With France.* 1909. Hamden, Conn.: Archon Books, 1967.

Allen, Thomas B. *George Washington, Spymaster: How the Americans Outspied the British and Won the Revolutionary War.* Washington, D.C.: National Geographic Society, 2004.

Amero, Richard W. "The Mexican-American War in Baja California." *Journal of San Diego History* 30, no. 1 (Winter 1984): 49–64.

Ames, George Walcott, Jr. "Horse Marines: California, 1846." *California Historical Society Quarterly*, March 1939, 1–13.

Anderson, Fred. *Crucible of War: The Seven Years' War and the Fate of Empire in British North America, 1754–1766*. New York: Knopf, 2000.

Antal, Sandy. *A Wampum Denied: Procter's War of 1812*. Montreal: McGill-Queens University Press, 2011.

Armed Forces Staff College Publication 1, *Joint Staff Officers Guide*. Norfolk, Va.: National Defense University, 1984.

Asprey, Robert B. "Assault on Fort Fisher." *Marine Corps Gazette*, November 1965, 30–31.

———. *Semper Fidelis*. New York: W. W. Norton, 1967.

Atwood, Rodney. *The Hessians: Mercenaries From Hessen-Kassel in the American Revolution*. Cambridge: Cambridge University Press, 1980.

Auchinleck, Gilbert. *A History of the War between Great Britain and the United States of American During the Years 1812, 1813, & 1814*. 1855. Toronto: Pendragon House Limited, 1972.

Bacon, Eugene H., and C. Joseph Bernardo. *American Military Policy: Its Development Since 1775*. Harrisburg, Pa.: Stackpole Books, 1955.

Banner, James M., Jr. *To the Hartford Convention: The Federalists and the Origins of Party Politics in Massachusetts, 1789–1815*. New York: Knopf, 1969.

Bartlett, Merrill L., ed. *Assault from the Sea: Essays on the History of Amphibious Warfare*. Annapolis, Md.: Naval Institute Press, 1983.

Barnes, Ian, and Charles Royster. *The Historical Atlas of the American Revolution*. New York: Routledge, 2000.

Bauer, Karl Jack. *The Mexican War, 1846–1848*. New York: Macmillan, 1974.

———. *Surfboats and Horse Marines: U.S. Naval Operations in the Mexican War, 1846–48*. Annapolis, Md.: Naval Institute Press, 1969.

———. "The Veracruz Expedition of 1847." *Military Affairs* 20, no. 3 (Fall 1956): 162–69.

Beale, Robert. *A Report of the Trial of Commodore David Porter: of the Navy of the United States, before a General Court Marshal, Held at Washington, in July 1825, to which is added a Review of the Court's Decision*. Washington, D.C., 1825.

Bill, Alfred Hoyt. *The Campaign of Princeton, 1776–1777.* Princeton, N.J.: Princeton University Press, 1948.

———. *The Mexican War, 1846–1848.* New York: Macmillan, 1974.

Billias, George Athan. *George Washington's Generals.* New York: William Morrow, 1964.

Birkner, Michael. "The 'Foxardo Affair' Revisited: Porter, Pirates and the Problem of Civilian Authority in the Early Republic." *American Neptune* 42, no. 3 (July 1982): 165–78.

———. *General John Glover and His Marblehead Mariners.* New York: Henry Holt, 1960.

Black, Jeremy. *America as a Military Power: From the American Revolution to the Civil War.* Westport, Conn.: Praeger, 2002.

———. *War for America: The Fight for Independence, 1775–1783.* New York: St. Martin's, 1991.

Blackmon, Richard D. *The Creek War, 1813–1814.* Washington, D.C.: Center of Military History, 2014.

Boot, Max. *The Savage Wars of Peace: Small Wars and the Rise of American Power.* New York: Basic Books, 2002.

Borneman, Walter K. *Polk: The Man Who Transformed the Presidency and America.* New York: Random House, 2008.

Bradford, James C., ed. *America, Sea Power, and the World.* Chichester, U.K.: John Wiley & Sons, 2016.

———, ed. *Atlas of American Military History.* Oxford: Oxford University Press, 2003.

———, ed. *A Companion to American Military History.* 2 vols. Chichester, U.K.: Wiley-Blackwell, 2010

———, ed. *Crucible of Empire: The Spanish-American War & Its Aftermath.* Annapolis, Md.: Naval Institute Press, 1993.

Brayall, Richard A. *"To the Uttermost of My Power": The Life and Times of Sir William Pepperrell, 1696–1759.* Westminster, Md.: Heritage Books, 2008.

Brown, Wilburt S. *The Amphibious Campaign for West Florida and Louisiana, 1814–1815: A Critical Review of Strategy and Tactics at New Orleans.* Tuscaloosa: University of Alabama Press, 1969.

Browning, Robert M., Jr. *From Cape Charles to Cape Fear: The North Atlantic Blockading Squadron during the Civil War.* Tuscaloosa: University of Alabama Press, 1993.

Brumwell, Stephen. *Paths of Glory: The Life and Death of General James Wolfe*. Montreal: McGill-Queen's University Press, 2006.

Buker, George E. *The Penobscot Expedition: Commodore Saltonstall and the Massachusetts Conspiracy of 1779*. Camden, Maine: Down East Books, 2002.

Bunn, Mike, and Clay Williams. *Battle for the Southern Frontier: The Creek War and the War of 1812*. Charleston, S.C.: History Press, 2008.

Burbank, Dale W. "Want of Proper Spirit and Energy: The Penobscot Expedition of 1779." Master's thesis, U.S. Army Command and General Staff College, 2011.

Caesar, Julius. *The Conquest of Gaul*. Edited by Jane P. Gardner, translated by S. A. Handford. London: Penguin Books, 1982.

Chaffin, Tom. *Pathfinder: John Charles Fremont and the Course of American Empire*. New York: Hill and Wang, 2002.

Chambers, John W., and G. Kurt Piehler, eds. *Major Problems in American Military History*. Boston: Houghton Mifflin Company, 1999.

Churchill, Winston S. *A History of the English-Speaking Peoples*. Vol. 1, *The Birth of Britain*. 1956. New York: Dodd, Mead & Company, 1966.

———. *A History of the English-Speaking Peoples*. Vol. 3, *The Age of Revolution. Read 1956. New York:* Dodd, Mead & Company, 1967.

Clark, Paul C., Jr., and Edward H. Moseley. "D-Day Veracruz, 1848—A Grand Design." *Joint Forces Quarterly* 10 (Winter 1995–96): 102–15.

Clark, William Bell, ed. *Naval Documents of the American Revolution*, vol. 2. Washington, D.C.: U.S. Navy Department, 1964.

Clausewitz, Carl von. *On War*. Princeton, N.J.: Princeton University Press, 1976.

Clifford, Kenneth J. *Progress and Purpose: A Developmental History of the United States Marine Corps 1900–1970*. Washington, D.C.: History and Museums Division United States Marine Corps, 1973.

Coles, Harry L. *The War of 1812*. Chicago: University of Chicago Press, 1965.

Conner, Philip S. P. *The Home Squadron under Commodore Conner in the War with Mexico: Being a Synopsis of Its Services*. Philadelphia: Privately printed, 1896.

Cooke, Philip St. George. *The Conquest of New Mexico and California: An Historical and Personal Narrative.* Oakland, Calif.: Biobooks, 1952.

Corbett, Julian S. *England in the Seven Years' War: A Study in Combined Strategy.* 2 vols. London: Longmans, Green and Co., 1918.

———. *Some Principles of Maritime Strategy.* London: Longmans, Green and Co., 1911.

Cornish, Dudley Taylor, and Virginia Jean Laas. *Lincoln's Lee: The Life of Samuel Phillips Lee, United States Navy, 1812–1897.* Lawrence: University Press of Kansas, 1986.

Craven, Tunis A. M. *A Naval Campaign in the Californias—1846–1849: The Journal of Lieutenant Tunis Augustus Macdonough Craven, U.S.N. United States Sloop of War, Dale.* Edited by John Haskell Kemble. San Francisco: Book Club of California, 1973.

Crawford, Mark, Jeanne T. Heidler, and David S. Heidler. *Encyclopedia of the Mexican-American War.* Santa Barbara, Calif.: ABC-CLIO, 1999.

Cray, Robert E., Jr. "Remembering the USS *Chesapeake:* The Politics of Maritime Death and Impressment." *Journal of the Early Republic* 25, no. 3 (Fall 2005): 445–74.

Curtin, Philip D. *The Atlantic Slave Trade: A Census.* Madison: University of Wisconsin Press, 1969.

Cutts, James Madison. *The Conquest of California and New Mexico by the Forces of the United States in the Years 1846 & 1847.* 1847. Albuquerque, N.M.: Horn & Wallace, 1965.

Dana, Richard Henry, Jr. *Two Years Before the Mast.* 1840. Danbury, Conn.: Grolier, 1980.

Dearden, Paul F. *The Rhode Island Campaign of 1778: Inauspicious Dawn of Alliance.* Providence: Rhode Island Publication Society, 1980.

DeConde, Alexander. *The Quasi-War: The Politics and Diplomacy of the Undeclared War with France 1797–1801.* New York: Charles Scribner's Sons, 1966.

Department of Defense. Joint Publication 1-02, *Department of Defense Dictionary of Military and Associated Terms.* Washington, D.C., 12 April 2001 (as Amended through 14 April 2006).

———. Joint Publication 1-02, *Department of Defense Dictionary of Military and Associated Terms.* Washington, D.C., 8 November 2010 (as Amended through 15 December 2012).

———. Joint Publication 3-02, *Amphibious Operations*. Washington, D.C., 19 September 2001.

———. Joint Publication 3-02, *Amphibious Operations*. Washington, D.C., 18 July 2014.

———. Joint Publication 3-02.1, *Amphibious Embarkation and Debarkation*. Washington, D.C., 25 November 2014.

Department of the Navy. *. . . From the Sea: Preparing the Naval Service for the 21st Century*. Washington, D.C.: Department of the Navy, September 1992.

———. Office of the Chief of Naval Operations and Headquarters U.S. Marine Corps. Naval Doctrine Publication 1, *Naval Warfare*. Washington, D.C., 28 March 1994.

Department of the Navy, U.S. Marine Corps. *Expeditionary Force 21*. Washington, D.C., 4 March 2014.

———. Marine Corps Doctrinal Publication 1, *Warfighting*. Washington, D.C., 20 June 1997.

———. Marine Corps Doctrinal Publication 1-0, *Marine Corps Operations*. Washington, D.C., 27 September 2001.

———. Marine Corps Doctrinal Publication 1-1, *Strategy*. Washington, D.C., 12 November 1997.

———. Marine Corps Doctrinal Publication 1-2, *Campaigning*. Washington, D.C., 1 August 1997.

———. Marine Corps Doctrinal Publication 1-3, *Tactics*. Washington, D.C., 30 July 1997.

———. Marine Corps Doctrinal Publication 3, *Expeditionary Operations*. Washington, D.C., 16 April 1998.

———. Marine Corps Doctrinal Publication 5, *Planning*. Washington, D.C., 21 July 1997.

———. *Marine Corps Vision & Strategy 2025*. Washington, D.C., undated.

———. Marine Corps Warfighting Publication 5-1, *Marine Corps Planning Process*. Washington, D.C., 24 September 2001.

———. *U.S. Marine Corps 36th Commandant's Planning Guidance 2015*. Washington, D.C., undated but issued in February 2015.

Drez, Ronald J. *The War of 1812: Conflict and Deception*. Baton Rouge: Louisiana State University Press, 2014.

Dudley, William S., and Michael J. Crawford, eds. *The Naval War of 1812: A Documentary History*. 3 vols. Washington, D.C.: U.S. Government Printing Office, 1985–2002.

Dull, Jonathan R. *A Diplomatic History of the American Revolution.* New Haven, Conn.: Yale University Press, 1985.

———. *The French Navy and American Independence: A Study of Arms and Diplomacy, 1774–1787.* Princeton, N.J.: Princeton University Press, 1975.

Dunnavent, R. Blake. *Brown Water Warfare: The U.S. Navy in Riverine Warfare and the Emergence of a Tactical Doctrine, 1775–1970.* Gainesville: University Press of Florida, 2003.

Edgar, Walter. *Partisans and Redcoats: The Southern Conflict That Turned the Tide of the American Revolution.* New York: HarperCollins, 2001.

Eglin, H. W. T. "General Scott's Landing at Veracruz." *Coast Artillery Journal* 68, no. 3 (March 1928): 244–47.

Eisenhower, John S. D. *Agent of Destiny: The Life and Times of General Winfield Scott.* New York: Free Press, 1997.

———. *So Far from God: The U.S. War with Mexico, 1846–1848.* New York: Random House, 1989.

Ellis, Joseph J. *His Excellency: George Washington.* New York: Alfred A. Knopf, 2004.

Eshelman, Ralph E., Scott S. Sheads, and Donald R. Hickey. *The War of 1812 in the Chesapeake.* Baltimore: Johns Hopkins University Press, 2010.

Fellman, Michael. *The Making of Robert E. Lee.* New York: Random House, 2000.

Ferling, John E. *Almost a Miracle: The American Victory in the War for Independence.* Oxford: Oxford University Press, 2007.

———. *The First of Men: A Life of George Washington.* Knoxville: University of Tennessee Press, 1988.

———. *John Adams: A Life.* Newtown, Conn.: American Political Biography Press, 1992.

———. *A Leap in the Dark: The Struggle to Create the American Republic.* Oxford: Oxford University Press, 2003.

———. *Struggle for a Continent: The Wars of Early America.* Arlington Heights, Ill.: Harlan Davidson, 1993.

———. *A Wilderness of Miseries: War and Warriors in Early America.* Westport, Conn.: Greenwood Press, 1980.

Fitzpatrick, John C., ed. *The Writings of George Washington from the Original Manuscripts*. 35 vols. Washington, D.C.: U.S. Government Printing Office, 1931–1940.

Fonvielle, Chris E., Jr. *The Wilmington Campaign: Last Rays of Departing Hope*. Mechanicsburg, Pa.: Stackpole Books, 1997.

Fowler, William M., Jr. *Rebels under Sail: The American Navy during the Revolution*. New York: Charles Scribner's Sons, 1976.

Freeman, Douglas Southall. *George Washington: A Biography*. 7 vols. New York: Charles Scribner's Sons, 1948–1957.

Gallagher, John J. *The Battle of Brooklyn, 1776*. New York: Sarpedon, 1995.

Gardiner, Robert. ed. *The Naval War of 1812*. London: Chatham Publishing, 1998.

George, Christopher T. *Terror on the Chesapeake: The War of 1812 on the Bay*. Shippensburg, Pa.: White Mane Books, 2000.

Gleig, George Robert. *A Narrative of the Campaigns of the British Army at Washington and New Orleans, under Generals Ross, Pakenham, and Lambert, in the Years 1814 and 1815; with Some Account of the Countries Visited*. London: John Murray, 1821.

Glover, John. *A Memoir of General John Glover of Marblehead*. From the Historical Collection of the Essex Institute, William P. Uphan, ed. Salem, Mass: Charles W. Swasey, 1863.

Goodwin, Doris Kearns. *Team of Rivals: The Political Genius of Abraham Lincoln*. New York: Simon & Schuster, 2005.

Gough, Barry. *Fighting Sail on Lake Huron and Georgian Bay: The War of 1812 and Its Aftermath*. Annapolis, Md.: Naval Institute Press, 2002.

Graebner, Norman A. *Empire of the Pacific: A Study in Continental Expansion*. 1955. Claremont, Calif.: Regina Books, 1983.

Gragg, Ron. *Confederate Goliath: The Battle of Fort Fisher*. New York: HarperCollins, 1991.

Grainger, John D. *The Battle of Yorktown, 1781: A Reassessment*. Woodbridge, Suffolk, U.K.: Boydell Press, 2005.

Grant, Ulysses S. *Personal Memoirs of U.S. Grant*. 2 vols. New York: Charles L. Webster, 1885.

Graves, Donald E. *Field of Glory: The Battle of Crysler's Farm, 1813*. Montreal: Robin Brass Studio, 1999.

Greeley & McElrath. "The Military Polka Dance—Annexation of Mexican Territory—Exciting Debate." *New-York Tribune*, 9 December 1846.

Greenberg, Amy S. *A Wicked War: Polk, Clay, Lincoln, and the 1846 U.S. Invasion of Mexico.* New York: Alfred A. Knopf, 2012.

Greenburg, Michael M. *The Court-Martial of Paul Revere: A Son of Liberty & America's Forgotten Military Disaster.* Lebanon, N.H.: ForeEdge, An Imprint of the University Press of New England, 2014.

Grenier, John. *The Far Reaches of Empire: War in Nova Scotia 1710–1760.* Norman: University of Oklahoma Press, 2008.

Grodzinski, John R. *Defender of Canada: Sir George Prevost and the War of 1812.* Norman: University of Oklahoma Press, 2013.

Gruber, Ira D. *The Howe Brothers and the American Revolution.* Chapel Hill: University of North Carolina Press, 1972.

Gwyn, Julian. *An Admiral for America: Sir Peter Warren, Vice Admiral of the Red, 1703–1752.* Gainesville: University Press of Florida, 2004.

Hagan, Kenneth J., and Michael T. McMaster, eds. *In Peace and War: Interpretations of American Naval History.* Westport, Conn.: Praeger Security International, 2008.

Hague, Harlan, and David J. Langrum. *Thomas O. Larkin: A Life of Patriotism and Profit in Old California.* Norman: University of Oklahoma Press, 1990.

Hall, Claude H. *Abel Parker Upshur: Conservative Virginian, 1790–1844.* Madison: State Historical Society of Wisconsin, 1964.

Hallahan, William H. *The Day the American Revolution Began, 19 April 1775.* New York: William Morrow, 2000.

Halleck, Henry W. *The Mexican War in Baja California: The Memorandum of Captain Henry W. Halleck Concerning His Expeditions in Lower California, 1846–1848.* Los Angeles: Dawson's Book Shop, 1977.

Hammond, George, P., ed. *The Larkin Papers: Personal, Business, and Official Correspondence of Thomas Oliver Larkin, Merchant and United States Consul in California.* 10 vols. Berkeley: University of California Press, 1951–1964.

Hammond, N. G. L. *A History of Greece to 322 B.C.* Oxford: Clarendon Press, 1991.

Harding, Richard. *Amphibious Warfare in the Eighteenth Century: The British Expedition to the West Indies 1740–1742.* Woodbridge, Suffolk, U.K.: Boydell Press, 1991.

Harlow, Neal. *California Conquered: War and Peace in the Pacific, 1846–1850.* Berkeley: University of California Press, 1982.

Hattendorf, John B. *Newport, the French Navy, and American Independence.* Newport, R.I.: Redwood Press, 2005.

Hearn, Chester G. *The Capture of New Orleans, 1862.* Baton Rouge: Louisiana State University Press, 1995.

Heidler, David S., and Jeanne T. Heidler, eds. *Encyclopedia of the American Civil War: A Political, Social, and Military History.* New York: W. W. Norton, 2000.

———, eds. *Encyclopedia of the War of 1812.* Santa Barbara, Calif.: ABC-CLIO, 1997.

———. *The War of 1812.* Westport, Conn.: Greenwood Press, 2002.

Heinl, Robert Debs, Jr. *Soldiers of the Sea: The United States Marine Corps, 1775–1962.* Annapolis, Md.: Naval Institute Press, 1962.

Henry, Robert Selph. *The Story of the Mexican War.* Indianapolis: Bobbs-Merrill, 1950.

Hickey, Donald R. *The War of 1812: A Forgotten Conflict.* Urbana: University of Illinois Press, 1989.

Higginbotham, Don. "The Early American Way of War: Reconnaissance and Appraisal." *William and Mary Quarterly*, 3rd Ser., 44, no. 2 (April 1987): 230–73.

———. *George Washington and the American Military Tradition.* Athens: University of Georgia Press, 1985.

———. *George Washington Reconsidered.* Charlottesville: University Press of Virginia, 2001.

Hittle, James D. "Jomini and Amphibious Thought." *Marine Corps Gazette*, May 1946, 35–38.

Hoffman, Jon T., ed. *USMC: A Complete History.* Quantico, Va.: Marine Corps Association, 2002.

Hollomon, Quinn G. "Union Joint Operations in North Carolina During the Civil War." Air War College Research Paper. Maxwell Air Force Base, Ala.: Air College, 1999.

Hollon, Cory S. "A Leap in the Dark: The Campaign to Conquer New Mexico and California, 1846–1847." *Army History* (Winter 2015): 7–25.

Horsman, Reginald. *The Causes of the War of 1812*. Philadelphia: University of Pennsylvania Press, 1962.

Hussey, John Adam. "The Origin of the Gillespie Mission." *California Historical Society Quarterly*, March 1940, 43–58.

Hutton, Paul Andrew, and Durwood Ball, eds. *Soldiers West: Biographies from the Military Frontier*. Norman: University of Oklahoma Press, 2009.

Irwin, Ray W. *The Diplomatic Relations of the United States with the Barbary Powers, 1776–1816*. New York: Russell & Russell, 1931.

Jackson, John W. *The Pennsylvania Navy 1775–1781: The Defense of Delaware*. New Brunswick, N.J.: Rutgers University Press, 1974.

Jackson, Shelton G. "The British and the California Dream: Rumors, Myths and Legends." *Southern California Quarterly* 57, no. 3 (Fall 1975): 251–70.

Jahncke, Ernest Lee. "The Battle of New Orleans." U.S. Naval Institute *Proceedings*, March 1931, 293–98.

"John Paul Jones." *Harpers New Monthly Magazine* 11, no. 1 (July 1855): 145–66.

Johnson, Robert Erwin. *Thence Round Cape Horn: The Story of the United States Naval Forces on Pacific Station, 1818–1923*. New York: Arno Press, 1980.

Johnson, Timothy D. *A Gallant Little Army: The Mexico City Campaign*. Lawrence: University Press of Kansas, 2007.

———. *Winfield Scott: The Quest for Military Glory*. Lawrence: University Press of Kansas, 1998.

Jomini, Antoine Henri. *The Art of War*. Westport, Conn.: Greenwood Press, 1862.

Keegan, John. *The Mask of Command*. New York: Viking Penguin, 1987.

Ketchum, Richard M. *Decisive Day: The Battle for Bunker Hill*. New York: Doubleday, 1991.

———. *Victory at Yorktown: The Campaign That Won the Revolution*. New York: Henry Holt, 2004.

Kilmeade, Brian, and Don Yaeger. *George Washington's Secret Six: The Spy Ring That Saved the American Revolution*. New York: Sentinel, 2013.

——. *Naval Documents Related to the Quasi-War between the United States and France.* 7 vols. Washington, D.C.: U.S. Government Printing Office, 1935–1938.

Knox, Dudley W. *Naval Documents Related to the United States Wars with the Barbary Powers.* 6 vols. Washington, D.C.: U.S. Government Printing Office, 1939–1944.

Kohn, Richard H. *Eagle and Sword: The Federalists and the Creation of the Military Establishment in America, 1783–1802.* New York: Free Press, 1975.

Lambert, Frank. *The Barbary Wars: American Independence in the Atlantic World.* New York: Hill and Wang, 2005.

Latour, Arsène Lacarrière. *Historical Memoir of the War in West Florida and Louisiana in 1814–15, with Atlas.* Gene A. Smith, ed. Gainesville, Fla.: Historic New Orleans Collection and University Press of Florida, 1999.

London, Joshua E. *Victory in Tripoli: How America's War with the Barbary Pirates Established the U.S. Navy and Shaped a Nation.* Hoboken, N.J.: John Wiley & Sons, 2005.

Long, David F. "'Martial Thunder': The First Official American Armed Intervention in Asia." *Pacific Historical Review* 42 (1973): 143–62.

——. *Nothing Too Daring: A Biography of Commodore David Porter, 1780-1843.* Annapolis, Md.: Naval Institute Press, 1970.

——. *Sailor-Diplomat: A Biography of Commodore James Biddle, 1783–1848.* Boston: Northeastern University Press, 1983.

Long, E. B., and Barbara Long. *The Civil War Day by Day: An Almanac 1861–1865.* Garden City, N.Y.: Doubleday, 1971.

Lookingbill, Brad D. *The American Military: A Narrative History.* West Sussex, U.K.: John Wiley & Sons, 2013.

Lord, Walter. *The Dawn's Early Light.* New York: W. W. Norton, 1972.

Lossing, Benson, J. *Pictorial Field Book of the War of 1812.* New York: Harper & Brothers, 1869.

Lowell, Edward J. *The Hessians and the Other German Auxiliaries of Great Britain in the Revolutionary War.* 1884. New York: Forgotten Books, 2012.

Mackesy, Piers. *The War for America, 1775–1783.* Cambridge, Mass.: Harvard University Press, 1965.

Mahan, Alfred T. *The Influence of Sea Power Upon History, 1660–1783.* Boston: Little, Brown, 1890.

———. *The Major Operations of the Navies in the War of American Independence.* Boston: Little, Brown, 1913.

———. *Sea Power in Its Relations to the War of 1812.* 2 vols. New York: Greenwood Press, 1903.

Malcomson, Robert. *Capital in Flames: The American Attack on York, 1813.* Montreal: Robin Brass Studio, 2008.

———. *Lords of the Lake: The Naval War on Lake Ontario, 1812–1814.* Annapolis, Md.: Naval Institute Press, 1998.

Manning, Stephen. *Quebec: The Story of Three Sieges.* Montreal: McGill-Queens University Press, 2009.

Mansfield, Edward Deering. *The Mexican War: A History of Its Origins, and a Detailed Account of the Victories which Terminated in the Surrender of the Capital; with the official dispatches of the generals. To which is added, the treaty of peace, and valuable tables of the strength and losses of the United States Army.* New York: A. S. Barnes and Company, 1849.

Marshall, Douglas W., and Howard H. Peckham. *Campaigns of the American Revolution: An Atlas of Manuscript Maps.* Ann Arbor: University of Michigan Press, 1976.

McCarty, William. *History of the War of 1812, from Commencement until the Final Termination Thereof, on the Memorable Eight of January, 1815 at New Orleans.* Freeport, N.Y.: Books for Libraries, 1816.

McClellan, Edwin N. "The Capture of Fort Fisher." *Marine Corps Gazette,* March 1920, 59–80.

McCranie, Kevin D. *Utmost Gallantry: The U.S. and Royal Navy in the War of 1812.* Annapolis, Md.: Naval Institute Press, 2011.

McDongall, James E. "The History of the Mameluke Sword of the United States Marine Corps." *Marine Corps Gazette,* November 2000. Web Site Exclusive.

McGuire, Thomas J. *The Philadelphia Campaign, Volume One: Brandywine and the Fall of Philadelphia.* Mechanicsburg, Pa.: Stackpole Books, 2014.

———. *Stop the Revolution: America in the Summer of Independence and the Conference for Peace.* Mechanicsburg, Pa.: Stackpole Books, 2011.

McKee, Christopher. *A Gentlemanly and Honorable Profession: The Creation of the U.S. Naval Officer Corps, 1794–1815.* Annapolis, Md.: Naval Institute Press, 1991.

McPherson, James M. *Battle Cry of Freedom: The Civil War Era.* New York: Oxford University Press, 1988.

———. *War on the Waters: The Union & Confederate Navies, 1861–1865.* Chapel Hill: University of North Carolina Press, 2012.

McWhiney, Grady, and Sue McWhiney, eds. *To Mexico with Taylor and Scott, 1845–1847.* Waltham, Mass.: Blaisdell Publishing, 1969.

Metcalf, Clyde H. *A History of the United States Marine Corps.* New York: G. P. Putnam's Sons, 1939.

Middlekauff, Robert. *The Glorious Cause: The American Revolution, 1763–1789.* New York: Oxford University Press, 1982.

Millett, Allan R. *Semper Fidelis: The History of the United States Marine Corps.* New York: Free Press, 1991.

Millett, Allan R., and Peter Maslowski. *For the Common Defense: A Military History of the United States of America.* New York: Free Press, 1984.

Millett, Allan R., and Jack Shulimson, eds. *Commandants of the Marine Corps.* Annapolis, Md.: Naval Institute Press, 2004.

Milligan, John D. *Gunboats down the Mississippi.* Annapolis, Md.: Naval Institute Press, 1965.

Molyneux, Thomas More. *Conjunct Expeditions: Or Expeditions That have been carried on jointly by the FLEET and ARMY with a Commentary on a Littoral War.* 2 vols. London: R. and J. Dodsley in Pall-Mall, 1759.

Morison, Samuel Eliot. *"Old Bruin" Commodore Matthew C. Perry, 1794–1858.* Boston: Little, Brown, 1967.

Morris, John D. *Sword of the Border: Major General Jacob Jennings Brown, 1775–1828.* Kent, Ohio: Kent State University Press, 2000.

Moskin, J. Robert. *The U.S. Marine Corps Story.* New York: McGraw-Hill, 1977.

Muller, Charles G. *The Darkest Day, 1814: The Washington–Baltimore Campaign.* New York: Lippincott, 1963.

Nash, Howard P., Jr. *The Forgotten Wars: The Role of the U.S. Navy in the Quasi War with France and the Barbary Wars 1798–1805.* New York: A. S. Barnes, 1968.

National Defense University, Joint Forces Staff College. *OP6500 Operational Art and Campaigning Case Study: Mexican-American War.* Norfolk, Va.: Joint Advance Warfighting School, 2006.

Naval War Records Office. *Official Records of the Union and Confederate Navies in the War of the Rebellion.* 30 vols. Washington, D.C.: Government Printing Office, 1894–1922. CD-ROM by Guild Press of Indiana, Inc., 1999. Republished by Oliver Computing LLC.

Nelson, Paul David. *General James Grant: Scottish Soldier and Royal Governor of East Florida.* Gainesville: University Press of Florida, 1993.

———. *The Life of William Alexander, Lord Stirling: George Washington's Noble General.* Tuscaloosa: University of Alabama Press, 1987.

Nevins, Allan, ed. *Polk: The Diary of a President 1845–1849 Covering the Mexican War, the Acquisition of Oregon, and the Conquest of California and the Southwest.* New York: Longmans, Green and Co., 1952.

Norton, Louis Arthur. *Joshua Barney: Hero of the Revolution and 1812.* Annapolis, Md.: Naval Institute Press, 2000.

O'Kelley, Patrick. *Nothing but Blood and Slaughter: The War in the Carolinas.* 4 vols. Bangor, Maine: Booklocker.com, Inc., 2004–2005.

Operational Maneuver from the Sea: A Concept for the Projection of Naval Power Ashore. Washington, D.C.: Headquarters, U.S. Marine Corps, 1996.

O'Shaughnessy, Andrew Jackson. *The Men Who Lost America: British Leadership, the American Revolution, and the Fate of the Empire.* New Haven, Conn.: Yale University Press, 2013.

Palmer, Dave Richard. *The Way of the Fox: American Strategy in the War for America, 1775–1783.* Westport, Conn.: Greenwood Press, 1975.

Palmer, Michael A. *Command at Sea: Naval Command and Control Since the Sixteenth Century.* Cambridge, Mass: Harvard University Press, 2005.

———. *Stoddert's War: Naval Operations During the Quasi-War with France, 1798–1801.* Columbia: University of South Carolina Press, 1987.

Pancake, John S. *Samuel Smith and the Politics of Business, 1752–1839.* Tuscaloosa: University of Alabama Press, 1972.

Parker, William D. *A Concise History of the United States Marine Corps 1775–1969.* Washington, D.C.: Historical Division, Headquarters, U.S. Marine Corps, 1970.

Parkman, Francis. *Montcalm and Wolfe.* 1884. New York: Atheneum, 1984.

Peckham, Howard H. *The Toll of Independence: Engagements & Battle Casualties of the American Revolution.* Chicago: University of Chicago Press, 1974.

Philbrick, Nathaniel. *Valiant Ambition: George Washington, Benedict Arnold, and the Fate of the American Revolution.* New York: Viking, 2016.

Pitch, Anthony, S. *The Burning of Washington: The British Invasion of 1814.* Annapolis, Md.: Naval Institute Press, 1998.

Polk, John Fleming. "Veracruz, 1847." *Marine Corps Gazette*, September 1979, 61–67.

Porter, David D. *Naval History of the Civil War.* 1886. Secaucus, N.J.: Castle, 1984.

Porter, Horace. *Campaigning with Grant.* New York: Century Club, 1897.

Pratt, Fletcher. *Preble's Boys: Commodore Preble and the Birth of American Sea Power.* New York: Sloane, 1950.

Pratt, Fletcher, and Hartley E. Howe. *The Compact History of the United States Navy.* 1957. New York: Hawthorn Books, 1962.

Quinby, Robert S. *The U.S. Army in the War of 1812: An Operational and Command Study.* 2 vols. East Lansing: Michigan State University Press, 1997.

Rawlyk, George A. *Yankees at Louisbourg: The Story of the First Siege 1745.* Englishtown, Nova Scotia: Breton Books, 1999.

Reed, Rowena. *Combined Operations in the Civil War.* Annapolis, Md.: Naval Institute Press, 1978.

Reid, Chipp. *Intrepid Sailors: The Legacy of Preble's Boys and the Tripoli Campaign.* Annapolis, Md.: Naval Institute Press, 2012.

Remini, Robert V. *The Battle of New Orleans: Andrew Jackson and America's First Military Victory.* New York: Penguin Putnam, 1999.

Richman, Irving Berdine. *California under Spain and Mexico, 1535–1847.* Boston: Houghton Mifflin, 1911.

Roberts, David. *A Newer World: Kit Carson, John C. Fremont, and the Claiming of the American West.* New York: Simon & Schuster, 2000.

Robinson, Charles M., III. *Hurricane of Fire: The Union Assault on Fort Fisher.* Annapolis, Md.: Naval Institute Press, 1998.

Roosevelt, Theodore. *The Naval War of 1812 or the History of the United States Navy during the Last War with Great Britain.* New York: G. P. Putnam's Sons, 1882.

Rose, Alexander. *Washington's Spies: The Story of America's First Spy Ring.* New York: Bantam Books, 2006.

Rukert, Norman G. *Fort McHenry: Home of the Brave.* Baltimore: Bodine, 1983.

Santelli, Gabrielle M. Neufeld. *Marines in the Mexican War.* Washington, D.C.: History and Museums Division, Headquarters, U.S. Marine Corps, 1991.

Schecter, Barnet. *The Battle for New York: The City at the Heart of the American Revolution.* New York: Walker & Company, 2002.

Schroeder, John H. *Commodore John Rodgers: Paragon of the Early American Navy.* Gainesville: University Press of Florida, 2006.

———. *Mr. Polk's War: American Opposition and Dissent, 1846–1848.* Madison: University of Wisconsin Press, 1973

Scott, Winfield. *Memoirs of Lieut.-General Scott, LL.D. Written by Himself.* 2 vols. 1864. Freeport, N.Y.: Books for Libraries Press, 1970.

Semmes, Raphael. *Service Afloat and Ashore During the Mexican War.* Cincinnati: W. H. Moore & Co., 1851.

Selby, John. *The Road to Yorktown.* New York: St. Martin's Press, 1976.

Shaw, Henry I., Jr. "Penobscot Assault–1779." *Military Affairs* 17, no. 2 (Summer 1953): 83–94.

Sheads, Scott S. *Fort McHenry: Home of the Brave.* Baltimore: Bodine, 1983.

———. *The Rockets' Red Glare: The Maritime Defense of Baltimore 1814.* Centerville, Md.: Tidewater Publishers, 1986.

Sherman, Edwin Allen. *The Life of the Late Rear-Admiral John Drake Sloat, of the United States Navy, Who Took Possession of California and Raised the American Flag at Monterey on July 7th, 1846.* Oakland, Calif.: Carruth & Carruth, 1902.

Shoman, Richard K., ed. *The Papers of General Nathanael Greene.* 13 vols. Chapel Hill: University of North Carolina Press, 1976–2005.

Simmons, Edwin H. "The Federals at Fort Fisher." *Marine Corps Gazette,* part 1, January 1951, 52–69, and part 2, February 1951, 47–53.

———. "Major Carmick at New Orleans." *Fortitudine*, Spring 1985, 3–7.

———. *The United States Marines: 1775–1975*. New York: Viking Press, 1976.

Simmons, Edwin H., and J. Robert Moskin, eds. *The Marines*. Quantico, Va.: Marine Corps Heritage Foundation, 1998.

Skaggs, Davis, and Gerard Altof. *A Signal Victory: The Lake Erie Campaign, 1812–13*. Annapolis, Md.: Naval Institute Press, 1997.

Sketch of the Life of Commodore Robert F. Stockton; with an appendix, comprising his correspondence with the Navy Department respecting his conquest of California; and extracts from the defense of Col. J.C. Fremont, in relation to the same subject; together with his speeches in the Senate of the United States, and his political letters. New York: Derby & Jackson, 1856.

Slagle, Jay. *Ironclad Captain: Seth Ledyard Phelps & the U.S. Navy, 1841–1864*. Kent, Ohio: Kent State University Press, 1996.

Smith, Charles R. *Marines in the Revolution: A History of the Continental Marines in the American Revolution 1775–1783*. Washington, D.C.: History and Museums Division, Headquarters, U.S. Marine Corps, 1975.

Smith, Cornelius C., Jr. "Our First Amphibious Assault." *Military Review* 38, no. 2 (February 1959): 18–28.

Smith, E. Kirby. *To Mexico With Scott: Letters of Captain E. Kirby Smith to his Wife*. Edited by Emma Jerome Blackwood. Cambridge, Mass: Harvard University Press, 1917.

Smith, Gene A. *Filibusters and Expansionists: Jeffersonian Manifest Destiny, 1800–1821*. Tuscaloosa: University of Alabama Press, 1997.

———. *"For the Purposes of Defense": The Politics of the Jeffersonian Gunboat Program*. Newark: University of Delaware Press, 1995.

———. *The Slaves' Gamble: Choosing Sides in the War of 1912*. New York: Palgrave Macmillan, 2013.

———. *Thomas ap Catesby Jones: Commodore of Manifest Destiny*. Annapolis, Md.: Naval Institute Press, 2000.

———. "The War That Wasn't: Thomas ap Catesby Jones's Seizure of Monterey." *California History* 66 (June 1987): 104–13, 155–57.

Smith, George Winston, and Charles Judah. *Chronicles of the Gringos: The U.S. Army in the Mexican War, 1846–1848: Accounts of*

Eyewitnesses and Combatants. Albuquerque: University of New Mexico Press, 1968.

Smith, Justin Harvey. *The War with Mexico.* 2 vols. New York: Macmillan, 1919.

Spivak, Burton. *Jefferson's English Crisis: Commerce, Embargo, and the Republican Revolution.* Charlottesville: University Press of Virginia, 1979.

Stagg, J. C. A. *The War of 1812: Conflict for a Continent.* New York: Cambridge University Press, 2012.

Steele, Matthew F. *American Campaigns.* 2 vols. Washington, D.C.: U.S. Infantry Association, 1943.

Stenberg, Richard R. "Polk and Frémont, 1845–1846." *Pacific Historical Review* 7, no. 3 (September 1938): 211–27.

Stinchcombe, William. *The XYZ Affair.* Westport, Conn.: Greenwood Press, 1980.

Stoker, Donald. *The Grand Design: Strategy and the U.S. Civil War.* New York: Oxford University Press, 2010.

Stryker, William S. *The Battles of Trenton and Princeton.* Boston: Houghton, Mifflin, 1898.

The Submarine in the United States Navy. Washington, D.C.: Naval History Division, 1969.

Sullivan, David M. *The United States Marine Corps in the Civil War—The Final Year.* Shippensburg, Pa.: White Mane Books, 2000.

Sun-tzu. *The Art of War: The First English Translation Incorporating the Recently Discovered Yun-ch'uch-shan Texts.* New York: Ballantine Books, 1993.

Symonds, Craig L. *The Civil War at Sea.* New York: Oxford University Press, 2009.

———. *Lincoln and His Admirals: Abraham Lincoln, The U.S. Navy, and the Civil War.* New York: Oxford University Press, 2008.

———. *Navalists and Antinavilists: The Naval Policy Debate in the United States, 1785–1827.* Newark: University of Delaware Press, 1980.

Syrett, David. "The British Armed Forces in the American Revolutionary War: Publications, 1875–1998." *Journal of Military History* 63, no. 1 (January 1999): 147–64.

———. *The Royal Navy in American Waters, 1775–1783.* Aldershot, U.K.: Scolar Press, 1989.

Tarleton, Banastre. *A History of the Campaigns of 1780 and 1781, in the Southern Provinces of North America.* Dublin: Colles, Exshaw, White, H. Whitestone, Burton, Moore, Jones, and Dornin, 1787.

Taylor, Alan. *The Civil War of 1812: American Citizens, British Subjects, Irish Rebels, and Indian Allies.* New York: Alfred A. Knopf, 2012.

Tays, George. "Frémont Had No Secret Instructions." *Pacific Historical Review* 9, no. 2 (June 1940): 157–71.

Thomas, Hugh. *The Slave Trade: The Story of the Atlantic Slave Trade, 1440–1870, 1887.* New York: Simon & Schuster, 1997.

Tilley, John A. *The British Navy and the American Revolution.* Columbia: University of South Carolina Press, 1987.

Toll, Ian W. *Six Frigates: The Epic History of the Founding of the U.S. Navy.* New York: W. W. Norton, 2006.

Triber, Jayne E. *A True Republican: The Life of Paul Revere.* Amherst: University of Massachusetts Press, 1998.

Tucker, Spencer C. *Handbook of 19th Century Naval Warfare.* Phoenix Hill Thrupp, U.K.: Sutton, 2000.

———. *The Jeffersonian Gunboat Navy.* Columbia: University of South Carolina Press, 1993.

Tucker, Spencer C., and Frank T. Reuter. *Injured Honor: The Chesapeake-Leopard Affair, June 22, 1807.* Annapolis, Md.: Naval Institute Press, 1996.

———. *Stephen Decatur: A Life Most Bold and Daring.* Annapolis, Md.: Naval Institute Press, 2005.

U.S. Congress, House of Representatives. *The War of the Rebellion: A Compilation of the Official Records of the Union and Confederate Armies*, 127 vols. Washington, D.C.: U.S. Government Printing Office, 1880–1901.

U.S. Marine Operations in Korea, 1950–1953, 5 vols. Washington, D.C.: Historical Branch, G-3, Headquarters, U.S. Marine Corps, 1954–1972.

U.S. War Department. *The War of the Rebellion: A Compilation of the Official Records of the Union and Confederate Armies.* Washington, D.C.: U.S. Government Printing Office, 1889. CD-ROM, *The Civil War CD-ROM*, edited by Philip Oliver, Frederick H. Dyer, Alan Conrad Aimone, Barbara A. Aimone, and William

F. Fox. Carmel: Guild Press of Indiana, 1997. Republished by Oliver Computing LLC.

Vagts, Alfred. *Landing Operations: Strategy, Psychology, Tactics, Politics, From Antiquity to 1945*. Washington, D.C.: Military Service Publishing Company, 1946.

Vauban, Sebastien. *The New Methods of Fortification as Practiced by Monfieur de Vauban, Engineer General of France, Together with a new Treatise of Geometry*. London: S. and E. Ballad, 1722.

Vego, Milan. "On Littoral Warfare." *Naval War College Review* 68, no. 2 (Spring 2015): 30–68.

Wagner, Margaret E., Gary W. Gallagher, and Paul Finkelman, eds. *The Library of Congress: Civil War Desk Reference*. New York: Simon & Schuster, 2002.

Watson, Henry Bulls. *The Journals of Marine Second Lieutenant Henry Bulls Watson, 1845–1848*. Edited by Charles R. Smith. Washington, D.C.: History and Museums Division, U.S. Marine Corps, 1990.

Weems, John E. *To Conquer a Peace: The War between the United States and Mexico*. Garden City, N.Y.: Doubleday, 1974.

Weigley, Russell F. *The American Way of War: A History of United States Military Strategy and Policy*. Bloomington: Indiana University Press, 1973.

West, Richard S., Jr. *Lincoln's Scapegoat General: A Life of Benjamin F. Butler, 1818–1893*. Boston: Houghton Mifflin Company, 1965.

Wheelan, Joseph. *Invading Mexico: America's Continental Dream and the Mexican War, 1846–1848*. New York: Carroll & Graf, 2007.

Whitehorne, Joseph A. *The Battle for Baltimore, 1814*. Baltimore: Nautical & Aviation Publishing Company of America, 1997.

Wilcox, Cadmus Marcellus. *History of the Mexican War*. Washington, D.C.: Church News Publishing, 1892.

Wilder, Patrick A. *The Battle of Sacketts Harbor*. Baltimore: Nautical & Aviation Publishing Company of America, 1994.

Winders, Richard Bruce. *Mr. Polk's Army: The American Military Experience in the Mexican War*. College Station: Texas A&M University Press, 1997.

Wise, Stephen R. *Lifeline of the Confederacy: Blockade Running during the Civil War*. Columbia: University of South Carolina Press, 1988.

Woodworth, Steven E., and Kenneth J. Winkle. *Atlas of the Civil War.* New York: Oxford University Press, 2004.

Yarnall, James L. *Newport History: The French in Newport.* Newport, R.I.: Newport Historical Society, 2004.

Young, George F. W. *The British Capture & Occupation of Downeast Maine, 1814–1815/1818.* Stonington, Maine: Penobscot Books, 2014.

Zacks, Richard. *The Pirate Coast: Thomas Jefferson, The First Marines, and the Secret Mission of 1805.* New York: Hyperion, 2005.

Zaslow, Morris. *The Defended Border: Upper Canada and the War of 1812.* Toronto: Macmillan Company of Canada, 1964.

Zimmerman, James Fulton. *Impressment of American Seamen.* New York: Columbia University Press, 1925.

Zook, David H., and Robin Higham. *A Short History of Warfare.* New York: Twayne, 1966.

Index

About the Author

Though born and raised in Kansas, **Dr. Gary Ohls** has lived in numerous locations throughout the United States and worldwide. His personal interests include reading, opera, travel, camping, fly fishing, hunting, and spending time with his two daughters and grandsons. In addition to a career in the Marine Corps and with the Naval War College/Naval Postgraduate School, Ohls has worked in management with the Aerospace Corporation and Northrop Grumman Corporation. Prior to teaching for the Naval War College, Ohls served as an assistant research professor in the Maritime History Department at the Naval War College in Newport. Additionally, he has taught undergraduate courses at the University of Colorado and Texas Christian University. Previous community involvement includes serving as a member of the Redondo Beach, California Harbor Commission.

The Naval Institute Press is the book-publishing arm of the U.S. Naval Institute, a private, nonprofit, membership society for sea service professionals and others who share an interest in naval and maritime affairs. Established in 1873 at the U.S. Naval Academy in Annapolis, Maryland, where its offices remain today, the Naval Institute has members worldwide.

Members of the Naval Institute support the education programs of the society and receive the influential monthly magazine *Proceedings* or the colorful bimonthly magazine *Naval History* and discounts on fine nautical prints and on ship and aircraft photos. They also have access to the transcripts of the Institute's Oral History Program and get discounted admission to any of the Institute-sponsored seminars offered around the country.

The Naval Institute's book-publishing program, begun in 1898 with basic guides to naval practices, has broadened its scope to include books of more general interest. Now the Naval Institute Press publishes about seventy titles each year, ranging from how-to books on boating and navigation to battle histories, biographies, ship and aircraft guides, and novels. Institute members receive significant discounts on the Press' more than eight hundred books in print.

Full-time students are eligible for special half-price membership rates. Life memberships are also available.

For a free catalog describing Naval Institute Press books currently available, and for further information about joining the U.S. Naval Institute, please write to:

Member Services
U.S. Naval Institute
291 Wood Road
Annapolis, MD 21402-5034
Telephone: (800) 233-8764
Fax: (410) 571-1703
Web address: www.usni.org